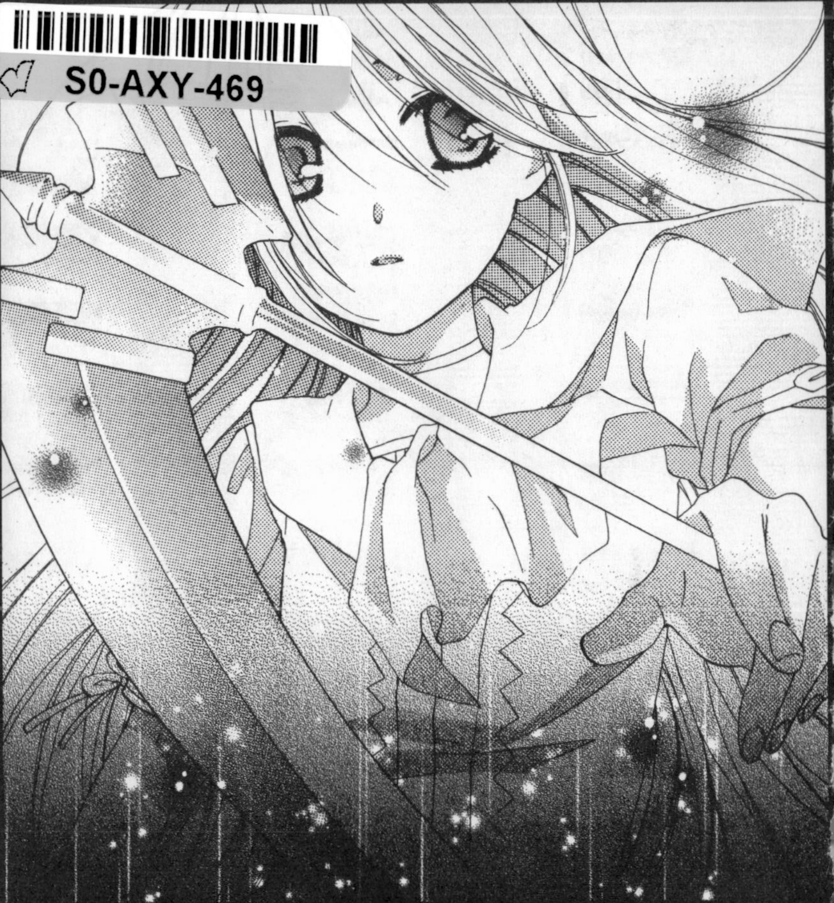

vol. 1

Ballad of a Shinigami

By Asuka Izumi

Original story by K-Ske Hasegawa

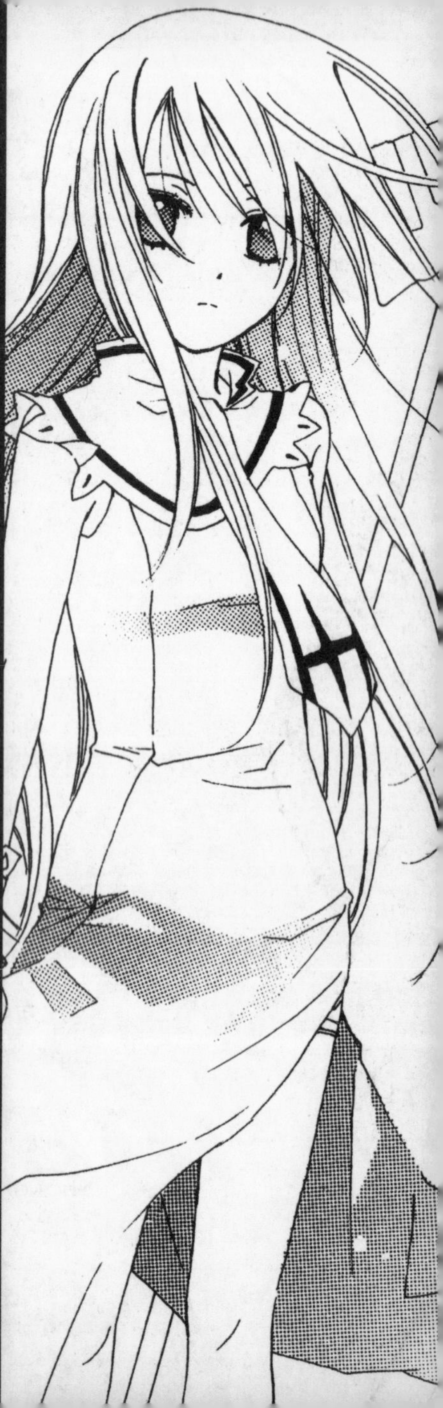

CONTENTS

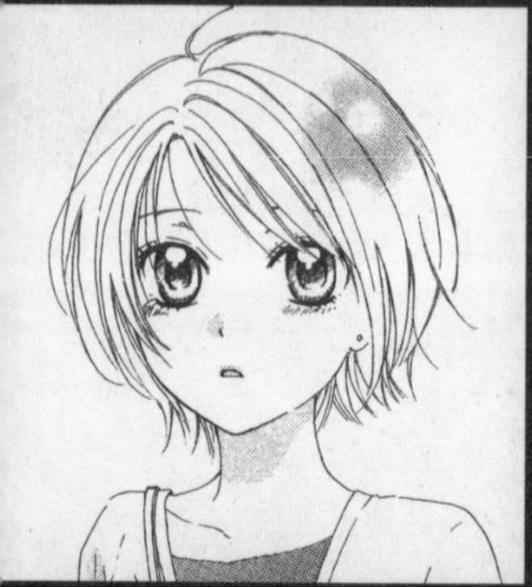

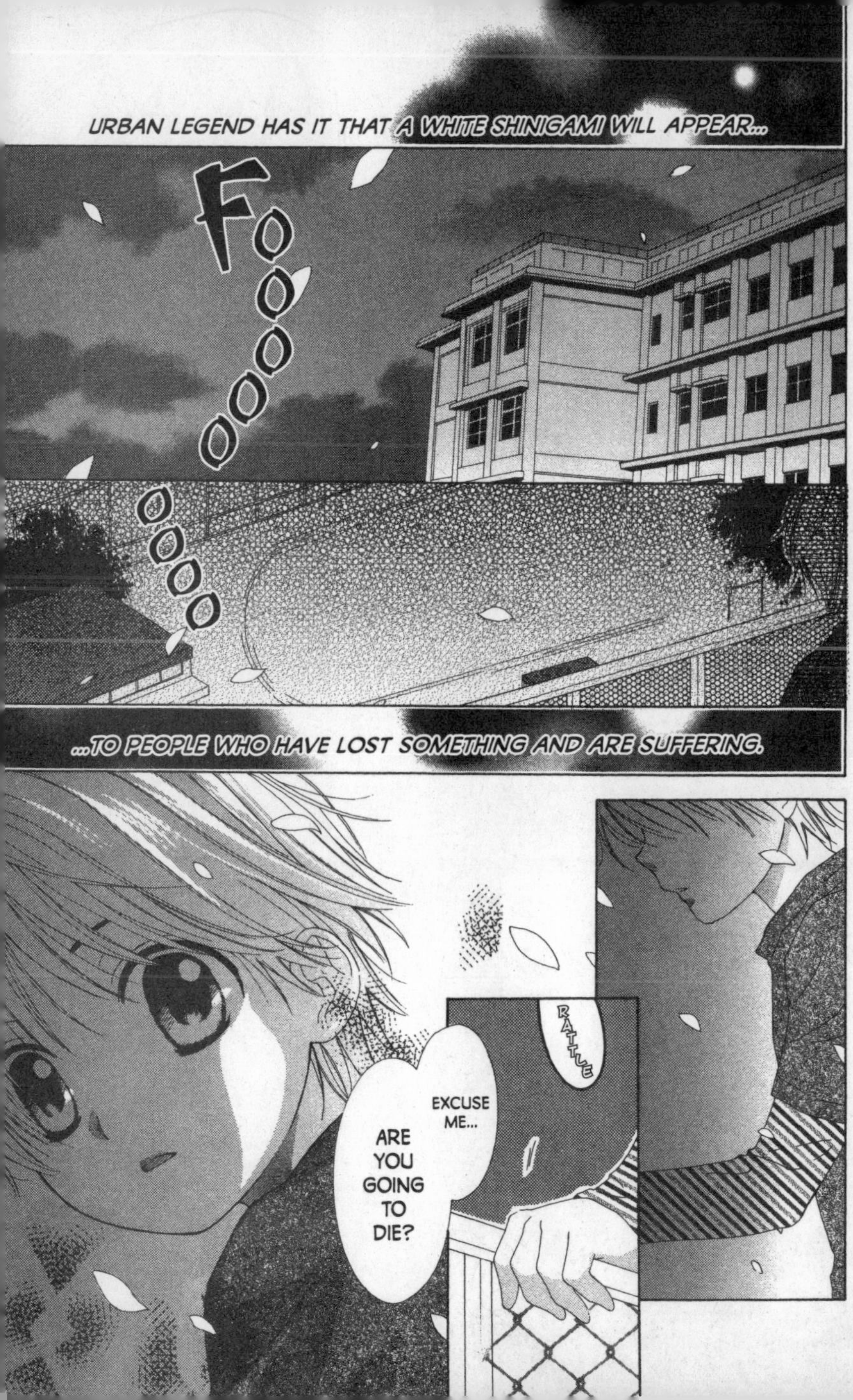
URBAN LEGEND HAS IT THAT A WHITE SHINIGAMI WILL APPEAR...
FOOOOOOOOOO
...TO PEOPLE WHO HAVE LOST SOMETHING AND ARE SUFFERING.
RATTLE
EXCUSE ME...
ARE YOU GOING TO DIE?

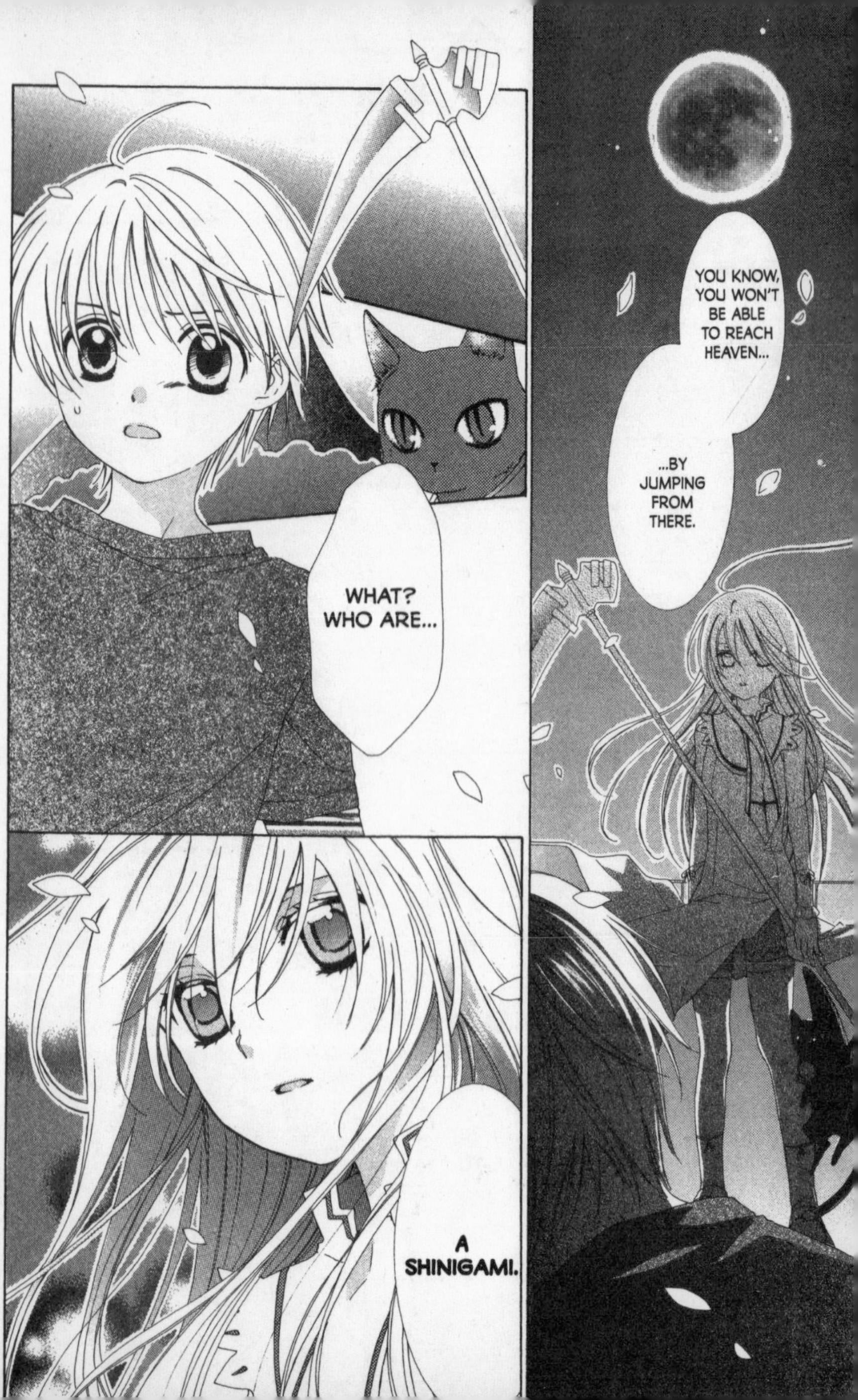
YOU KNOW, YOU WON'T BE ABLE TO REACH HEAVEN...
...BY JUMPING FROM THERE.
WHAT? WHO ARE...
A SHINIGAMI.

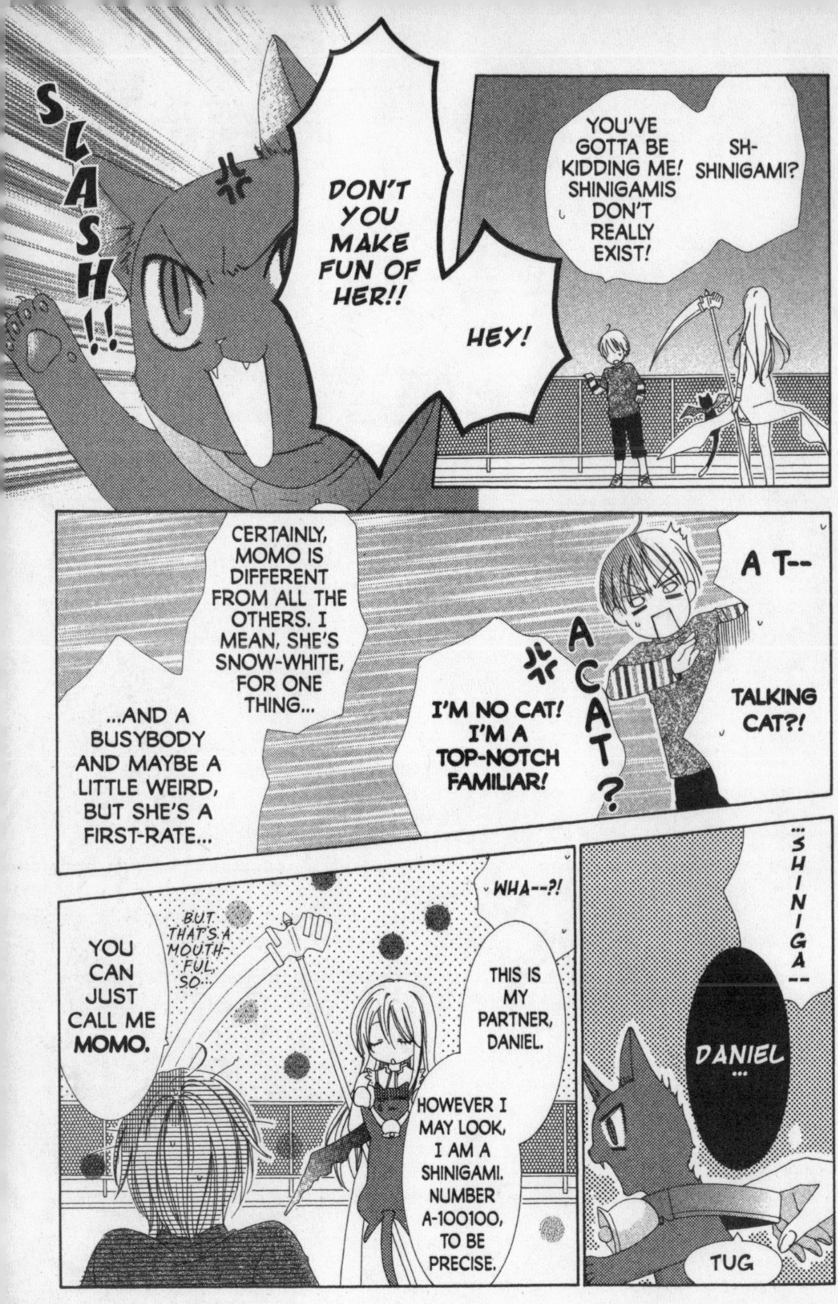
SH-SHINIGAMI?
YOU'VE GOTTA BE KIDDING ME! SHINIGAMIS DON'T REALLY EXIST!
HEY!
DON'T YOU MAKE FUN OF HER!!
SLASH!!
A T--
TALKING CAT?!
A CAT?
I'M NO CAT! I'M A TOP-NOTCH FAMILIAR!
CERTAINLY, MOMO IS DIFFERENT FROM ALL THE OTHERS. I MEAN, SHE'S SNOW-WHITE, FOR ONE THING...
...AND A BUSYBODY AND MAYBE A LITTLE WEIRD, BUT SHE'S A FIRST-RATE...
...SHINIGA--
DANIEL...
TUG
WHA--?!
THIS IS MY PARTNER, DANIEL.
HOWEVER I MAY LOOK, I AM A SHINIGAMI. NUMBER A-100100, TO BE PRECISE.
BUT THAT'S A MOUTHFUL, SO...
YOU CAN JUST CALL ME MOMO.

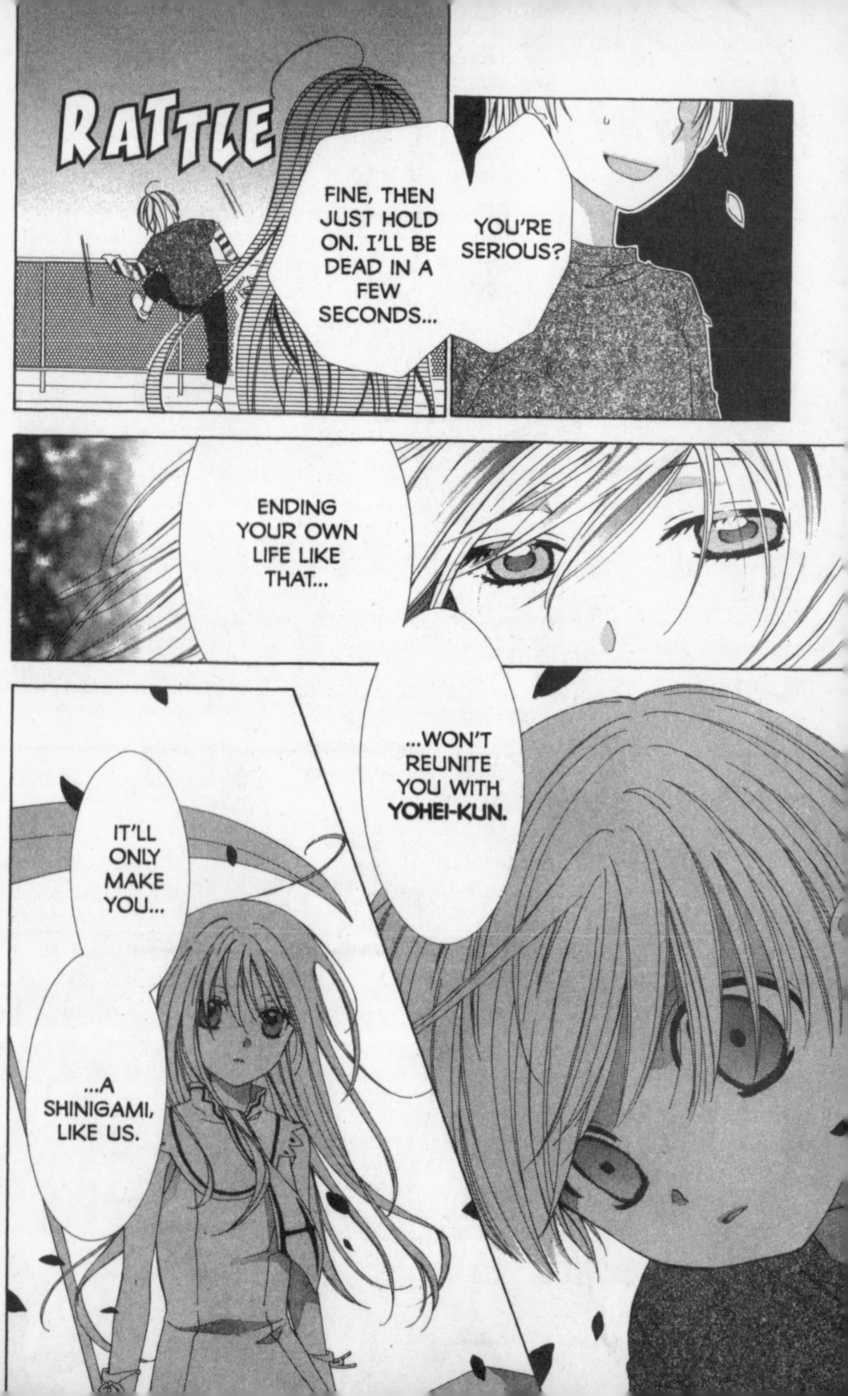
YOU'RE SERIOUS?
FINE, THEN JUST HOLD ON. I'LL BE DEAD IN A FEW SECONDS...
RATTLE
ENDING YOUR OWN LIFE LIKE THAT...
...WON'T REUNITE YOU WITH YOHEI-KUN.
IT'LL ONLY MAKE YOU...
...A SHINIGAMI, LIKE US.

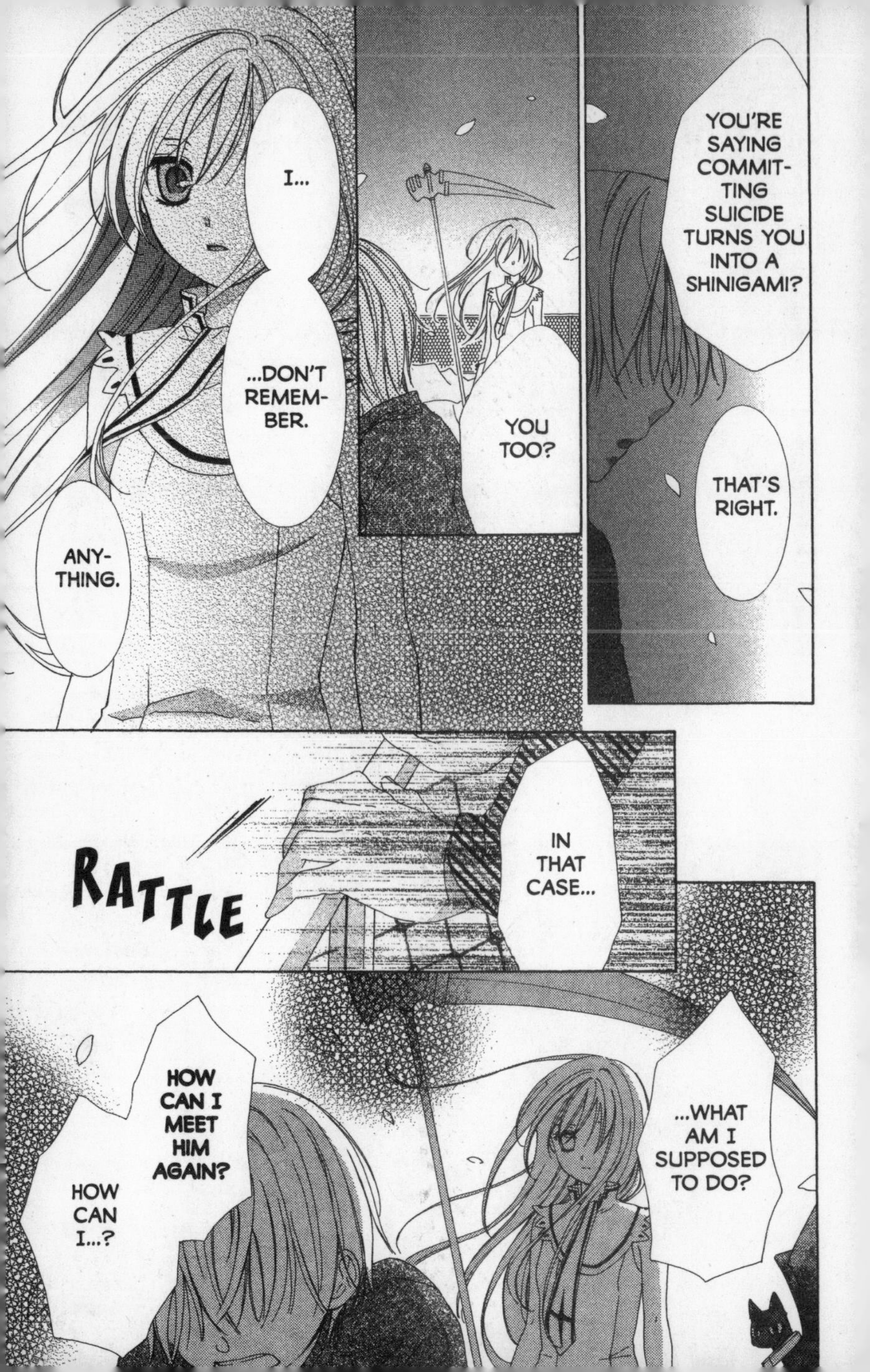
YOU'RE SAYING COMMITTING SUICIDE TURNS YOU INTO A SHINIGAMI?
THAT'S RIGHT.
YOU TOO?
I...
...DON'T REMEMBER.
ANYTHING.
IN THAT CASE...
RATTLE
...WHAT AM I SUPPOSED TO DO?
HOW CAN I MEET HIM AGAIN?
HOW CAN I...?

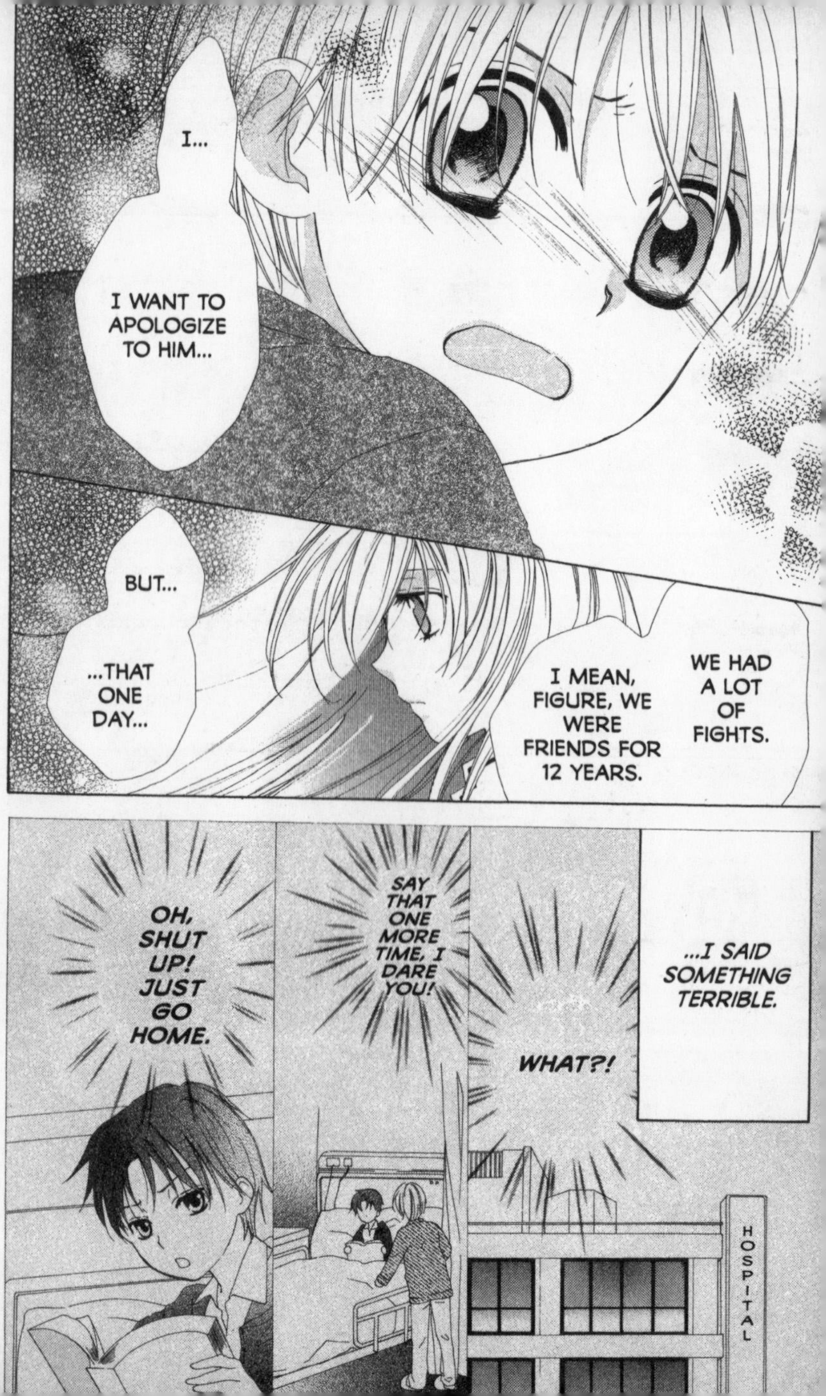
I...
I WANT TO APOLOGIZE TO HIM...
WE HAD A LOT OF FIGHTS.
I MEAN, FIGURE, WE WERE FRIENDS FOR 12 YEARS.
BUT...
...THAT ONE DAY...
...I SAID SOMETHING TERRIBLE.
WHAT?!
HOSPITAL
SAY THAT ONE MORE TIME, I DARE YOU!
OH, SHUT UP! JUST GO HOME.

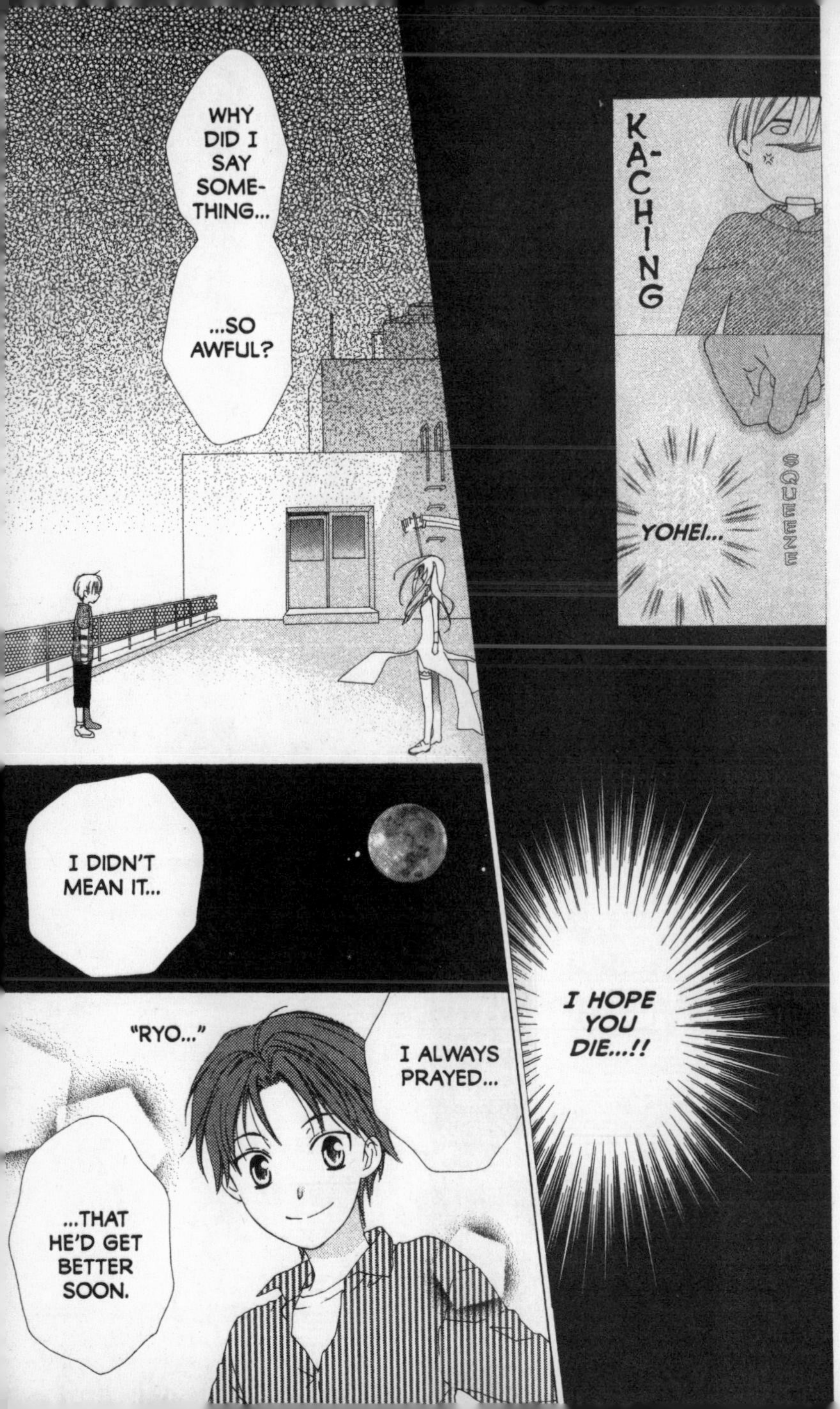
KA-CHING
SQUEEEZE
YOHEI...
I HOPE YOU DIE...!!
WHY DID I SAY SOMETHING...
...SO AWFUL?
I DIDN'T MEAN IT...
"RYO..."
I ALWAYS PRAYED...
...THAT HE'D GET BETTER SOON.

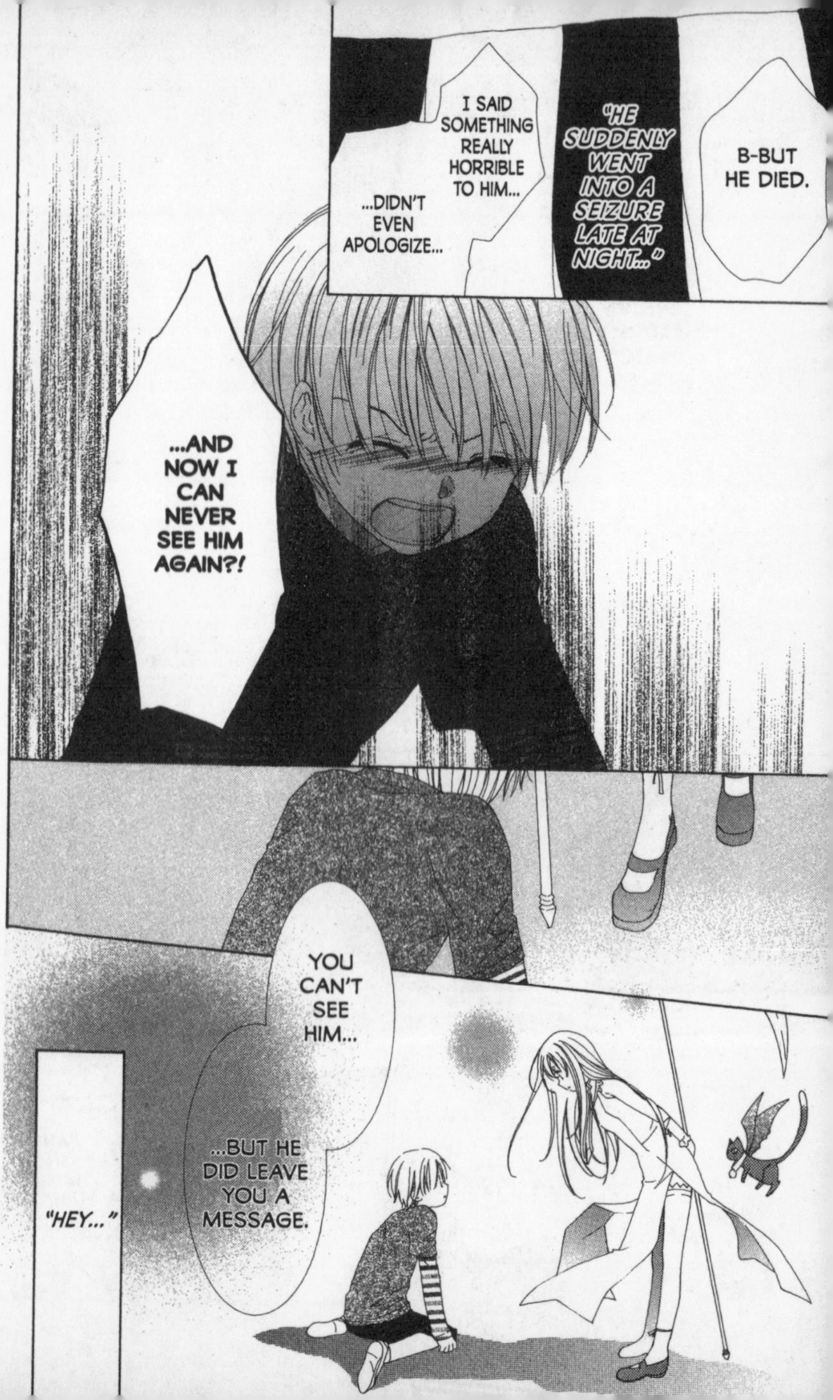
B-BUT HE DIED.
"HE SUDDENLY WENT INTO A SEIZURE LATE AT NIGHT..."
I SAID SOMETHING REALLY HORRIBLE TO HIM...
...DIDN'T EVEN APOLOGIZE...
...AND NOW I CAN NEVER SEE HIM AGAIN?!
YOU CAN'T SEE HIM...
...BUT HE DID LEAVE YOU A MESSAGE.
"HEY..."

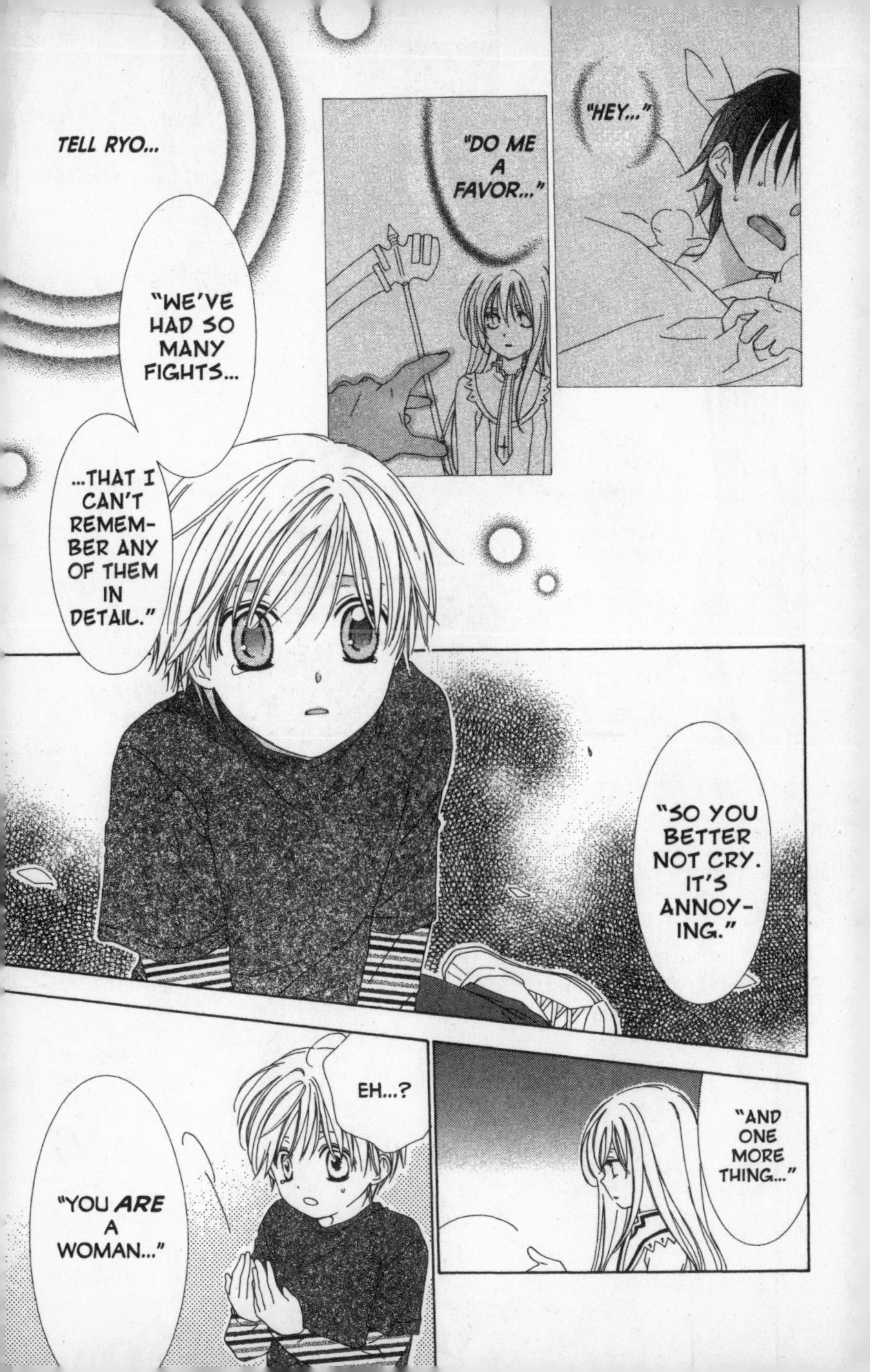
"HEY..."
"DO ME A FAVOR..."
TELL RYO...
"WE'VE HAD SO MANY FIGHTS...
...THAT I CAN'T REMEMBER ANY OF THEM IN DETAIL."
"SO YOU BETTER NOT CRY. IT'S ANNOYING."
"AND ONE MORE THING..."
EH...?
"YOU *ARE* A WOMAN..."

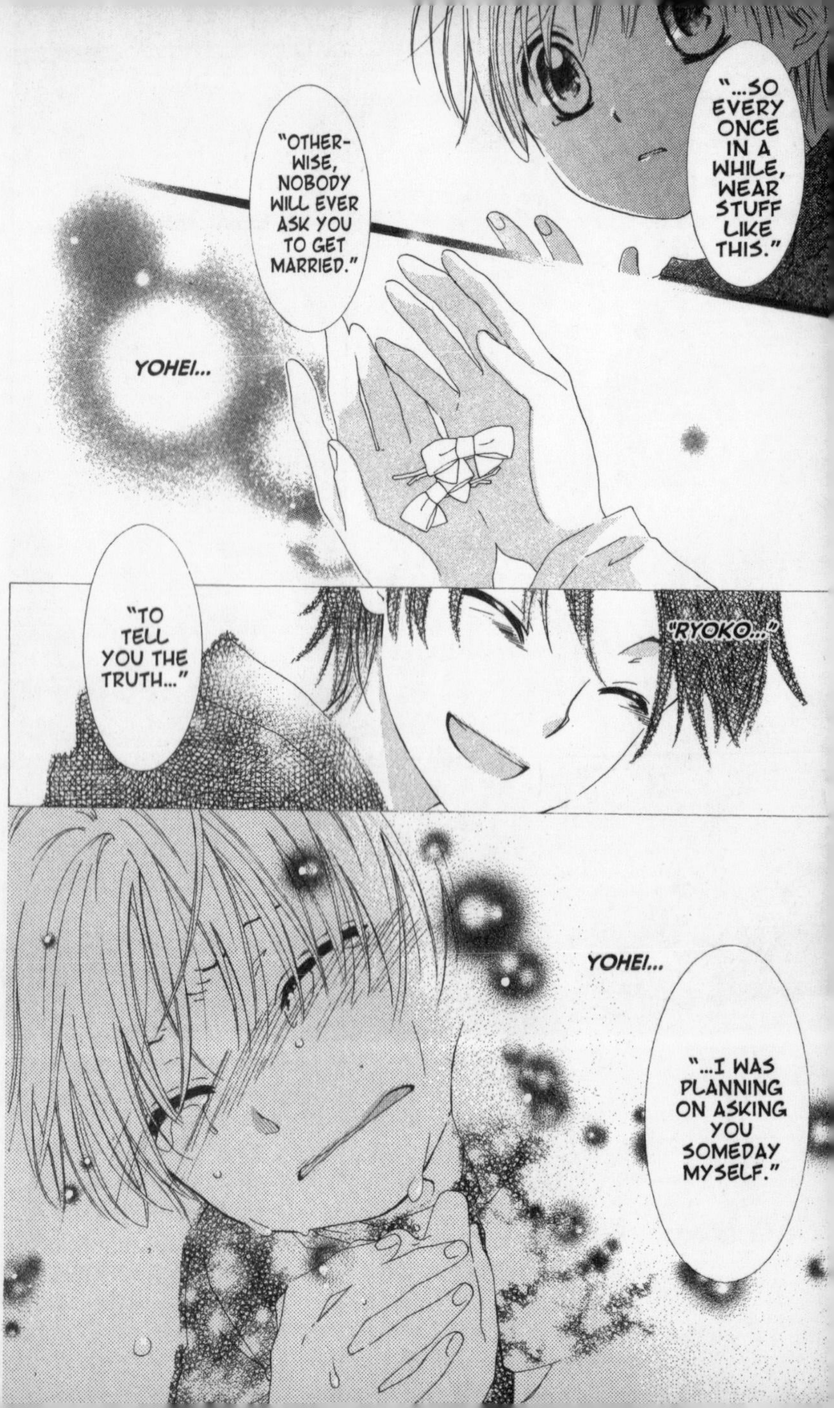
"...SO EVERY ONCE IN A WHILE, WEAR STUFF LIKE THIS."
"OTHER-WISE, NOBODY WILL EVER ASK YOU TO GET MARRIED."
YOHEI...
"RYOKO..."
"TO TELL YOU THE TRUTH..."
"...I WAS PLANNING ON ASKING YOU SOMEDAY MYSELF."
YOHEI...

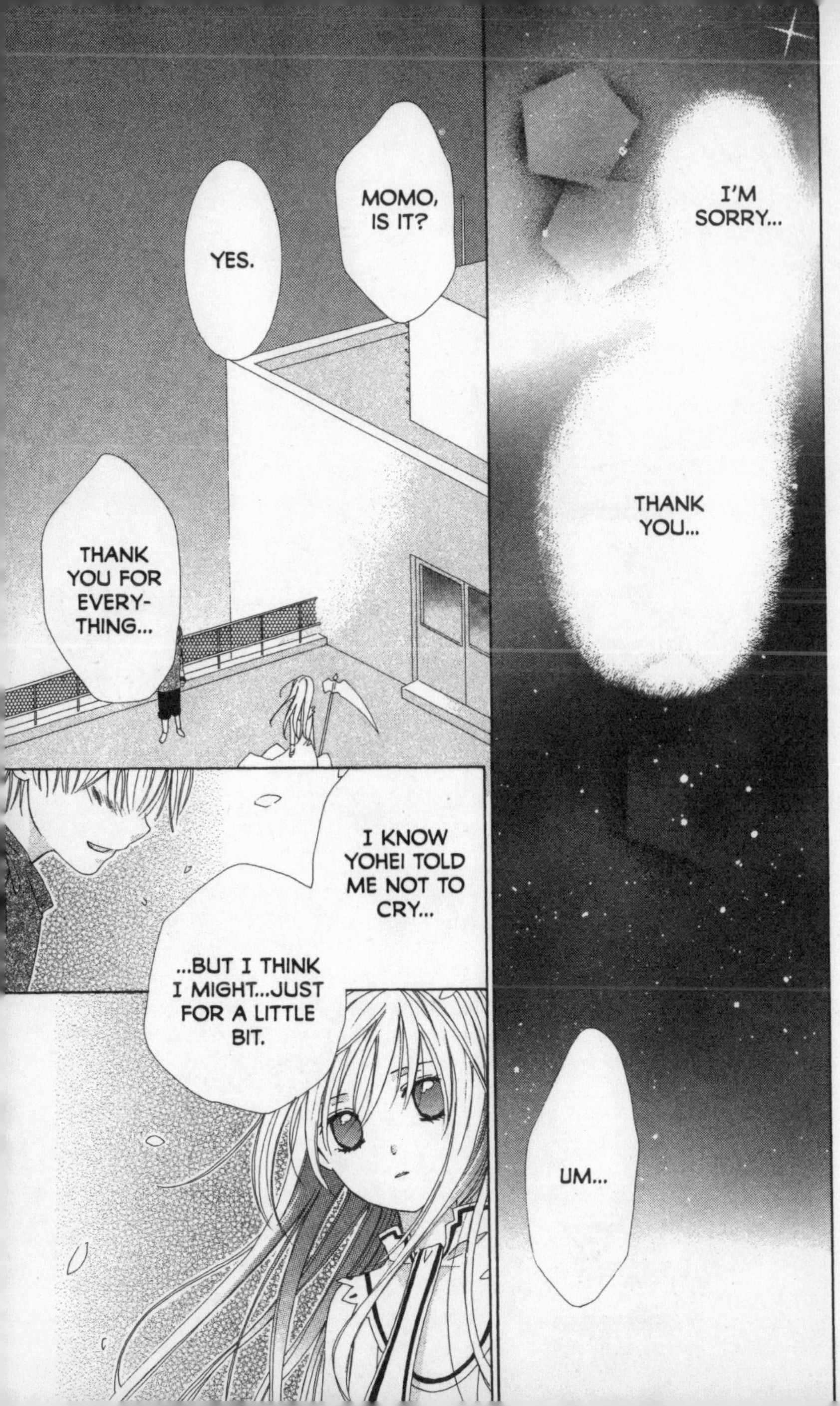
I'M SORRY...
THANK YOU...
UM...
MOMO, IS IT?
YES.
THANK YOU FOR EVERY-THING...
I KNOW YOHEI TOLD ME NOT TO CRY...
...BUT I THINK I MIGHT...JUST FOR A LITTLE BIT.

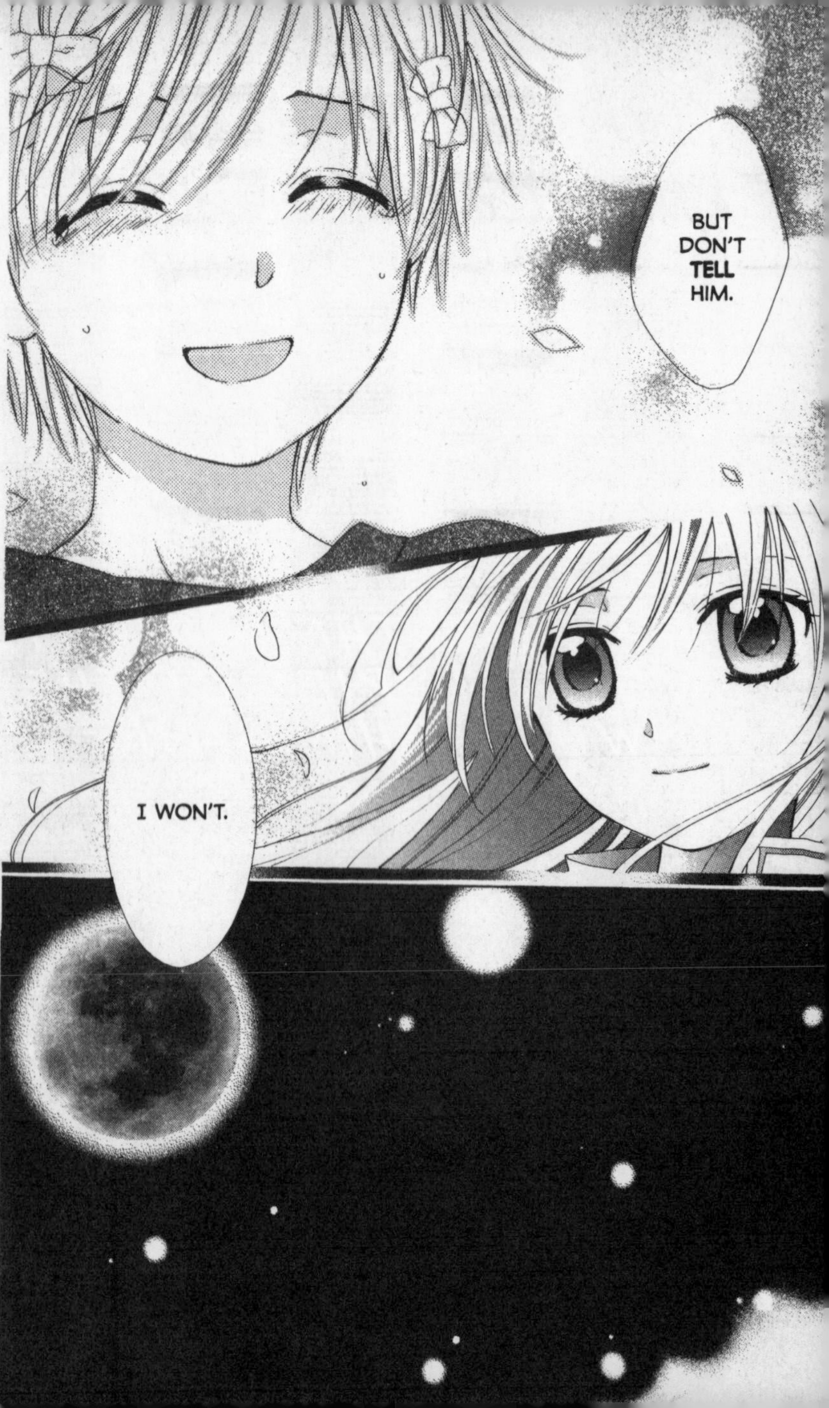
BUT DON'T **TELL** HIM.
I WON'T.

THESE ARE THE SAD BUT SWEET STORIES OF THE WHITE SHINIGAMI.

THE BALLAD OF A SHINIGAMI: PROLOGUE / THE END

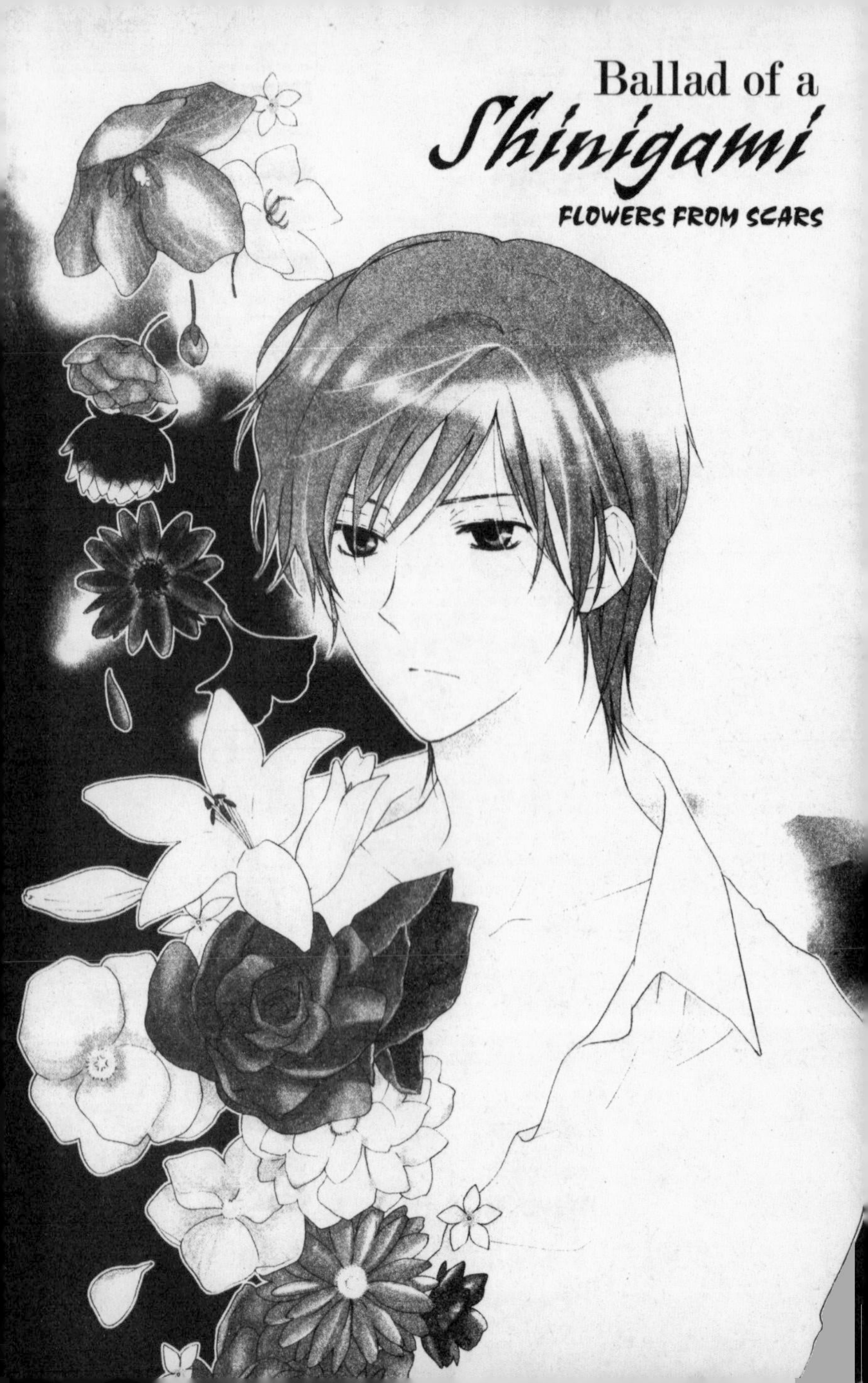
Ballad of a
Shinigami
FLOWERS FROM SCARS

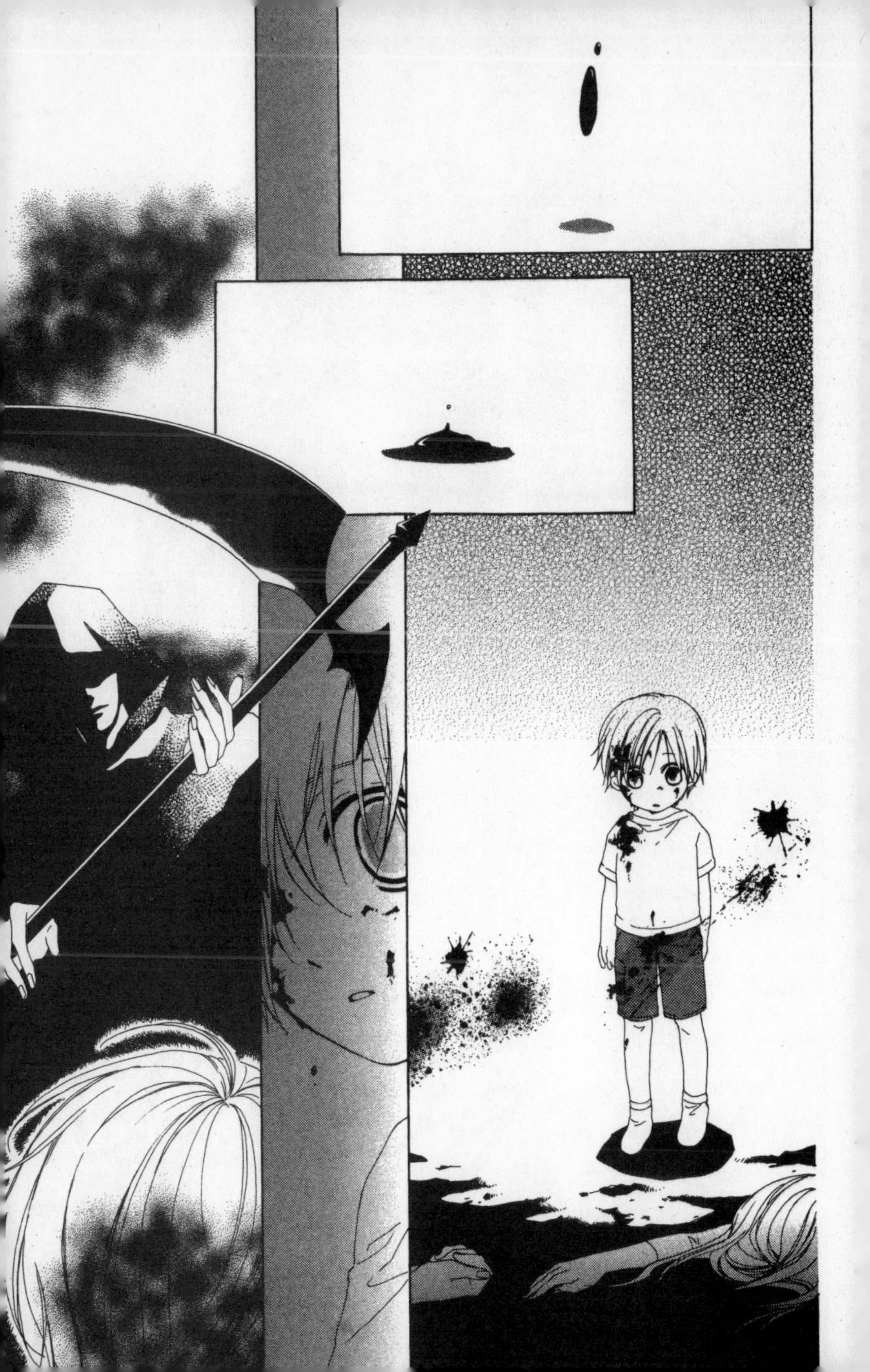

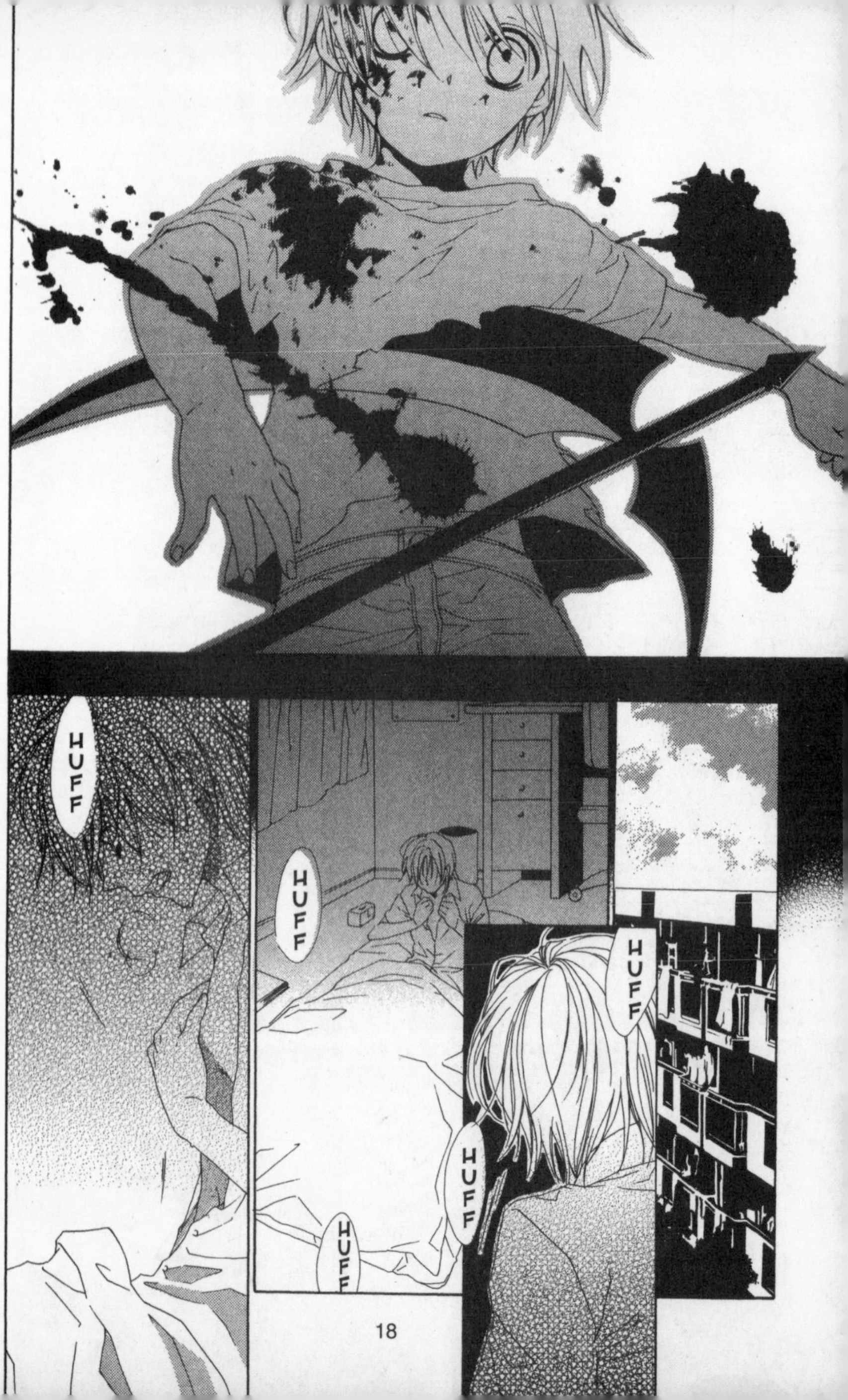
HUFF
HUFF
HUFF
HUFF
HUFF

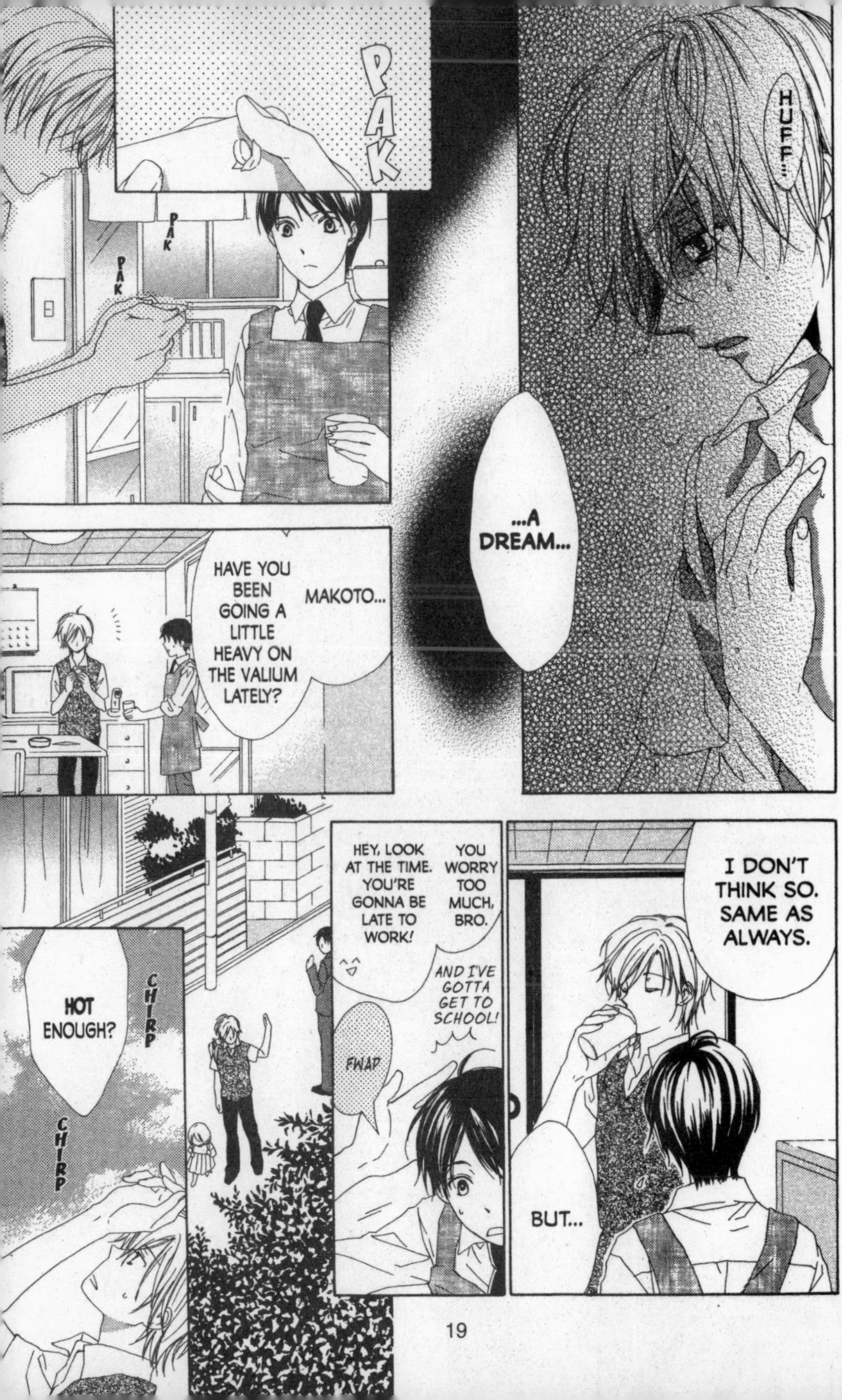
HUFF...
...A DREAM...
PAK
PAK
PAK
MAKOTO...
HAVE YOU BEEN GOING A LITTLE HEAVY ON THE VALIUM LATELY?
I DON'T THINK SO. SAME AS ALWAYS.
BUT...
YOU WORRY TOO MUCH, BRO.
HEY, LOOK AT THE TIME. YOU'RE GONNA BE LATE TO WORK!
AND I'VE GOTTA GET TO SCHOOL!
FWAP
HOT ENOUGH?
CHIRP
CHIRP

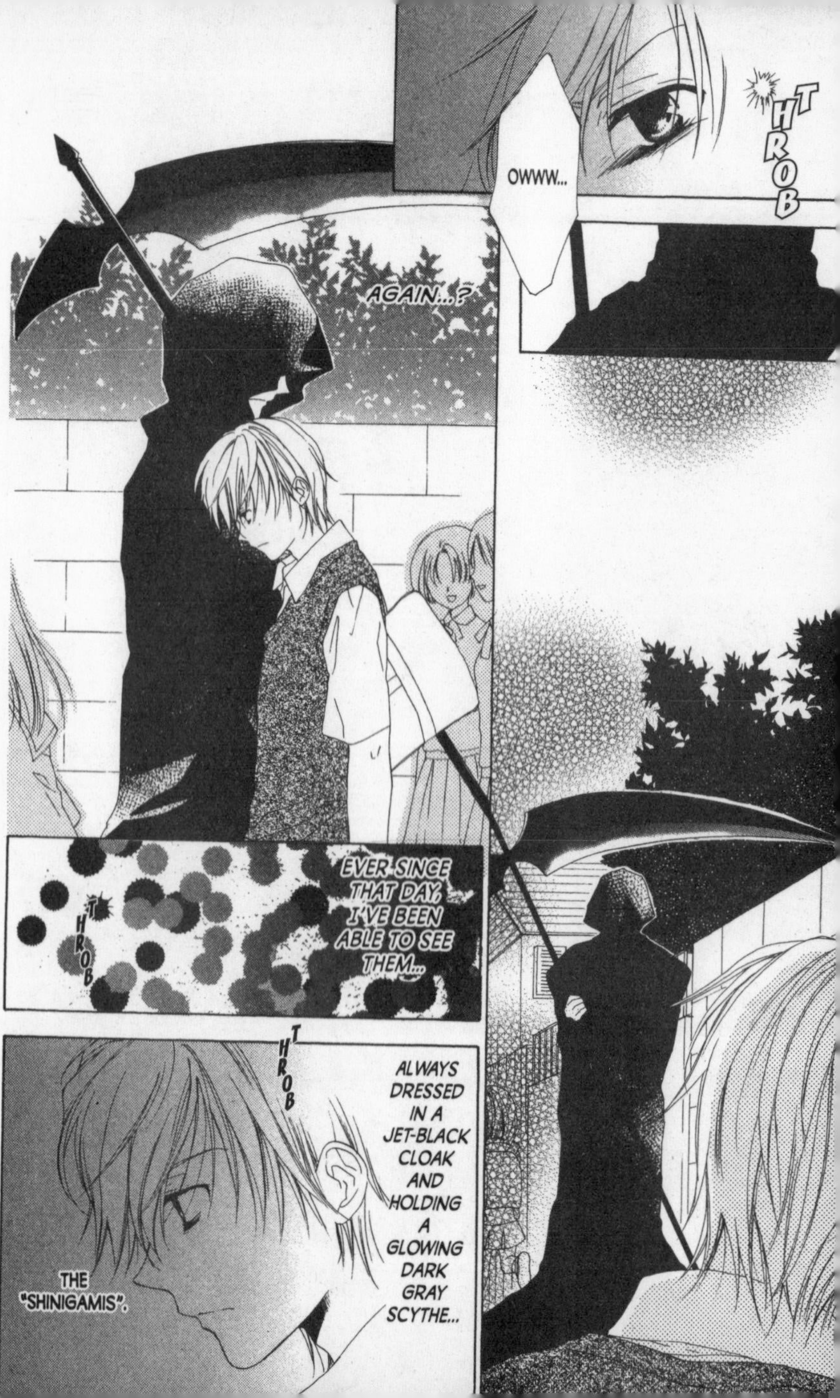
THROB
OWWW...
AGAIN...?
EVER SINCE THAT DAY, I'VE BEEN ABLE TO SEE THEM...
THROB
THROB
ALWAYS DRESSED IN A JET-BLACK CLOAK AND HOLDING A GLOWING DARK GRAY SCYTHE...
THE "SHINIGAMIS".

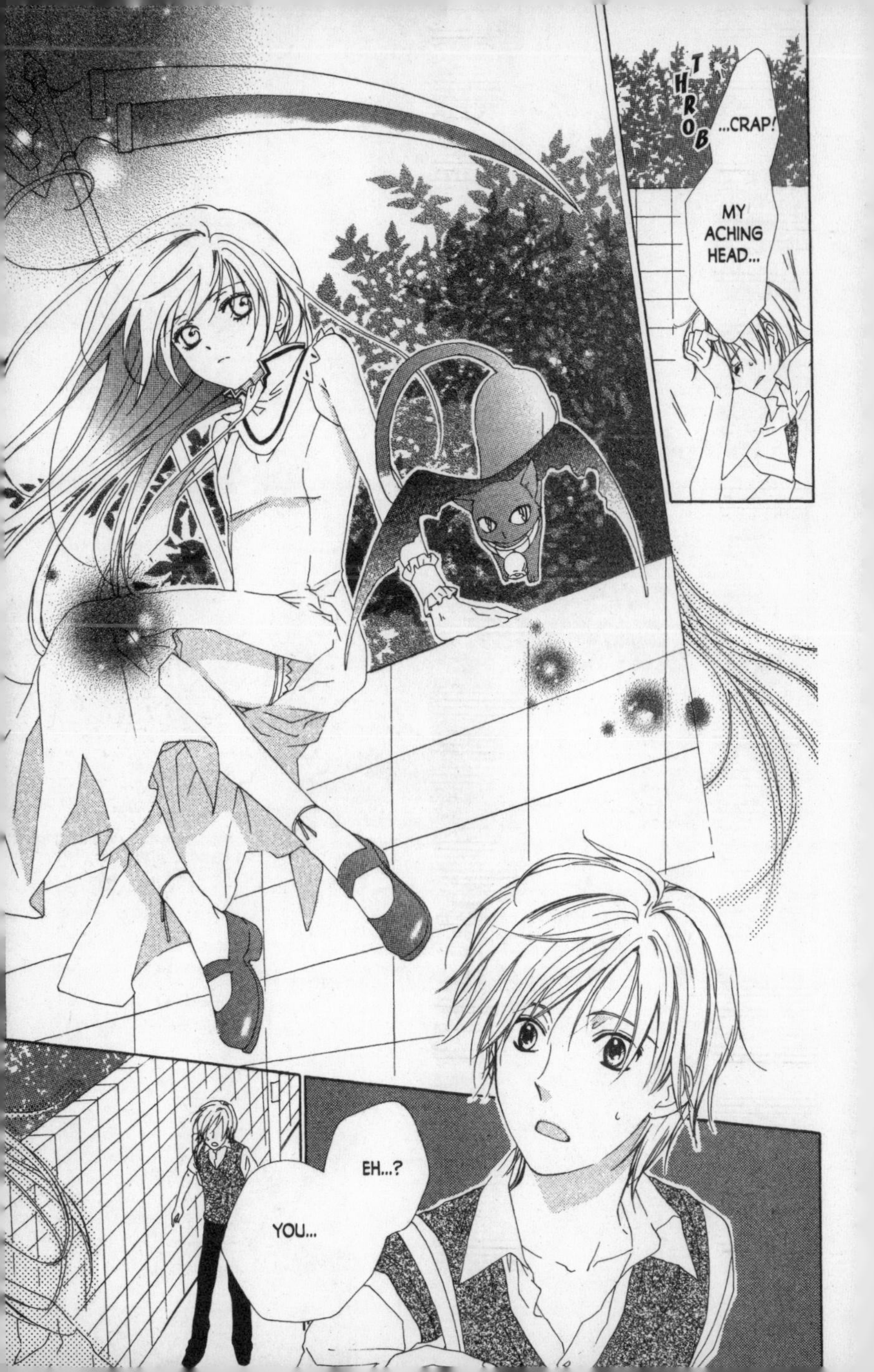
THROB
...CRAP!
MY ACHING HEAD...
EH...?
YOU...

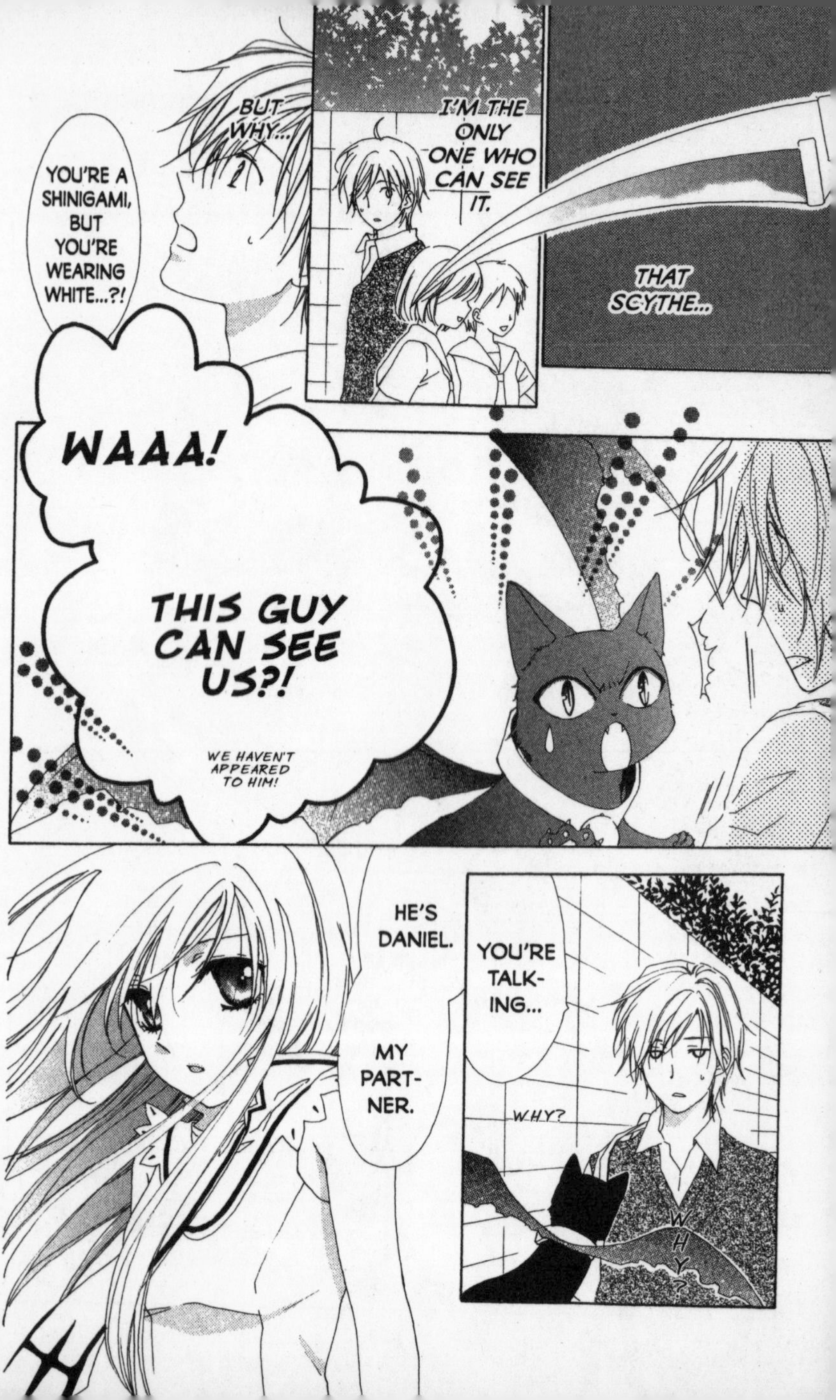
THAT SCYTHE...
I'M THE ONLY ONE WHO CAN SEE IT.
BUT WHY...
YOU'RE A SHINIGAMI, BUT YOU'RE WEARING WHITE...?!
WAAA!
THIS GUY CAN SEE US?!
WE HAVEN'T APPEARED TO HIM!
YOU'RE TALKING...
WHY?
WHY?
HE'S DANIEL.
MY PARTNER.

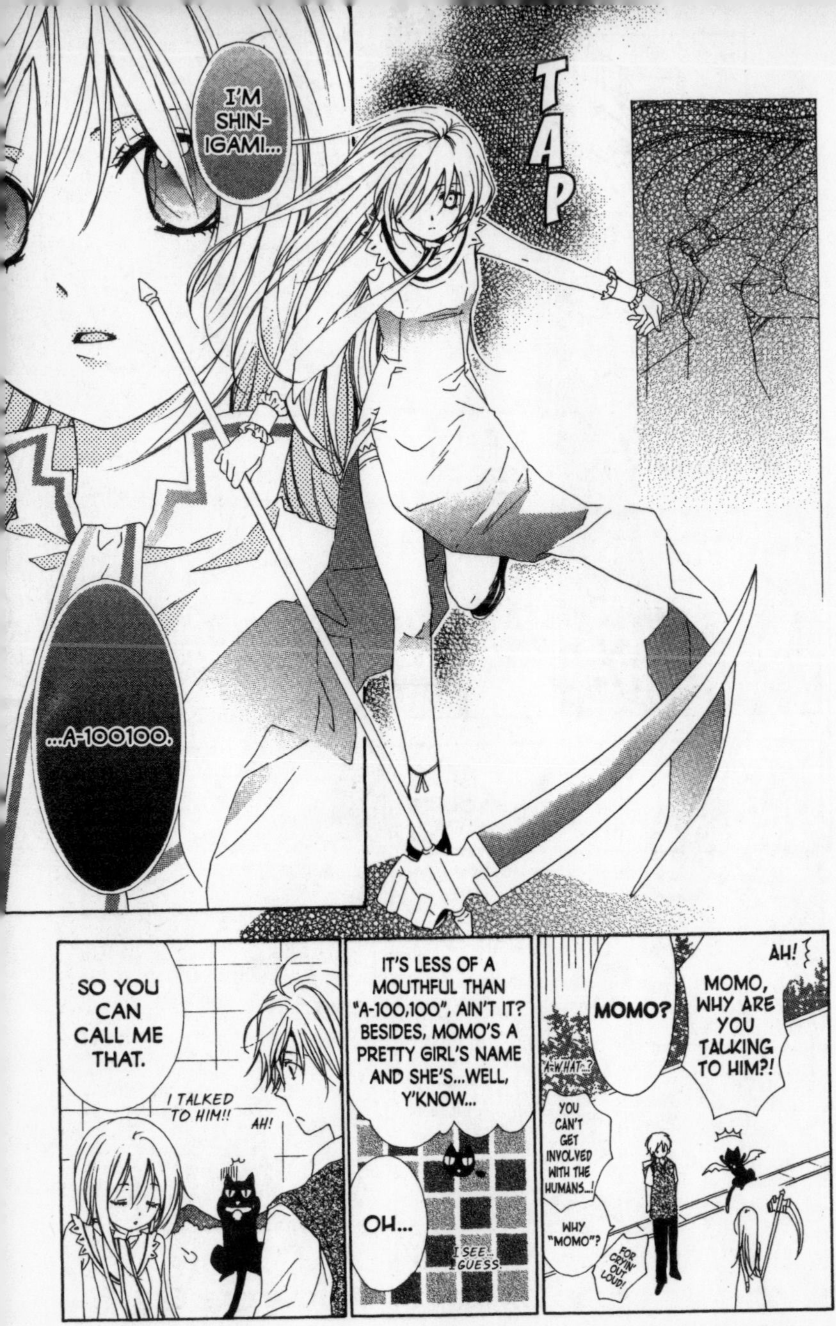
TAP
I'M SHIN-IGAMI...
...A-100100.
AH!
MOMO, WHY ARE YOU TALKING TO HIM?!
MOMO?
A-WHAT...?
YOU CAN'T GET INVOLVED WITH THE HUMANS...!
WHY "MOMO"?
FOR CRYIN' OUT LOUD!
IT'S LESS OF A MOUTHFUL THAN "A-100,100", AIN'T IT? BESIDES, MOMO'S A PRETTY GIRL'S NAME AND SHE'S...WELL, Y'KNOW...
OH...
I SEE... I GUESS.
SO YOU CAN CALL ME THAT.
AH!
I TALKED TO HIM!!

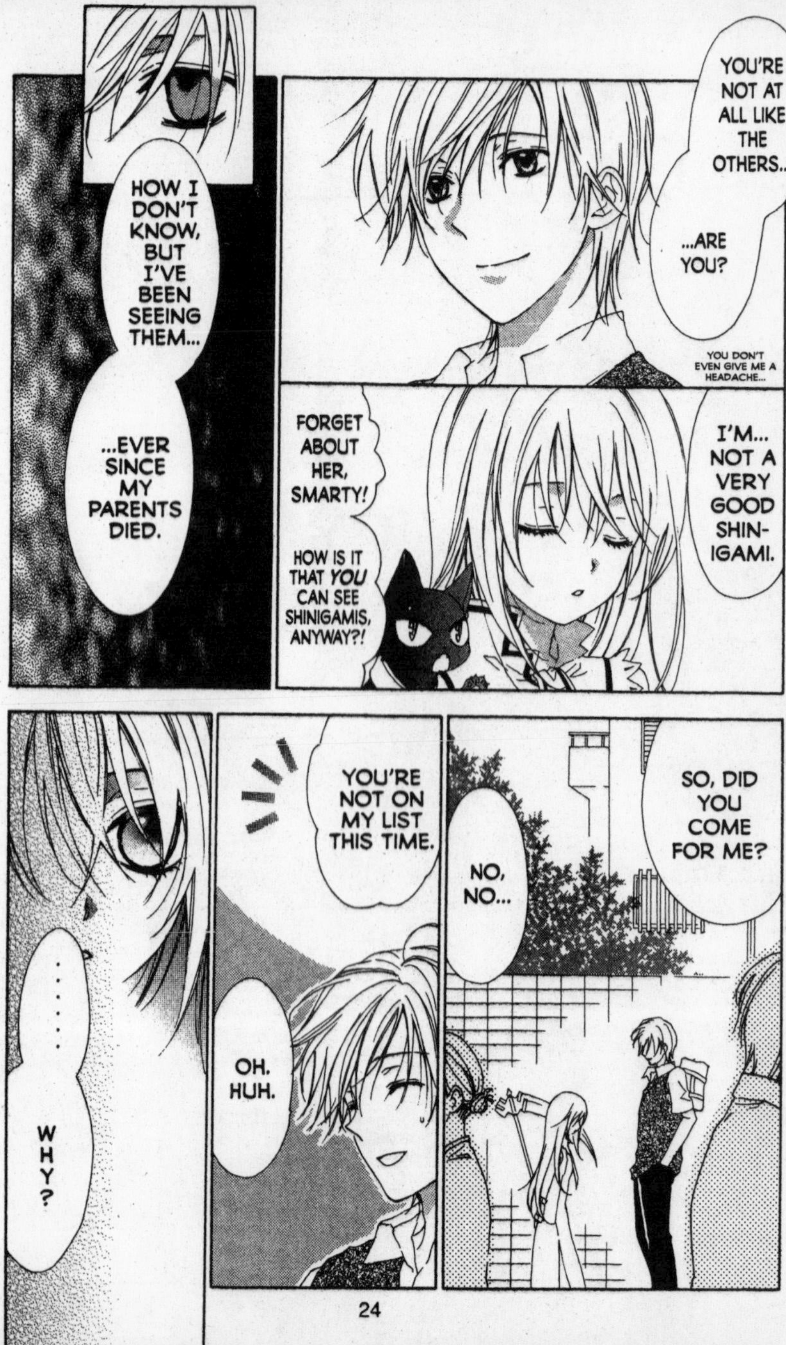
YOU'RE NOT AT ALL LIKE THE OTHERS...
...ARE YOU?
YOU DON'T EVEN GIVE ME A HEADACHE...
I'M... NOT A VERY GOOD SHINIGAMI.
FORGET ABOUT HER, SMARTY!
HOW IS IT THAT *YOU* CAN SEE SHINIGAMIS, ANYWAY?!
HOW I DON'T KNOW, BUT I'VE BEEN SEEING THEM...
...EVER SINCE MY PARENTS DIED.
SO, DID YOU COME FOR ME?
NO, NO...
YOU'RE NOT ON MY LIST THIS TIME.
OH. HUH.
......
WHY?

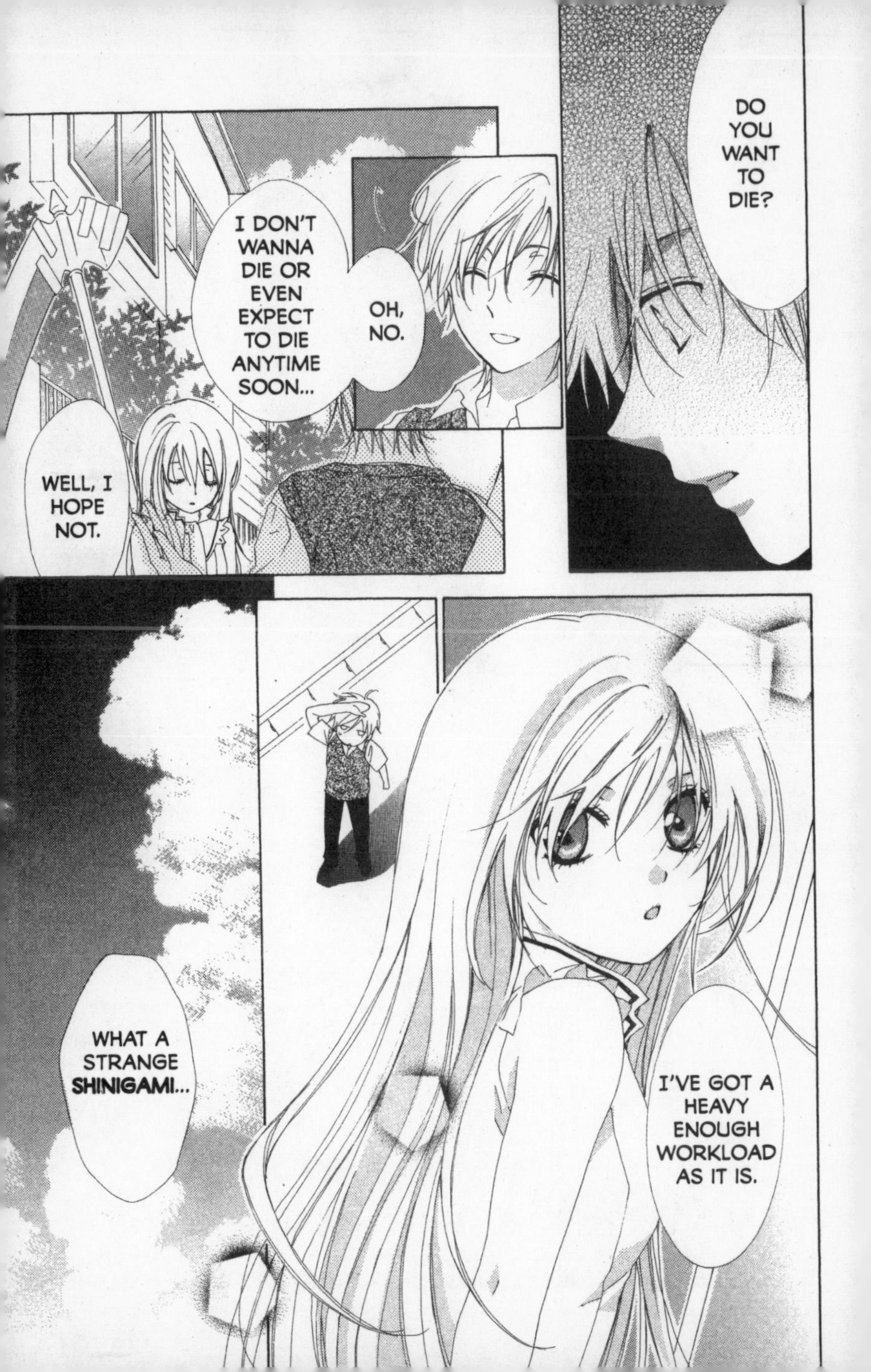
DO YOU WANT TO DIE?
OH, NO.
I DON'T WANNA DIE OR EVEN EXPECT TO DIE ANYTIME SOON...
WELL, I HOPE NOT.
I'VE GOT A HEAVY ENOUGH WORKLOAD AS IT IS.
WHAT A STRANGE **SHINIGAMI**...

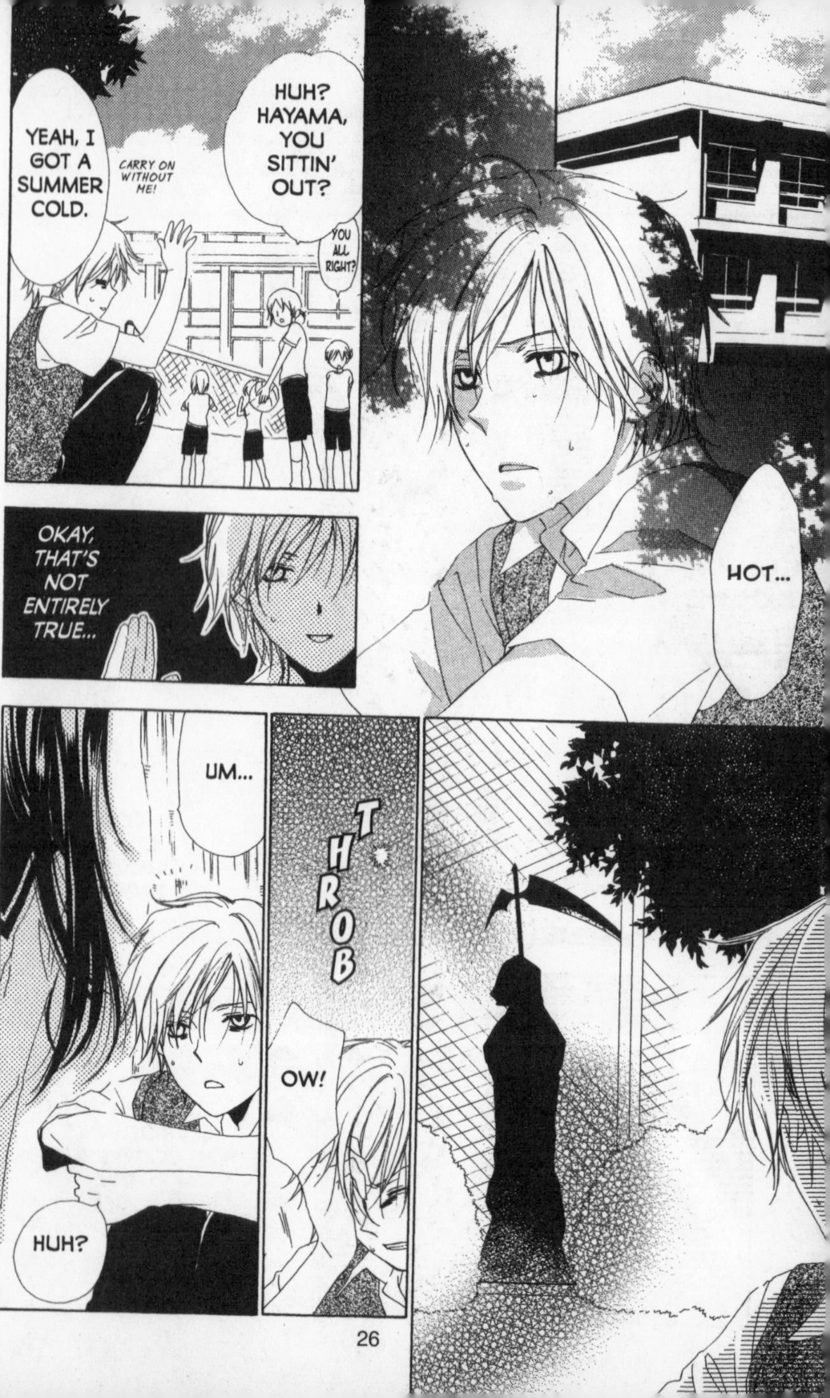
HOT...
HUH? HAYAMA, YOU SITTIN' OUT?
YOU ALL RIGHT?
CARRY ON WITHOUT ME!
YEAH, I GOT A SUMMER COLD.
OKAY, THAT'S NOT ENTIRELY TRUE...
THROB
OW!
UM...
HUH?

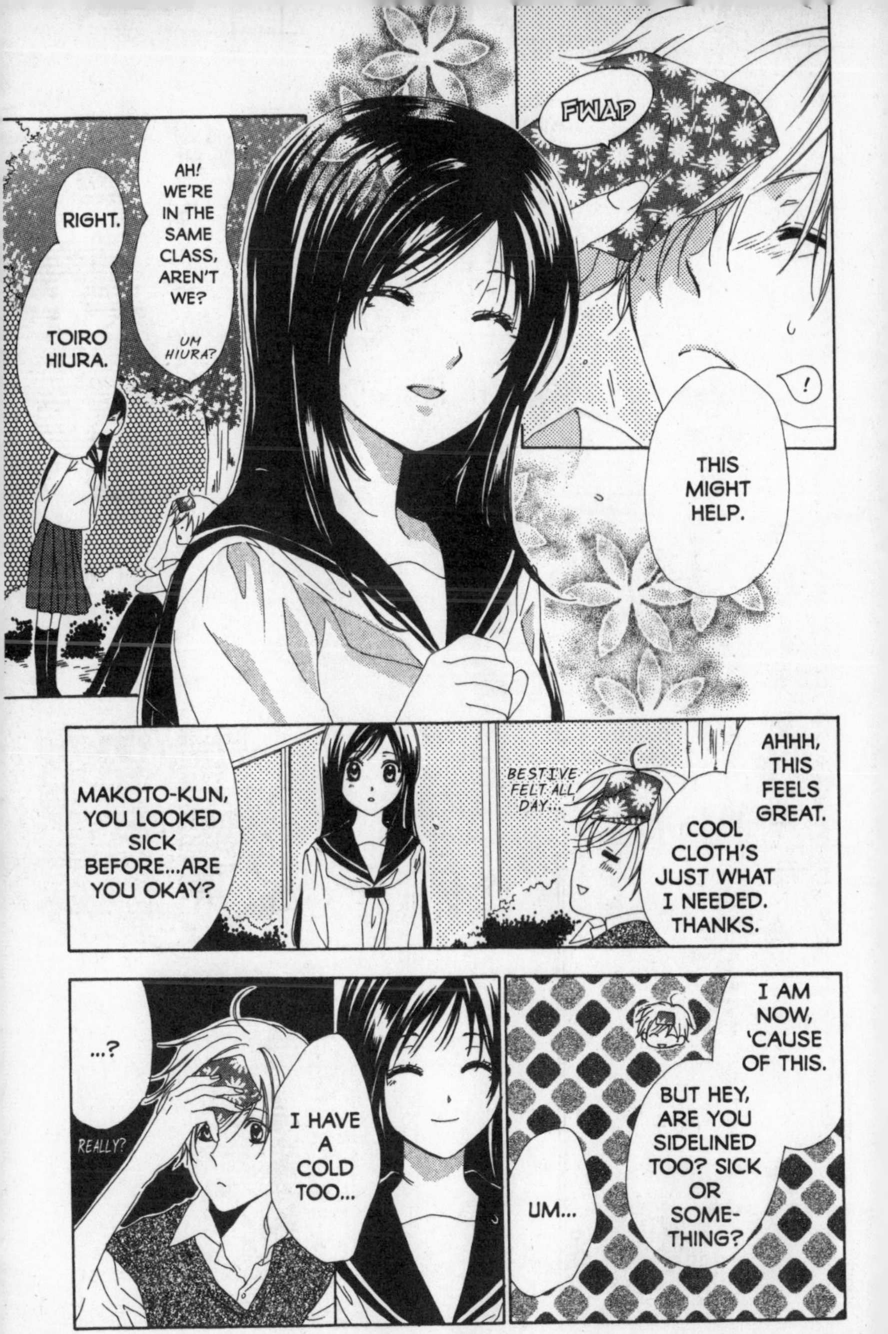
FWAP
!
THIS MIGHT HELP.
AH! WE'RE IN THE SAME CLASS, AREN'T WE?
UM HIURA?
RIGHT.
TOIRO HIURA.
AHHH, THIS FEELS GREAT.
COOL CLOTH'S JUST WHAT I NEEDED. THANKS.
BEST I'VE FELT ALL DAY...
MAKOTO-KUN, YOU LOOKED SICK BEFORE...ARE YOU OKAY?
I AM NOW, 'CAUSE OF THIS.
BUT HEY, ARE YOU SIDELINED TOO? SICK OR SOME-THING?
UM...
I HAVE A COLD TOO...
...?
REALLY?

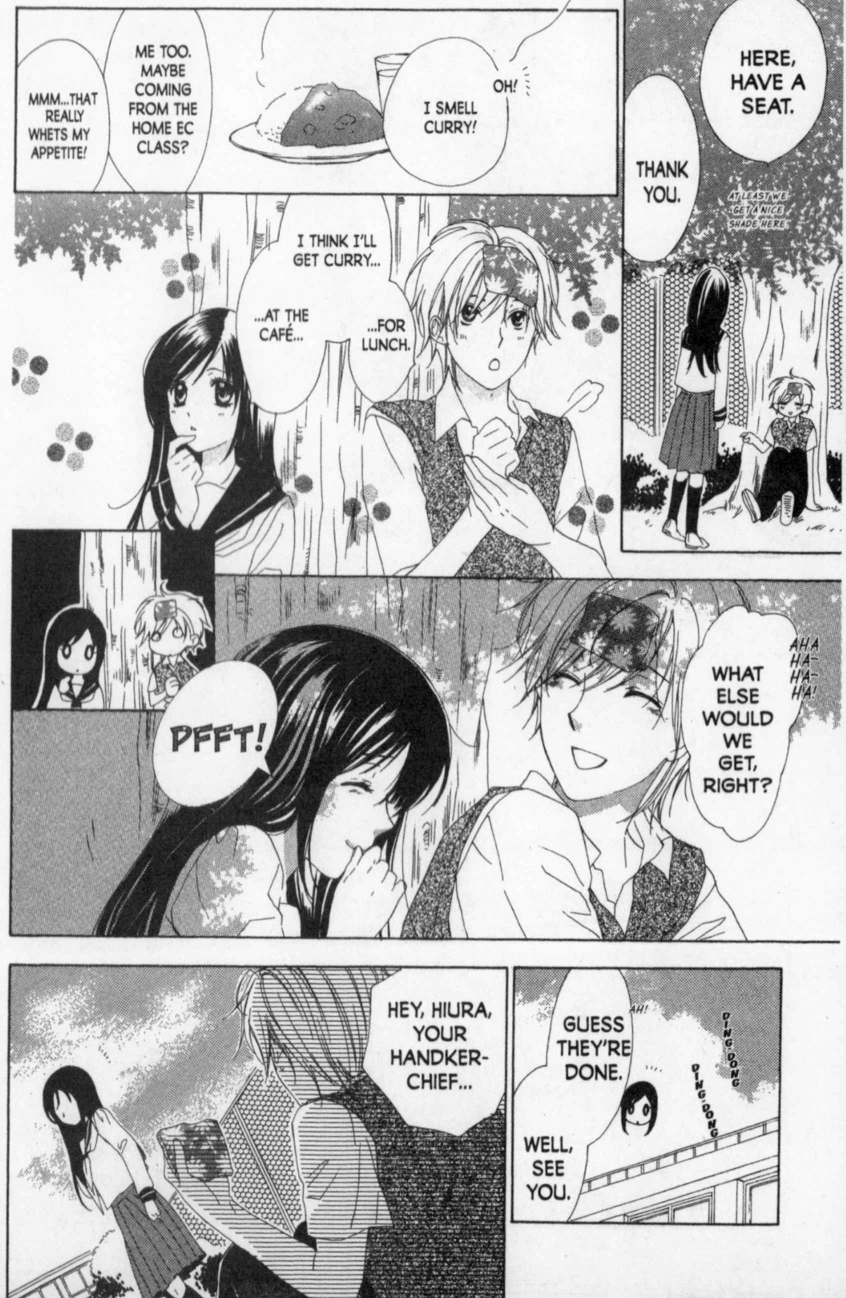
HERE, HAVE A SEAT.
THANK YOU.
AT LEAST WE GET A NICE SHADE HERE.
OH!
I SMELL CURRY!
ME TOO. MAYBE COMING FROM THE HOME EC CLASS?
MMM...THAT REALLY WHETS MY APPETITE!
I THINK I'LL GET CURRY...
...FOR LUNCH.
...AT THE CAFÉ...
AHAHAHA!
WHAT ELSE WOULD WE GET, RIGHT?
PFFT!
DING DONG
DING DONG
AH!
GUESS THEY'RE DONE.
WELL, SEE YOU.
HEY, HIURA, YOUR HANDKER-CHIEF...

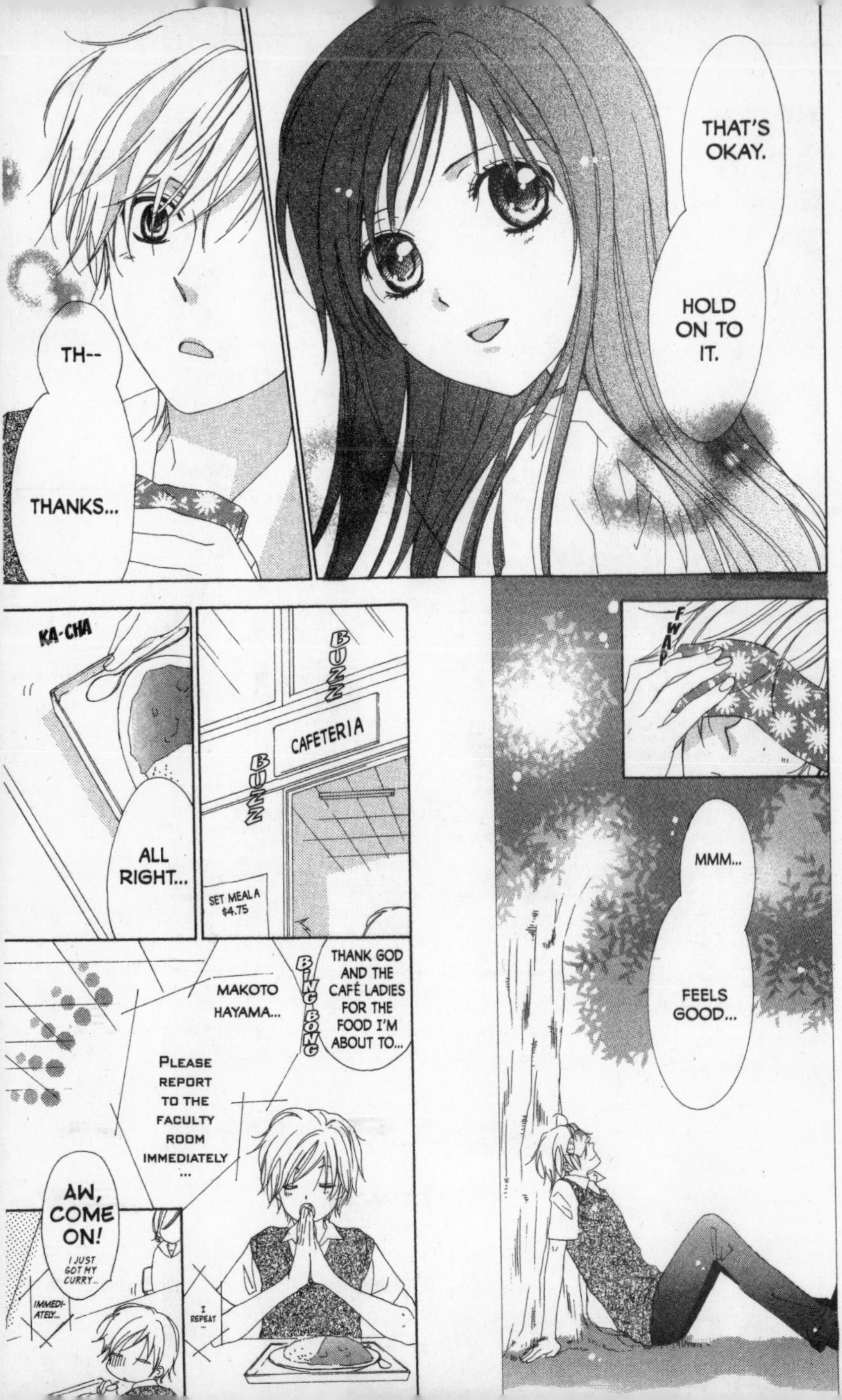

THAT'S OKAY.
HOLD ON TO IT.
TH--
THANKS...
FWAP
MMM...
FEELS GOOD...
BUZZ
BUZZ
CAFETERIA
SET MEAL A $4.75
KA-CHA
ALL RIGHT...
THANK GOD AND THE CAFÉ LADIES FOR THE FOOD I'M ABOUT TO...
BING BONG
MAKOTO HAYAMA...
PLEASE REPORT TO THE FACULTY ROOM IMMEDIATELY...
I REPEAT...
AW, COME ON!
I JUST GOT MY CURRY...
IMMEDIATELY...

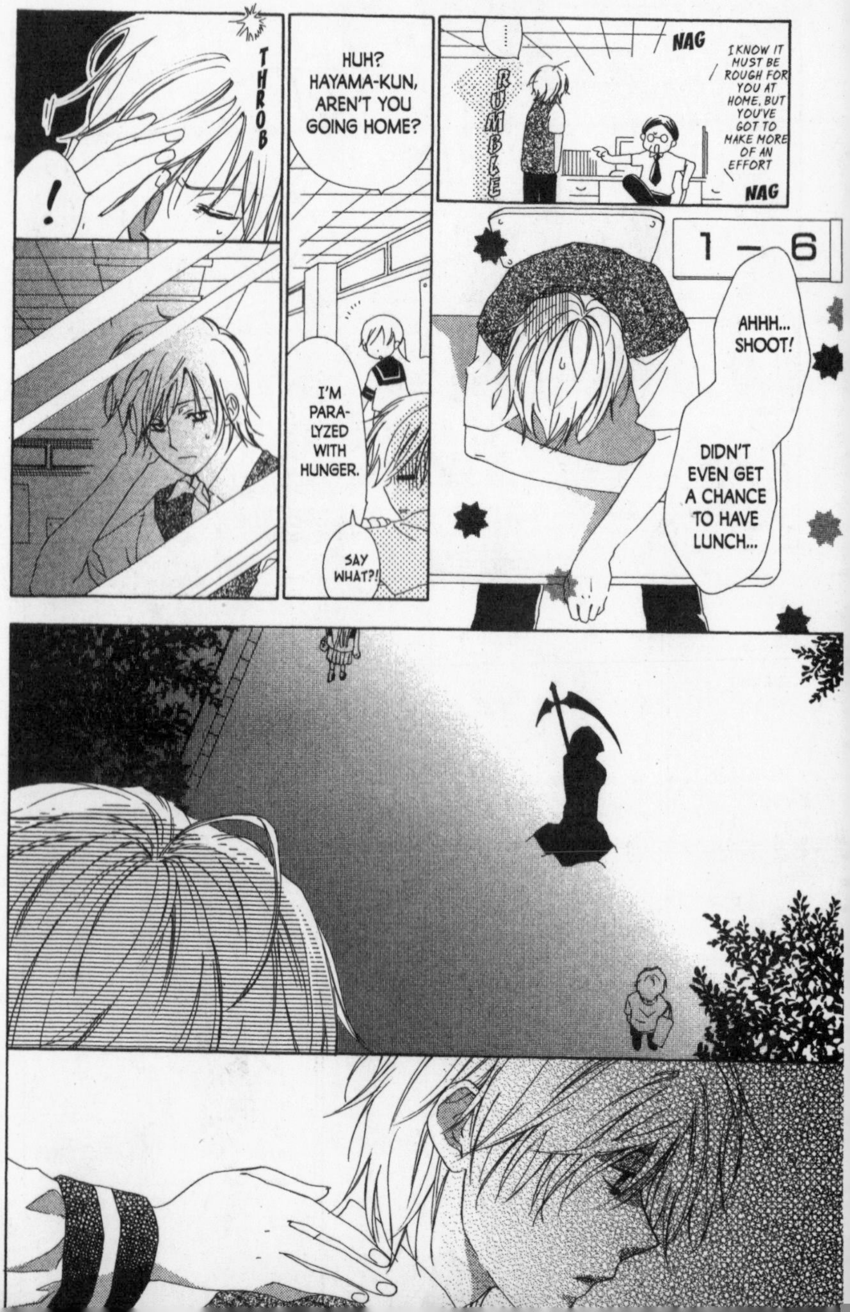
...
RUMBLE
NAG
I KNOW IT MUST BE ROUGH FOR YOU AT HOME, BUT YOU'VE GOT TO MAKE MORE OF AN EFFORT
NAG
1 - 6
AHHH... SHOOT!
DIDN'T EVEN GET A CHANCE TO HAVE LUNCH...
HUH? HAYAMA-KUN, AREN'T YOU GOING HOME?
I'M PARALYZED WITH HUNGER.
SAY WHAT?!
THROB
!

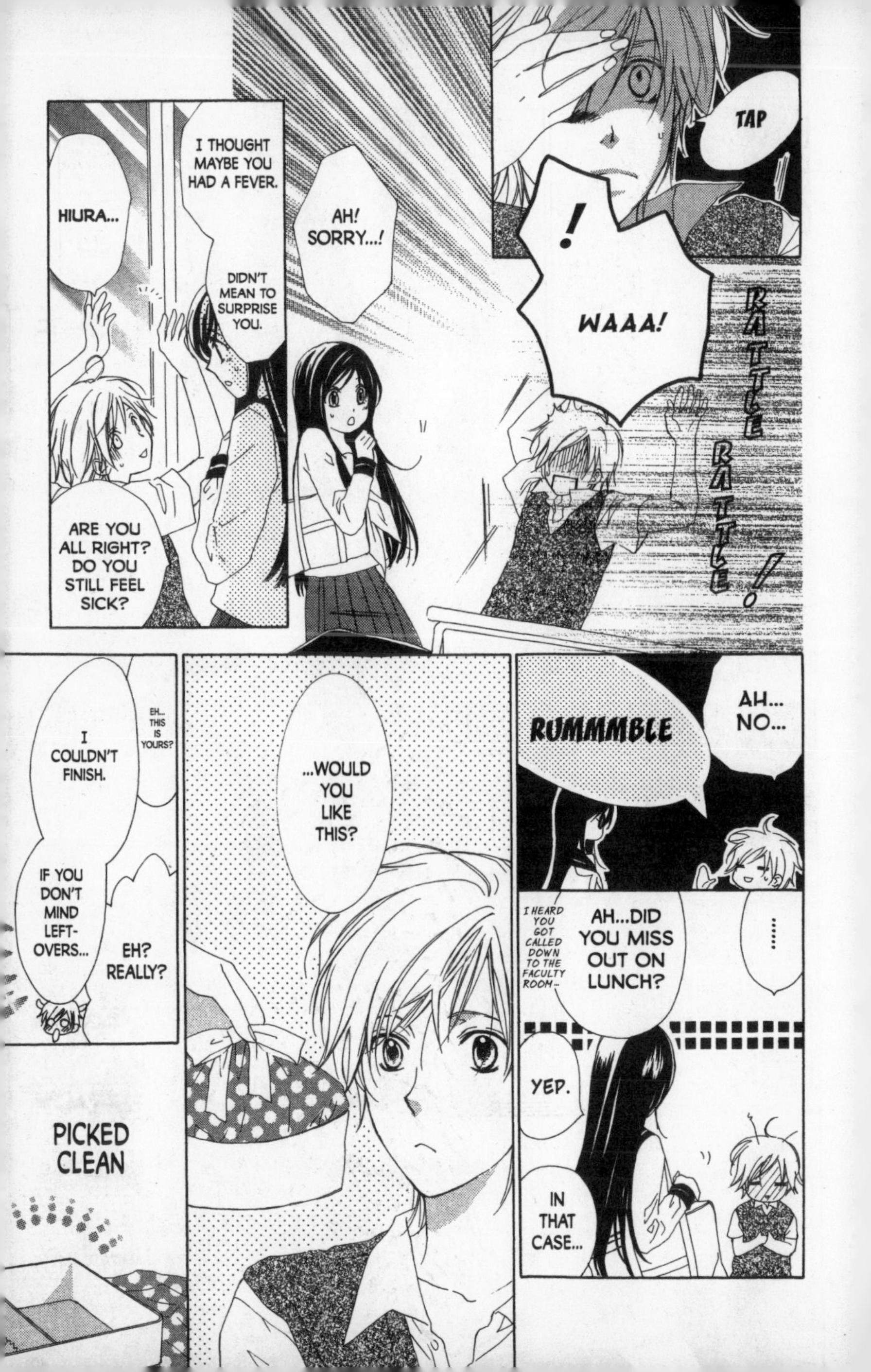
TAP
!
WAAA!
RATTLE RATTLE!
AH! SORRY...!
DIDN'T MEAN TO SURPRISE YOU.
I THOUGHT MAYBE YOU HAD A FEVER.
HIURA...
ARE YOU ALL RIGHT? DO YOU STILL FEEL SICK?
AH... NO...
RUMMMBLE
......
AH...DID YOU MISS OUT ON LUNCH?
I HEARD YOU GOT CALLED DOWN TO THE FACULTY ROOM...
YEP.
IN THAT CASE...
...WOULD YOU LIKE THIS?
EH... THIS IS YOURS?
I COULDN'T FINISH.
EH? REALLY?
IF YOU DON'T MIND LEFT-OVERS...
PICKED CLEAN

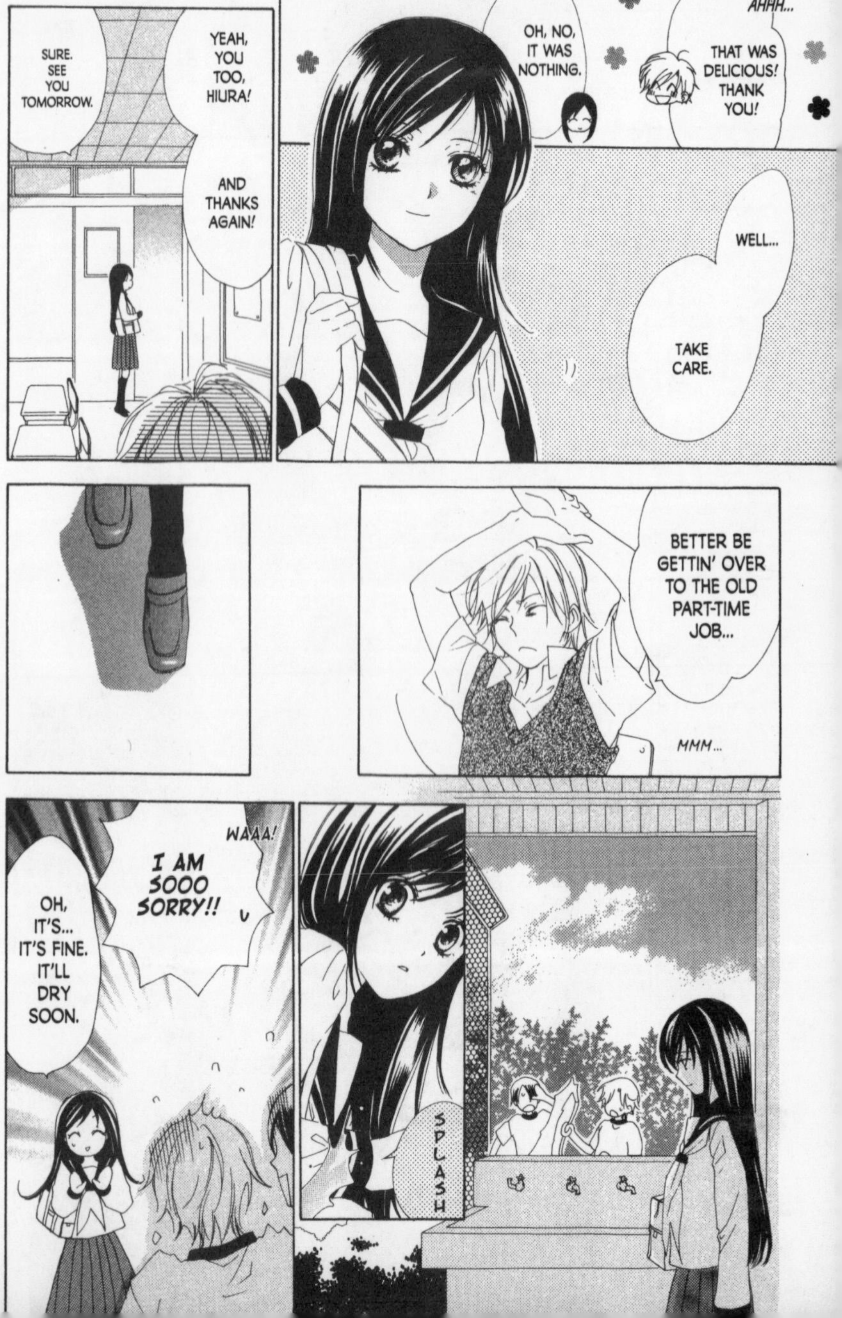
AHHH...
THAT WAS DELICIOUS! THANK YOU!
OH, NO, IT WAS NOTHING.
WELL...
TAKE CARE.
YEAH, YOU TOO, HIURA!
AND THANKS AGAIN!
SURE. SEE YOU TOMORROW.
BETTER BE GETTIN' OVER TO THE OLD PART-TIME JOB...
MMM...
SPLASH
WAAA!
I AM SOOO SORRY!!
OH, IT'S... IT'S FINE. IT'LL DRY SOON.

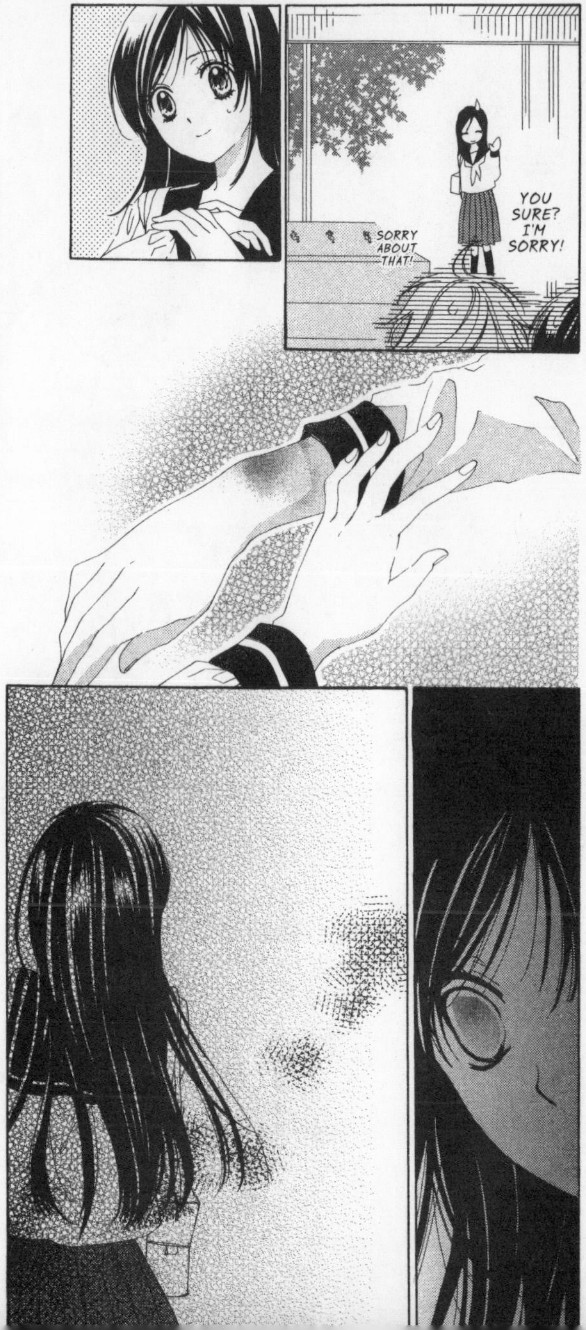
YOU SURE? I'M SORRY!
SORRY ABOUT THAT!

1

NICE TO MEET YOU.
HELLO.
I'M ASUKA IZUMI.

I'M HAPPY TO BRING YOU THE COLLECTED EDITION OF "BALLAD OF A SHINIGAMI"! THANK YOU FOR GETTING IT!

THIS VOLUME HAS SIX COLUMN SPACES, SO I THOUGHT I'D USE THEM TO SHOW YOU HOW MOMO-SAN WOULD LOOK IN VARIOUS OUTFITS.

I HOPE YOU ENJOY THE BOOK.

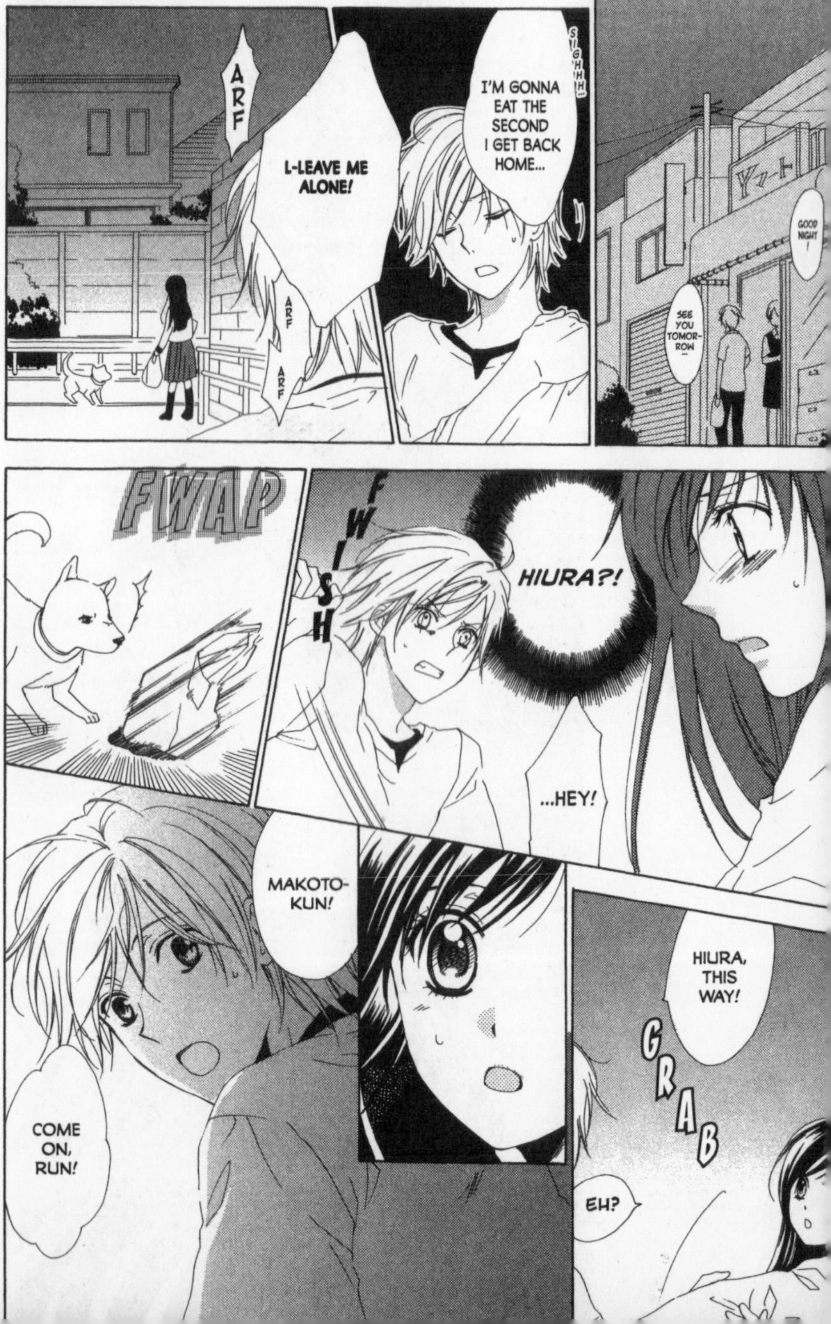
GOOD NIGHT!
SEE YOU TOMOR-ROW...
SIGHHH...
I'M GONNA EAT THE SECOND I GET BACK HOME...
ARF
L-LEAVE ME ALONE!
ARF
ARF
HIURA?!
...HEY!
FWISH
FWAP
HIURA, THIS WAY!
GRAB
EH?
MAKOTO-KUN!
COME ON, RUN!

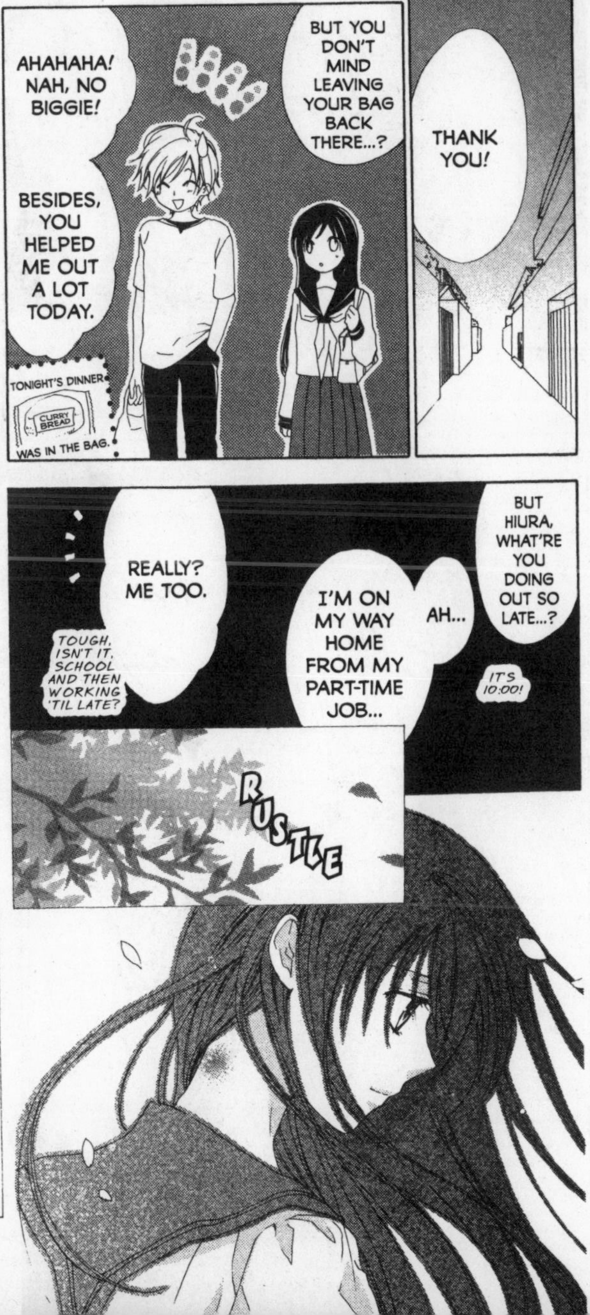
THANK YOU!
BUT YOU DON'T MIND LEAVING YOUR BAG BACK THERE...?
AHAHAHA! NAH, NO BIGGIE!
BESIDES, YOU HELPED ME OUT A LOT TODAY.
TONIGHT'S DINNER
CURRY BREAD
WAS IN THE BAG.
BUT HIURA, WHAT'RE YOU DOING OUT SO LATE...?
IT'S 10:00!
AH...
I'M ON MY WAY HOME FROM MY PART-TIME JOB...
REALLY? ME TOO.
TOUGH, ISN'T IT, SCHOOL AND THEN WORKING 'TIL LATE?
RUSTLE

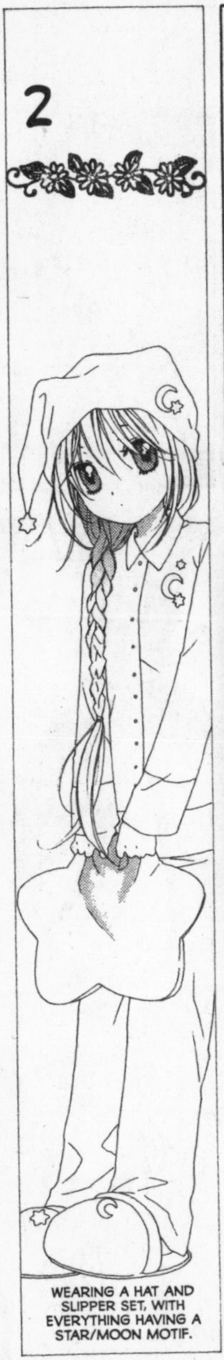
2
WEARING A HAT AND SLIPPER SET, WITH EVERYTHING HAVING A STAR/MOON MOTIF.

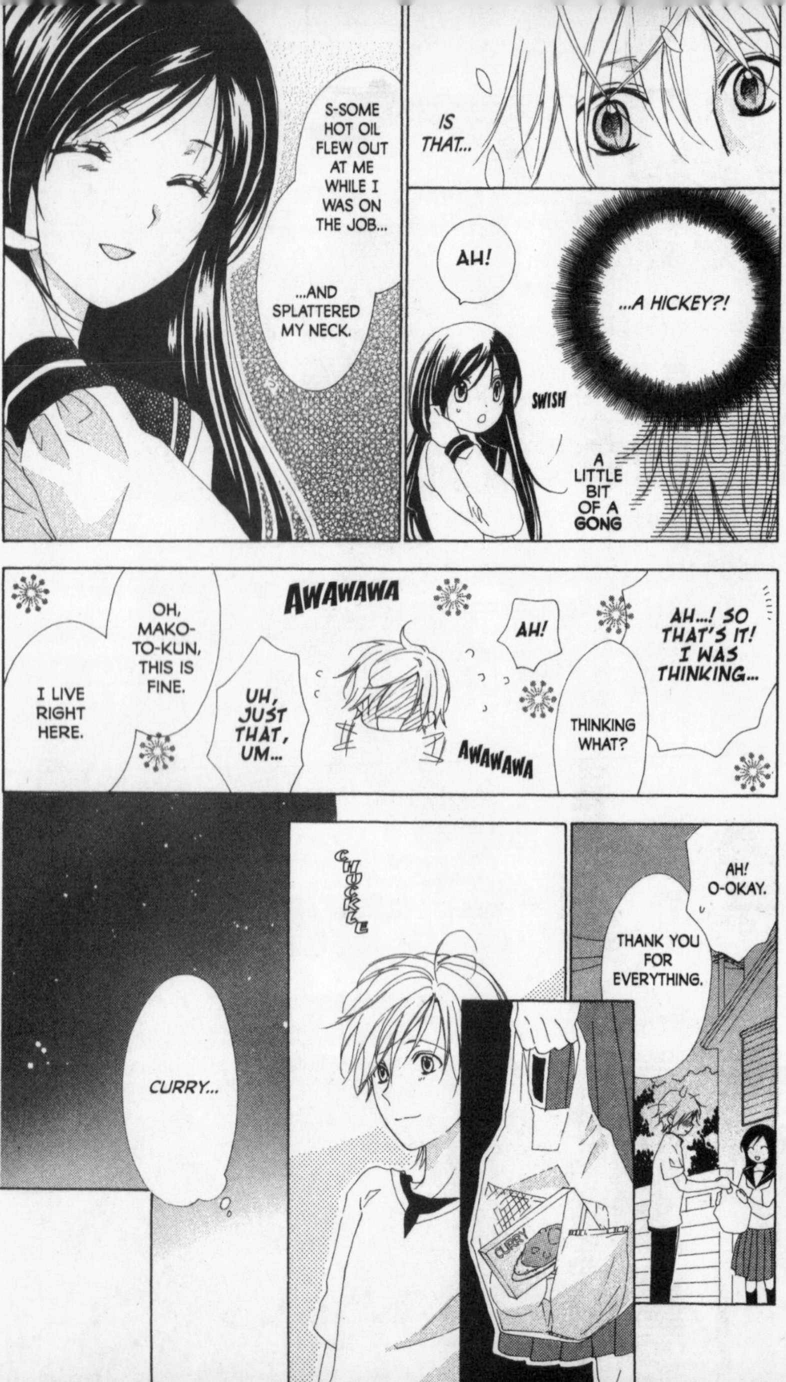
IS THAT...
AH!
...A HICKEY?!
SWISH
A LITTLE BIT OF A GONG
S-SOME HOT OIL FLEW OUT AT ME WHILE I WAS ON THE JOB...
...AND SPLATTERED MY NECK.
AH...! SO THAT'S IT! I WAS THINKING...
THINKING WHAT?
AH!
AWAWAWA
AWAWAWA
UH, JUST THAT, UM...
OH, MAKO-TO-KUN, THIS IS FINE.
I LIVE RIGHT HERE.
AH! O-OKAY.
THANK YOU FOR EVERYTHING.
CHUCKLE
CURRY
CURRY...

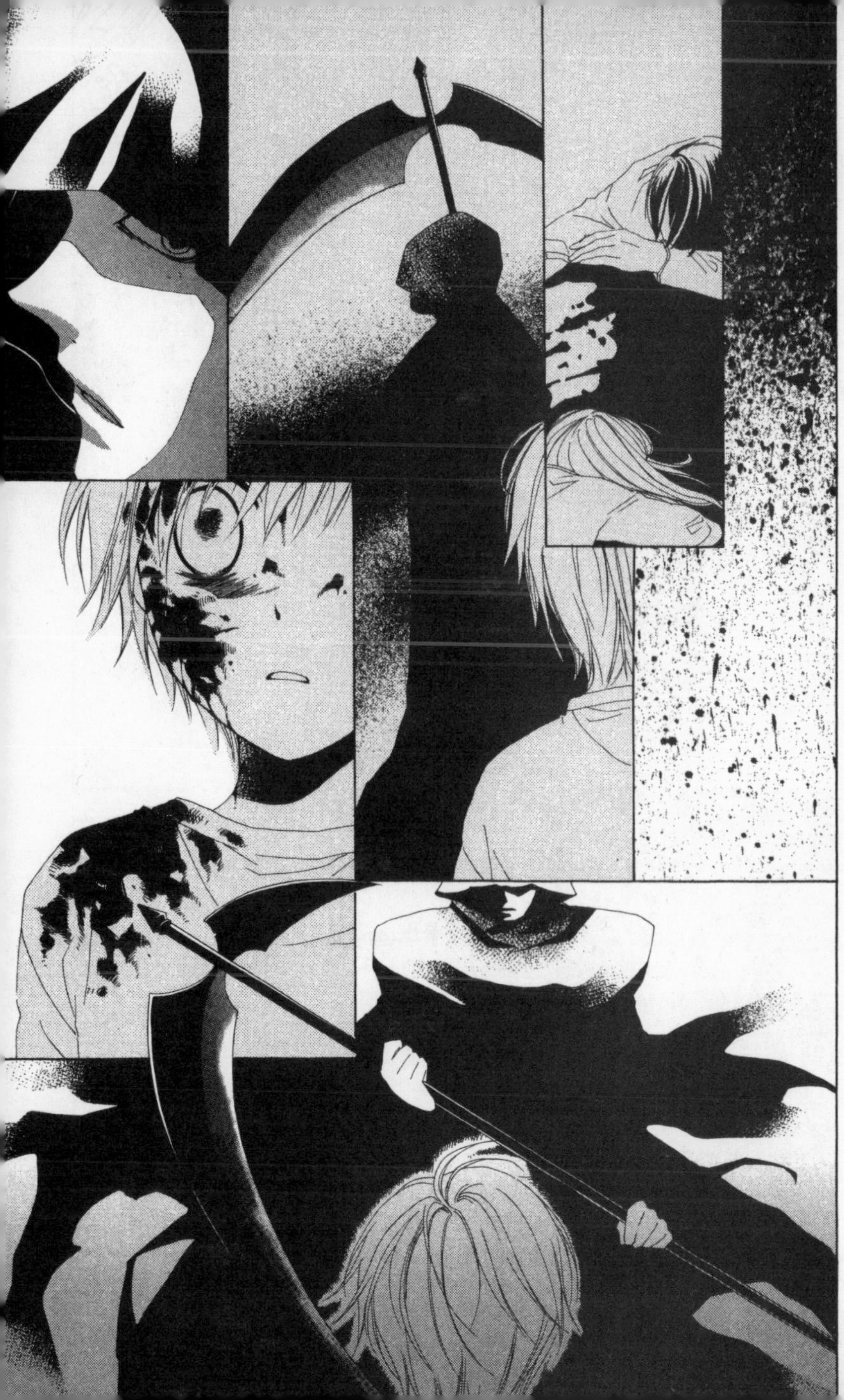

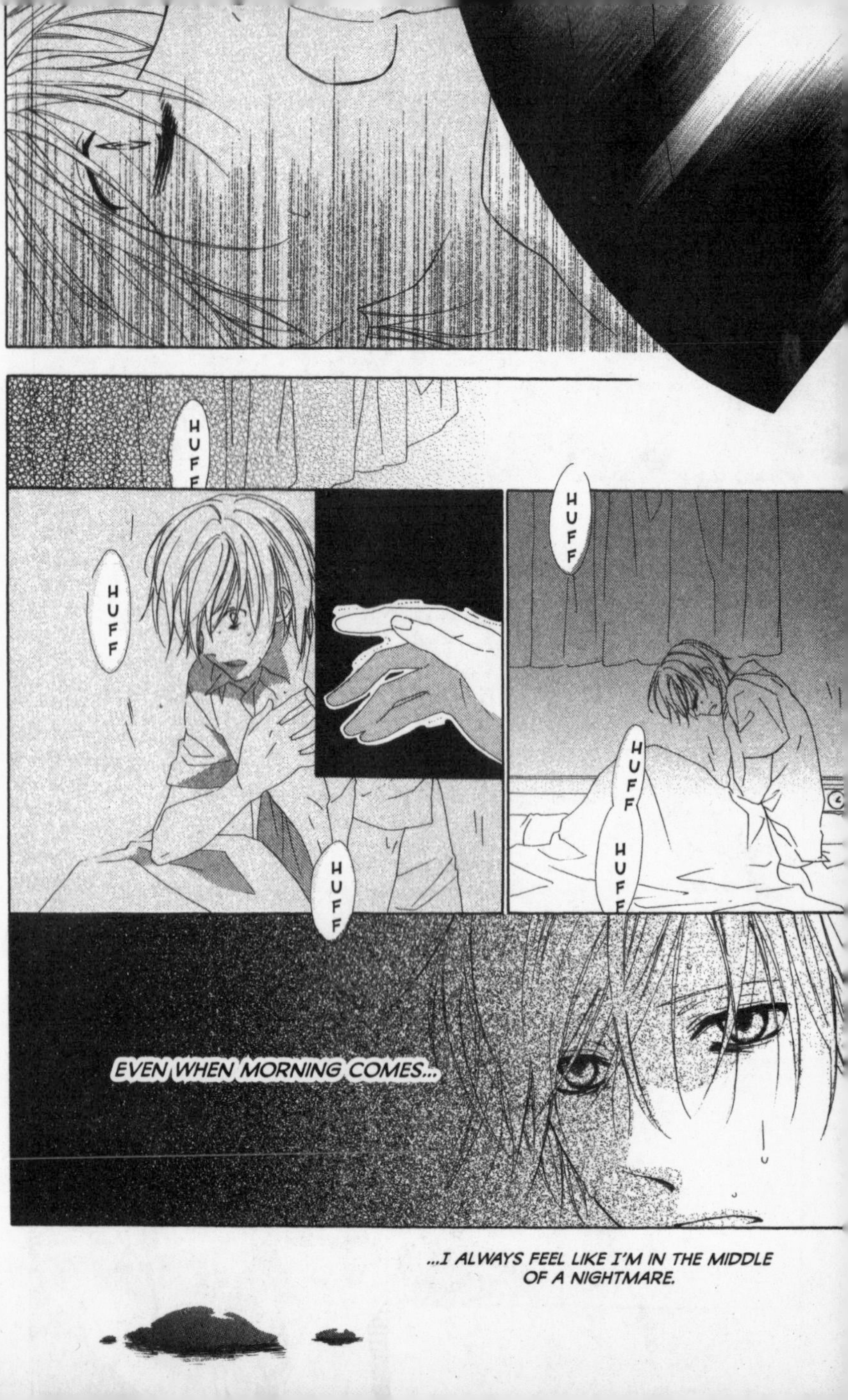
HUFF
HUFF
HUFF
HUFF
HUFF
HUFF
EVEN WHEN MORNING COMES...
...I ALWAYS FEEL LIKE I'M IN THE MIDDLE OF A NIGHTMARE.

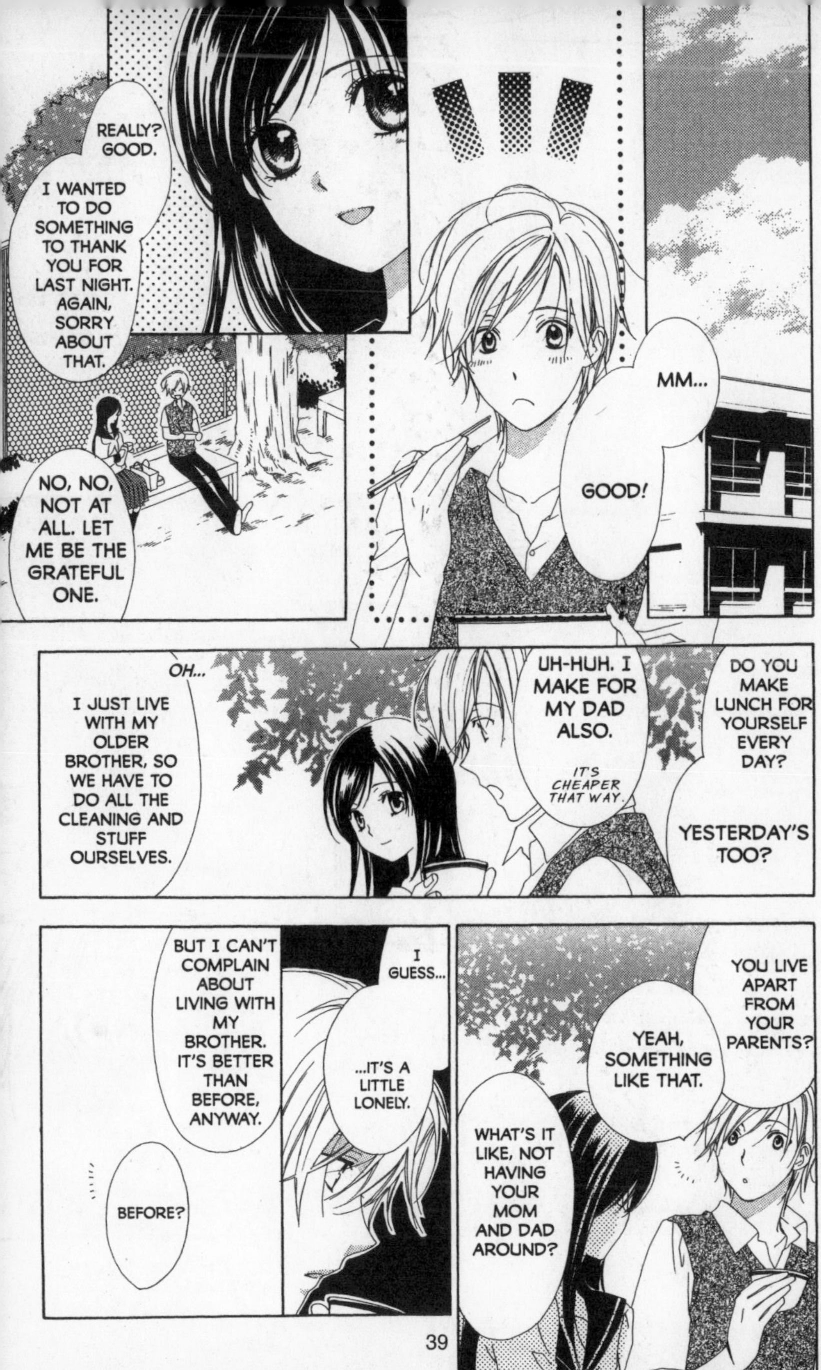
MM...
GOOD!
REALLY? GOOD.
I WANTED TO DO SOMETHING TO THANK YOU FOR LAST NIGHT. AGAIN, SORRY ABOUT THAT.
NO, NO, NOT AT ALL. LET ME BE THE GRATEFUL ONE.
DO YOU MAKE LUNCH FOR YOURSELF EVERY DAY?
YESTERDAY'S TOO?
UH-HUH. I MAKE FOR MY DAD ALSO.
IT'S CHEAPER THAT WAY.
OH...
I JUST LIVE WITH MY OLDER BROTHER, SO WE HAVE TO DO ALL THE CLEANING AND STUFF OURSELVES.
YOU LIVE APART FROM YOUR PARENTS?
YEAH, SOMETHING LIKE THAT.
WHAT'S IT LIKE, NOT HAVING YOUR MOM AND DAD AROUND?
I GUESS...
...IT'S A LITTLE LONELY.
BUT I CAN'T COMPLAIN ABOUT LIVING WITH MY BROTHER. IT'S BETTER THAN BEFORE, ANYWAY.
BEFORE?

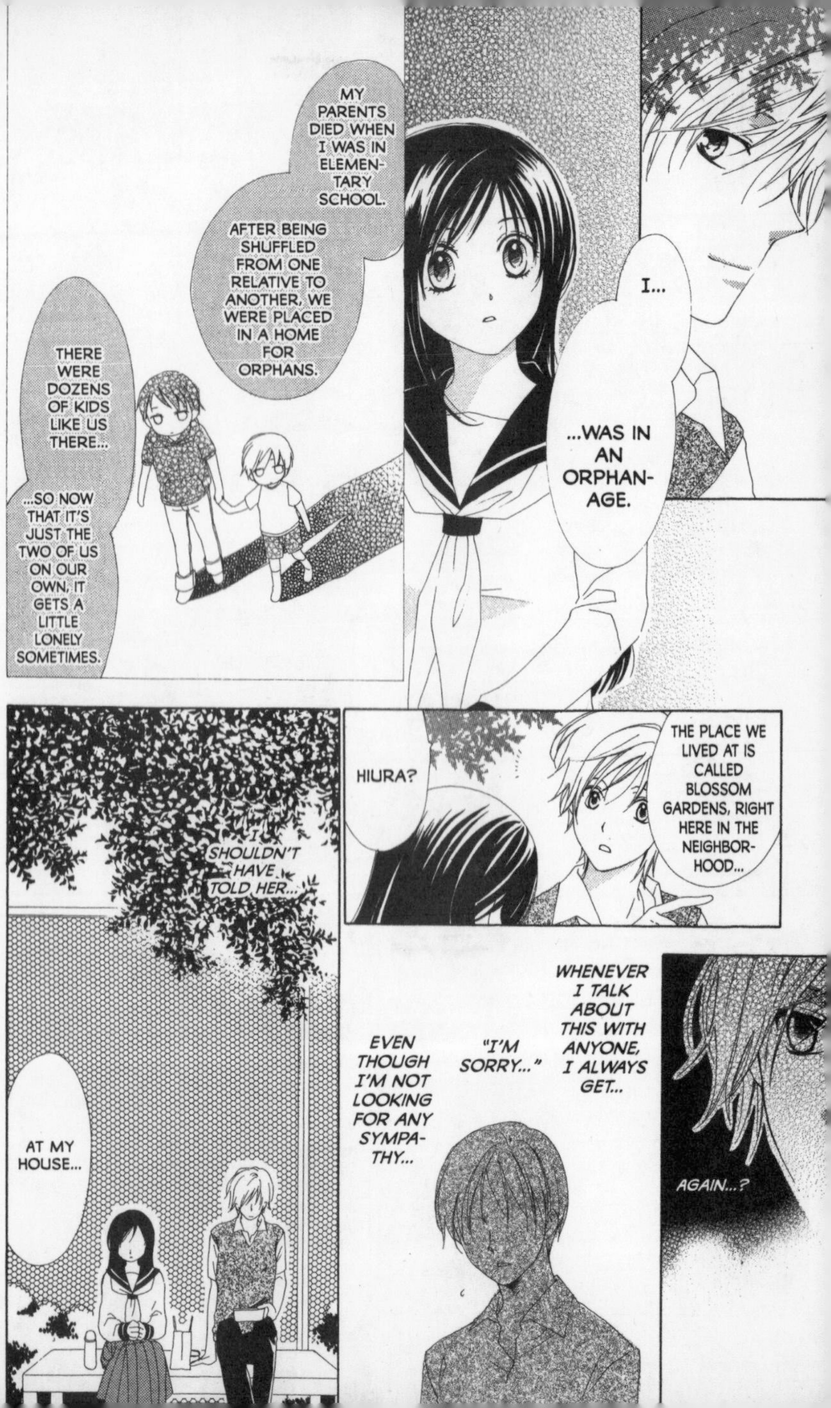
I...
...WAS IN AN ORPHANAGE.
MY PARENTS DIED WHEN I WAS IN ELEMENTARY SCHOOL.
AFTER BEING SHUFFLED FROM ONE RELATIVE TO ANOTHER, WE WERE PLACED IN A HOME FOR ORPHANS.
THERE WERE DOZENS OF KIDS LIKE US THERE...
...SO NOW THAT IT'S JUST THE TWO OF US ON OUR OWN, IT GETS A LITTLE LONELY SOMETIMES.
THE PLACE WE LIVED AT IS CALLED BLOSSOM GARDENS, RIGHT HERE IN THE NEIGHBORHOOD...
HIURA?
WHENEVER I TALK ABOUT THIS WITH ANYONE, I ALWAYS GET...
"I'M SORRY..."
AGAIN...?
EVEN THOUGH I'M NOT LOOKING FOR ANY SYMPATHY...
I SHOULDN'T HAVE TOLD HER...
AT MY HOUSE...

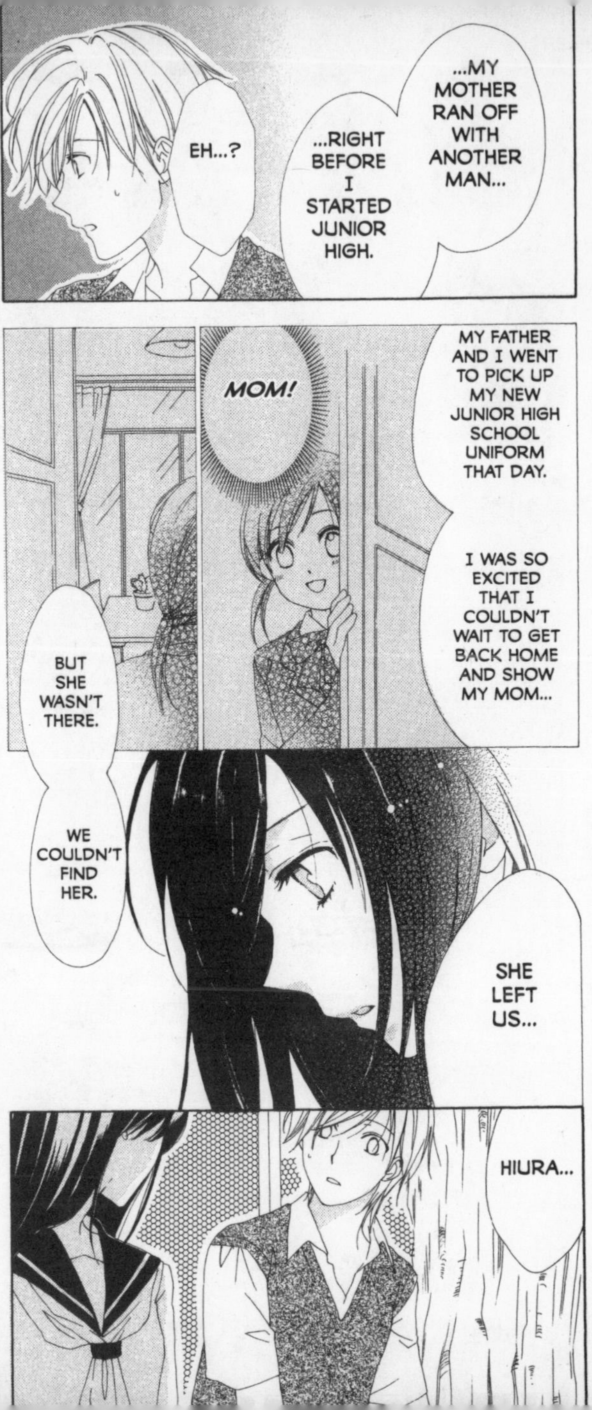
...MY MOTHER RAN OFF WITH ANOTHER MAN...
...RIGHT BEFORE I STARTED JUNIOR HIGH.
EH...?
MY FATHER AND I WENT TO PICK UP MY NEW JUNIOR HIGH SCHOOL UNIFORM THAT DAY.
I WAS SO EXCITED THAT I COULDN'T WAIT TO GET BACK HOME AND SHOW MY MOM...
MOM!
BUT SHE WASN'T THERE.
WE COULDN'T FIND HER.
SHE LEFT US...
HIURA...

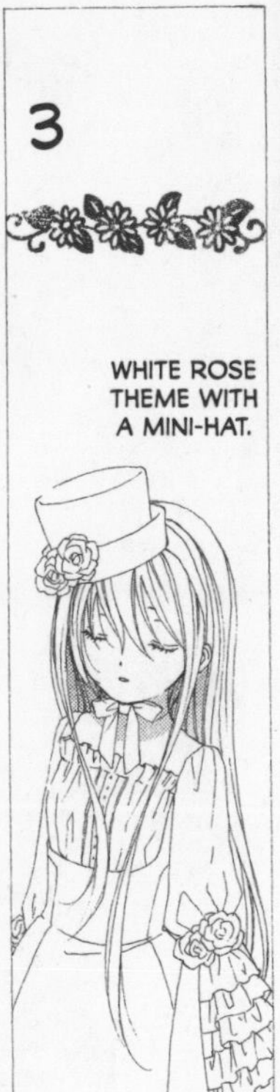
3
WHITE ROSE THEME WITH A MINI-HAT.

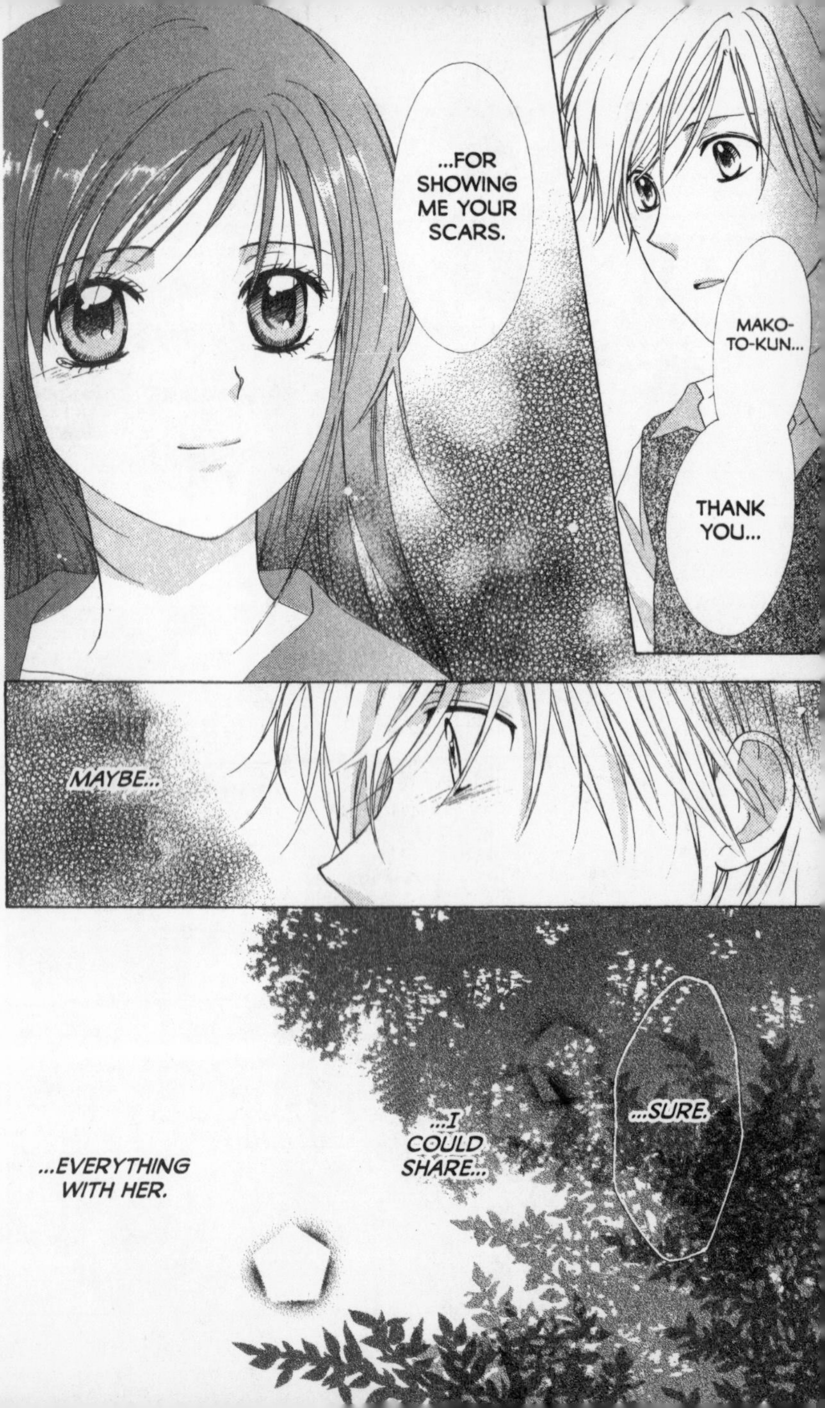
MAKO-TO-KUN...
THANK YOU...
...FOR SHOWING ME YOUR SCARS.
MAYBE...
...SURE.
...I COULD SHARE...
...EVERYTHING WITH HER.

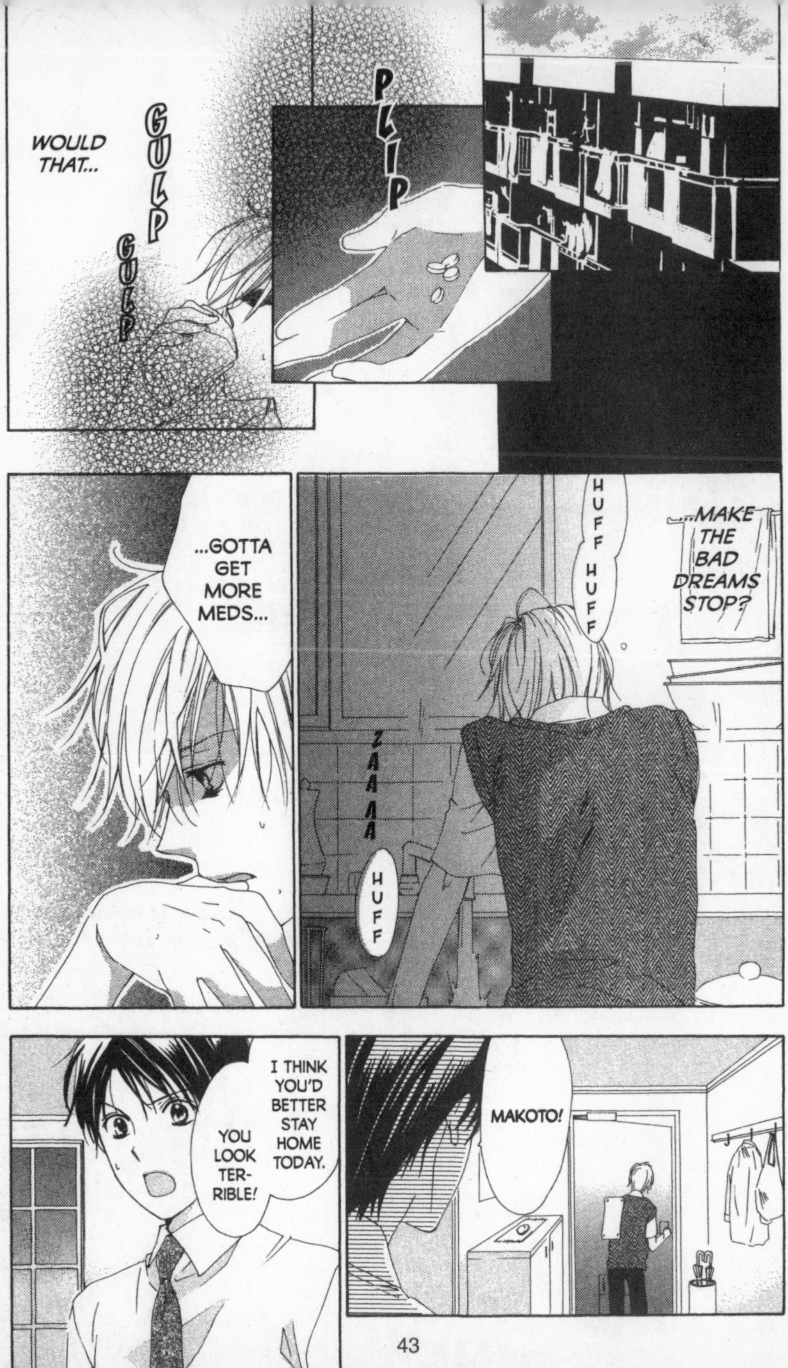
PLIP
WOULD THAT...
GULP
GULP
...MAKE THE BAD DREAMS STOP?
HUFF HUFF
ZAAAA
HUFF HUFF
...GOTTA GET MORE MEDS...
MAKOTO!
I THINK YOU'D BETTER STAY HOME TODAY.
YOU LOOK TER-RIBLE!

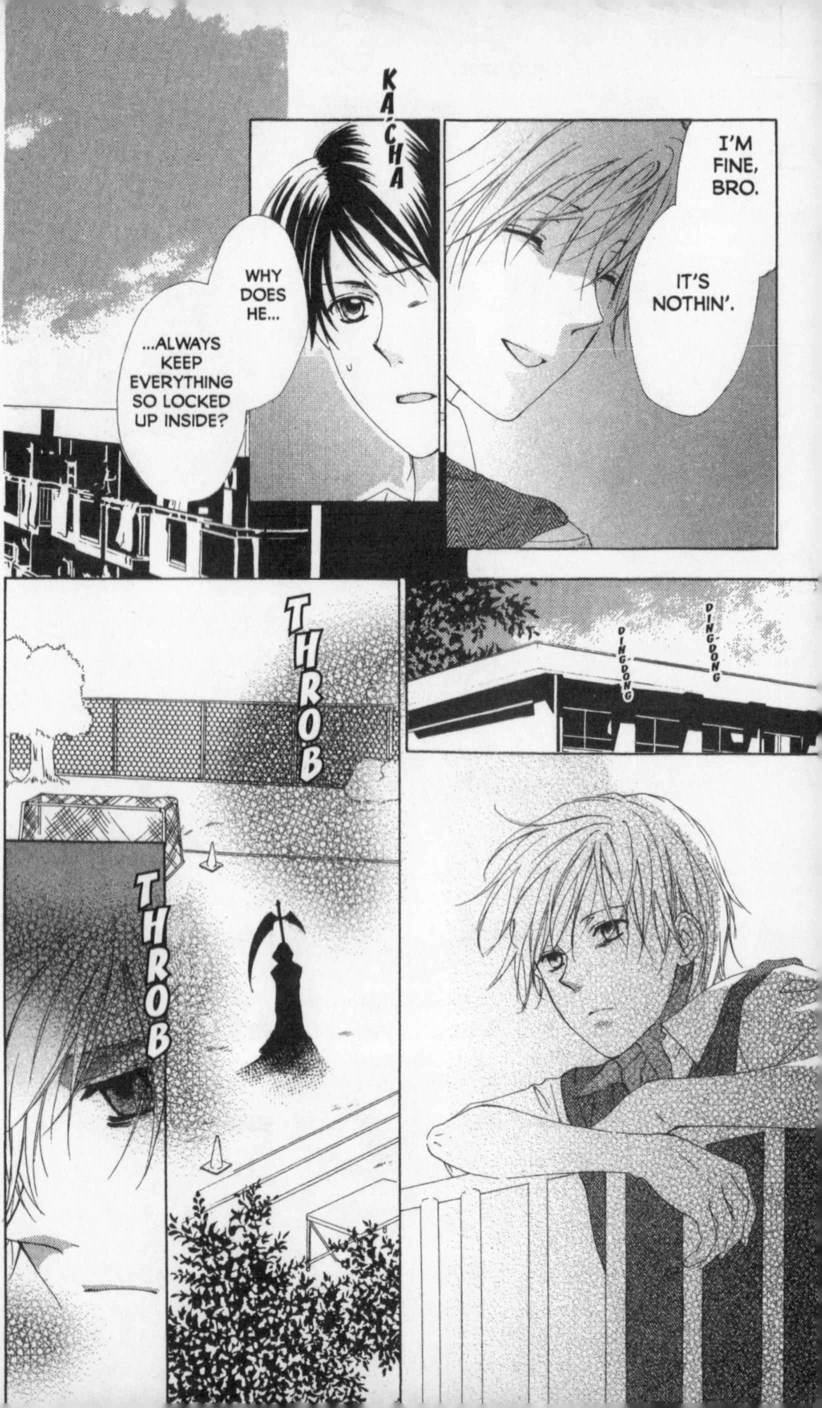
I'M FINE, BRO.
IT'S NOTHIN'.
KACHA
WHY DOES HE...
...ALWAYS KEEP EVERYTHING SO LOCKED UP INSIDE?
DING-DONG
DING-DONG
THROB
THROB

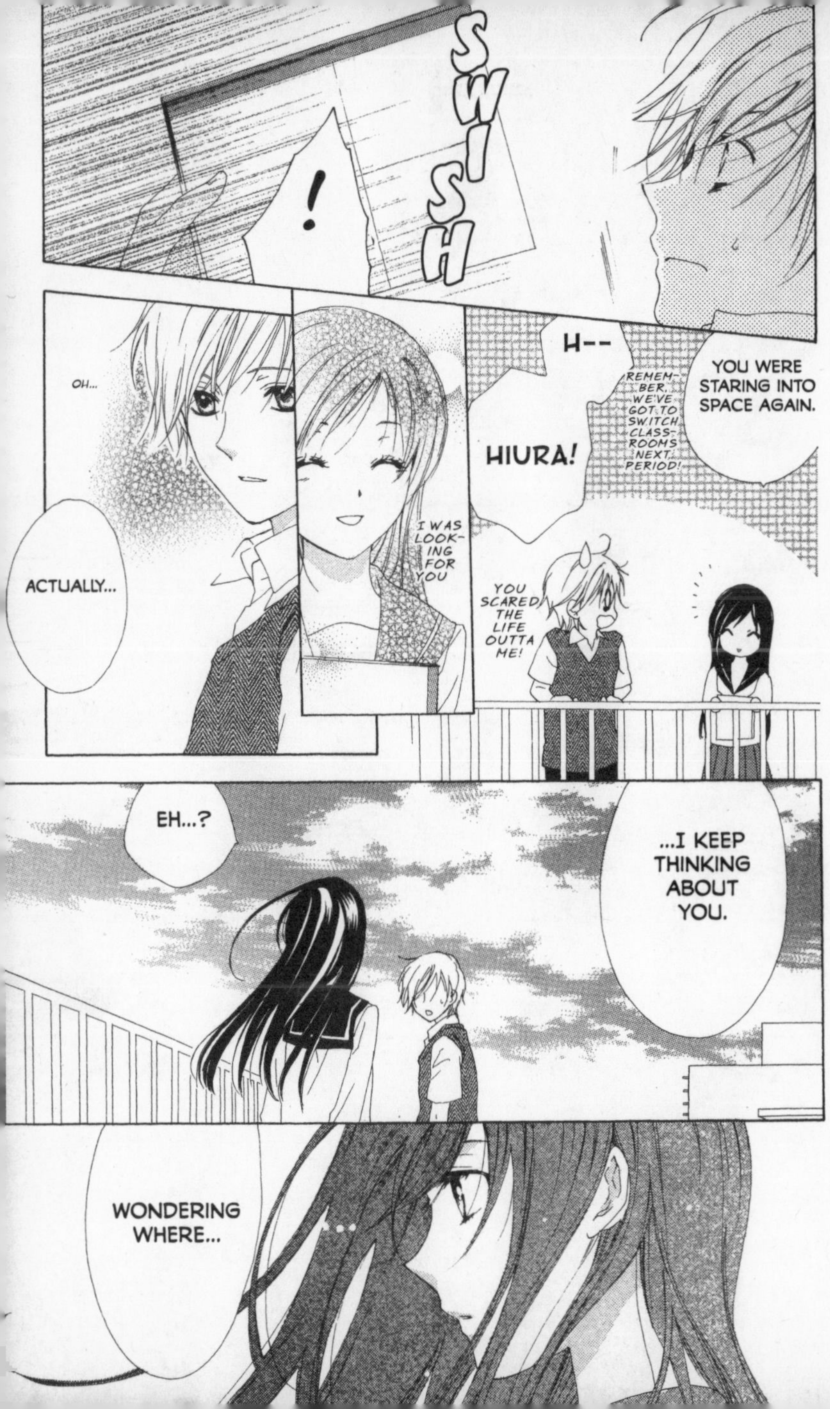
SWISH
!
YOU WERE STARING INTO SPACE AGAIN.
H--
REMEMBER, WE'VE GOT TO SWITCH CLASSROOMS NEXT PERIOD!
HIURA!
YOU SCARED THE LIFE OUTTA ME!
I WAS LOOKING FOR YOU
OH...
ACTUALLY...
...I KEEP THINKING ABOUT YOU.
EH...?
WONDERING WHERE...
...

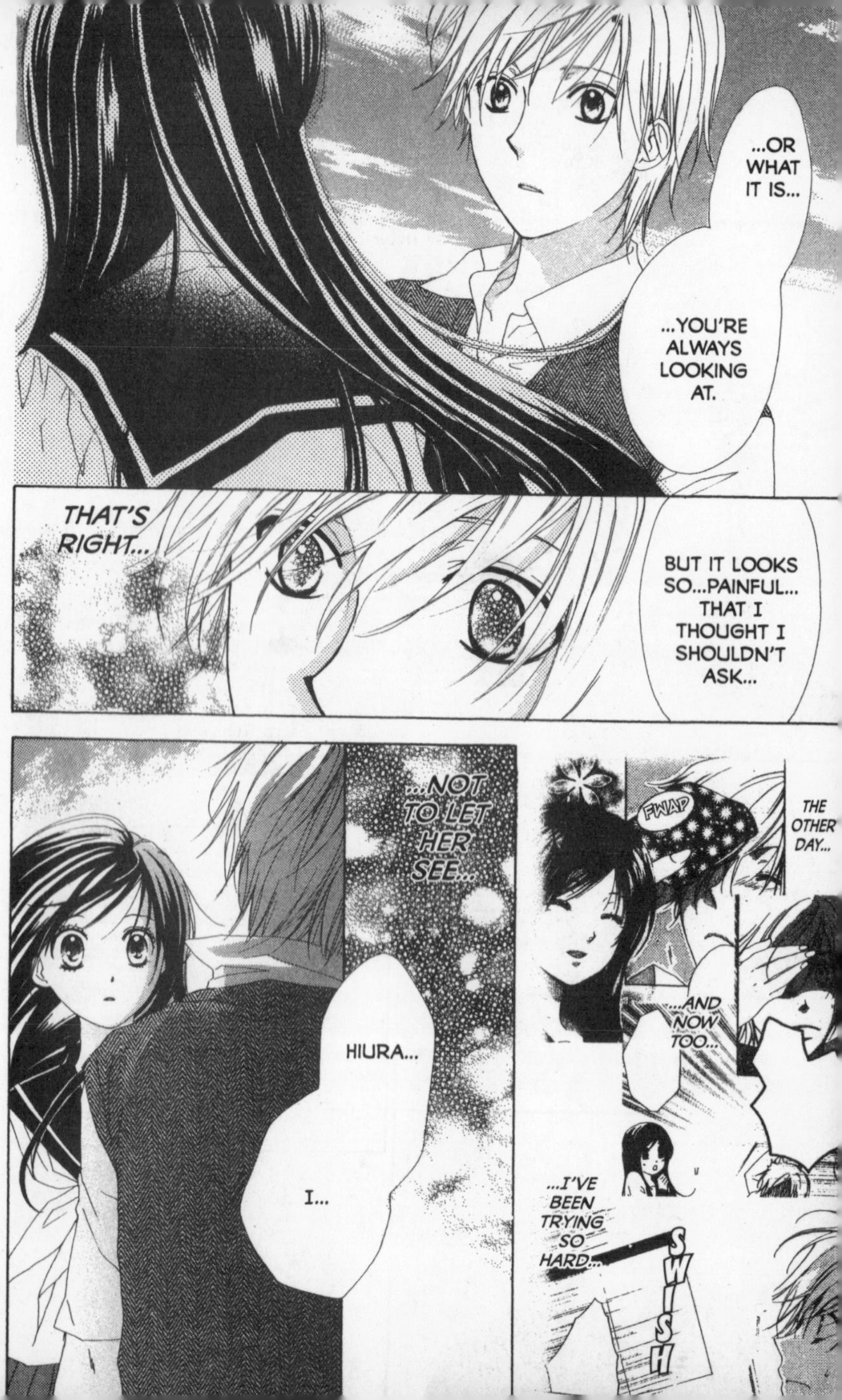
...OR WHAT IT IS...
...YOU'RE ALWAYS LOOKING AT.
BUT IT LOOKS SO...PAINFUL... THAT I THOUGHT I SHOULDN'T ASK...
THAT'S RIGHT...
THE OTHER DAY...
FWAP
...AND NOW TOO...
...I'VE BEEN TRYING SO HARD...
SWISH
...NOT TO LET HER SEE...
HIURA...
I...

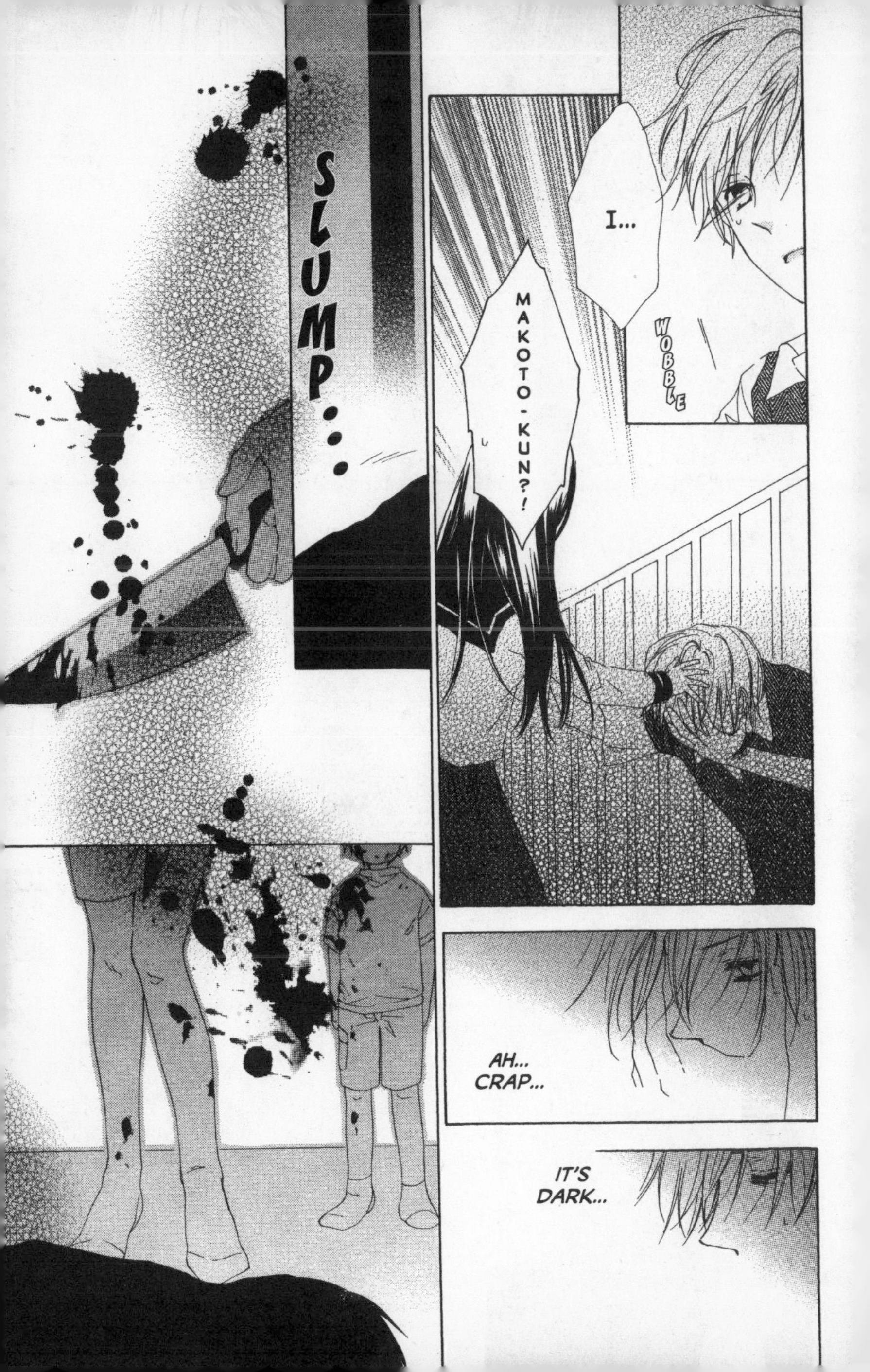
I...
WOBBLE
MAKOTO-KUN?!
AH... CRAP...
IT'S DARK...
SLUMP...

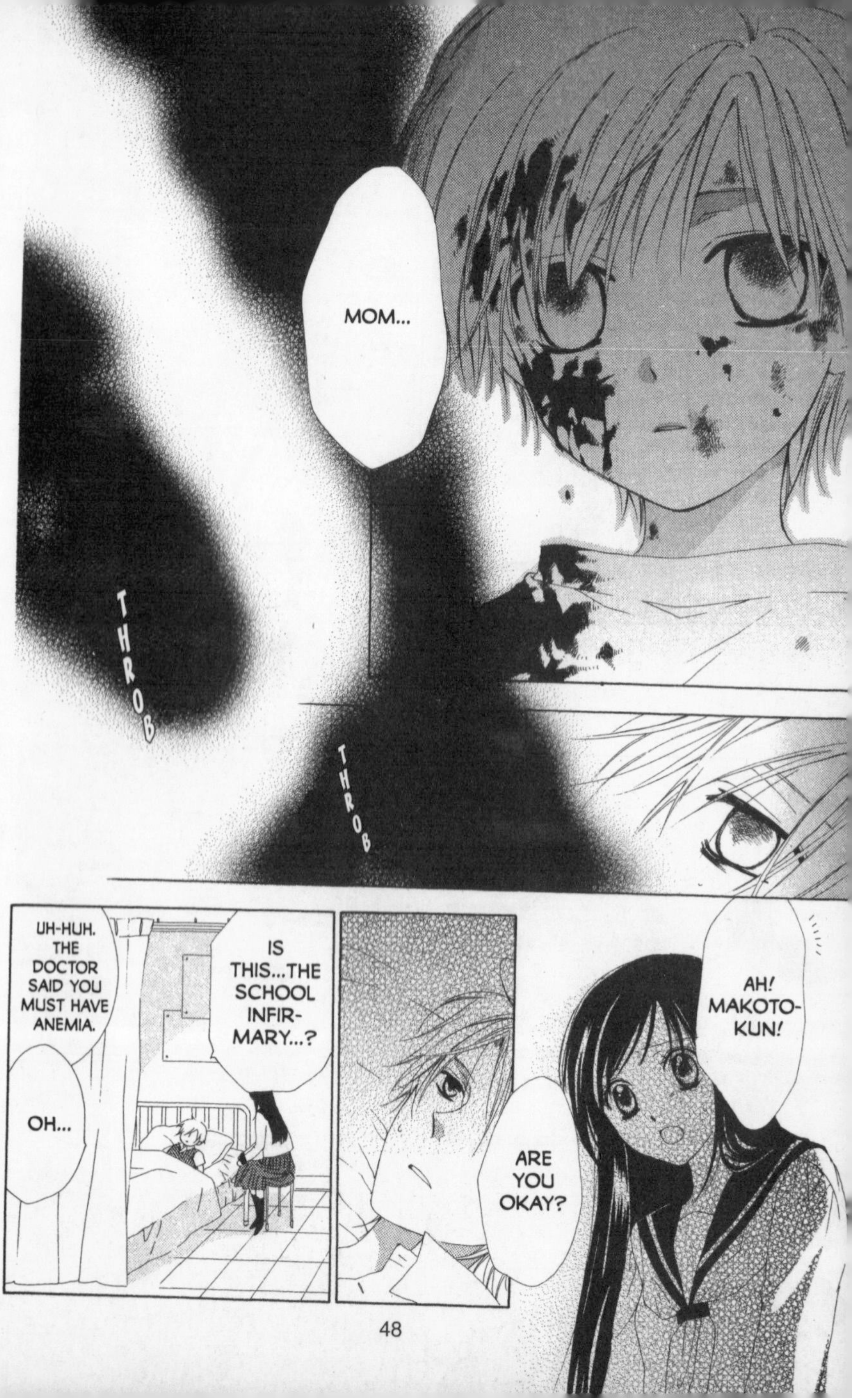
MOM...
THROB
THROB
AH! MAKOTO-KUN!
ARE YOU OKAY?
IS THIS...THE SCHOOL INFIRMARY...?
UH-HUH. THE DOCTOR SAID YOU MUST HAVE ANEMIA.
OH...

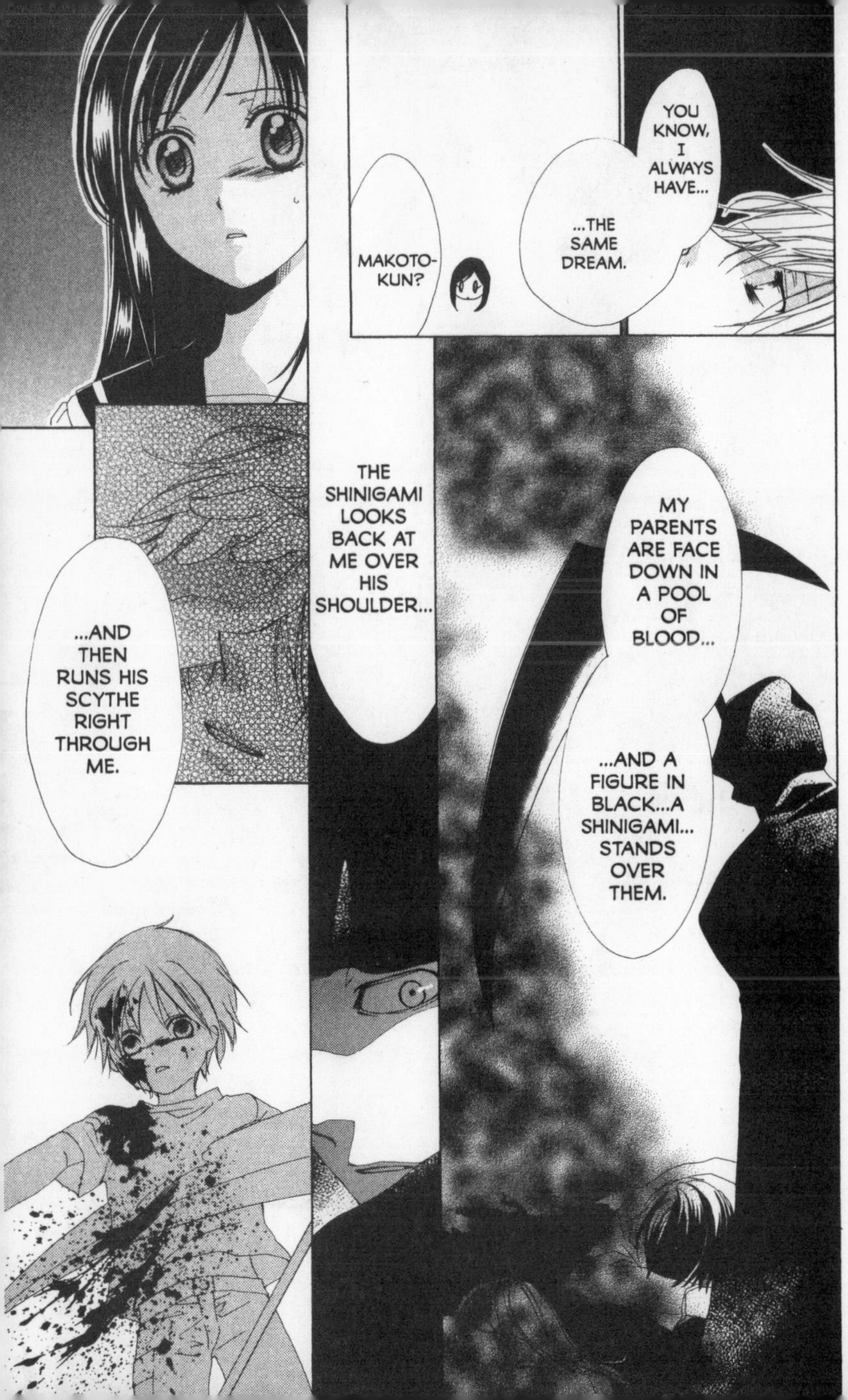
YOU KNOW, I ALWAYS HAVE...
...THE SAME DREAM.
MAKOTO-KUN?
MY PARENTS ARE FACE DOWN IN A POOL OF BLOOD...
...AND A FIGURE IN BLACK...A SHINIGAMI... STANDS OVER THEM.
THE SHINIGAMI LOOKS BACK AT ME OVER HIS SHOULDER...
...AND THEN RUNS HIS SCYTHE RIGHT THROUGH ME.

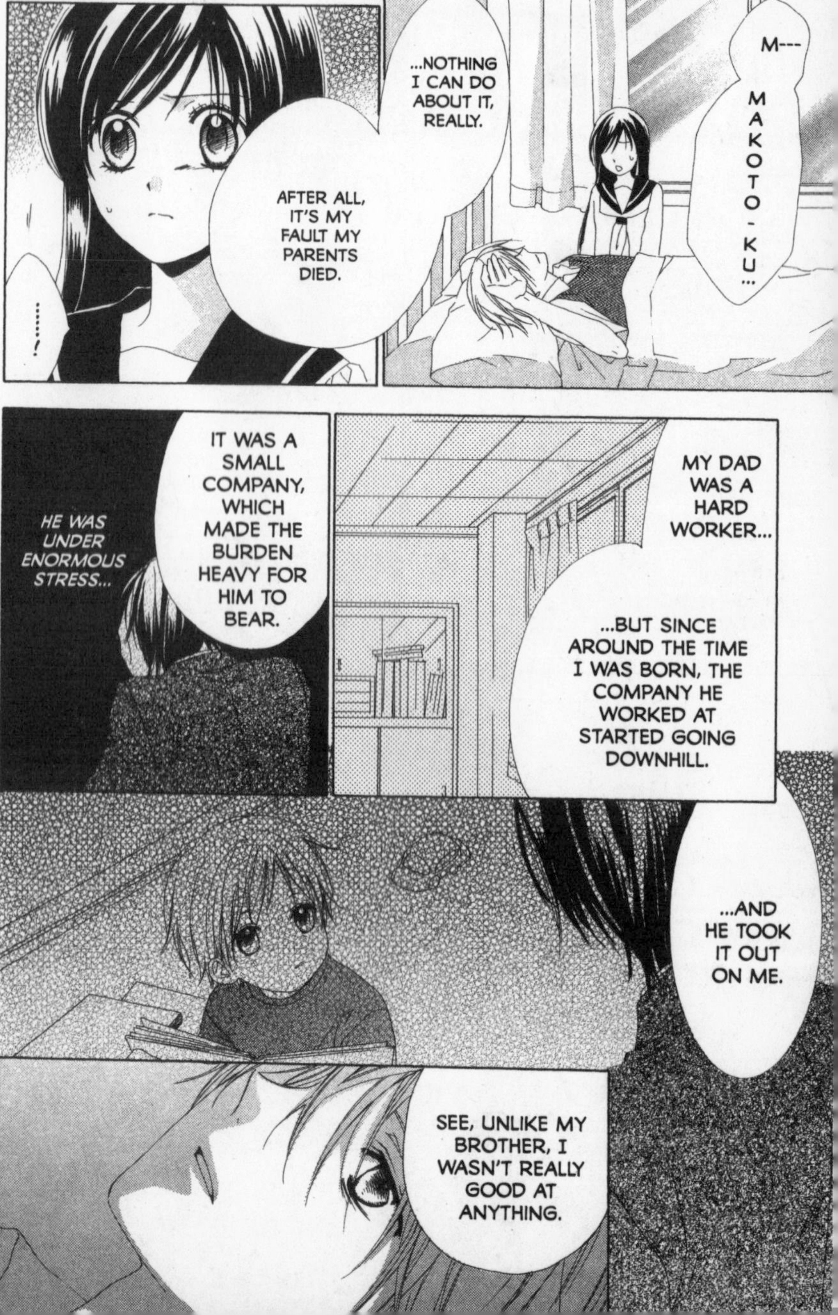
M--- MAKOTO-KU...
...NOTHING I CAN DO ABOUT IT, REALLY.
AFTER ALL, IT'S MY FAULT MY PARENTS DIED.
......!
MY DAD WAS A HARD WORKER...
...BUT SINCE AROUND THE TIME I WAS BORN, THE COMPANY HE WORKED AT STARTED GOING DOWNHILL.
IT WAS A SMALL COMPANY, WHICH MADE THE BURDEN HEAVY FOR HIM TO BEAR.
HE WAS UNDER ENORMOUS STRESS...
...AND HE TOOK IT OUT ON ME.
SEE, UNLIKE MY BROTHER, I WASN'T REALLY GOOD AT ANYTHING.

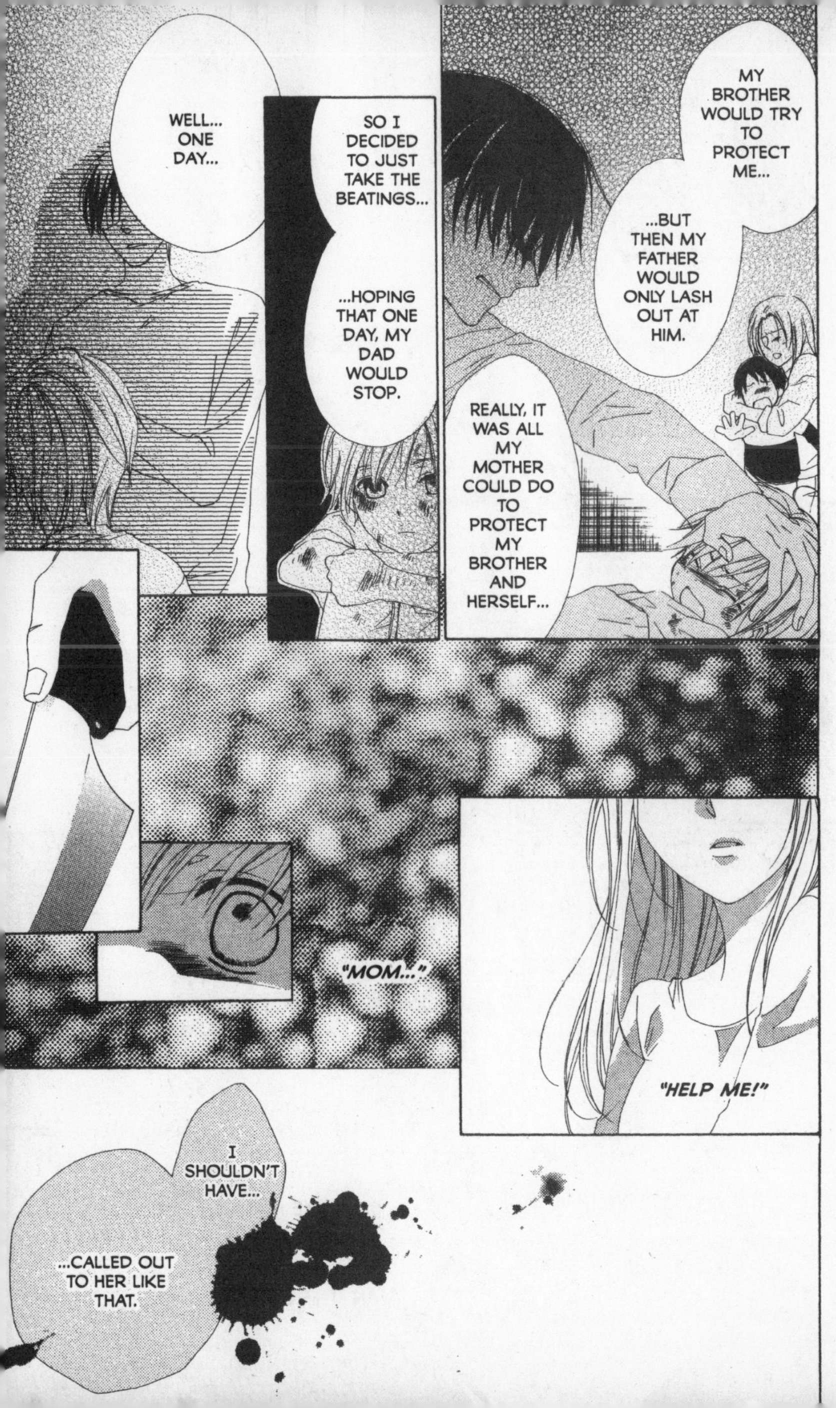
MY BROTHER WOULD TRY TO PROTECT ME...
...BUT THEN MY FATHER WOULD ONLY LASH OUT AT HIM.
REALLY, IT WAS ALL MY MOTHER COULD DO TO PROTECT MY BROTHER AND HERSELF...
SO I DECIDED TO JUST TAKE THE BEATINGS...
...HOPING THAT ONE DAY, MY DAD WOULD STOP.
WELL... ONE DAY...
"MOM..."
"HELP ME!"
I SHOULDN'T HAVE...
...CALLED OUT TO HER LIKE THAT.

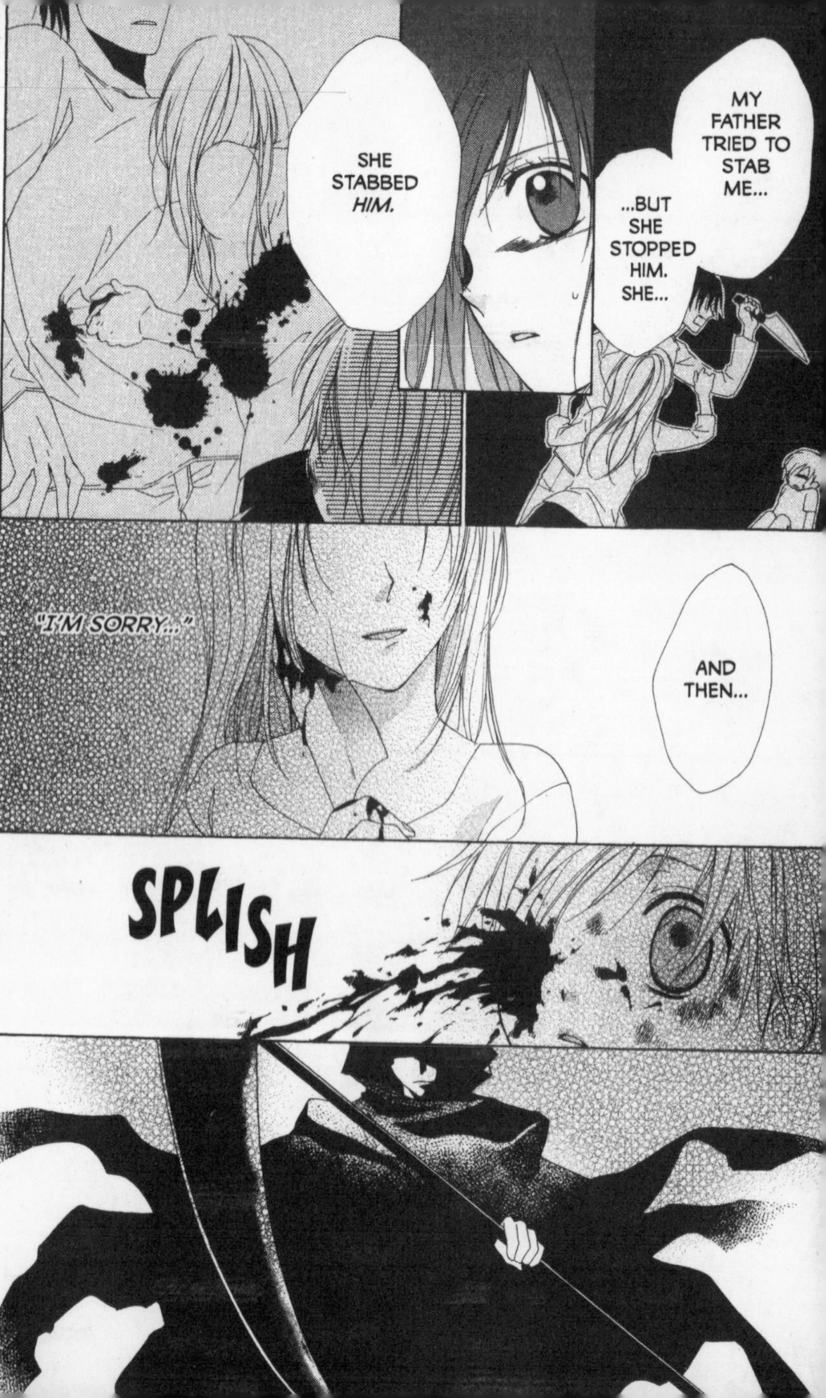
MY FATHER TRIED TO STAB ME...
...BUT SHE STOPPED HIM. SHE...
SHE STABBED *HIM.*
AND THEN...
"I'M SORRY..."
SPLISH

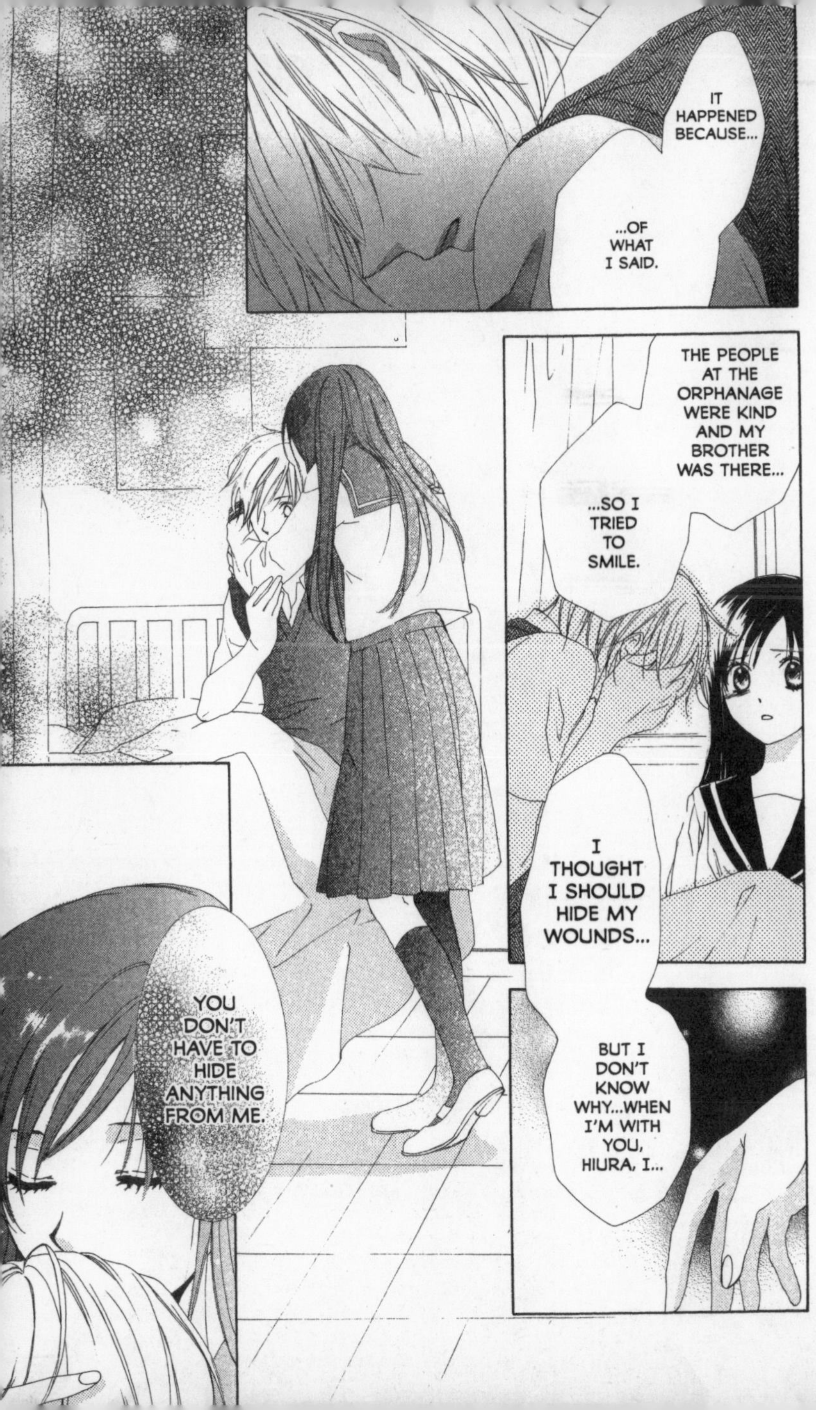
IT HAPPENED BECAUSE...
...OF WHAT I SAID.
THE PEOPLE AT THE ORPHANAGE WERE KIND AND MY BROTHER WAS THERE...
...SO I TRIED TO SMILE.
I THOUGHT I SHOULD HIDE MY WOUNDS...
BUT I DON'T KNOW WHY...WHEN I'M WITH YOU, HIURA, I...
YOU DON'T HAVE TO HIDE ANYTHING FROM ME.

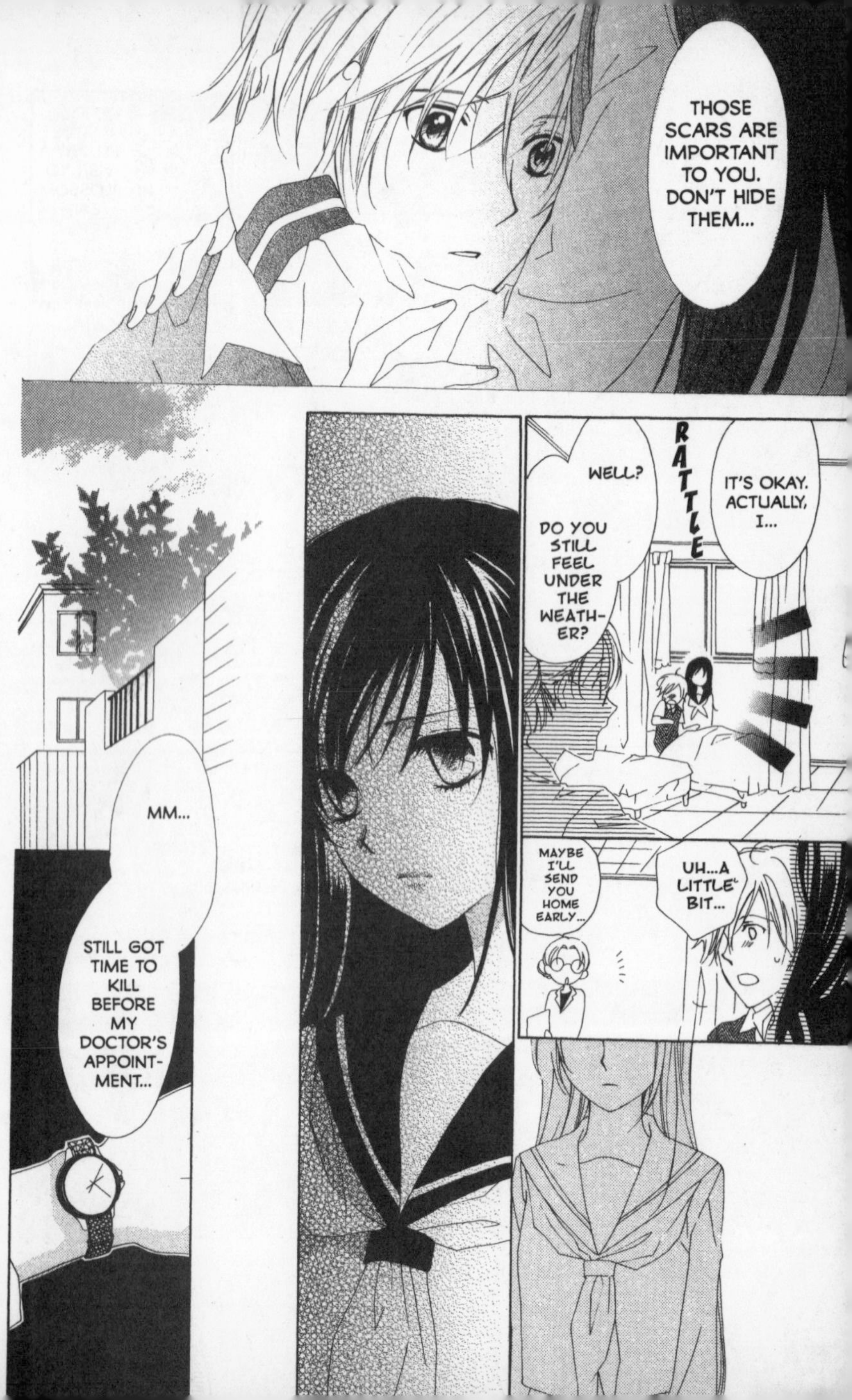
THOSE SCARS ARE IMPORTANT TO YOU. DON'T HIDE THEM...
IT'S OKAY. ACTUALLY, I...
RATTLE
WELL?
DO YOU STILL FEEL UNDER THE WEATH-ER?
UH...A LITTLE BIT...
MAYBE I'LL SEND YOU HOME EARLY...
MM...
STILL GOT TIME TO KILL BEFORE MY DOCTOR'S APPOINT-MENT...

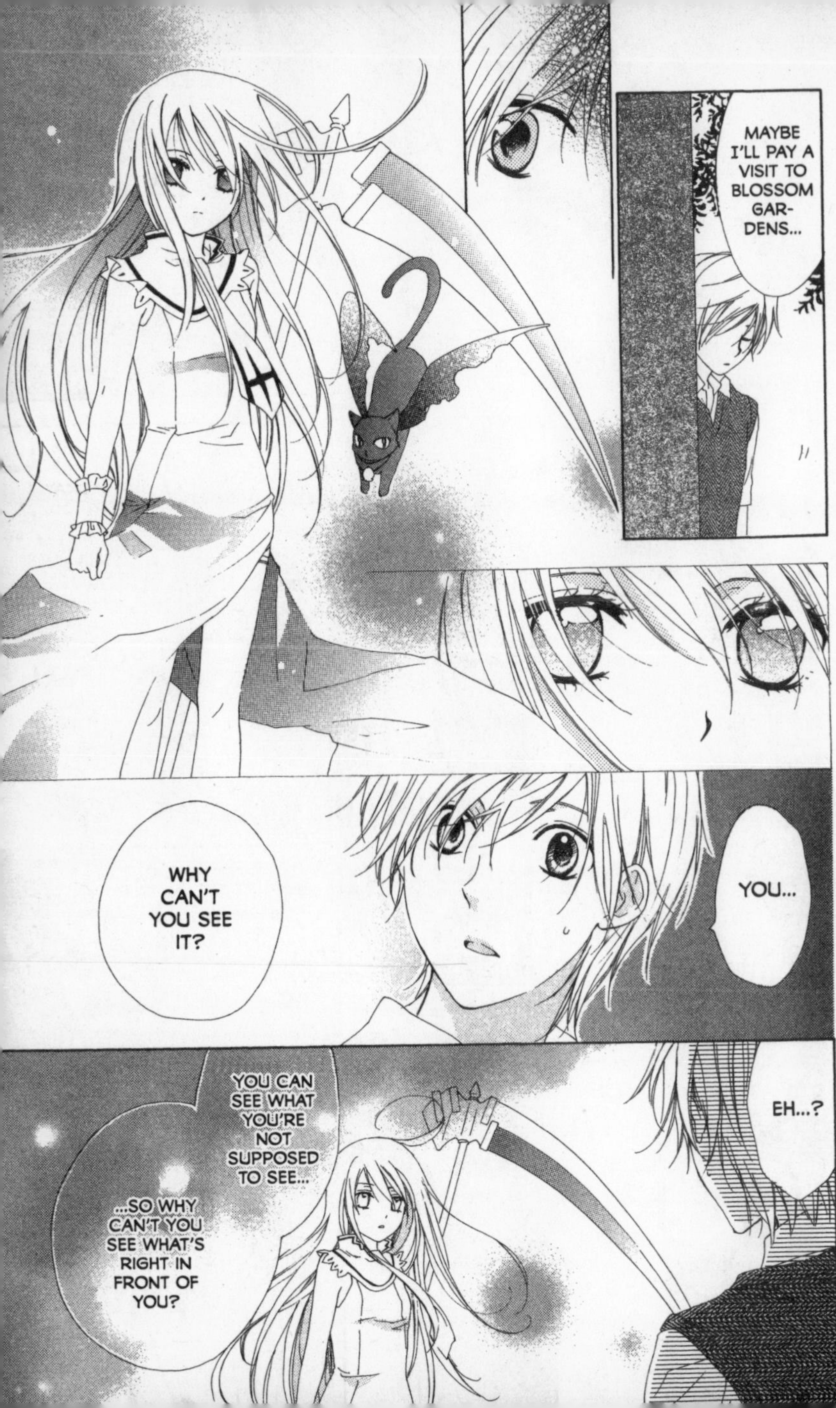
MAYBE I'LL PAY A VISIT TO BLOSSOM GAR-DENS...
YOU...
WHY CAN'T YOU SEE IT?
EH...?
YOU CAN SEE WHAT YOU'RE NOT SUPPOSED TO SEE...
...SO WHY CAN'T YOU SEE WHAT'S RIGHT IN FRONT OF YOU?

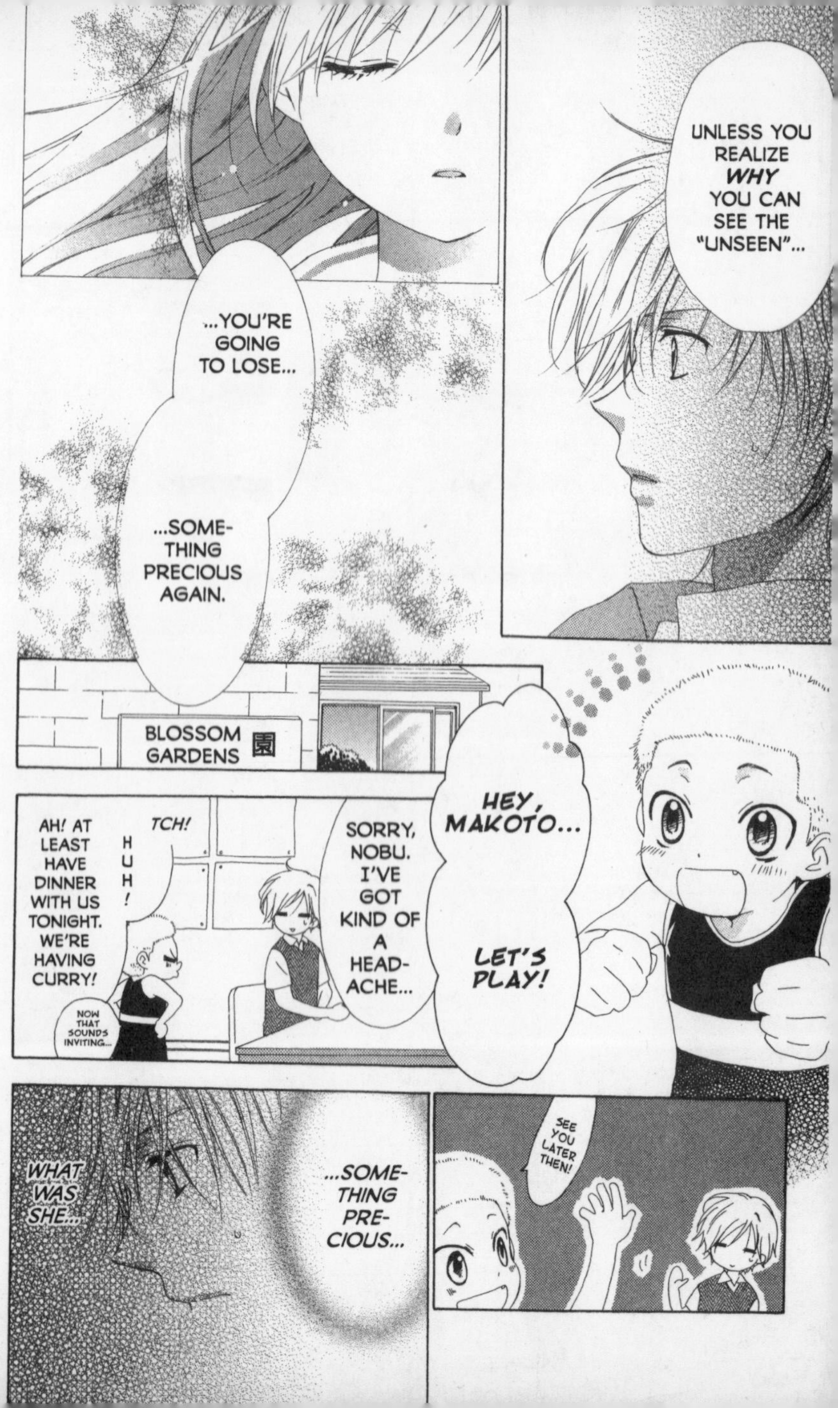
UNLESS YOU REALIZE *WHY* YOU CAN SEE THE "UNSEEN"...
...YOU'RE GOING TO LOSE...
...SOME-THING PRECIOUS AGAIN.
HEY, MAKOTO...
LET'S PLAY!
BLOSSOM GARDENS 園
SORRY, NOBU. I'VE GOT KIND OF A HEAD-ACHE...
TCH!
HUH!
AH! AT LEAST HAVE DINNER WITH US TONIGHT. WE'RE HAVING CURRY!
NOW THAT SOUNDS INVITING...
SEE YOU LATER THEN!
...SOME-THING PRE-CIOUS...
WHAT WAS SHE...

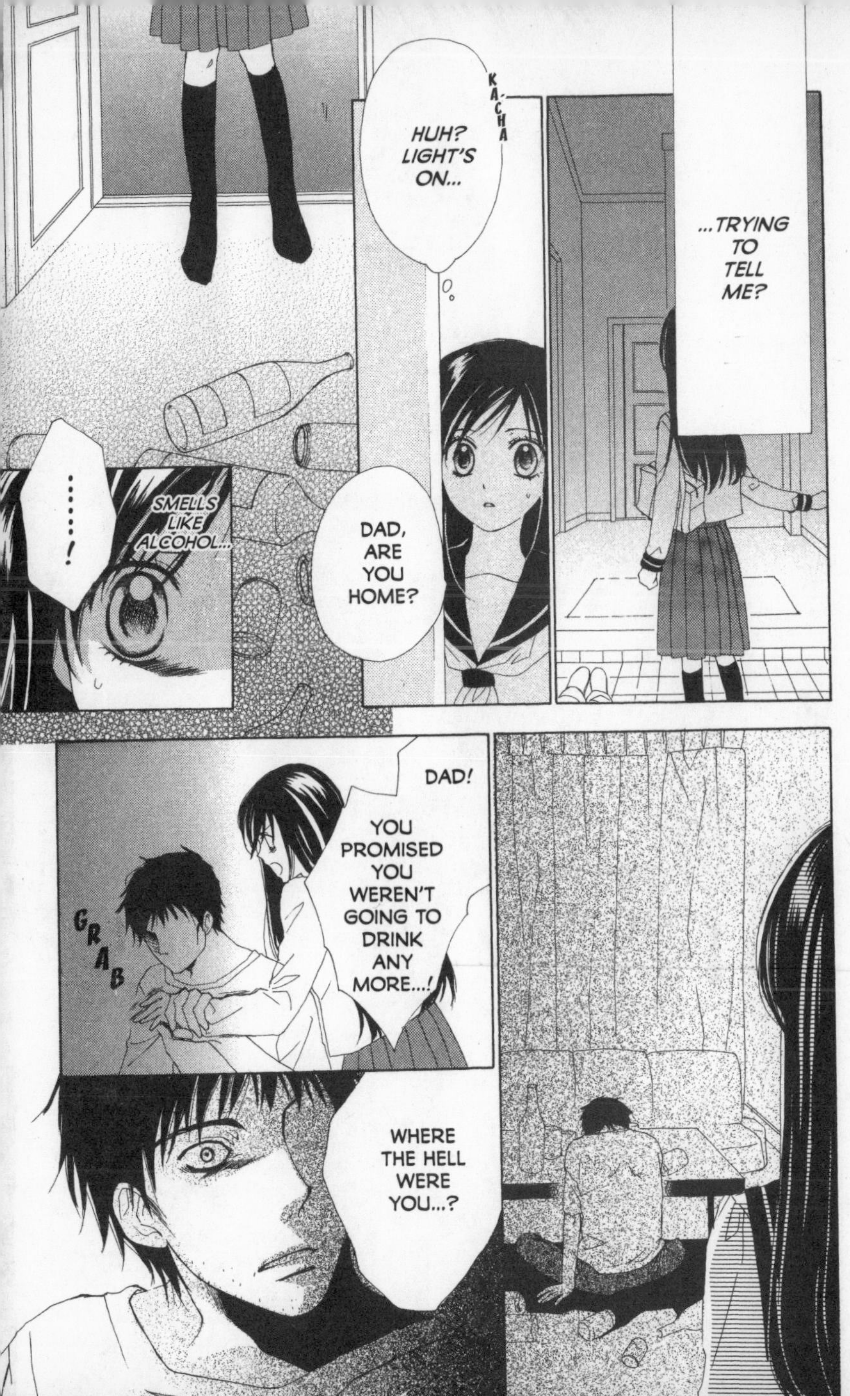
...TRYING TO TELL ME?
KACHA
HUH? LIGHT'S ON...
DAD, ARE YOU HOME?
SMELLS LIKE ALCOHOL...
......!
DAD!
YOU PROMISED YOU WEREN'T GOING TO DRINK ANY MORE...!
GRAB
WHERE THE HELL WERE YOU...?

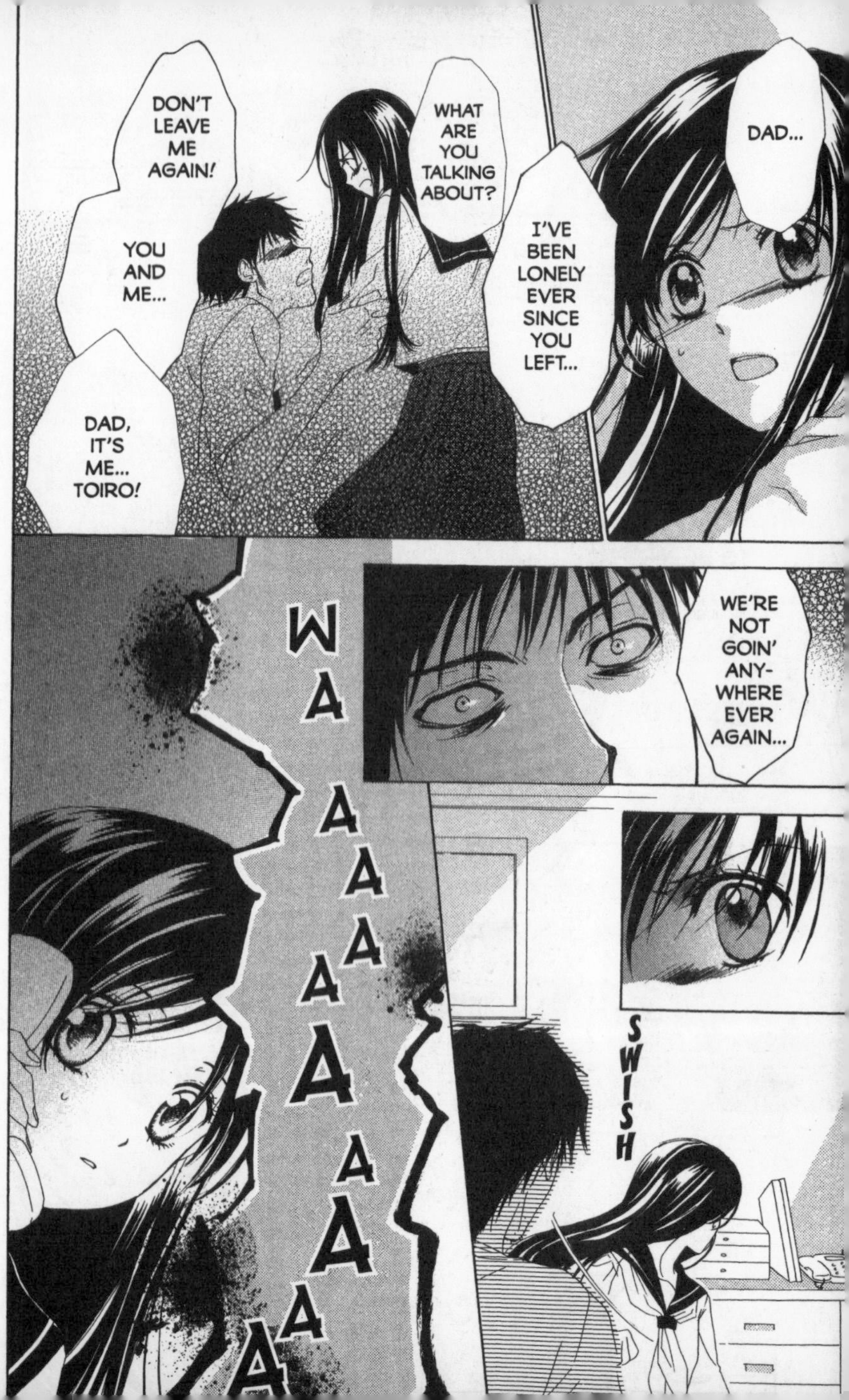
DAD...
I'VE BEEN LONELY EVER SINCE YOU LEFT...
WHAT ARE YOU TALKING ABOUT?
DON'T LEAVE ME AGAIN!
YOU AND ME...
DAD, IT'S ME... TOIRO!
WE'RE NOT GOIN' ANY-WHERE EVER AGAIN...
SWISH
WAAAAAAAAAAA

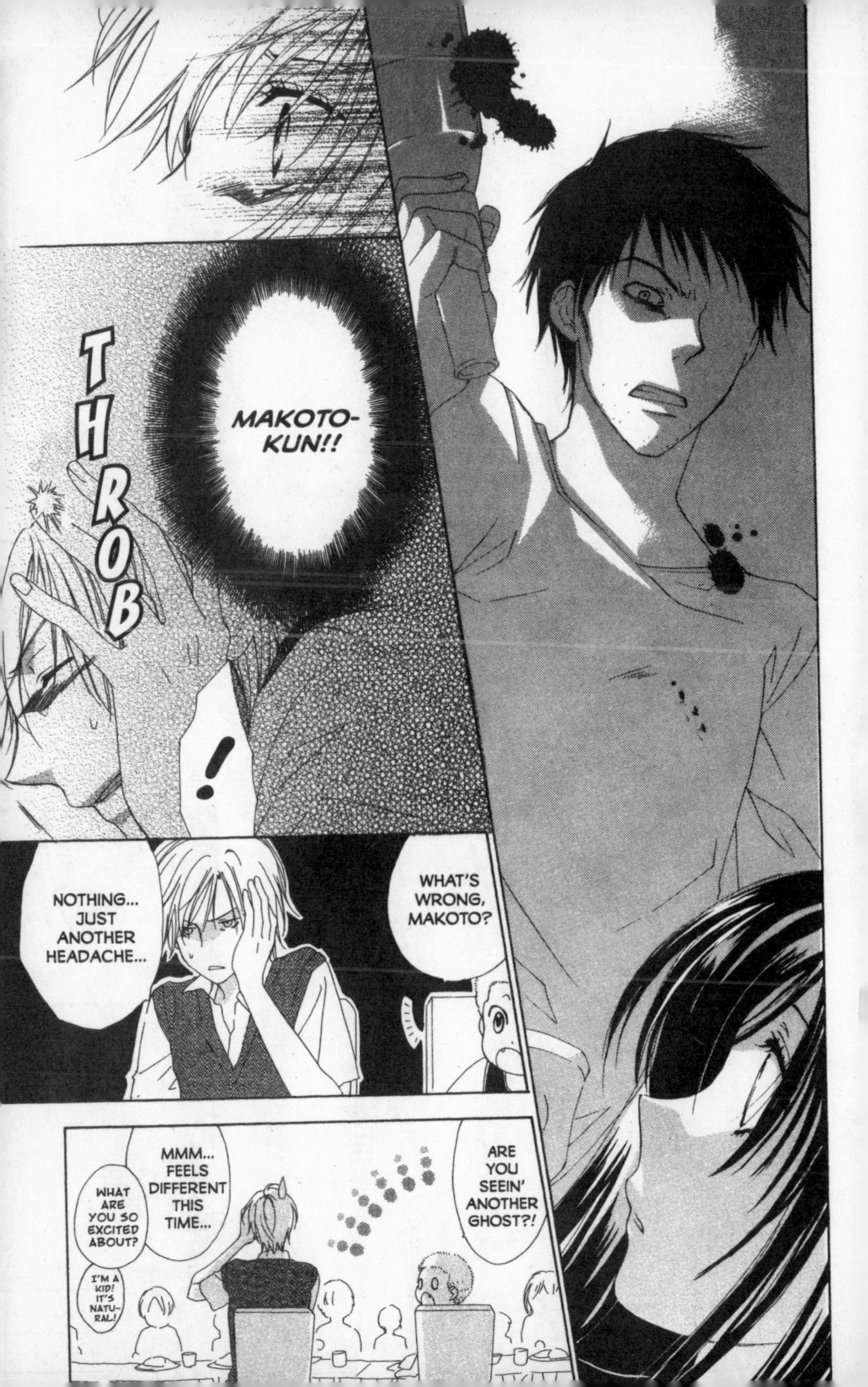
MAKOTO-KUN!!
THROB
!
WHAT'S WRONG, MAKOTO?
NOTHING... JUST ANOTHER HEADACHE...
ARE YOU SEEIN' ANOTHER GHOST?!
MMM... FEELS DIFFERENT THIS TIME...
WHAT ARE YOU SO EXCITED ABOUT?
I'M A KID! IT'S NATU-RAL!

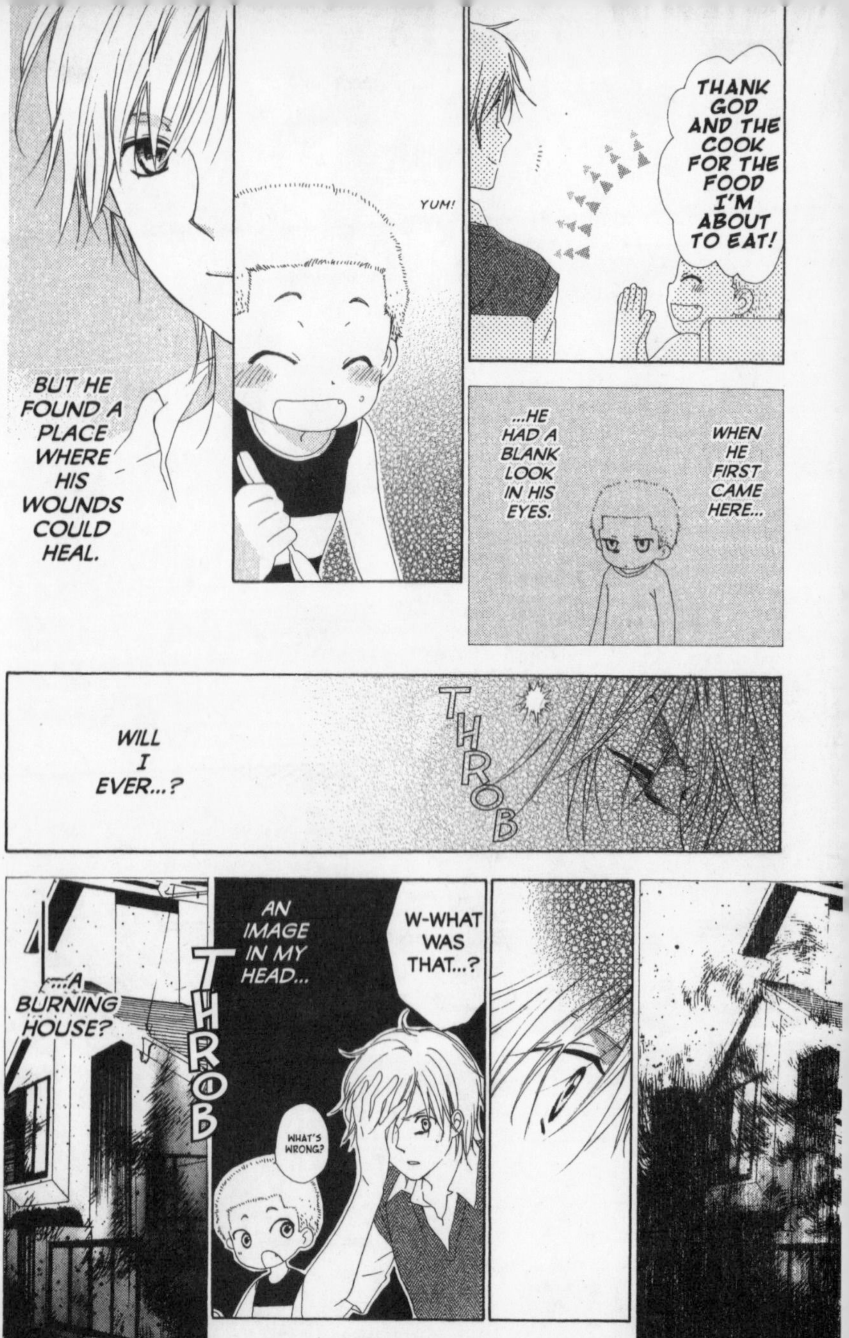
THANK GOD AND THE COOK FOR THE FOOD I'M ABOUT TO EAT!
WHEN HE FIRST CAME HERE...
...HE HAD A BLANK LOOK IN HIS EYES.
YUM!
BUT HE FOUND A PLACE WHERE HIS WOUNDS COULD HEAL.
THROB
WILL I EVER...?
W-WHAT WAS THAT...?
AN IMAGE IN MY HEAD...
THROB
WHAT'S WRONG?
...A BURNING HOUSE?

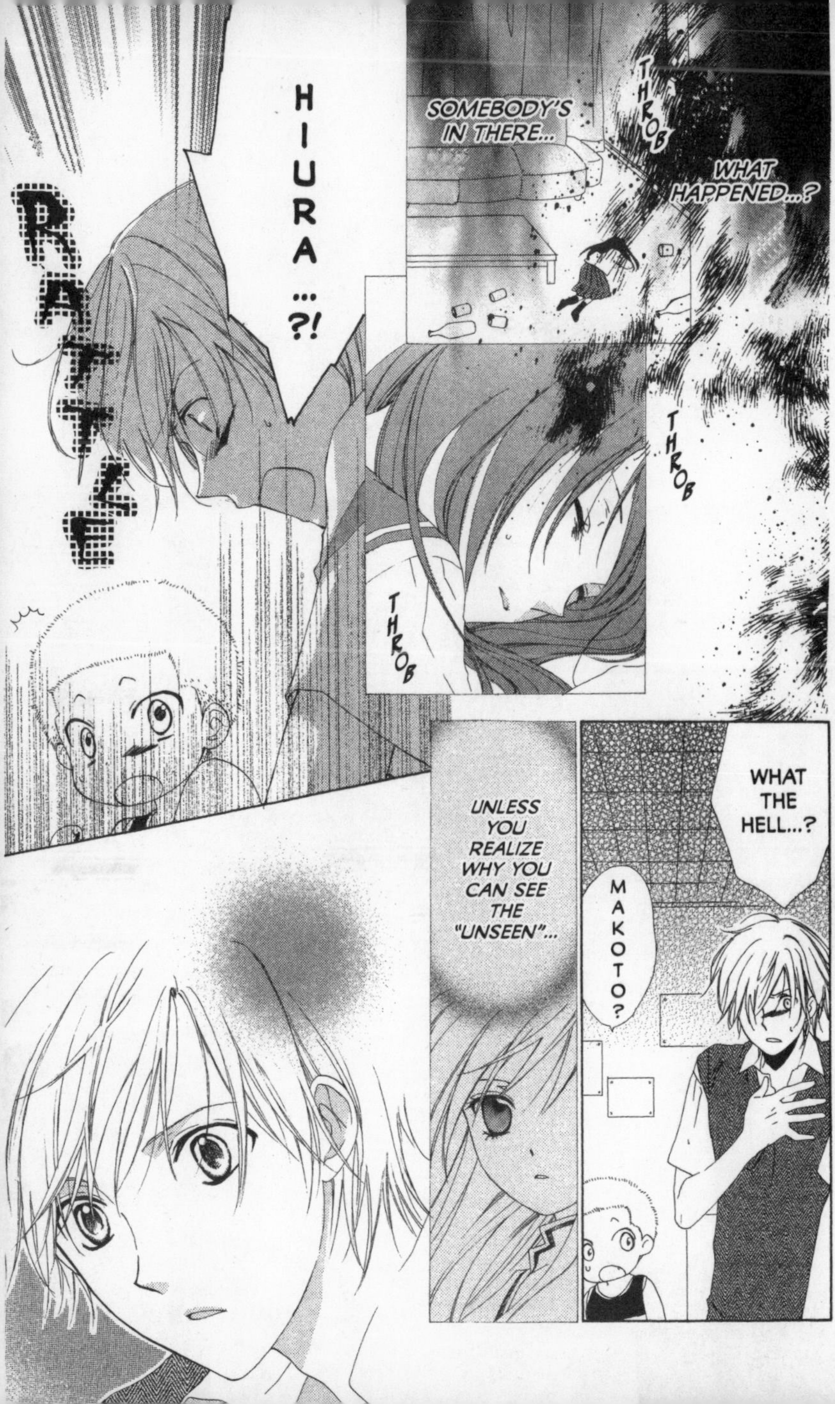
THROB
WHAT HAPPENED...?
SOMEBODY'S IN THERE...
THROB
THROB
HIURA ...?!
RATTLE
WHAT THE HELL...?
MAKOTO?
UNLESS YOU REALIZE WHY YOU CAN SEE THE "UNSEEN"...

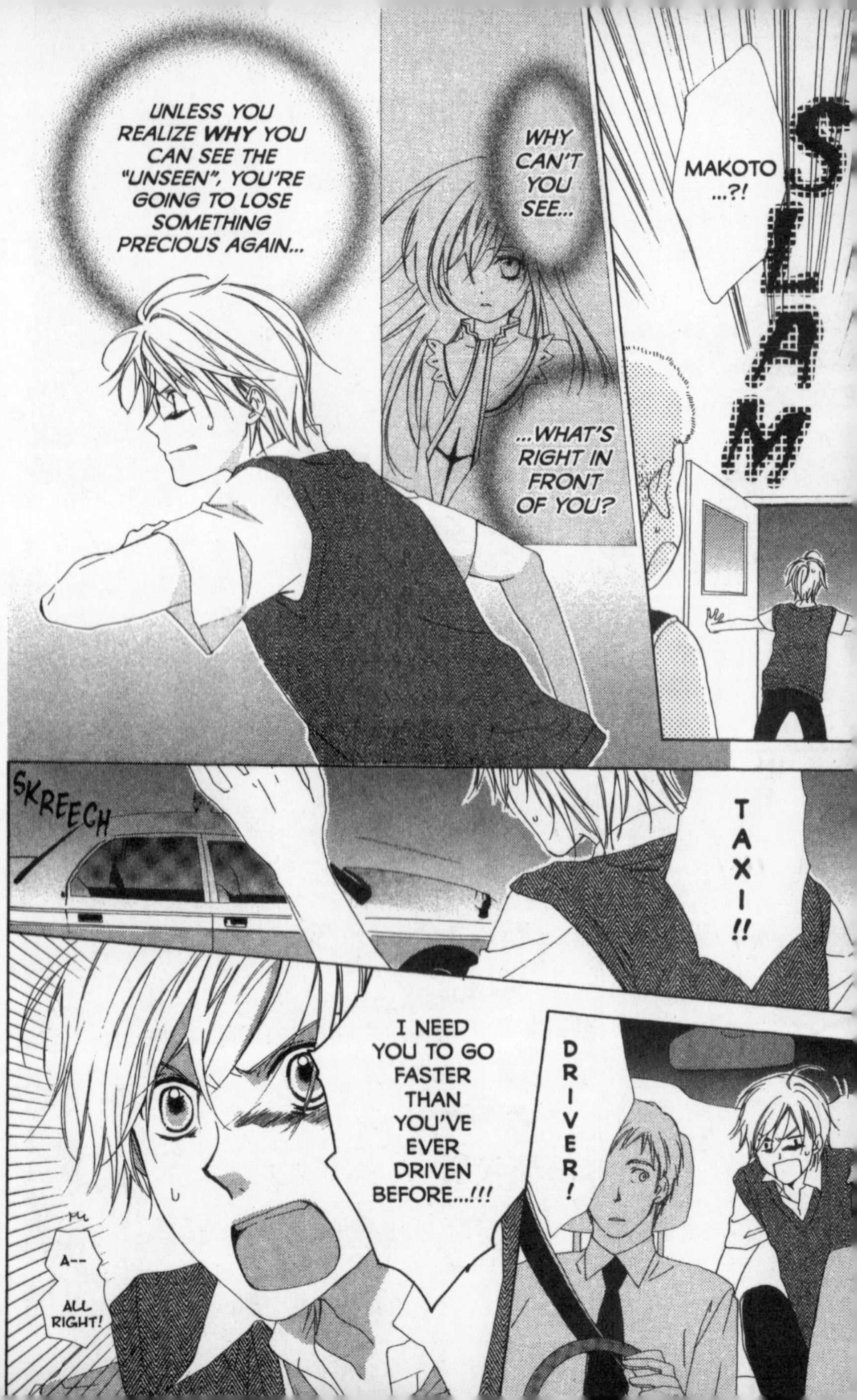
MAKOTO ...?!
SLAM
WHY CAN'T YOU SEE...
...WHAT'S RIGHT IN FRONT OF YOU?
UNLESS YOU REALIZE WHY YOU CAN SEE THE "UNSEEN", YOU'RE GOING TO LOSE SOMETHING PRECIOUS AGAIN...
TAXI!!
SKREECH
DRIVER!
I NEED YOU TO GO FASTER THAN YOU'VE EVER DRIVEN BEFORE...!!!
A--
ALL RIGHT!

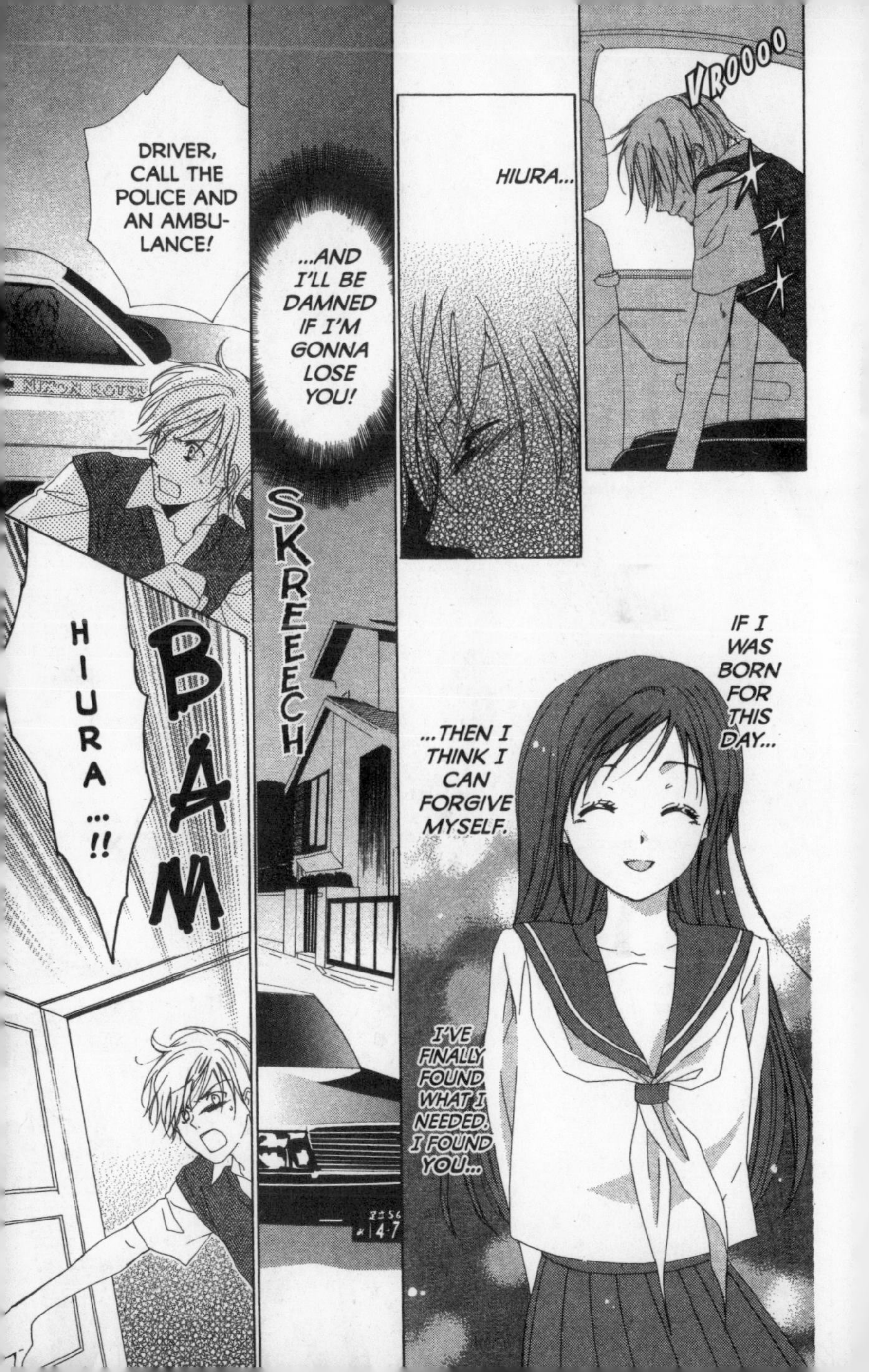
VROOOO
HIURA...
IF I WAS BORN FOR THIS DAY...
...THEN I THINK I CAN FORGIVE MYSELF.
I'VE FINALLY FOUND WHAT I NEEDED. I FOUND YOU...
...AND I'LL BE DAMNED IF I'M GONNA LOSE YOU!
SKREEECH
DRIVER, CALL THE POLICE AND AN AMBULANCE!
BAM
HIURA...!!

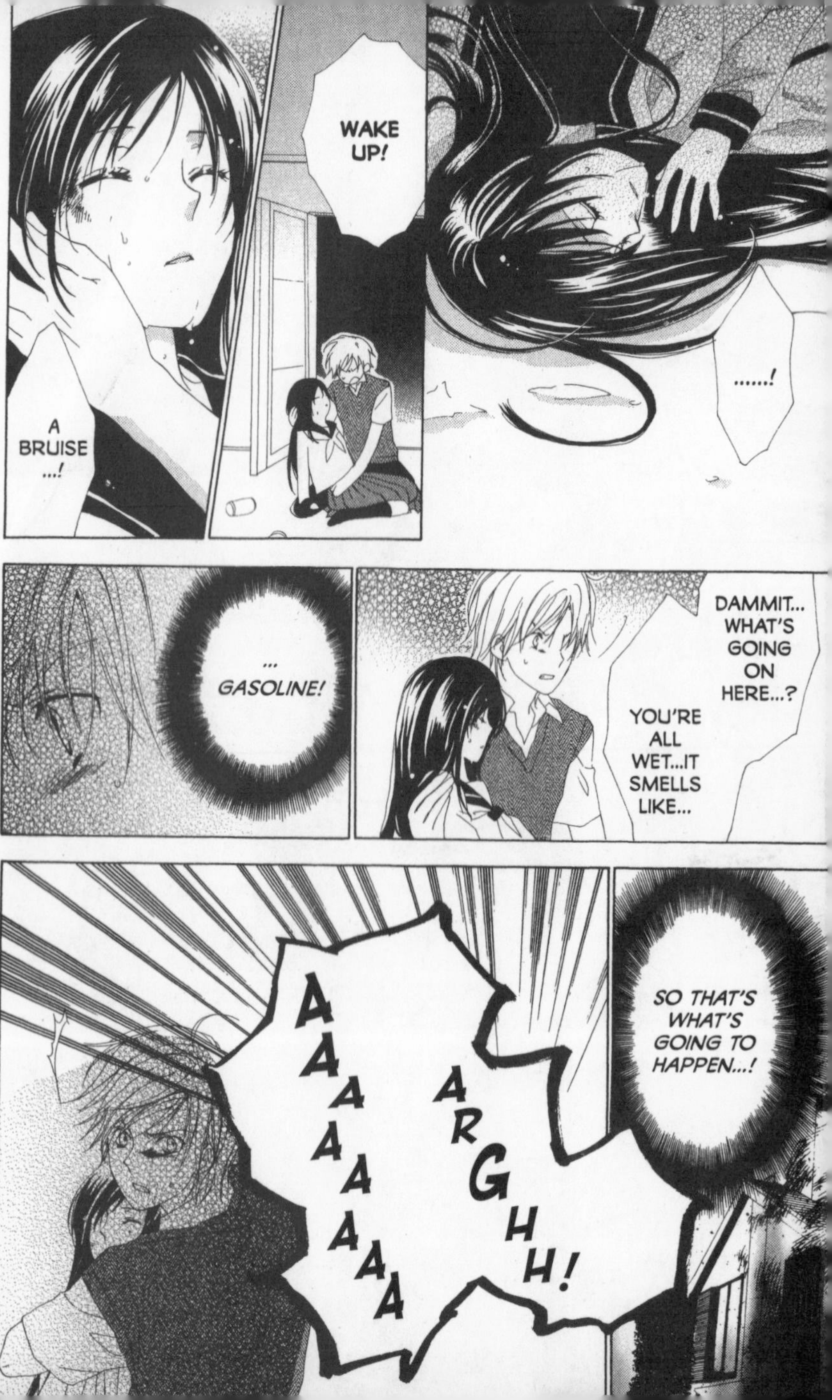
......!
WAKE UP!
A BRUISE ...!
DAMMIT... WHAT'S GOING ON HERE...?
YOU'RE ALL WET...IT SMELLS LIKE...
... GASOLINE!
SO THAT'S WHAT'S GOING TO HAPPEN...!
AAAAAAAAARGHH!

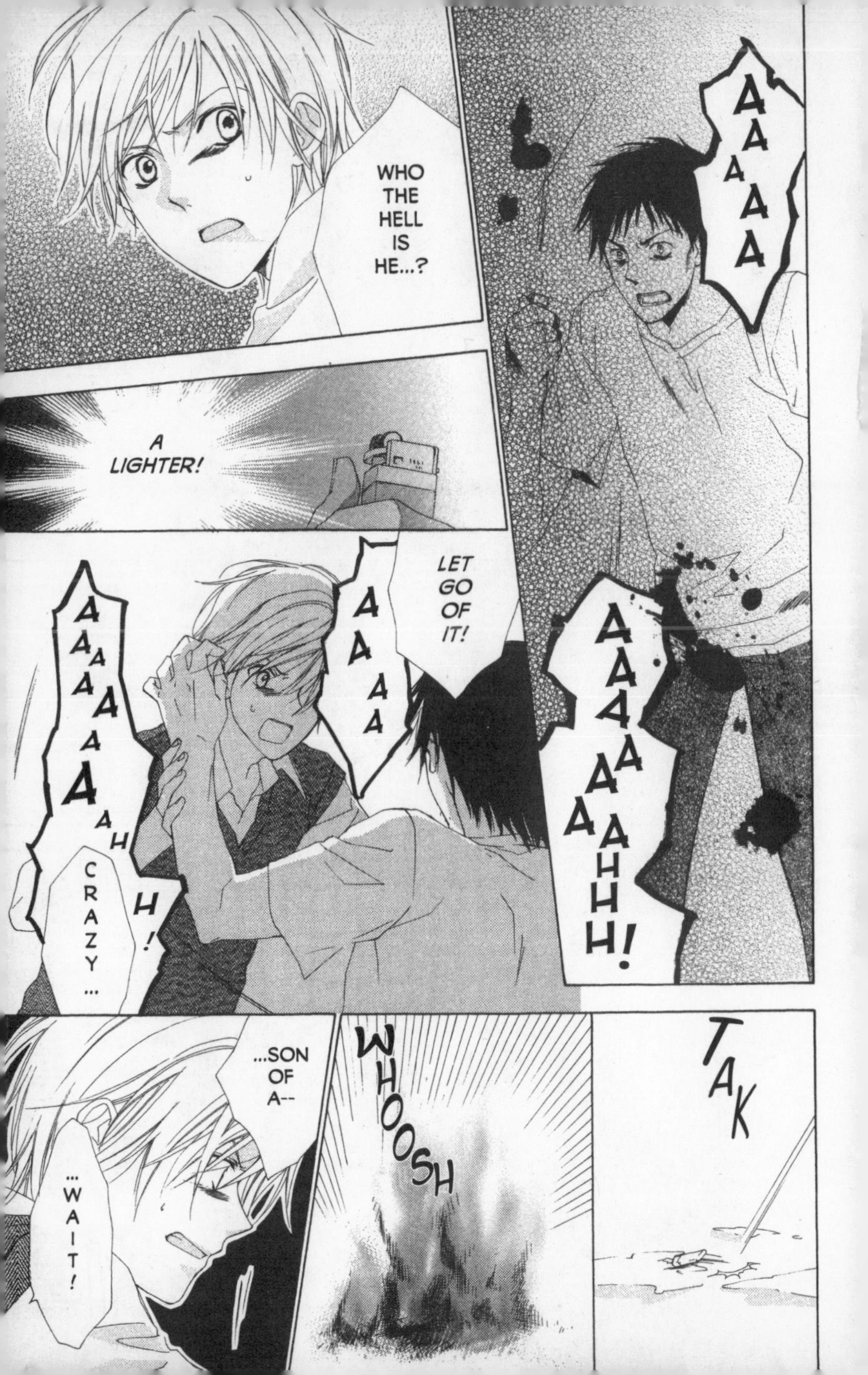

AAAAAA
AAAAAAAAAHHHH!
WHO THE HELL IS HE...?
A LIGHTER!
LET GO OF IT!
AAAAA
AAAAAAAAAAHH!
CRAZY...
TAK
WHOOSH
...SON OF A--
...WAIT!

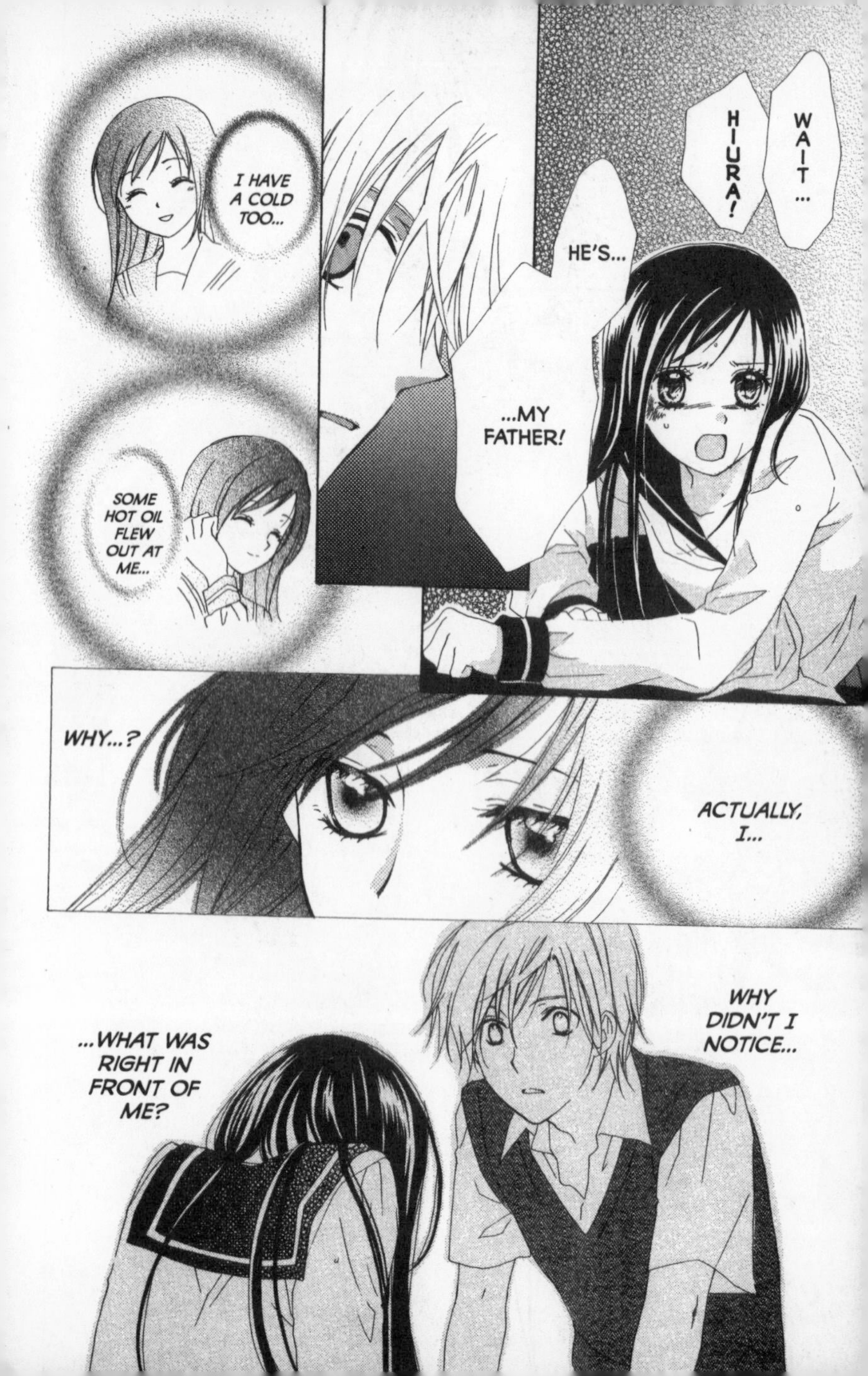
WAIT...
HIURA!
HE'S...
...MY FATHER!
I HAVE A COLD TOO...
SOME HOT OIL FLEW OUT AT ME...
ACTUALLY, I...
WHY...?
WHY DIDN'T I NOTICE...
...WHAT WAS RIGHT IN FRONT OF ME?

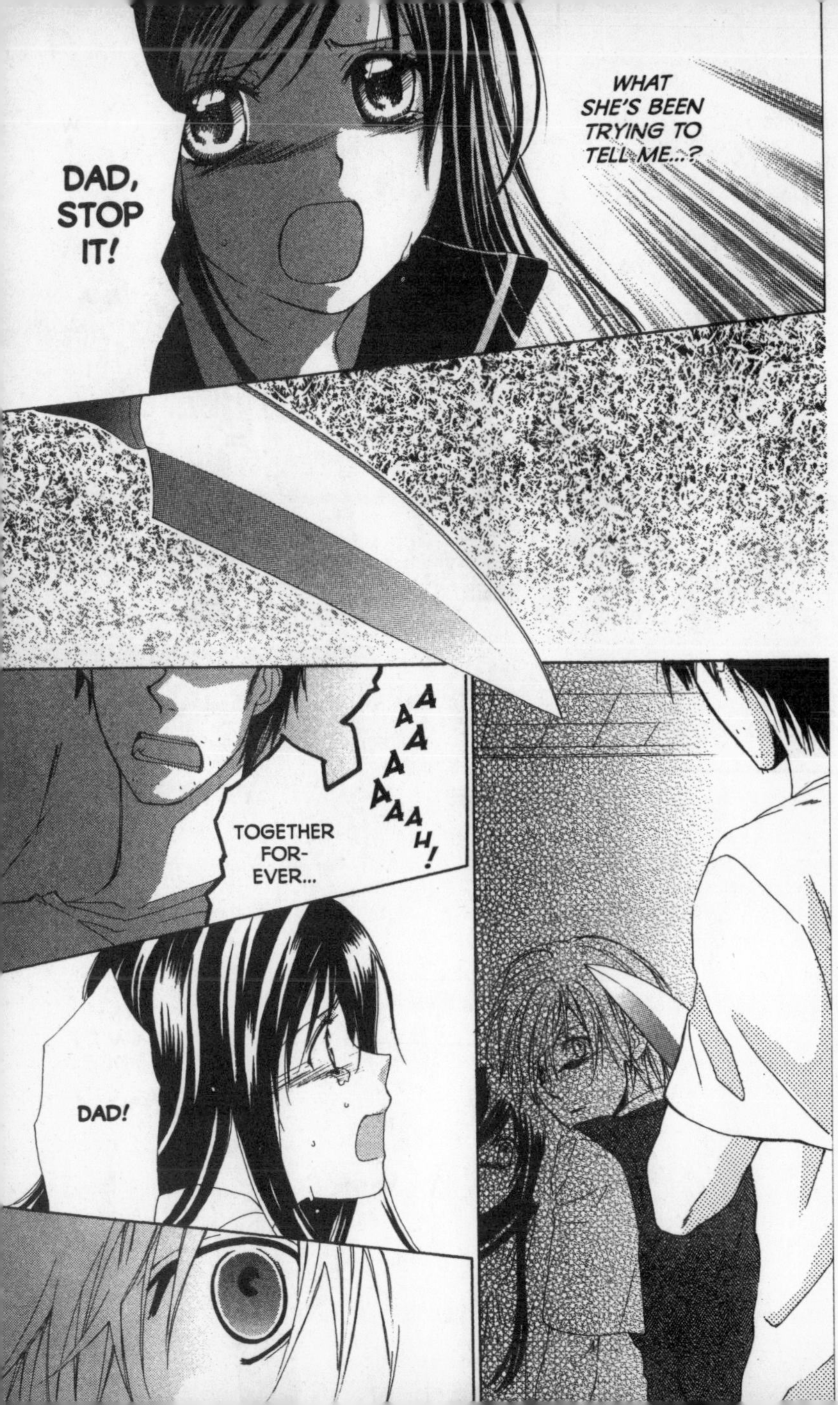
WHAT SHE'S BEEN TRYING TO TELL ME...?
DAD, STOP IT!
AAAAAAAH!
TOGETHER FOR-EVER...
DAD!

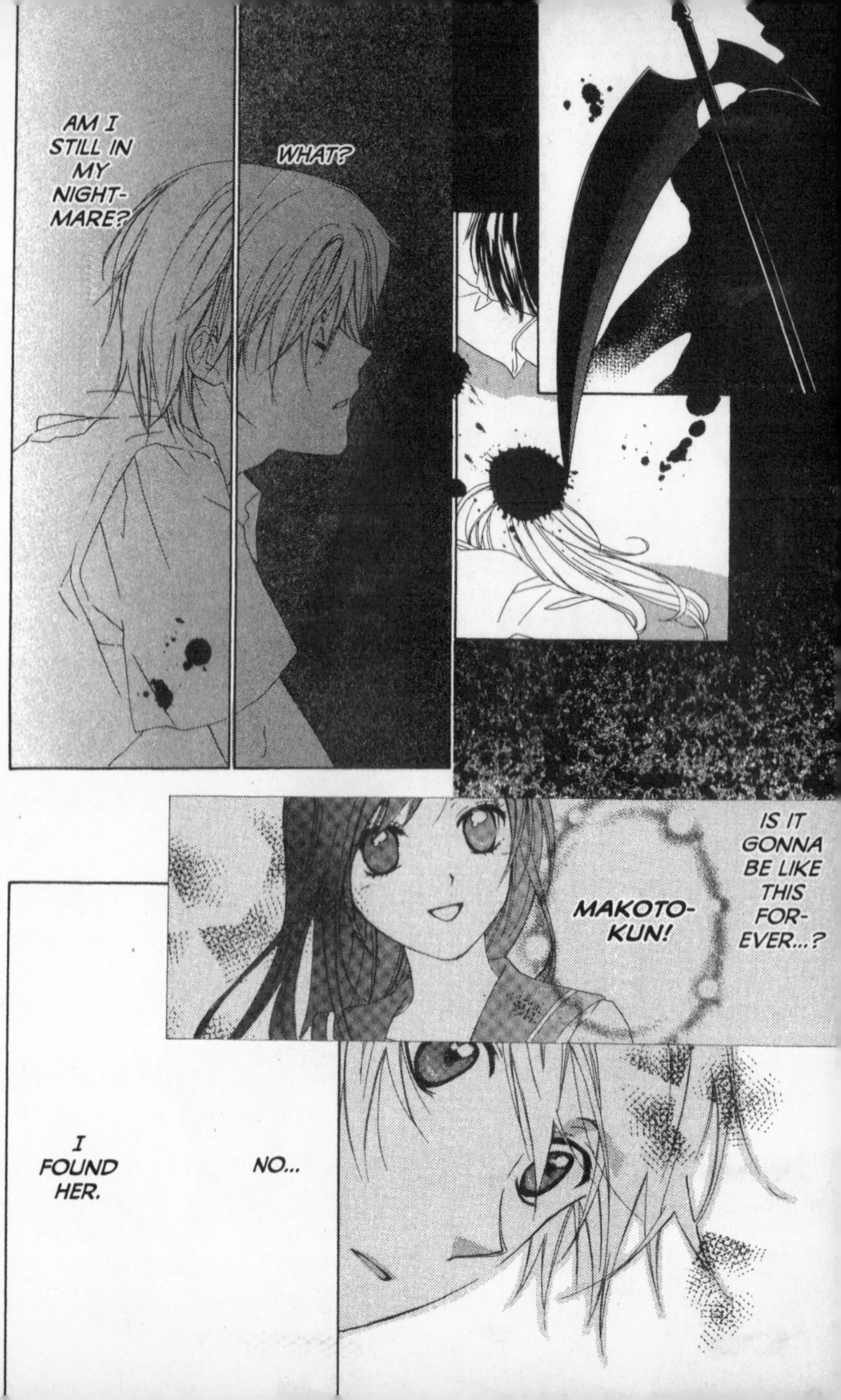
WHAT?
AM I STILL IN MY NIGHT-MARE?
IS IT GONNA BE LIKE THIS FOR-EVER...?
MAKOTO-KUN!
NO...
I FOUND HER.

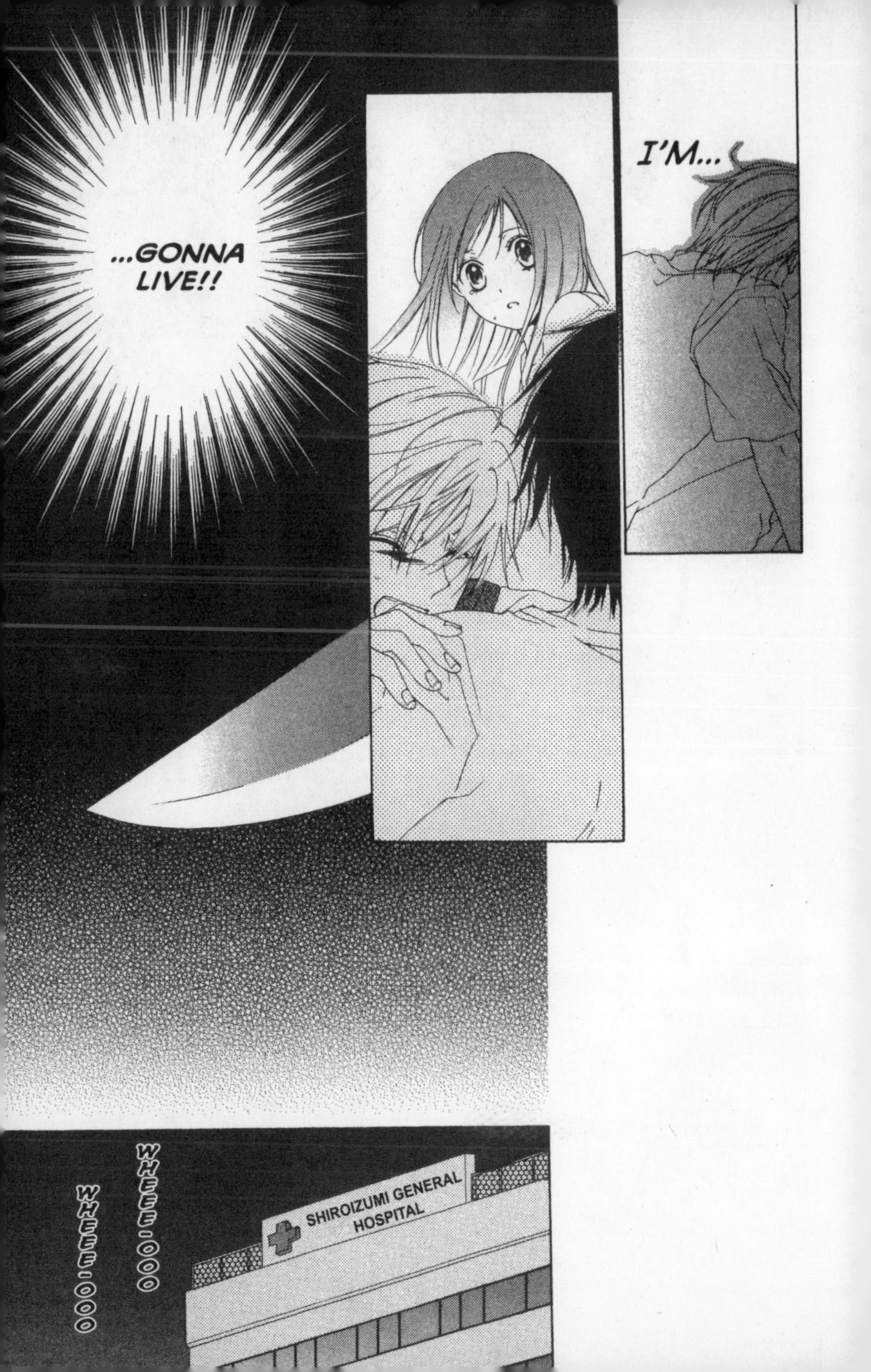
I'M...
...GONNA LIVE!!
SHIROIZUMI GENERAL HOSPITAL
WHEEE-OOO
WHEEE-OOO

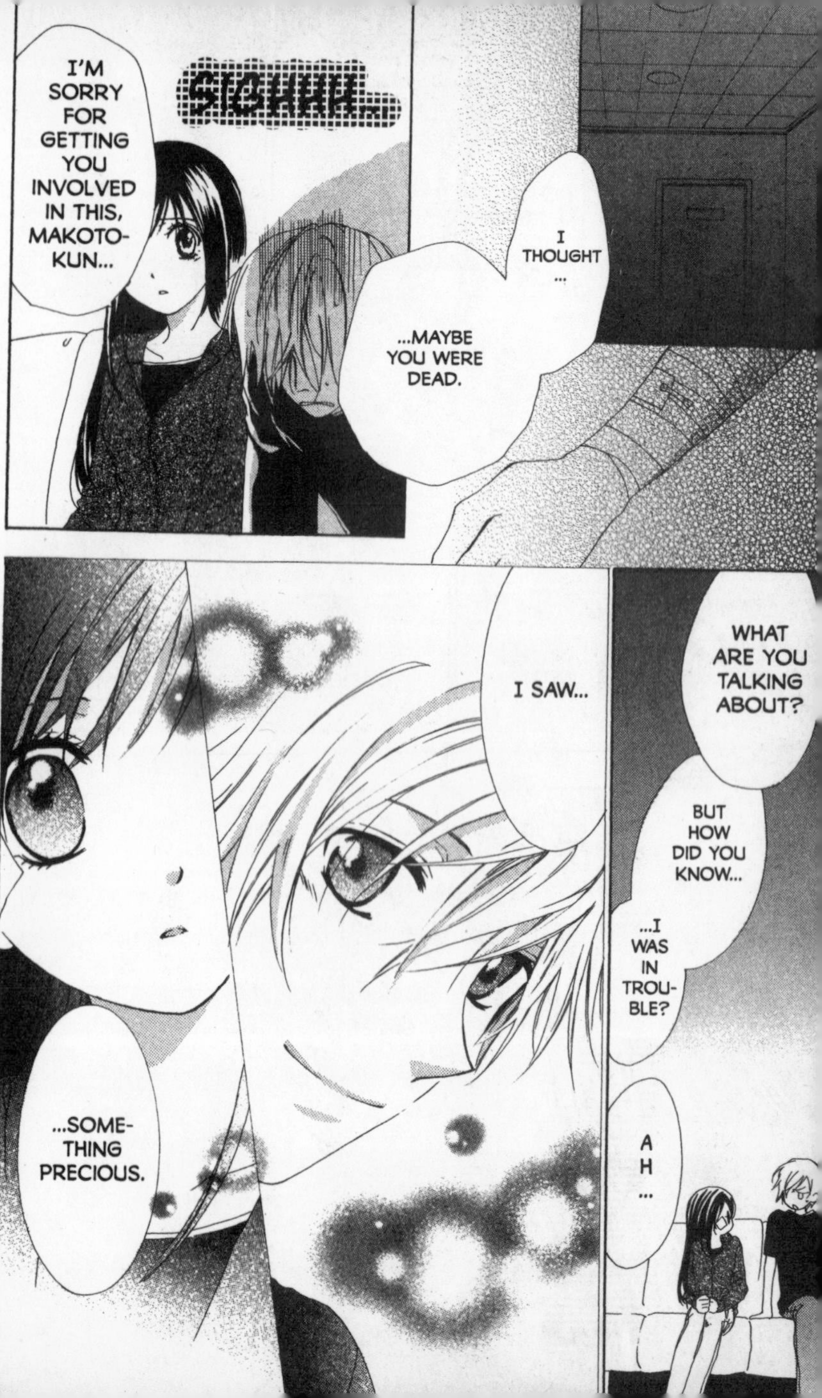
I THOUGHT ...
...MAYBE YOU WERE DEAD.
SIGHHH...
I'M SORRY FOR GETTING YOU INVOLVED IN THIS, MAKOTO-KUN...
WHAT ARE YOU TALKING ABOUT?
BUT HOW DID YOU KNOW...
...I WAS IN TROUBLE?
AH ...
I SAW...
...SOMETHING PRECIOUS.

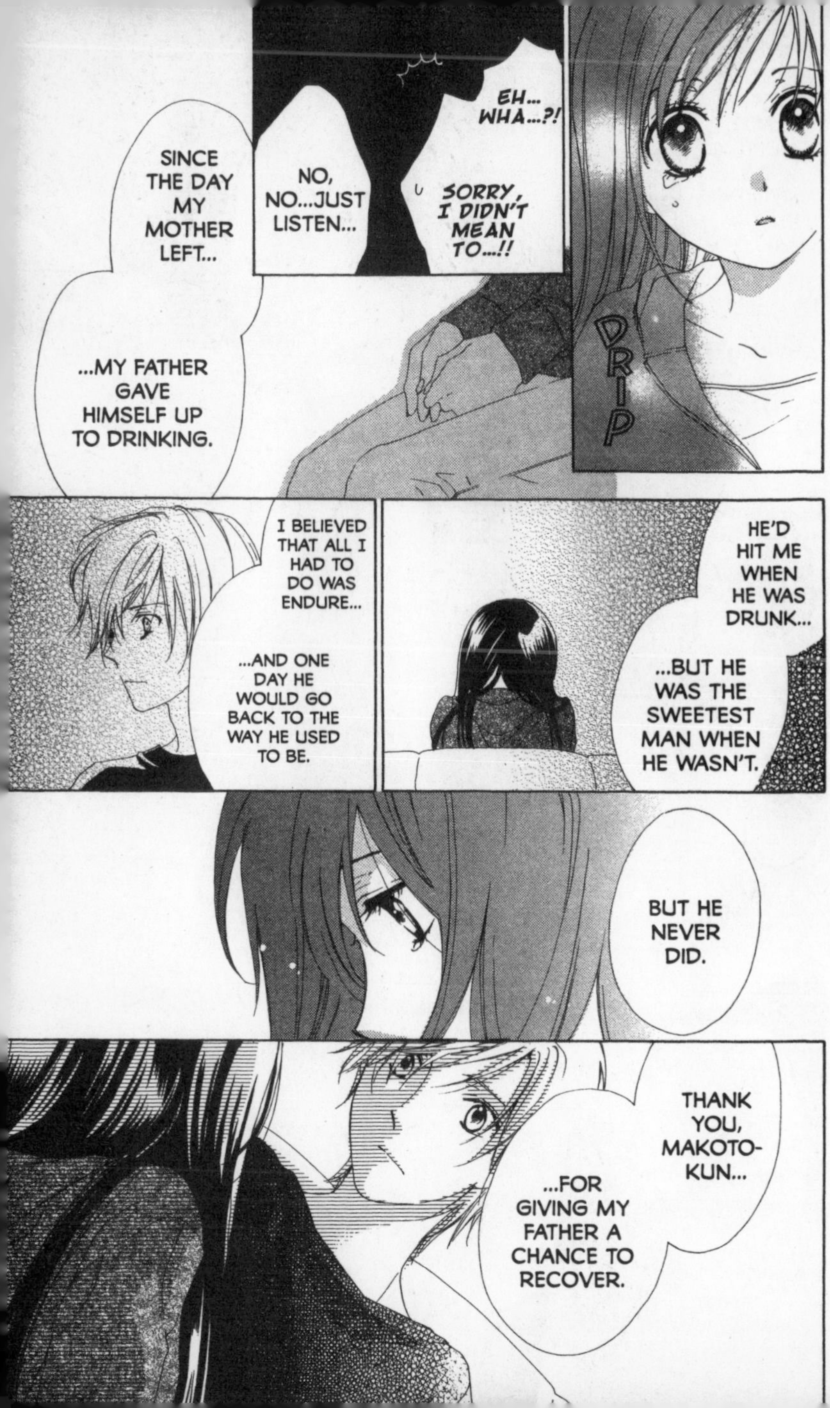
EH... WHA...?!
SORRY, I DIDN'T MEAN TO...!!
DRIP
NO, NO...JUST LISTEN...
SINCE THE DAY MY MOTHER LEFT...
...MY FATHER GAVE HIMSELF UP TO DRINKING.
HE'D HIT ME WHEN HE WAS DRUNK...
...BUT HE WAS THE SWEETEST MAN WHEN HE WASN'T.
I BELIEVED THAT ALL I HAD TO DO WAS ENDURE...
...AND ONE DAY HE WOULD GO BACK TO THE WAY HE USED TO BE.
BUT HE NEVER DID.
THANK YOU, MAKOTO-KUN...
...FOR GIVING MY FATHER A CHANCE TO RECOVER.

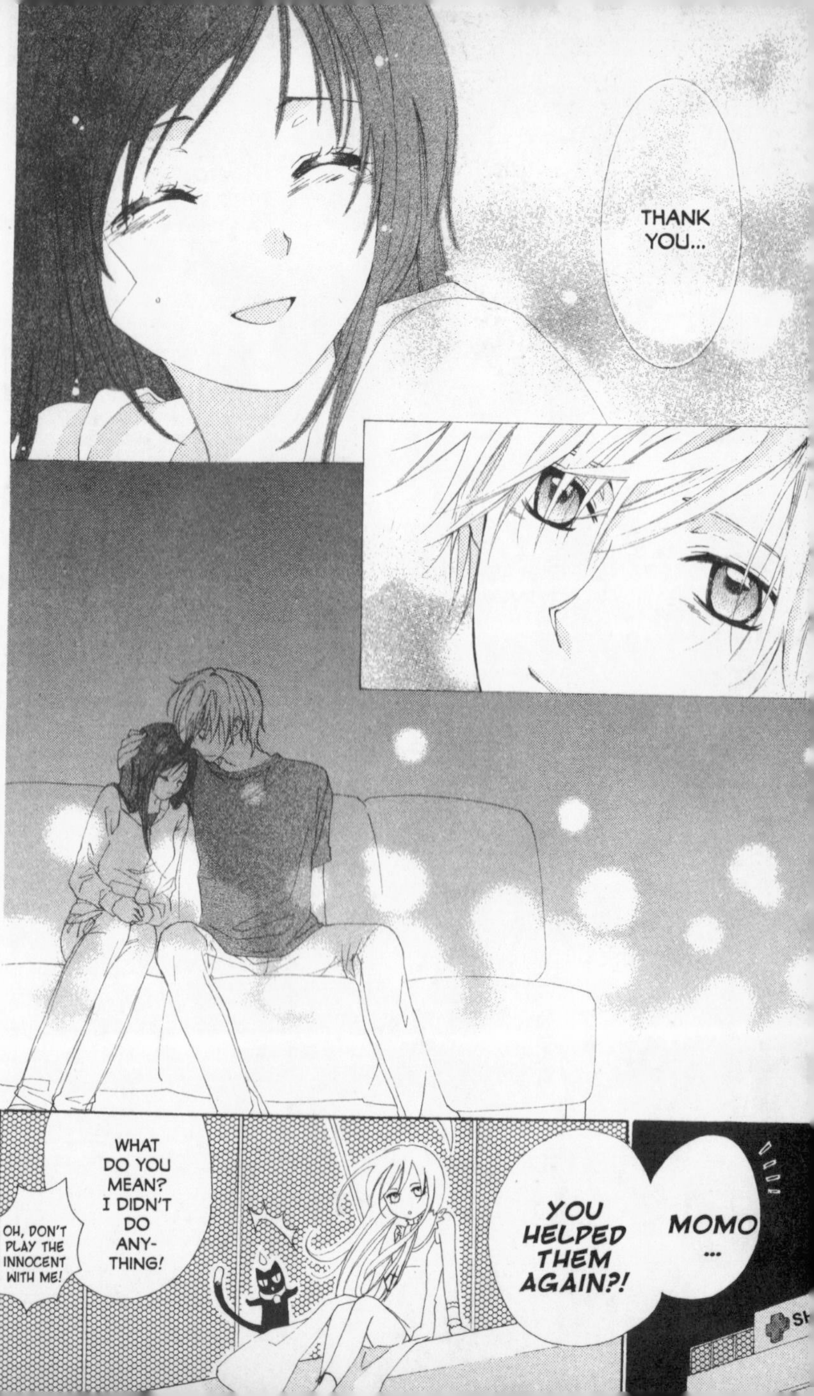
THANK YOU...
MOMO...
YOU HELPED THEM AGAIN?!
WHAT DO YOU MEAN? I DIDN'T DO ANY-THING!
OH, DON'T PLAY THE INNOCENT WITH ME!

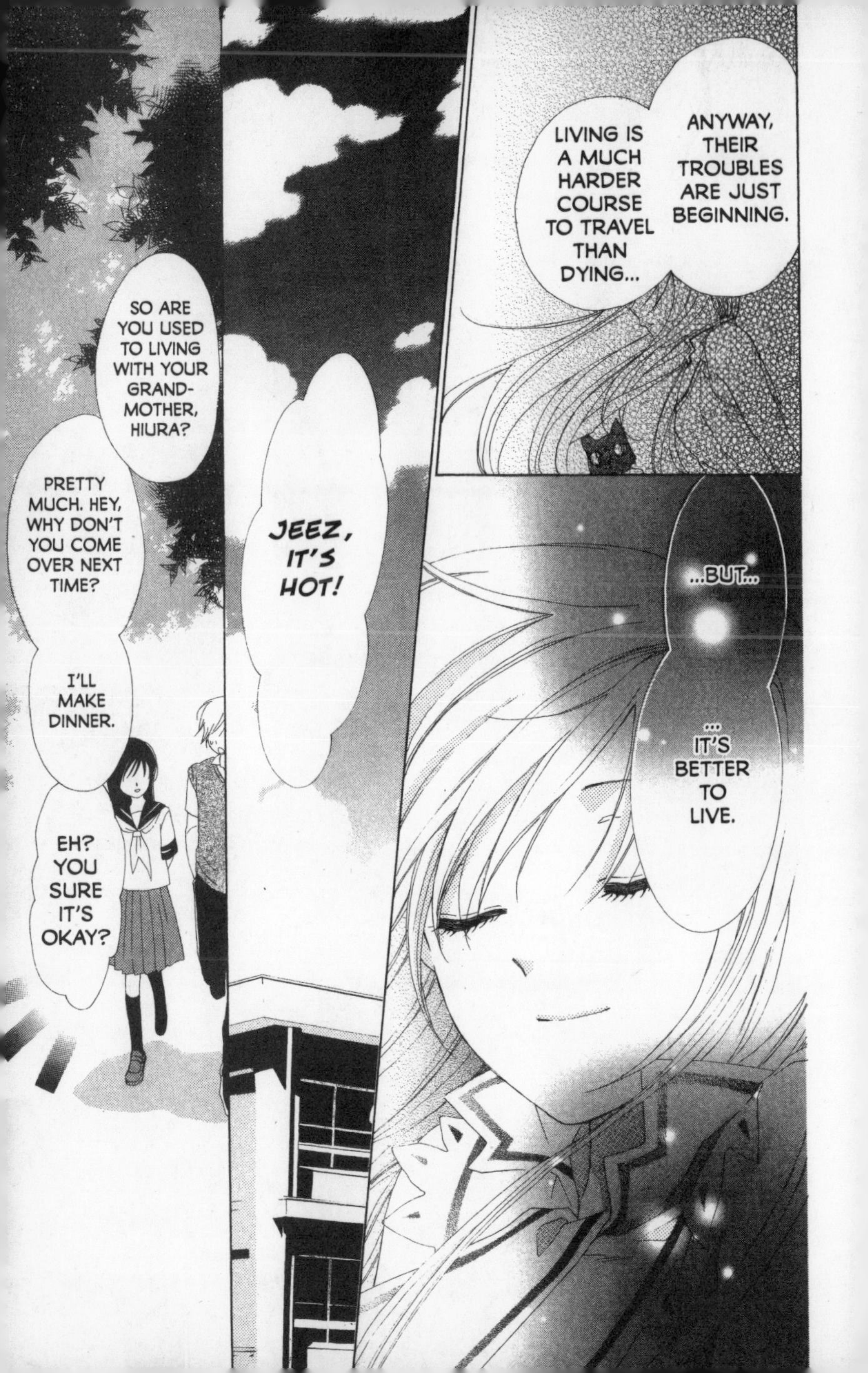
ANYWAY, THEIR TROUBLES ARE JUST BEGINNING.
LIVING IS A MUCH HARDER COURSE TO TRAVEL THAN DYING...
...BUT...
...IT'S BETTER TO LIVE.
JEEZ, IT'S HOT!
SO ARE YOU USED TO LIVING WITH YOUR GRAND-MOTHER, HIURA?
PRETTY MUCH. HEY, WHY DON'T YOU COME OVER NEXT TIME?
I'LL MAKE DINNER.
EH? YOU SURE IT'S OKAY?

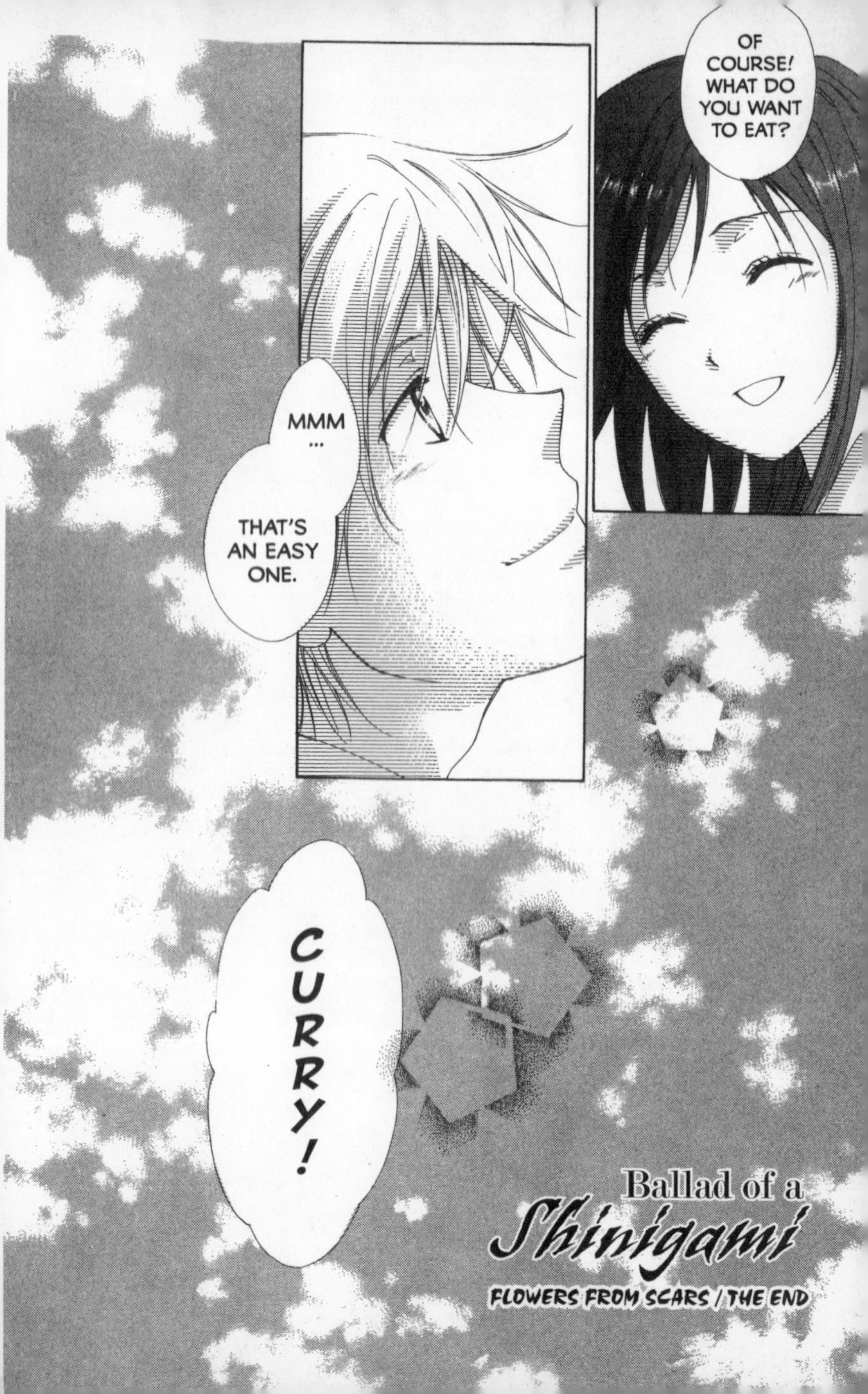
OF COURSE! WHAT DO YOU WANT TO EAT?
MMM ...
THAT'S AN EASY ONE.
CURRY!
Ballad of a Shinigami
FLOWERS FROM SCARS / THE END

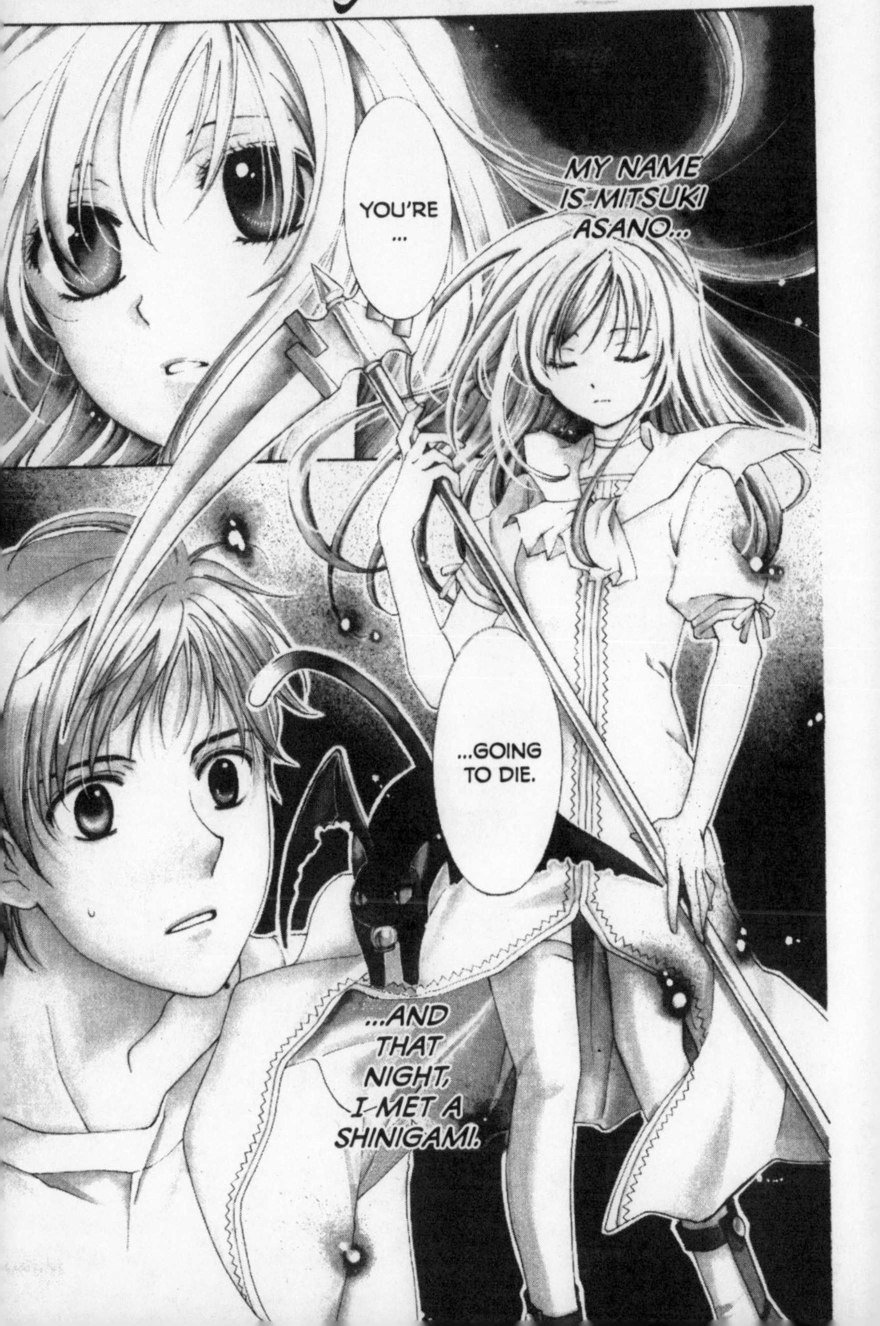
MY NAME IS MITSUKI ASANO...
YOU'RE ...
...GOING TO DIE.
...AND THAT NIGHT, I MET A SHINIGAMI.

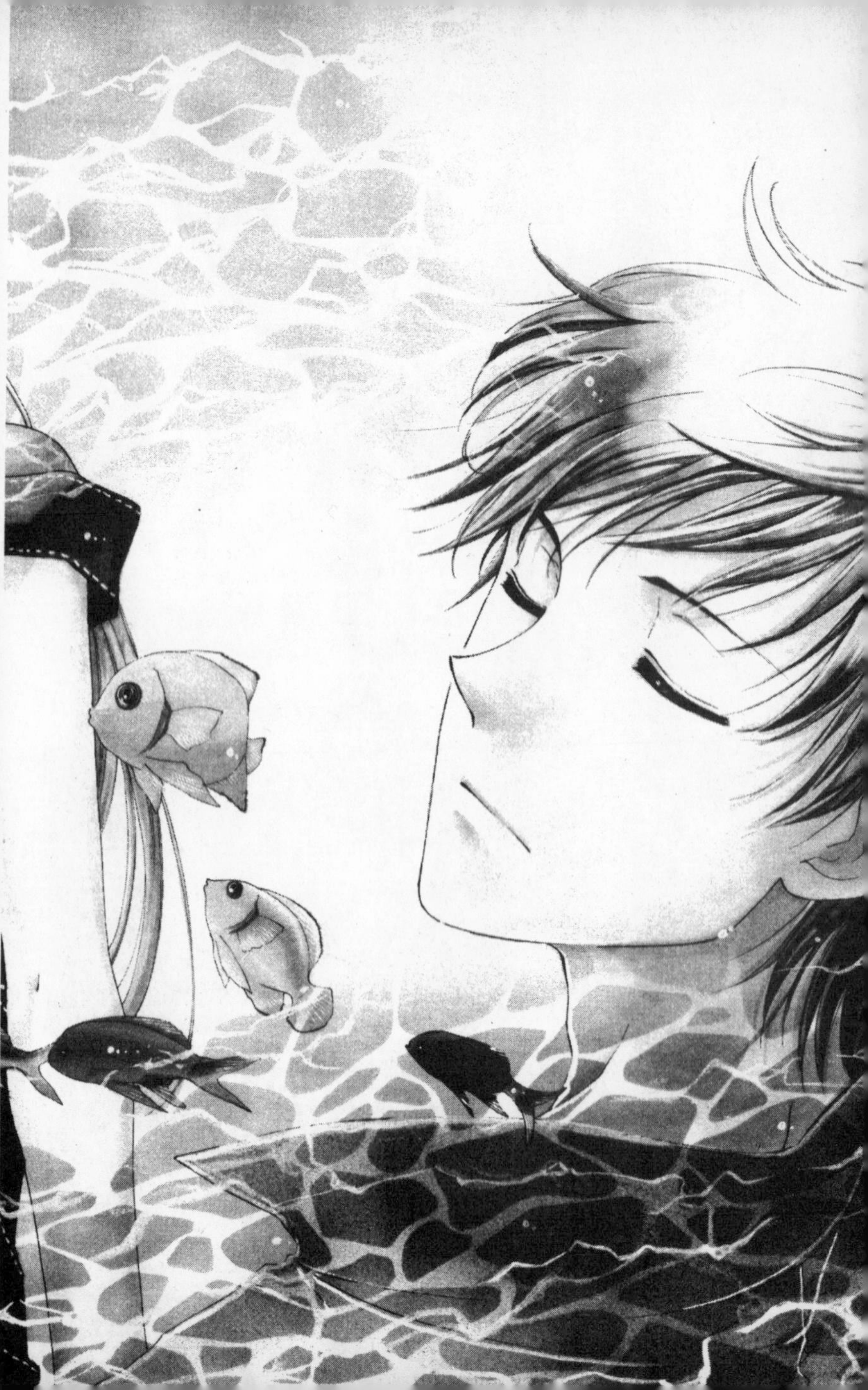

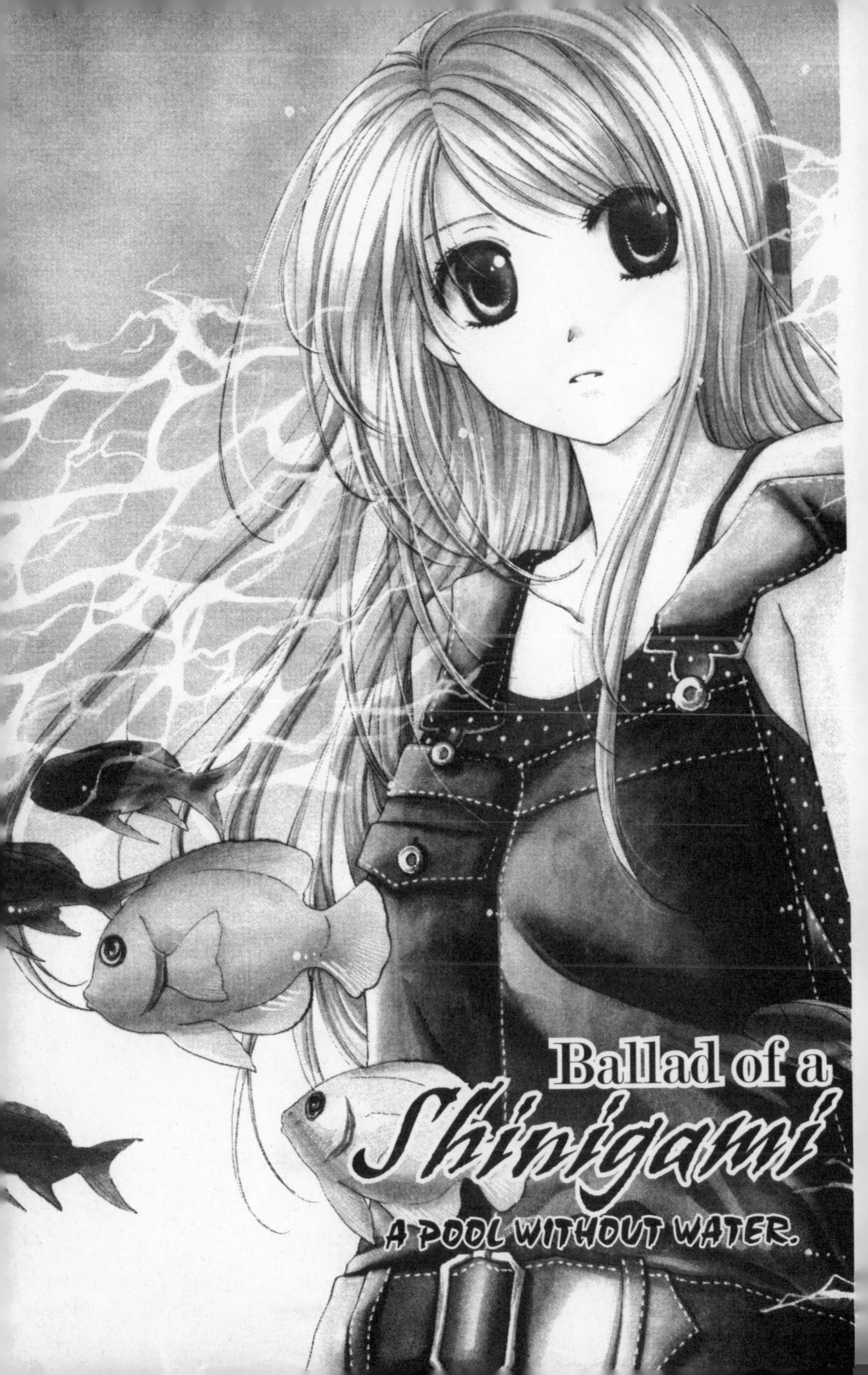
Ballad of a
Shinigami
A POOL WITHOUT WATER.

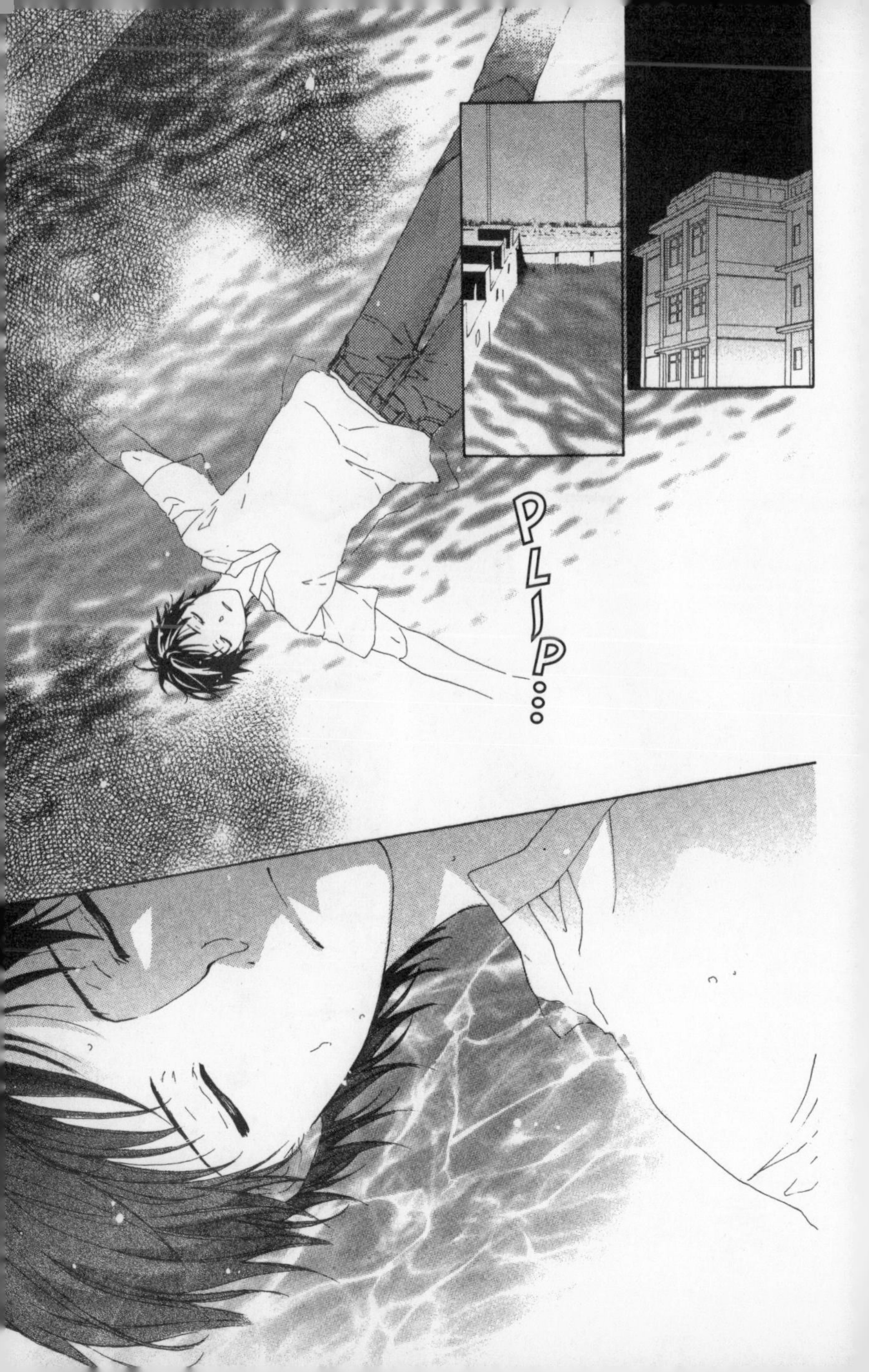
PLIP...

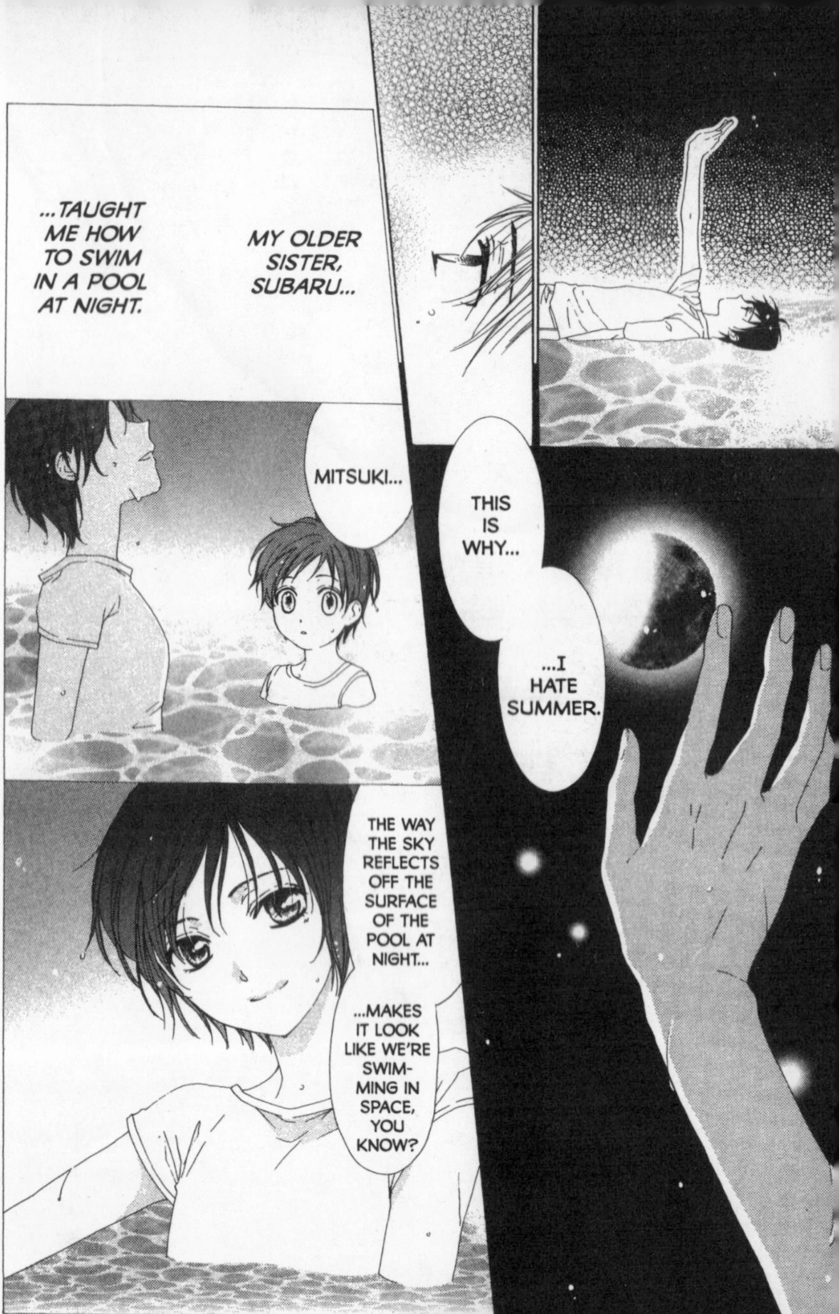
MY OLDER SISTER, SUBARU...
...TAUGHT ME HOW TO SWIM IN A POOL AT NIGHT.
THIS IS WHY...
...I HATE SUMMER.
MITSUKI...
THE WAY THE SKY REFLECTS OFF THE SURFACE OF THE POOL AT NIGHT...
...MAKES IT LOOK LIKE WE'RE SWIM-MING IN SPACE, YOU KNOW?

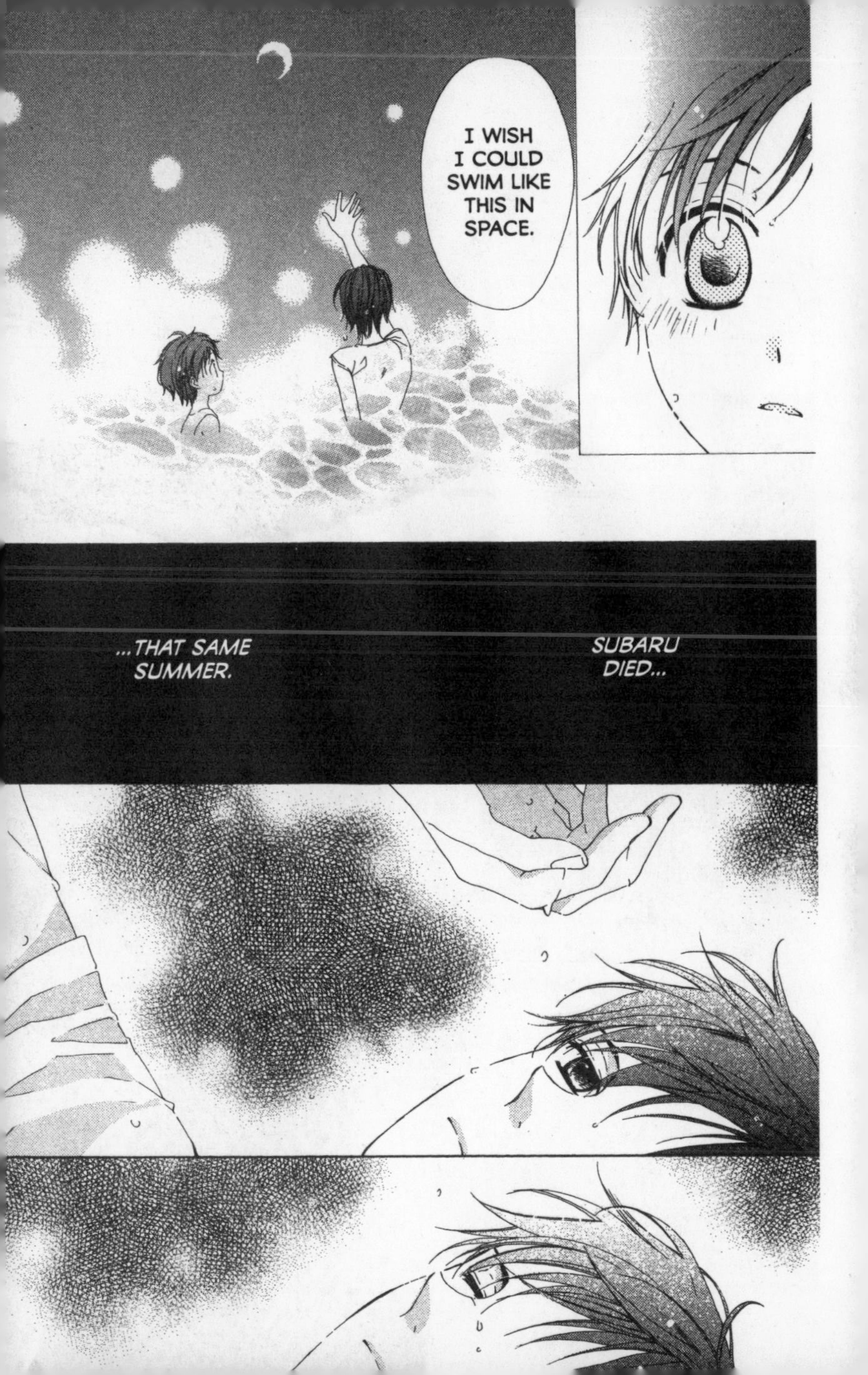
I WISH I COULD SWIM LIKE THIS IN SPACE.
SUBARU DIED...
...THAT SAME SUMMER.

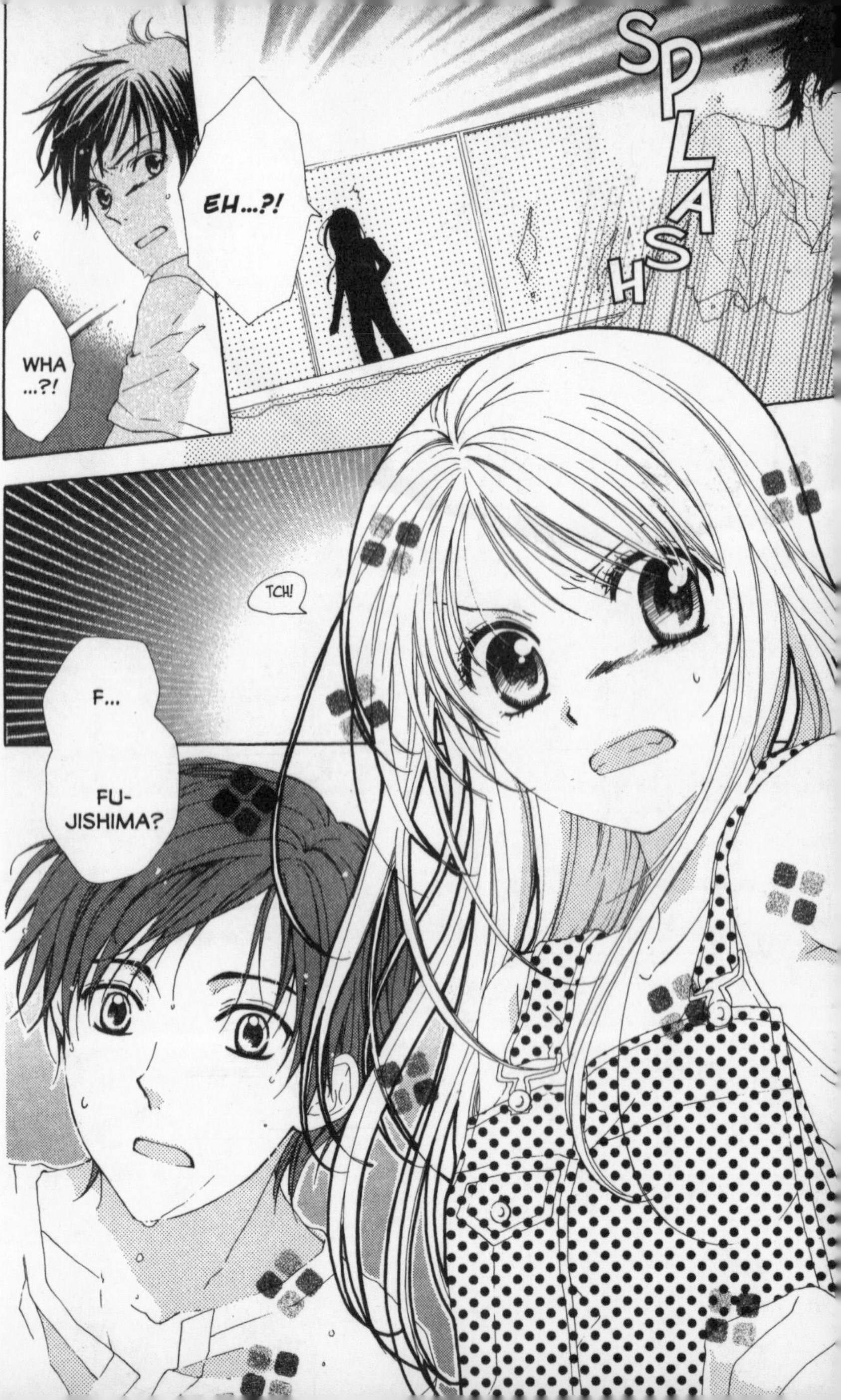
SPLASH
EH...?!
WHA...?!
TCH!
F... FU-JISHIMA?

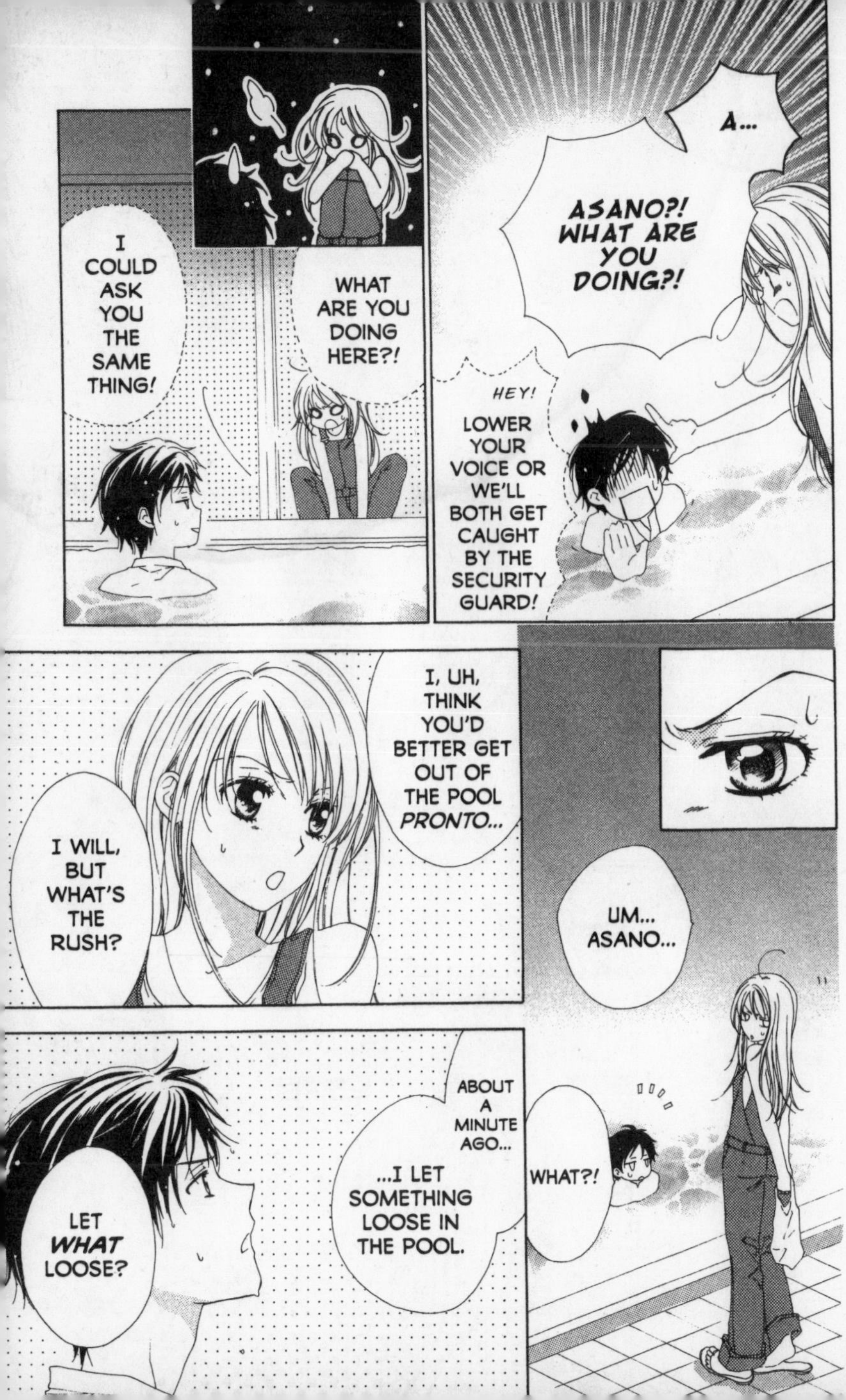
A...
ASANO?! WHAT ARE YOU DOING?!
HEY!
LOWER YOUR VOICE OR WE'LL BOTH GET CAUGHT BY THE SECURITY GUARD!
WHAT ARE YOU DOING HERE?!
I COULD ASK YOU THE SAME THING!
UM... ASANO...
WHAT?!
I, UH, THINK YOU'D BETTER GET OUT OF THE POOL *PRONTO*...
I WILL, BUT WHAT'S THE RUSH?
ABOUT A MINUTE AGO...
...I LET SOMETHING LOOSE IN THE POOL.
LET ***WHAT*** LOOSE?

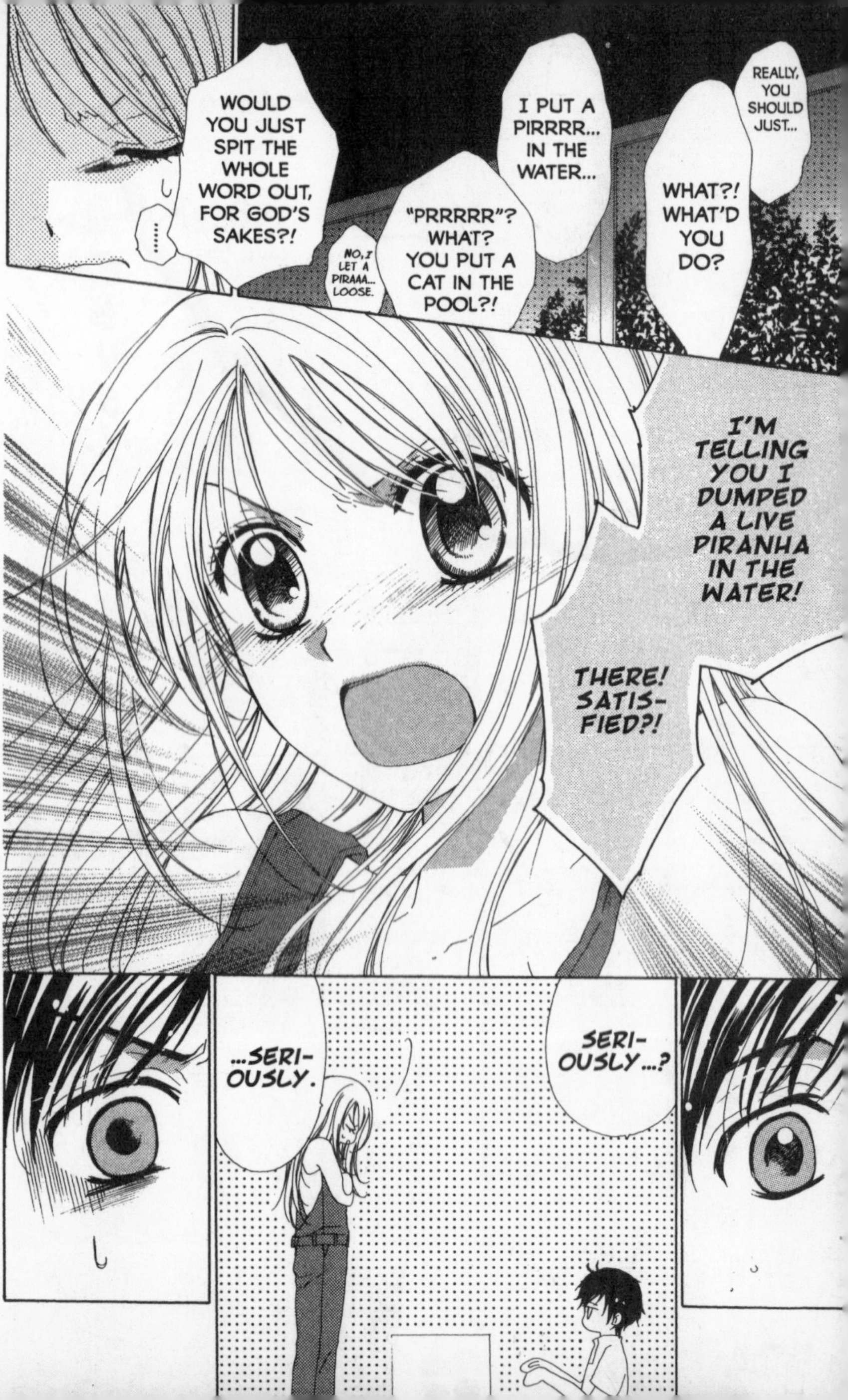

REALLY, YOU SHOULD JUST...
WHAT?! WHAT'D YOU DO?
I PUT A PIRRRR... IN THE WATER...
"PRRRRR"? WHAT? YOU PUT A CAT IN THE POOL?!
NO, I LET A PIRAAA... LOOSE.
WOULD YOU JUST SPIT THE WHOLE WORD OUT, FOR GOD'S SAKES?!
......
I'M TELLING YOU I DUMPED A LIVE PIRANHA IN THE WATER!
THERE! SATIS-FIED?!
SERI-OUSLY...?
...SERI-OUSLY.

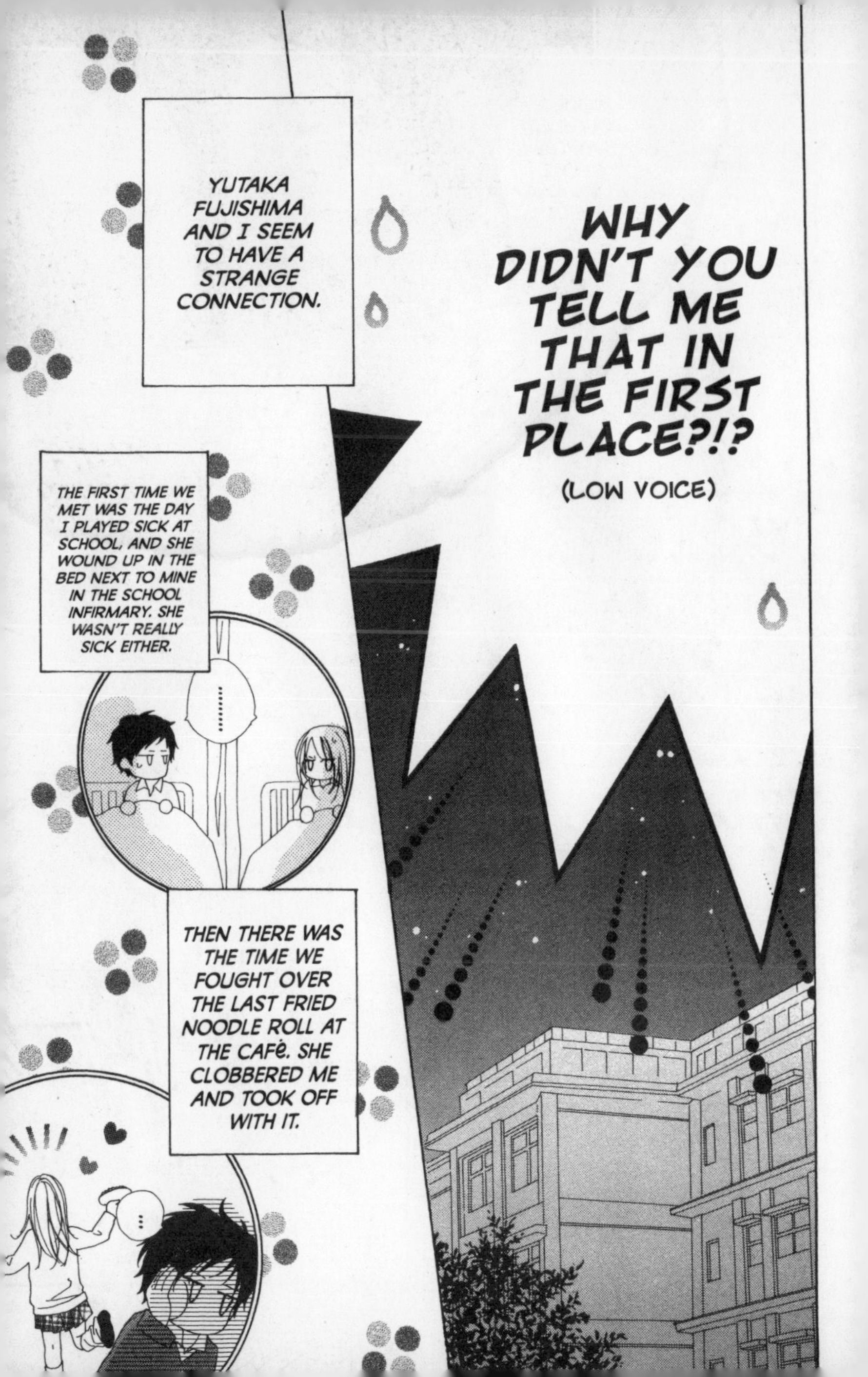
WHY DIDN'T YOU TELL ME THAT IN THE FIRST PLACE?!?
(LOW VOICE)
YUTAKA FUJISHIMA AND I SEEM TO HAVE A STRANGE CONNECTION.
THE FIRST TIME WE MET WAS THE DAY I PLAYED SICK AT SCHOOL, AND SHE WOUND UP IN THE BED NEXT TO MINE IN THE SCHOOL INFIRMARY. SHE WASN'T REALLY SICK EITHER.
THEN THERE WAS THE TIME WE FOUGHT OVER THE LAST FRIED NOODLE ROLL AT THE CAFè. SHE CLOBBERED ME AND TOOK OFF WITH IT.

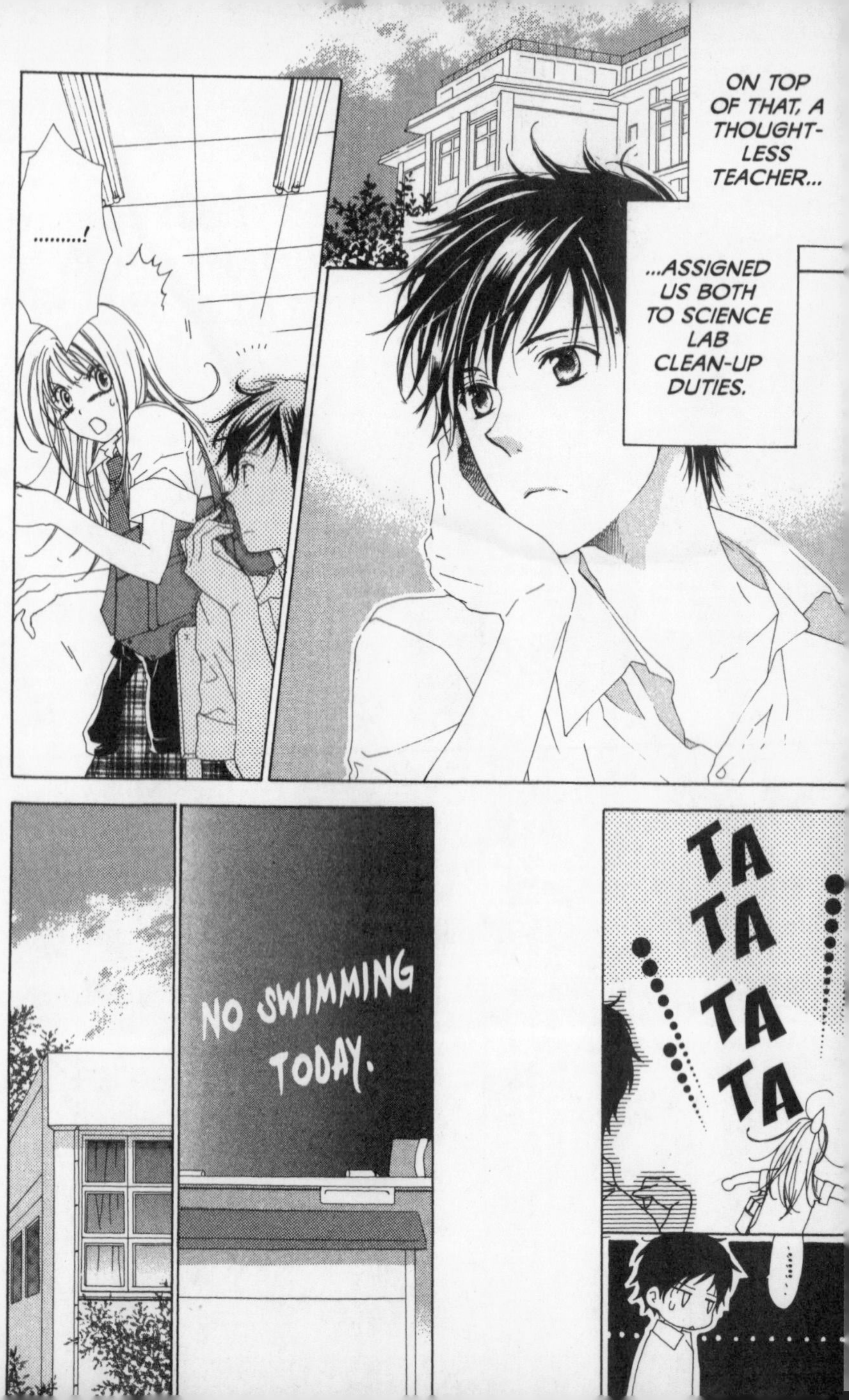
ON TOP OF THAT, A THOUGHT-LESS TEACHER...
...ASSIGNED US BOTH TO SCIENCE LAB CLEAN-UP DUTIES.
.........!
TA TA TA TA
NO SWIMMING TODAY.

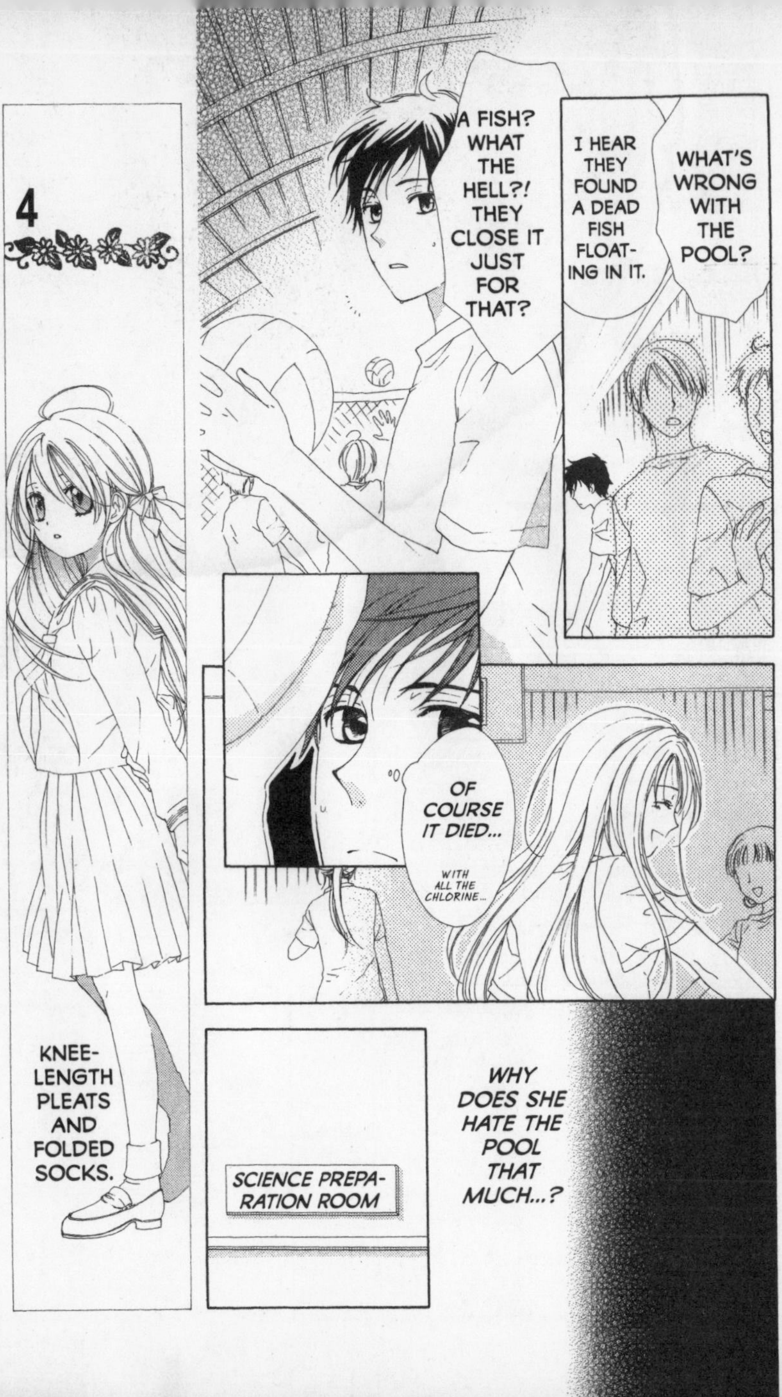
WHAT'S WRONG WITH THE POOL?
I HEAR THEY FOUND A DEAD FISH FLOAT-ING IN IT.
A FISH? WHAT THE HELL?! THEY CLOSE IT JUST FOR THAT?
OF COURSE IT DIED...
WITH ALL THE CHLORINE...
WHY DOES SHE HATE THE POOL THAT MUCH...?
SCIENCE PREPA-RATION ROOM
4
KNEE-LENGTH PLEATS AND FOLDED SOCKS.

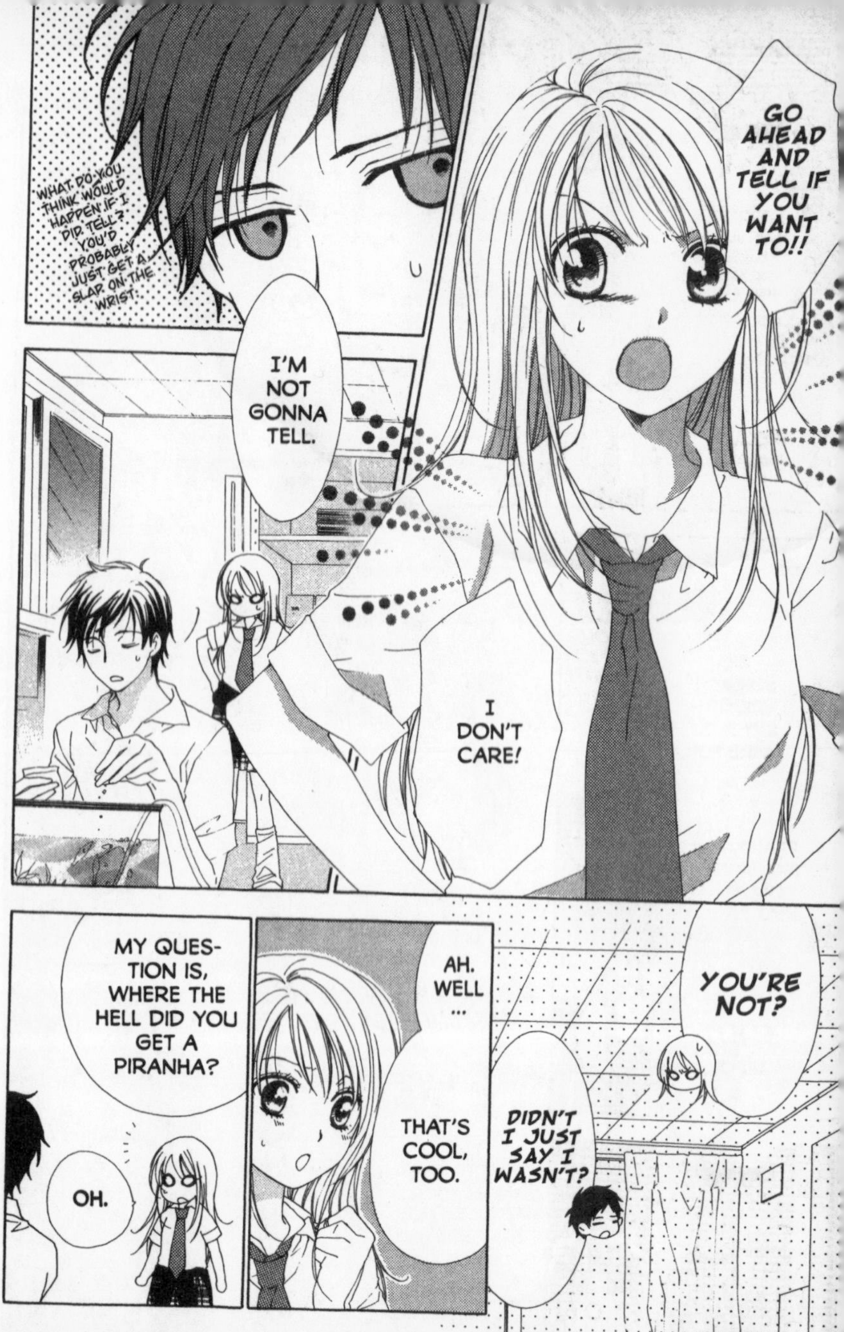
GO AHEAD AND TELL IF YOU WANT TO!!
I DON'T CARE!
I'M NOT GONNA TELL.
WHAT DO YOU THINK WOULD HAPPEN IF I DID TELL? YOU'D PROBABLY JUST GET A SLAP ON THE WRIST.
YOU'RE NOT?
DIDN'T I JUST SAY I WASN'T?
AH. WELL ...
THAT'S COOL, TOO.
MY QUES-TION IS, WHERE THE HELL DID YOU GET A PIRANHA?
OH.

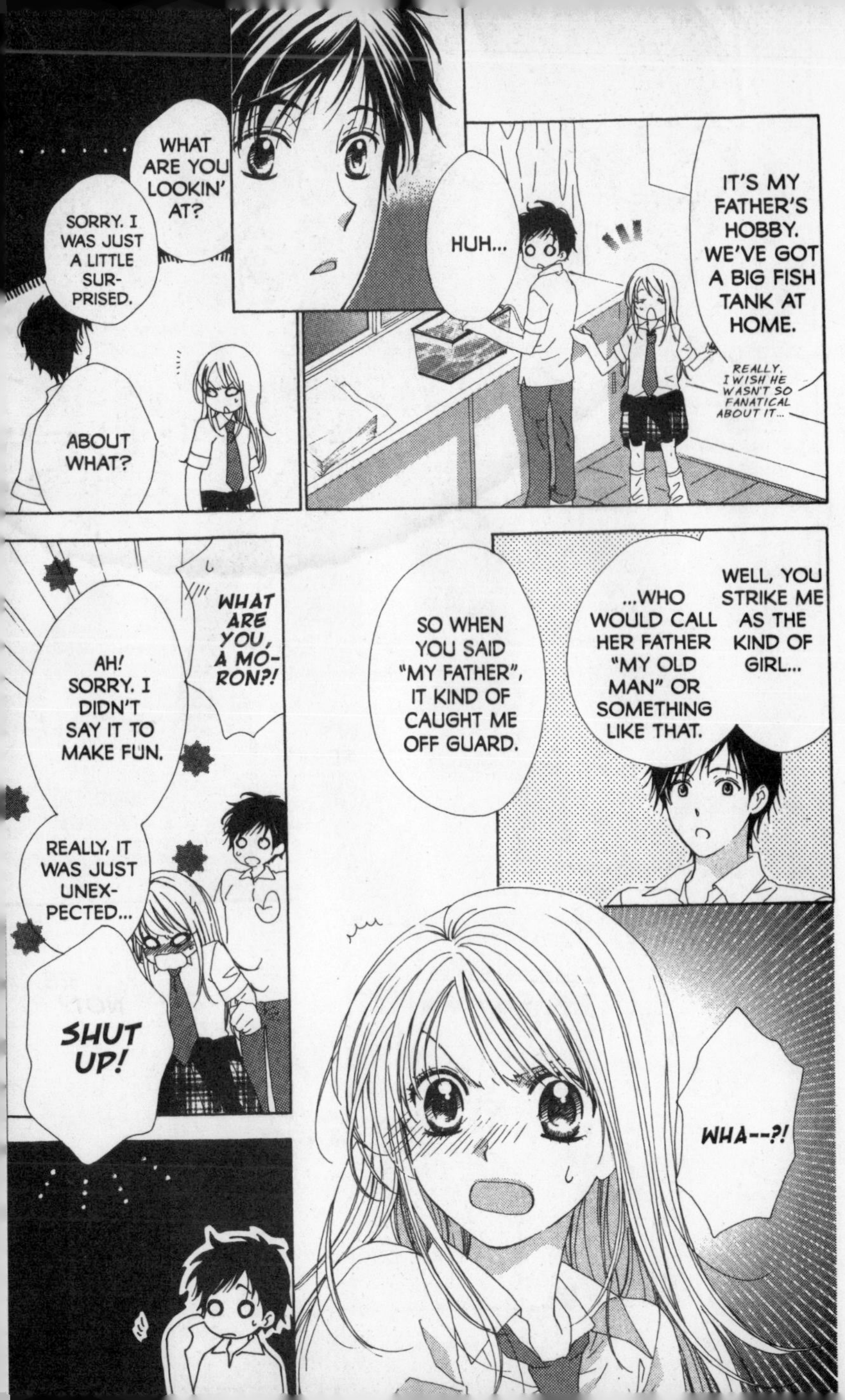
IT'S MY FATHER'S HOBBY. WE'VE GOT A BIG FISH TANK AT HOME.
REALLY, I WISH HE WASN'T SO FANATICAL ABOUT IT...
HUH...
WHAT ARE YOU LOOKIN' AT?
SORRY. I WAS JUST A LITTLE SUR-PRISED.
ABOUT WHAT?
WELL, YOU STRIKE ME AS THE KIND OF GIRL...
...WHO WOULD CALL HER FATHER "MY OLD MAN" OR SOMETHING LIKE THAT.
SO WHEN YOU SAID "MY FATHER", IT KIND OF CAUGHT ME OFF GUARD.
WHA--?!
WHAT ARE YOU, A MO-RON?!
AH! SORRY. I DIDN'T SAY IT TO MAKE FUN.
REALLY, IT WAS JUST UNEX-PECTED...
SHUT UP!

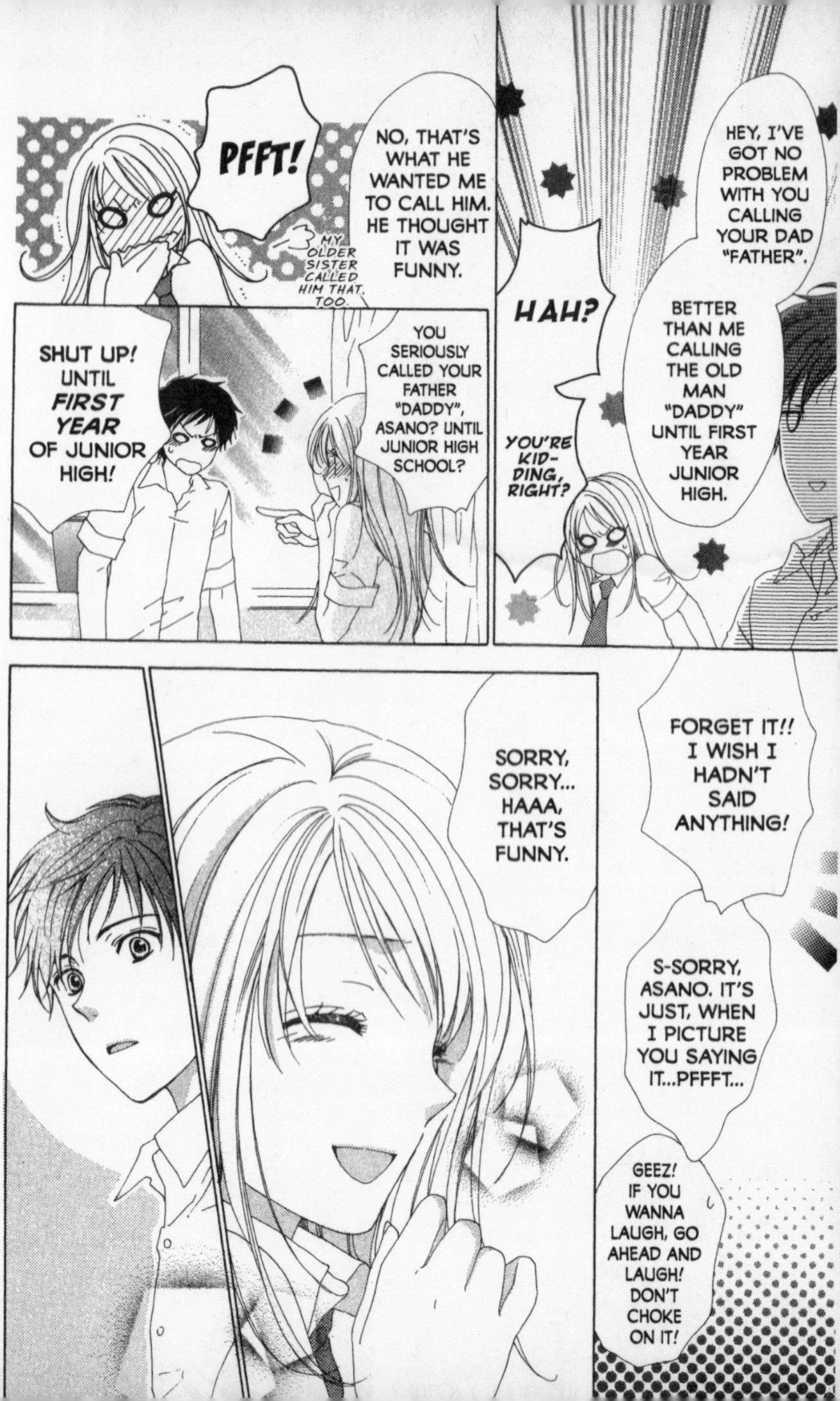
HEY, I'VE GOT NO PROBLEM WITH YOU CALLING YOUR DAD "FATHER".
BETTER THAN ME CALLING THE OLD MAN "DADDY" UNTIL FIRST YEAR JUNIOR HIGH.
HAH?
YOU'RE KID-DING, RIGHT?
PFFT!
NO, THAT'S WHAT HE WANTED ME TO CALL HIM. HE THOUGHT IT WAS FUNNY.
MY OLDER SISTER CALLED HIM THAT, TOO.
YOU SERIOUSLY CALLED YOUR FATHER "DADDY", ASANO? UNTIL JUNIOR HIGH SCHOOL?
SHUT UP! UNTIL FIRST YEAR OF JUNIOR HIGH!
FORGET IT!! I WISH I HADN'T SAID ANYTHING!
SORRY, SORRY... HAAA, THAT'S FUNNY.
S-SORRY, ASANO. IT'S JUST, WHEN I PICTURE YOU SAYING IT...PFFFT...
GEEZ! IF YOU WANNA LAUGH, GO AHEAD AND LAUGH! DON'T CHOKE ON IT!

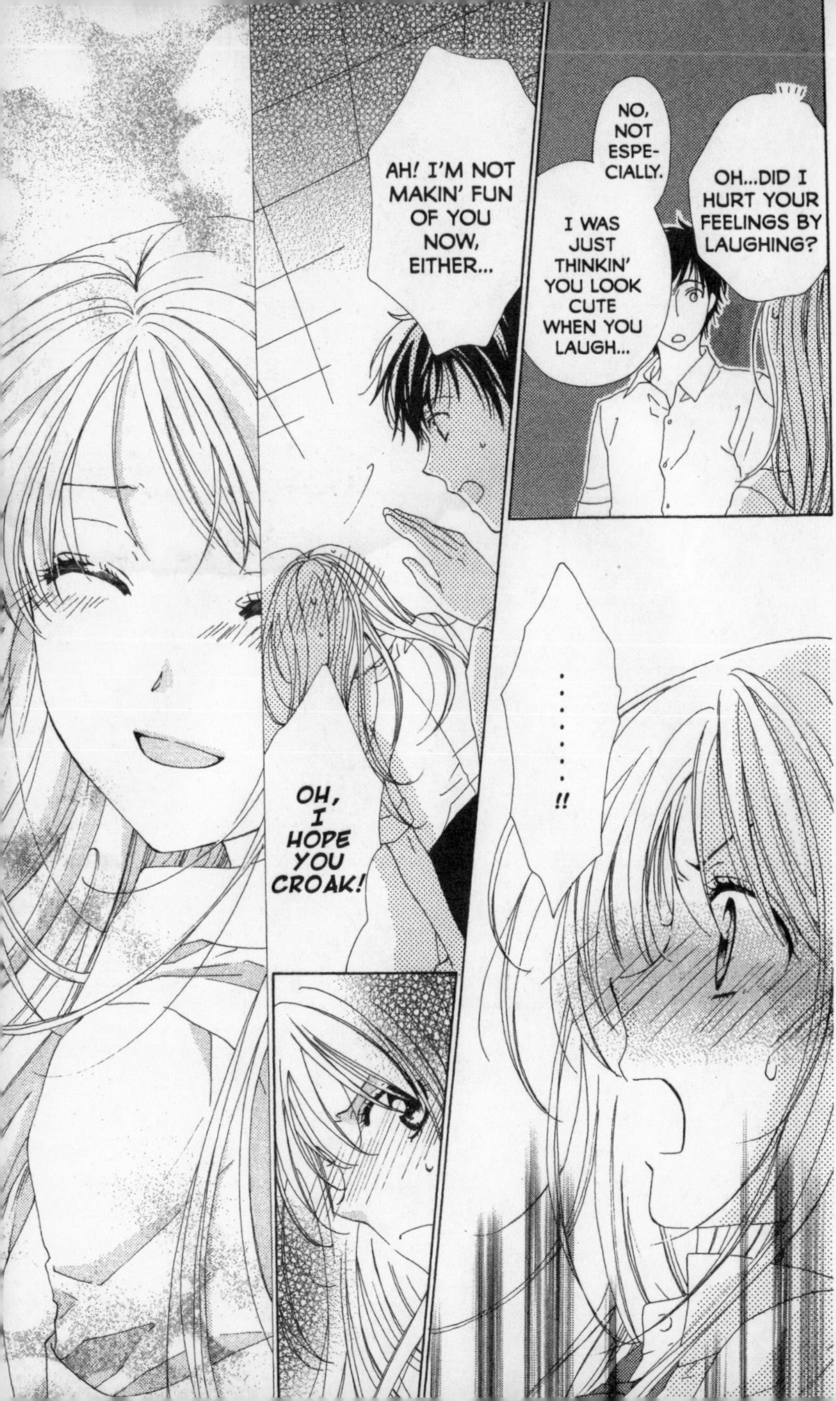
OH...DID I HURT YOUR FEELINGS BY LAUGHING?
NO, NOT ESPE-CIALLY.
I WAS JUST THINKIN' YOU LOOK CUTE WHEN YOU LAUGH...
AH! I'M NOT MAKIN' FUN OF YOU NOW, EITHER...
......!!
OH, I HOPE YOU CROAK!

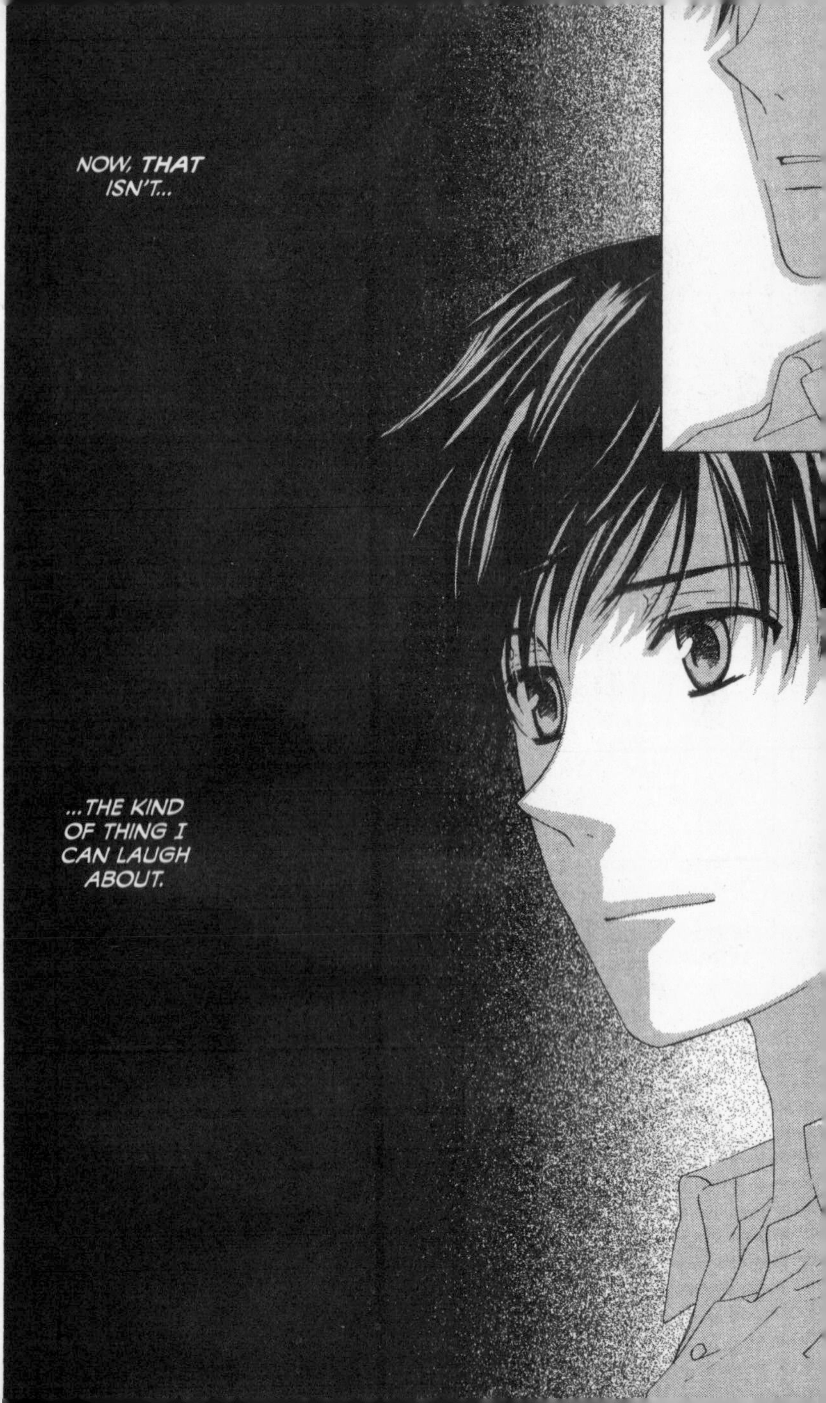
NOW, THAT ISN'T...
...THE KIND OF THING I CAN LAUGH ABOUT.

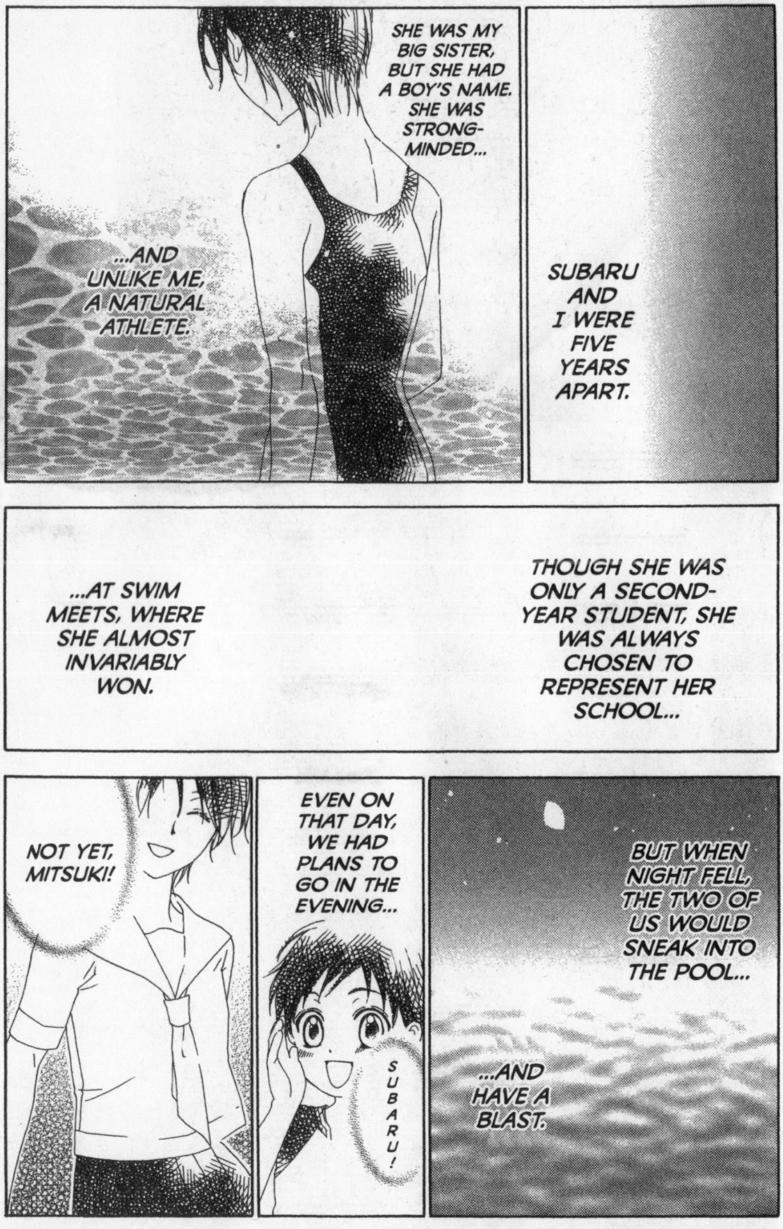
SUBARU AND I WERE FIVE YEARS APART.
SHE WAS MY BIG SISTER, BUT SHE HAD A BOY'S NAME. SHE WAS STRONG-MINDED...
...AND UNLIKE ME, A NATURAL ATHLETE.
THOUGH SHE WAS ONLY A SECOND-YEAR STUDENT, SHE WAS ALWAYS CHOSEN TO REPRESENT HER SCHOOL...
...AT SWIM MEETS, WHERE SHE ALMOST INVARIABLY WON.
BUT WHEN NIGHT FELL, THE TWO OF US WOULD SNEAK INTO THE POOL...
...AND HAVE A BLAST.
EVEN ON THAT DAY, WE HAD PLANS TO GO IN THE EVENING...
SUBARU!
NOT YET, MITSUKI!

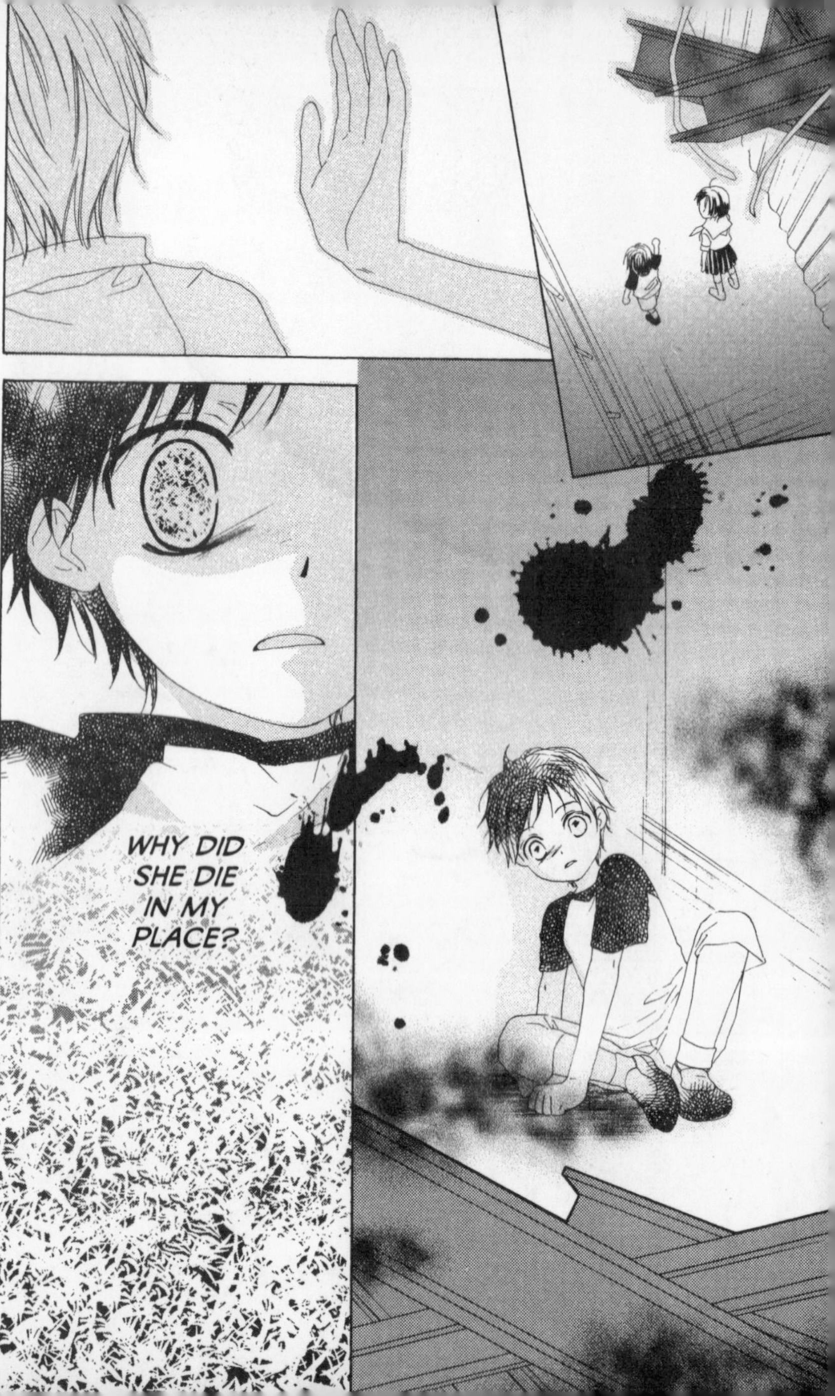
WHY DID SHE DIE IN MY PLACE?

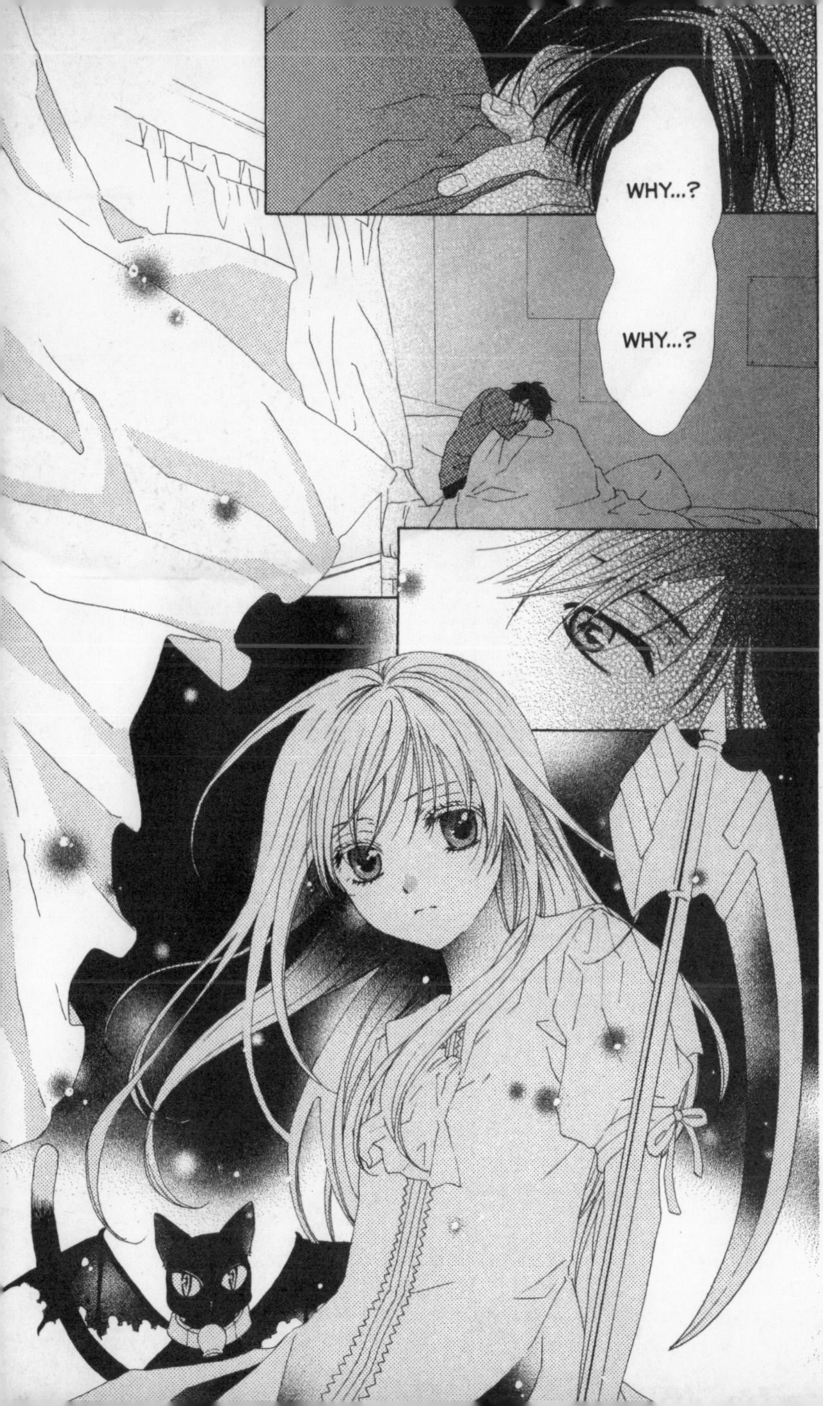
WHY...?
WHY...?

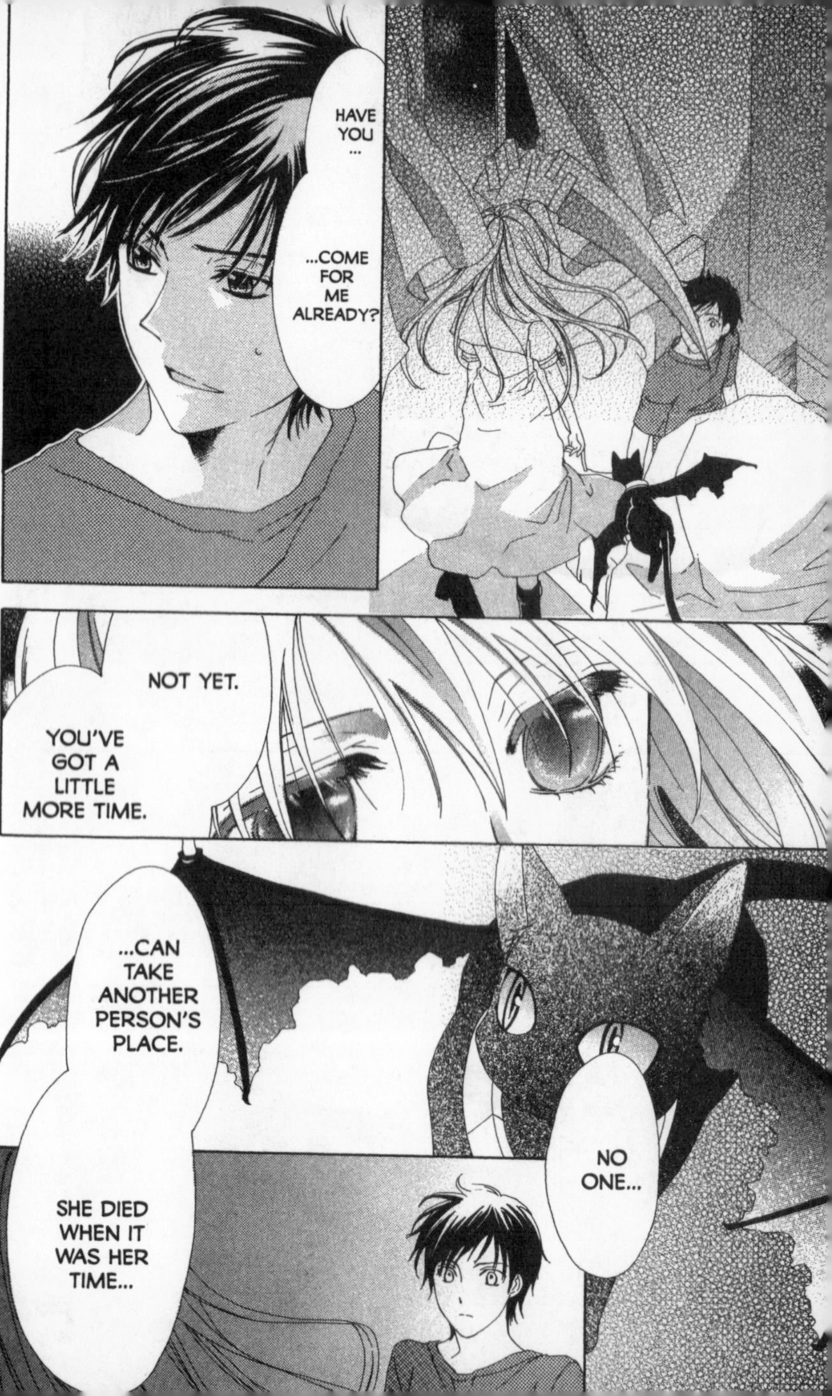
HAVE YOU ...
...COME FOR ME ALREADY?
NOT YET.
YOU'VE GOT A LITTLE MORE TIME.
NO ONE...
...CAN TAKE ANOTHER PERSON'S PLACE.
SHE DIED WHEN IT WAS HER TIME...

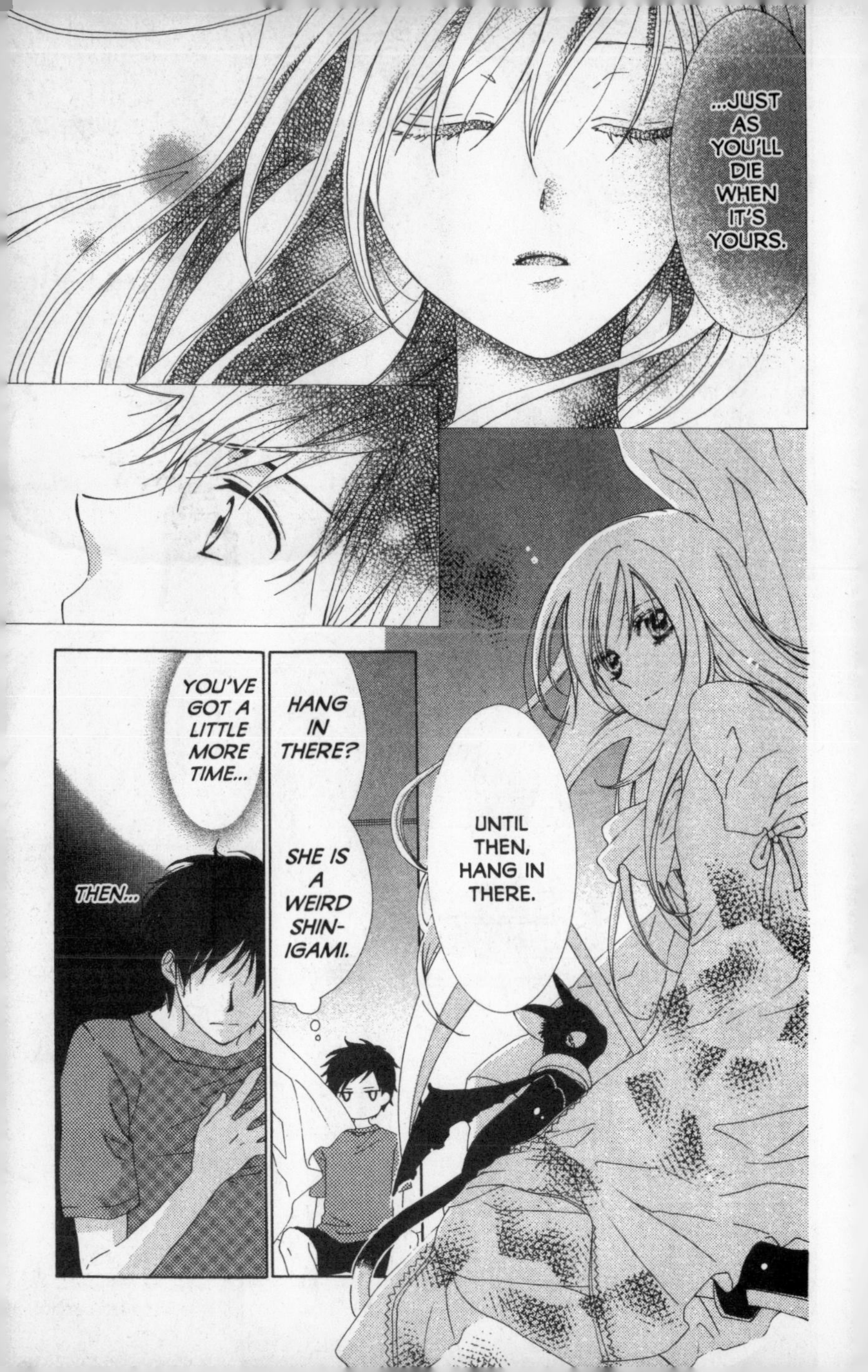
...JUST AS YOU'LL DIE WHEN IT'S YOURS.
UNTIL THEN, HANG IN THERE.
HANG IN THERE?
SHE IS A WEIRD SHINIGAMI.
YOU'VE GOT A LITTLE MORE TIME...
THEN...

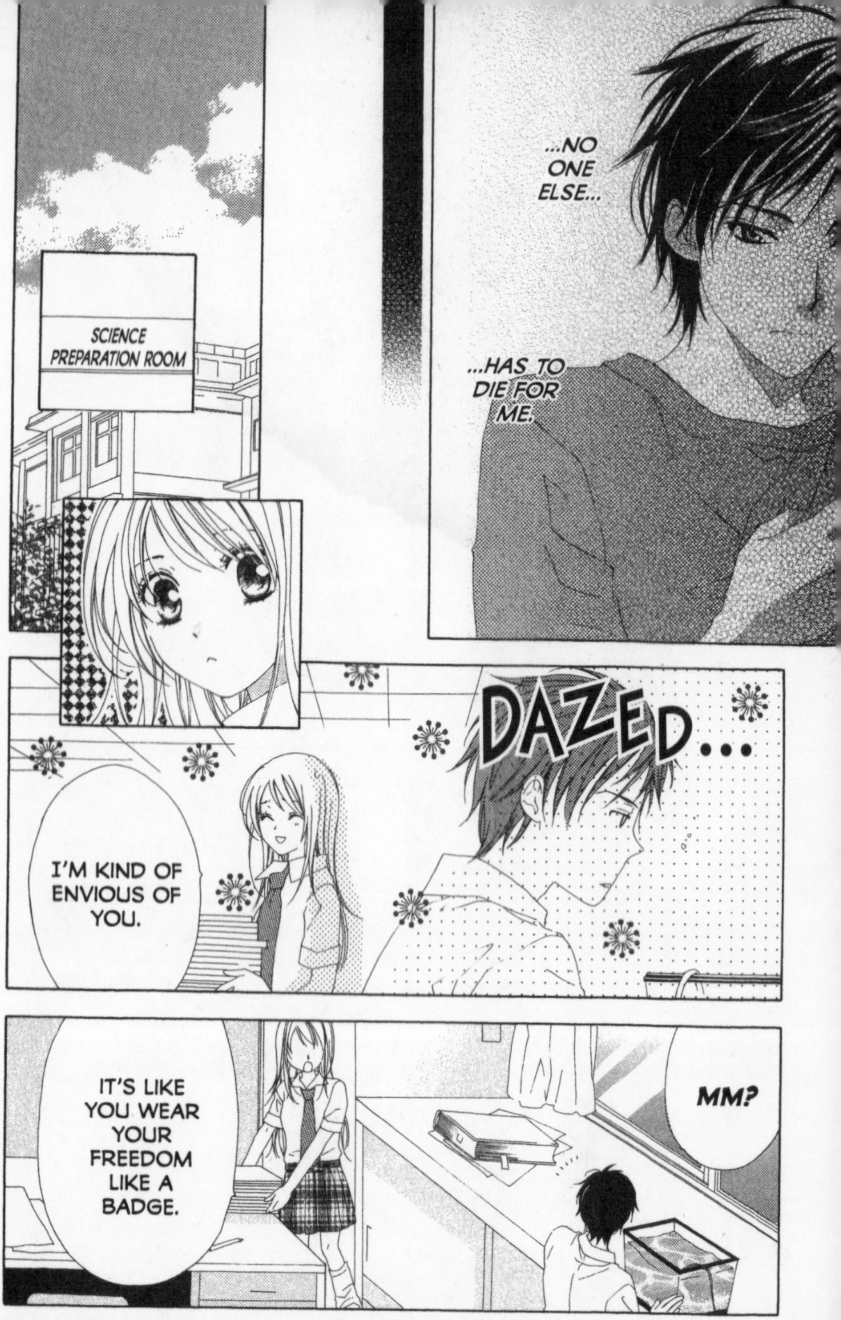
...NO ONE ELSE...
...HAS TO DIE FOR ME.
SCIENCE PREPARATION ROOM
DAZED...
I'M KIND OF ENVIOUS OF YOU.
MM?
IT'S LIKE YOU WEAR YOUR FREEDOM LIKE A BADGE.

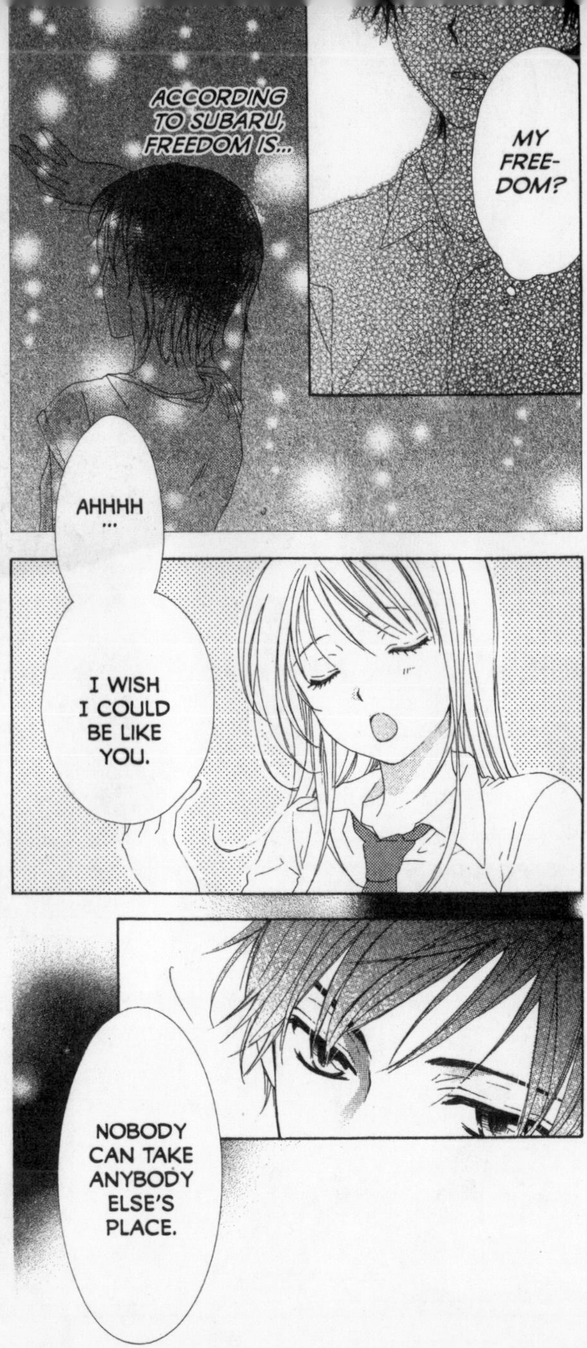
MY FREE-DOM?
ACCORDING TO SUBARU, FREEDOM IS...
AHHHH ...
I WISH I COULD BE LIKE YOU.
NOBODY CAN TAKE ANYBODY ELSE'S PLACE.
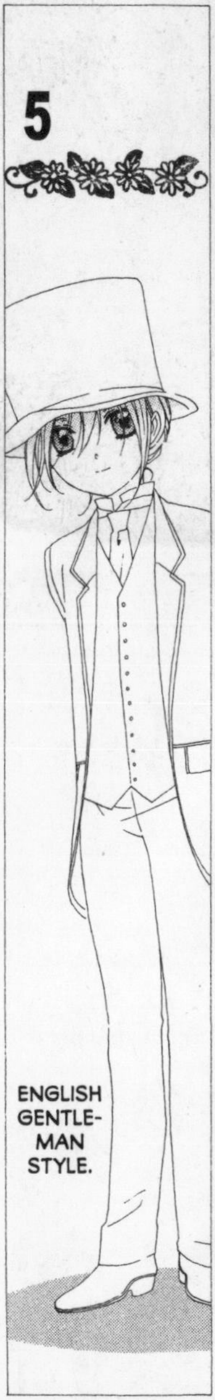
5
ENGLISH GENTLE-MAN STYLE.

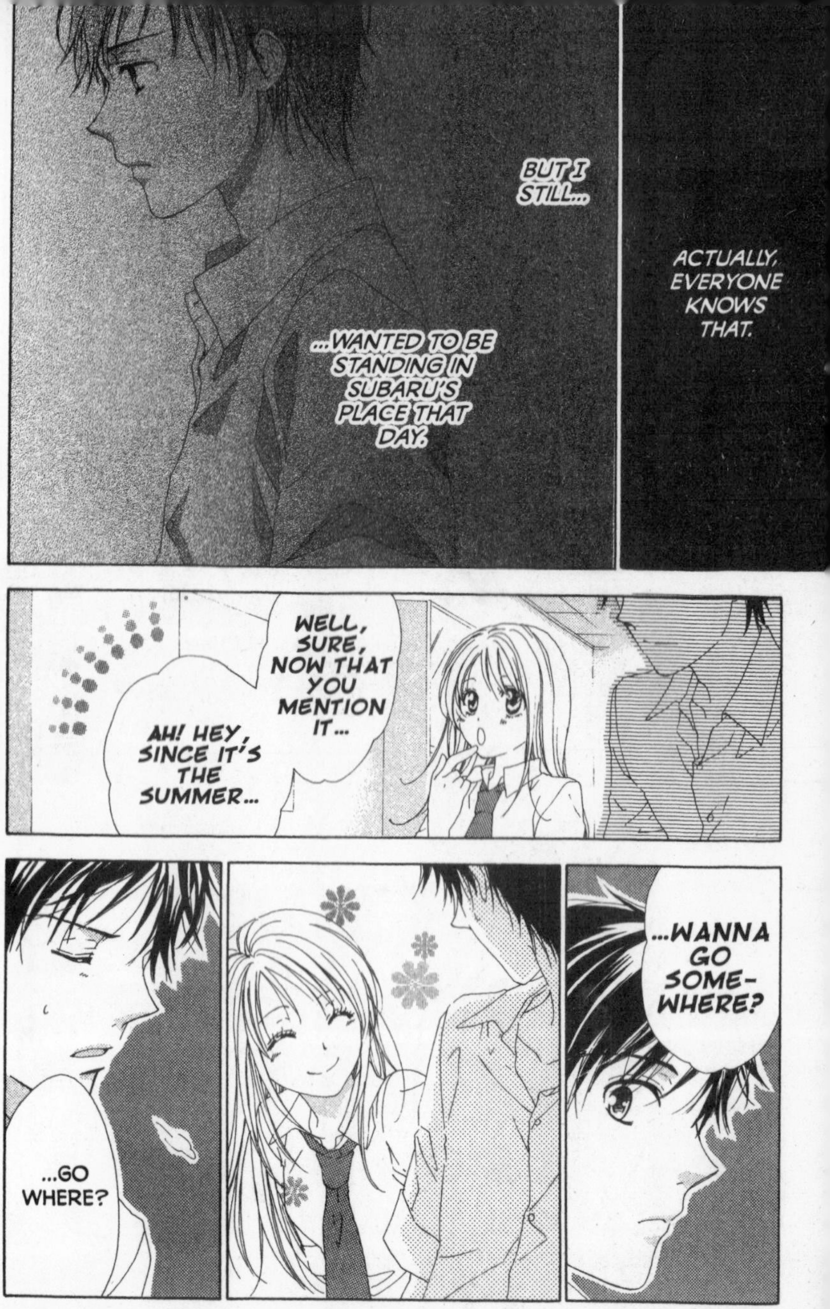
ACTUALLY, EVERYONE KNOWS THAT.
BUT I STILL...
...WANTED TO BE STANDING IN SUBARU'S PLACE THAT DAY.
WELL, SURE, NOW THAT YOU MENTION IT...
AH! HEY, SINCE IT'S THE SUMMER...
...WANNA GO SOME-WHERE?
...GO WHERE?

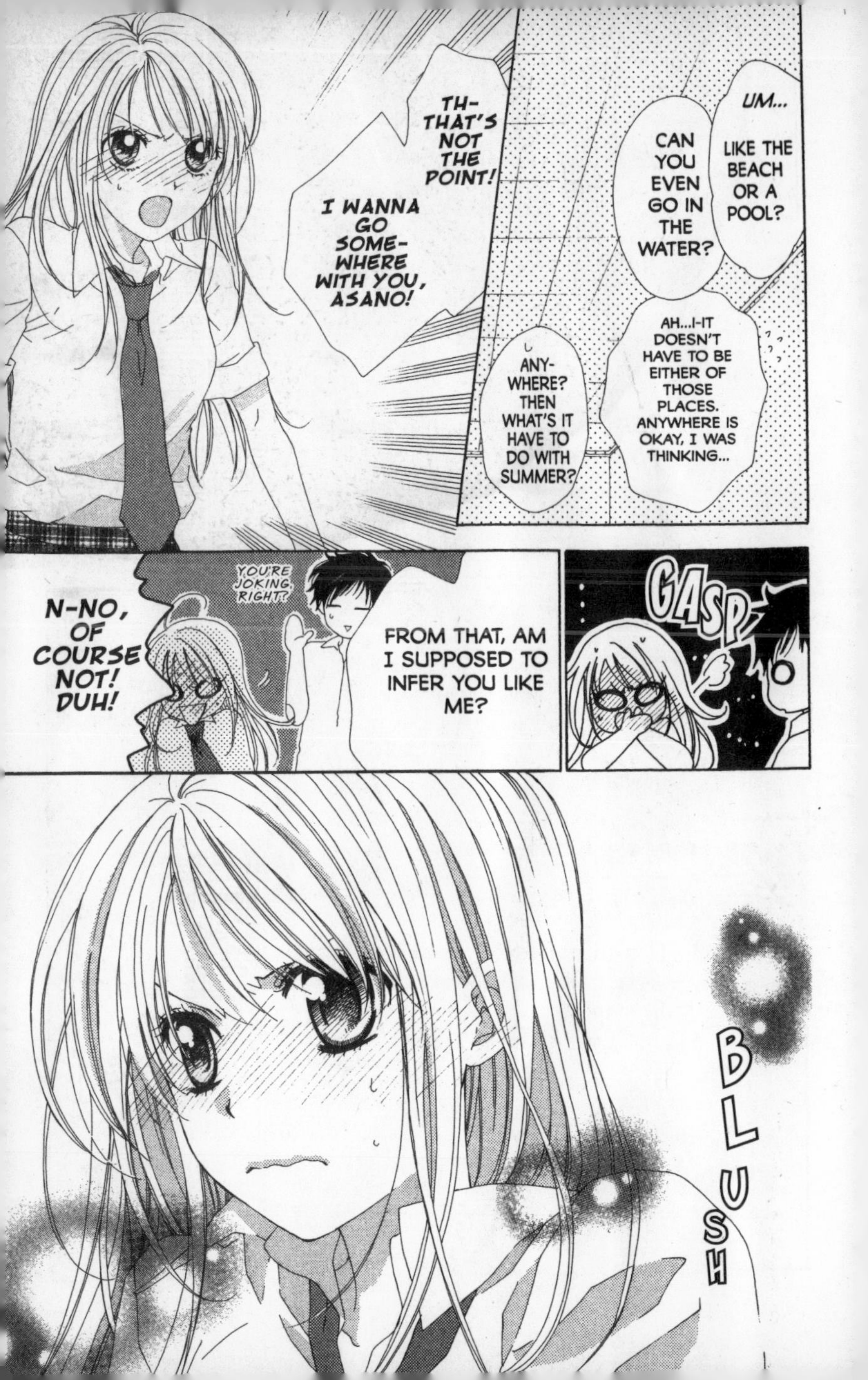
UM...
LIKE THE BEACH OR A POOL?
CAN YOU EVEN GO IN THE WATER?
AH...I-IT DOESN'T HAVE TO BE EITHER OF THOSE PLACES. ANYWHERE IS OKAY, I WAS THINKING...
ANY-WHERE? THEN WHAT'S IT HAVE TO DO WITH SUMMER?
TH-THAT'S NOT THE POINT!
I WANNA GO SOME-WHERE WITH YOU, ASANO!
GASP
FROM THAT, AM I SUPPOSED TO INFER YOU LIKE ME?
YOU'RE JOKING, RIGHT!?
N-NO, OF COURSE NOT! DUH!
BLUSH

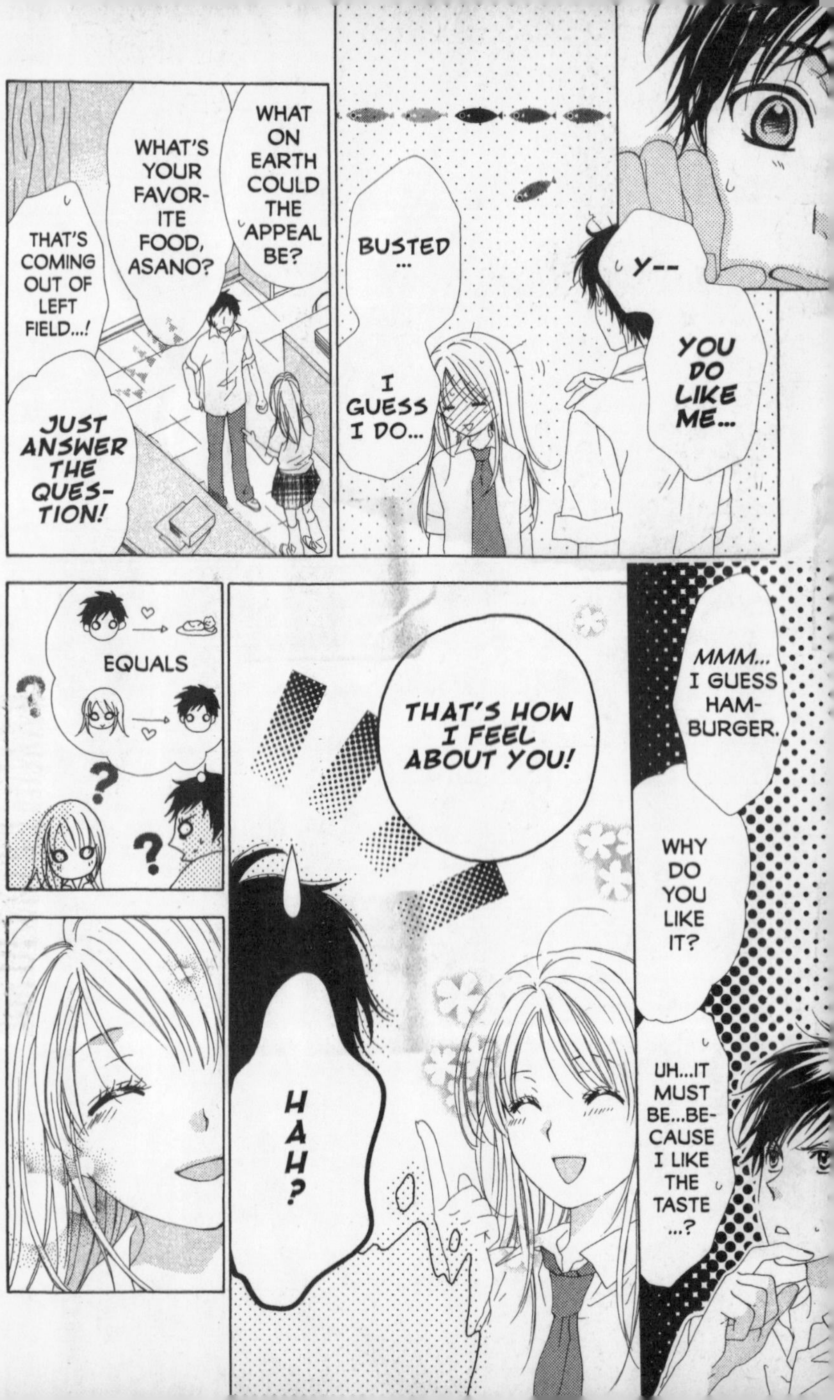
Y--
YOU DO LIKE ME...
BUSTED...
I GUESS I DO...
WHAT ON EARTH COULD THE APPEAL BE?
WHAT'S YOUR FAVOR-ITE FOOD, ASANO?
THAT'S COMING OUT OF LEFT FIELD...!
JUST ANSWER THE QUES-TION!
MMM... I GUESS HAM-BURGER.
WHY DO YOU LIKE IT?
UH...IT MUST BE...BE-CAUSE I LIKE THE TASTE...?
THAT'S HOW I FEEL ABOUT YOU!
HAH?
EQUALS

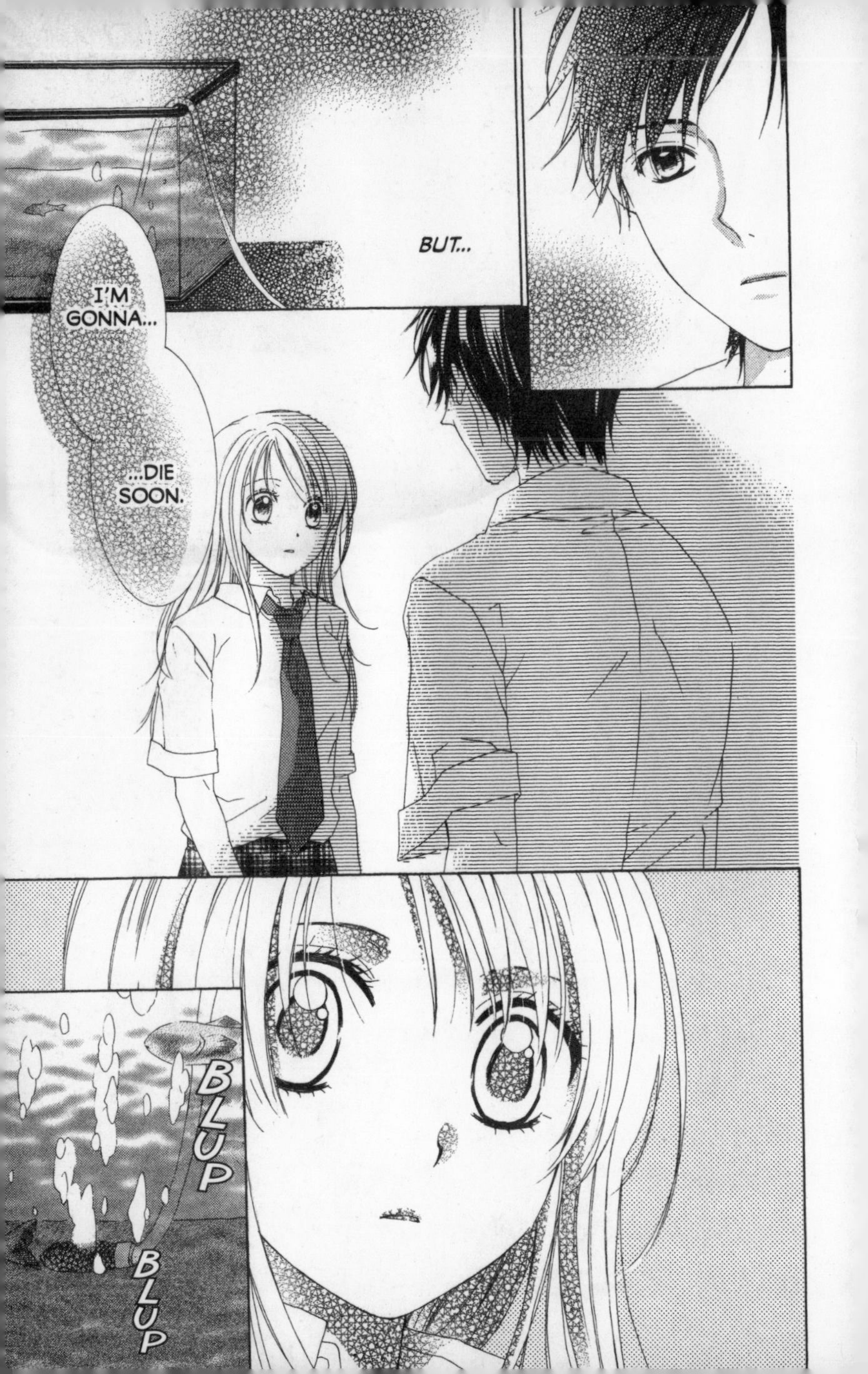
BUT...
I'M GONNA...
...DIE SOON.
BLUP
BLUP

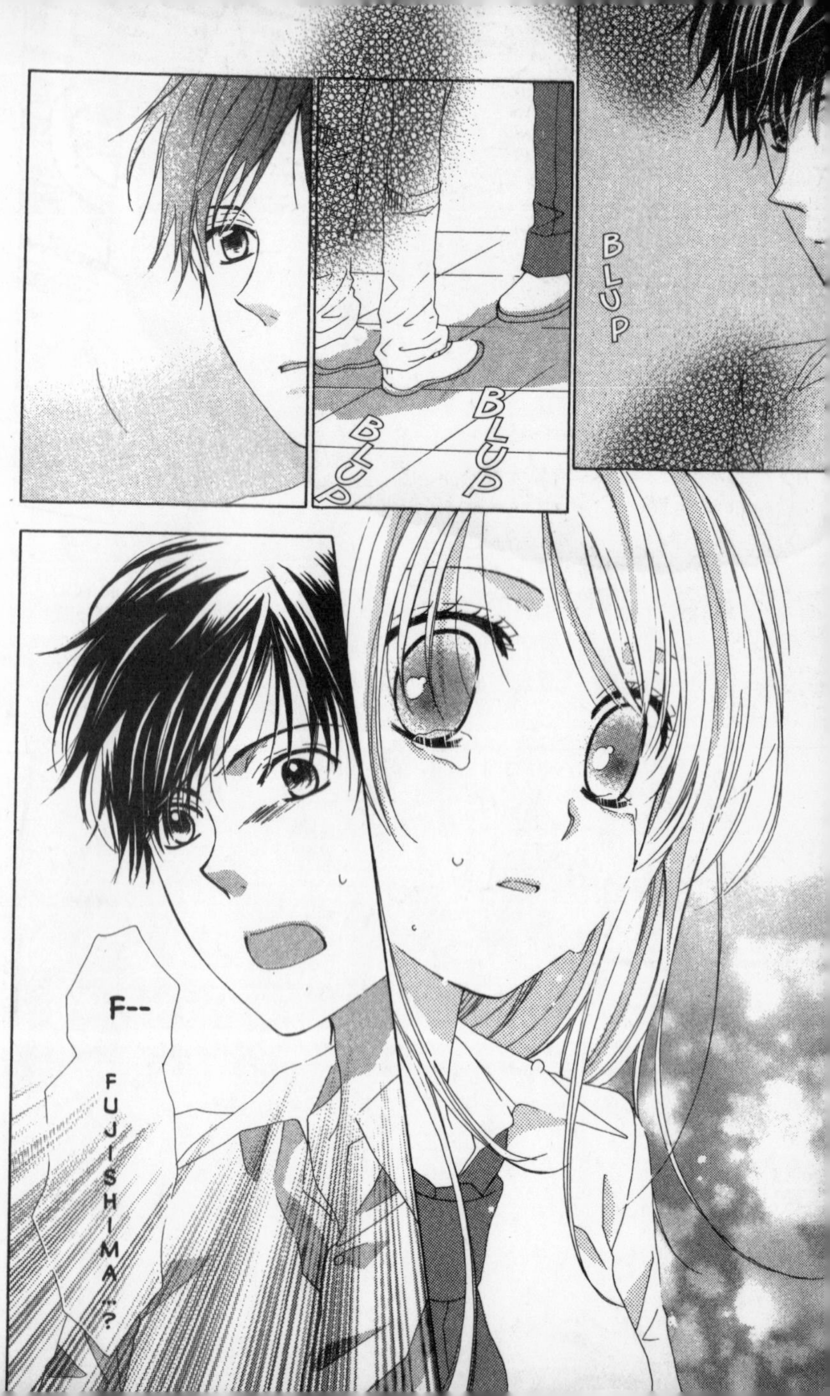
BLUP
BLUP
BLUP
F--
FUJISHIMA...?

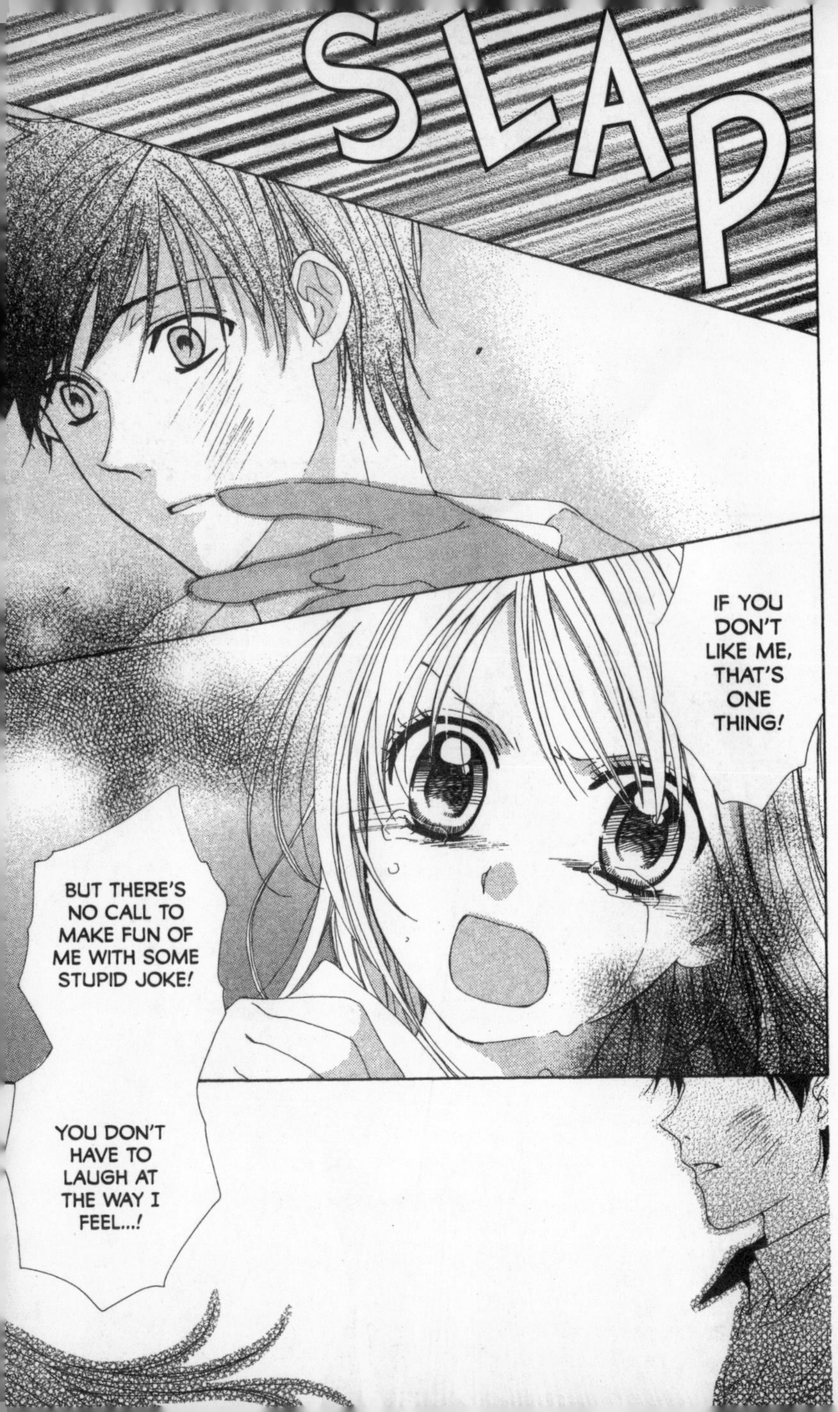
SLAP
IF YOU DON'T LIKE ME, THAT'S ONE THING!
BUT THERE'S NO CALL TO MAKE FUN OF ME WITH SOME STUPID JOKE!
YOU DON'T HAVE TO LAUGH AT THE WAY I FEEL...!

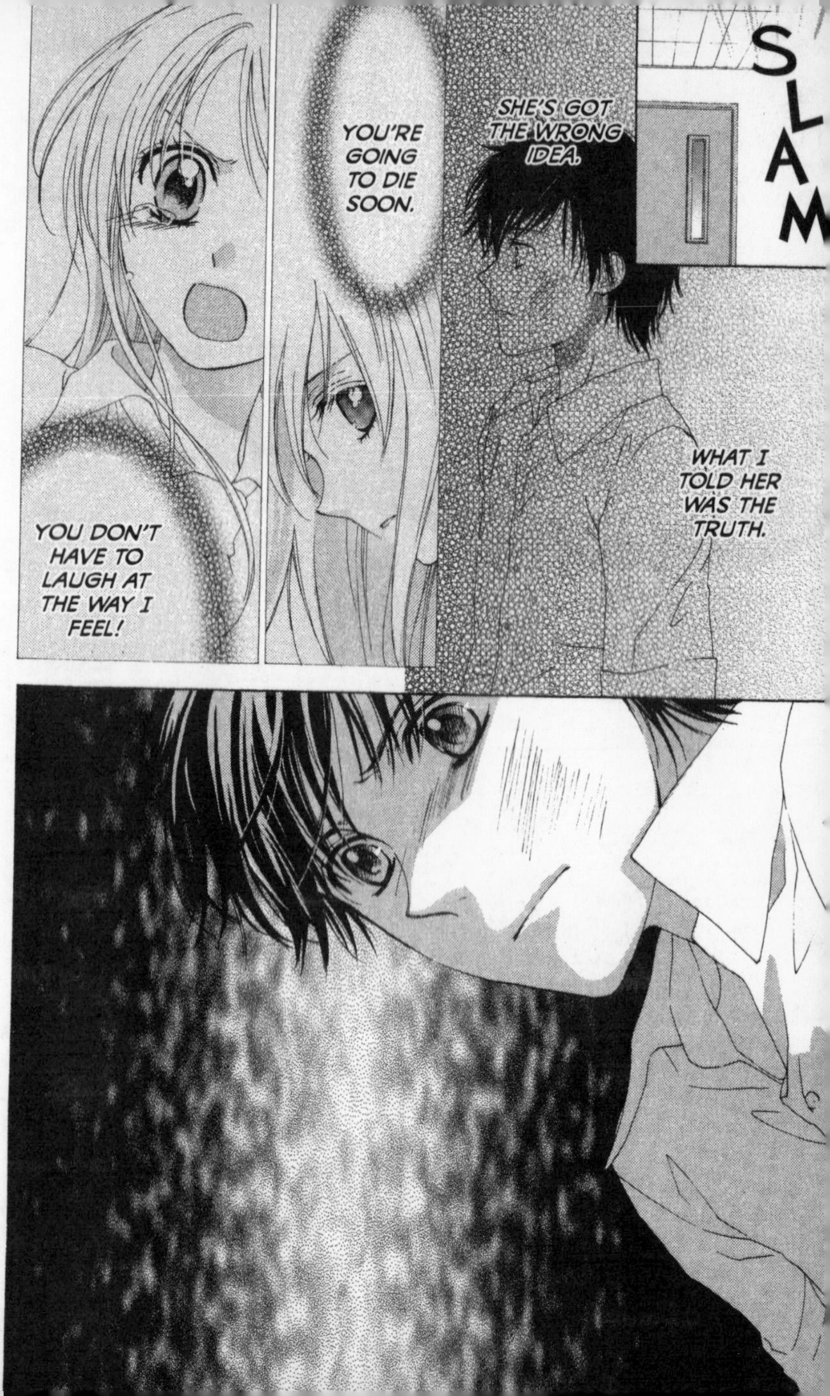
SLAM
SHE'S GOT THE WRONG IDEA.
WHAT I TOLD HER WAS THE TRUTH.
YOU'RE GOING TO DIE SOON.
YOU DON'T HAVE TO LAUGH AT THE WAY I FEEL!

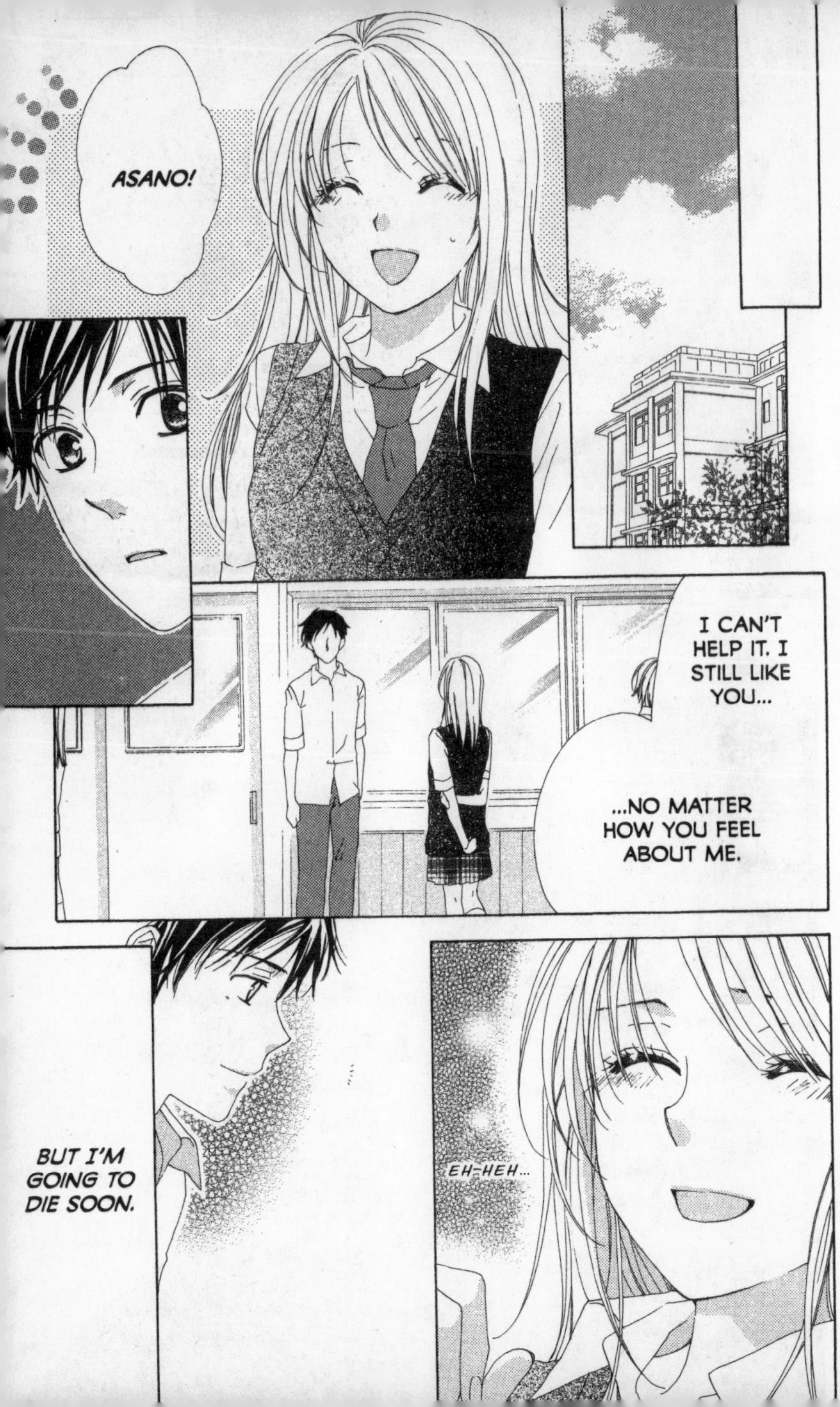
ASANO!
I CAN'T HELP IT. I STILL LIKE YOU...
...NO MATTER HOW YOU FEEL ABOUT ME.
EH-HEH...
BUT I'M GOING TO DIE SOON.

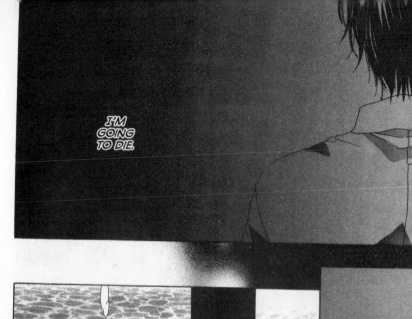

I'M GOING TO DIE.

BLUP

IT SEEMS...

"IT HURTS..."

"I FEEL SO SAD..."

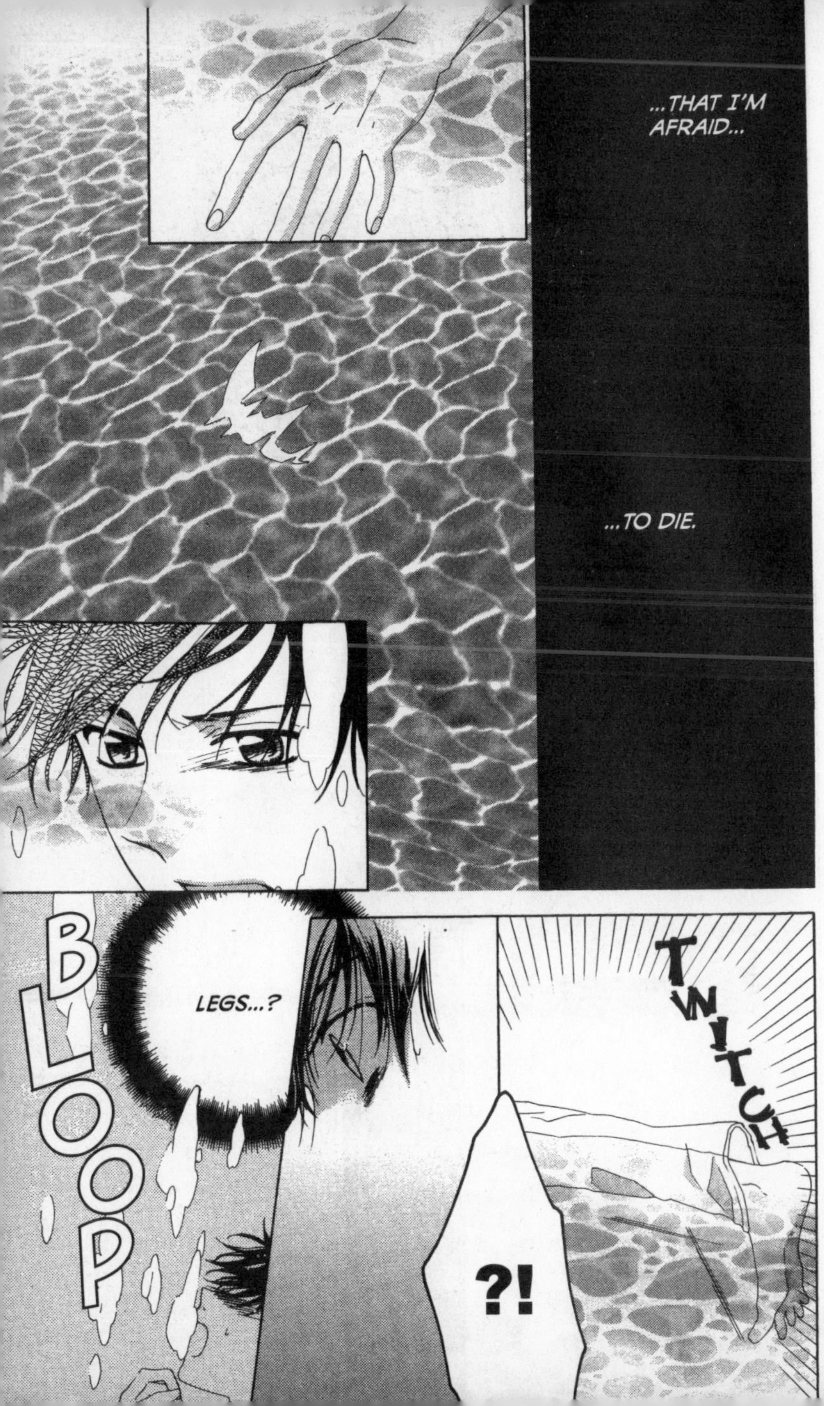
...THAT I'M AFRAID...
...TO DIE.
TWITCH
?!
LEGS...?
BLOOP

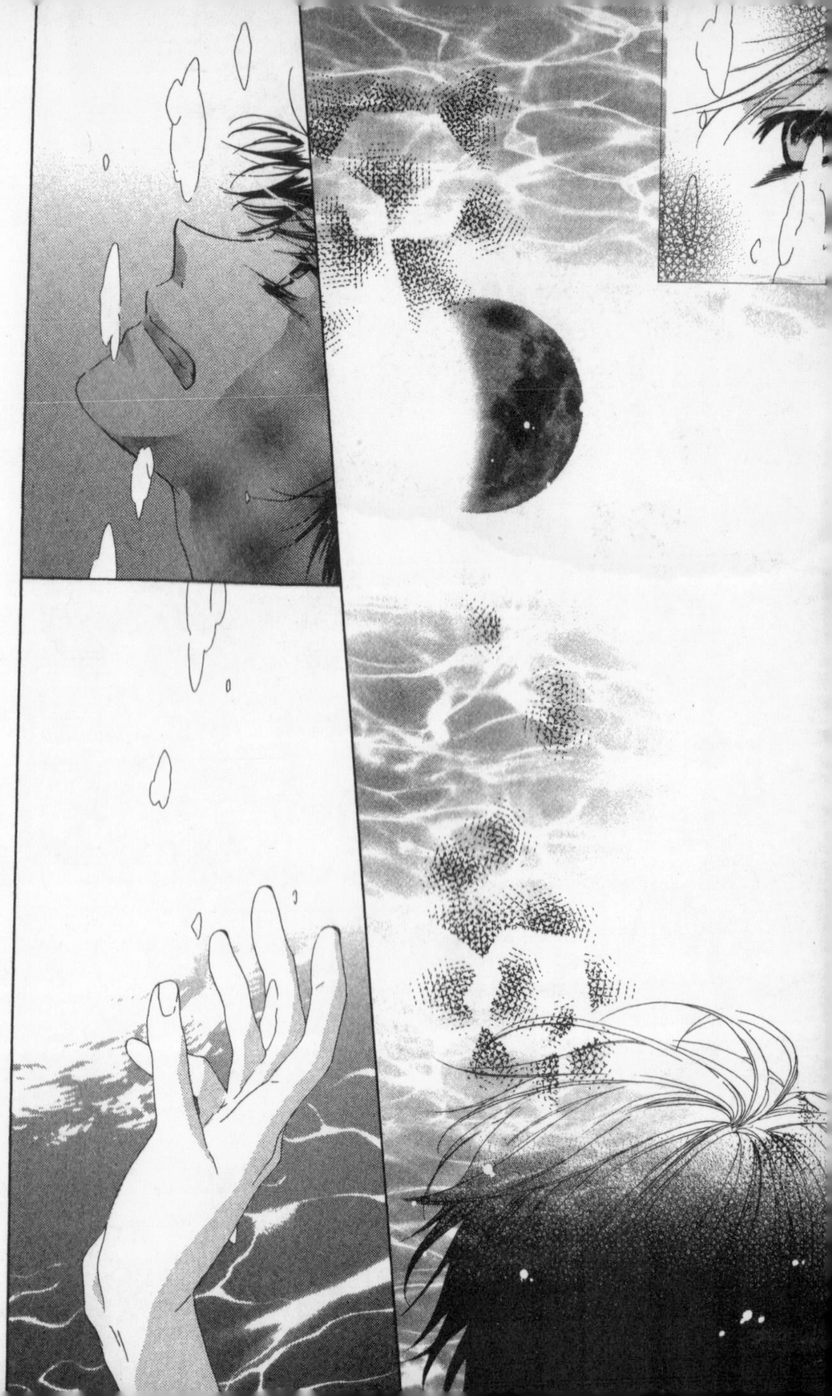

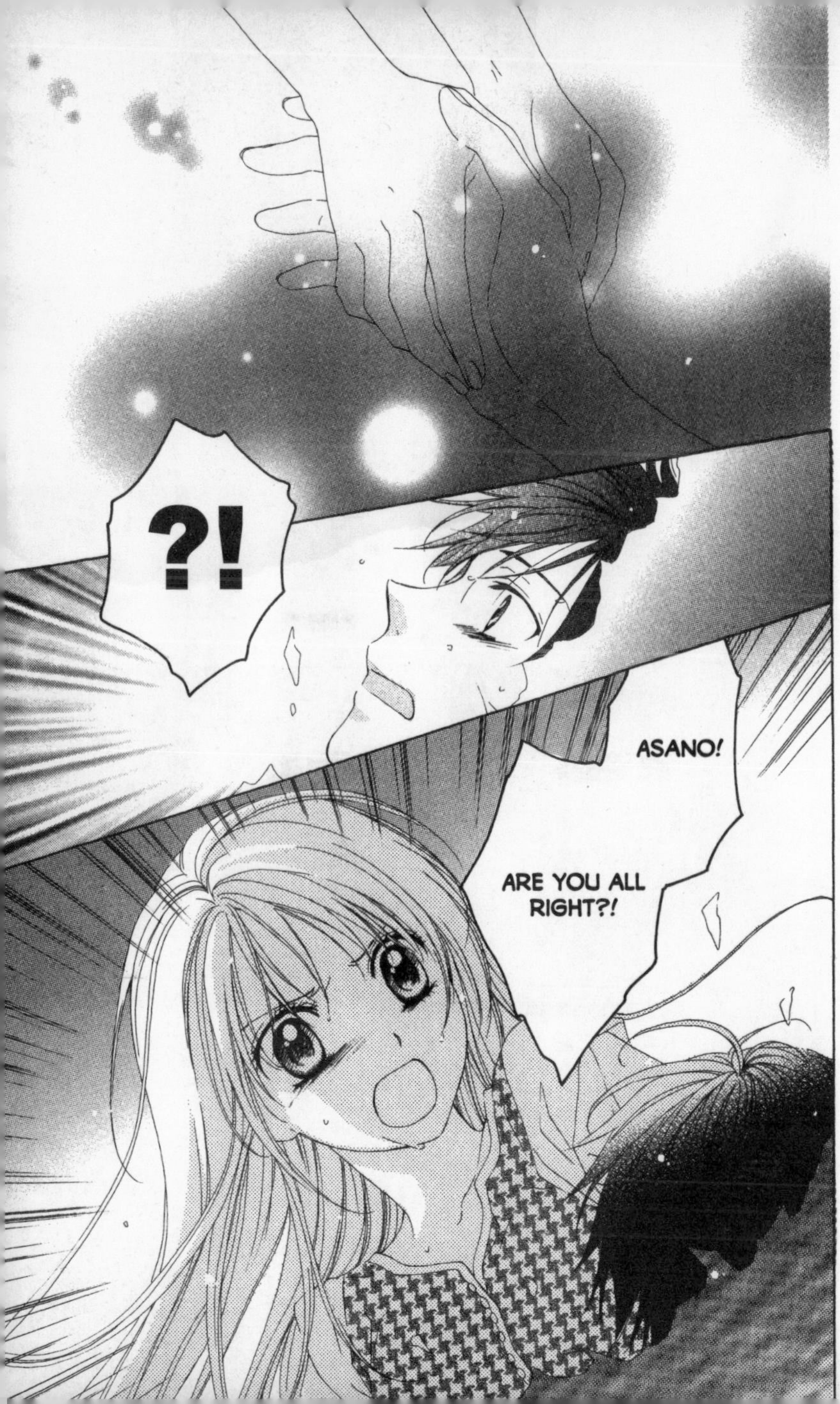
?!
ASANO!
ARE YOU ALL RIGHT?!

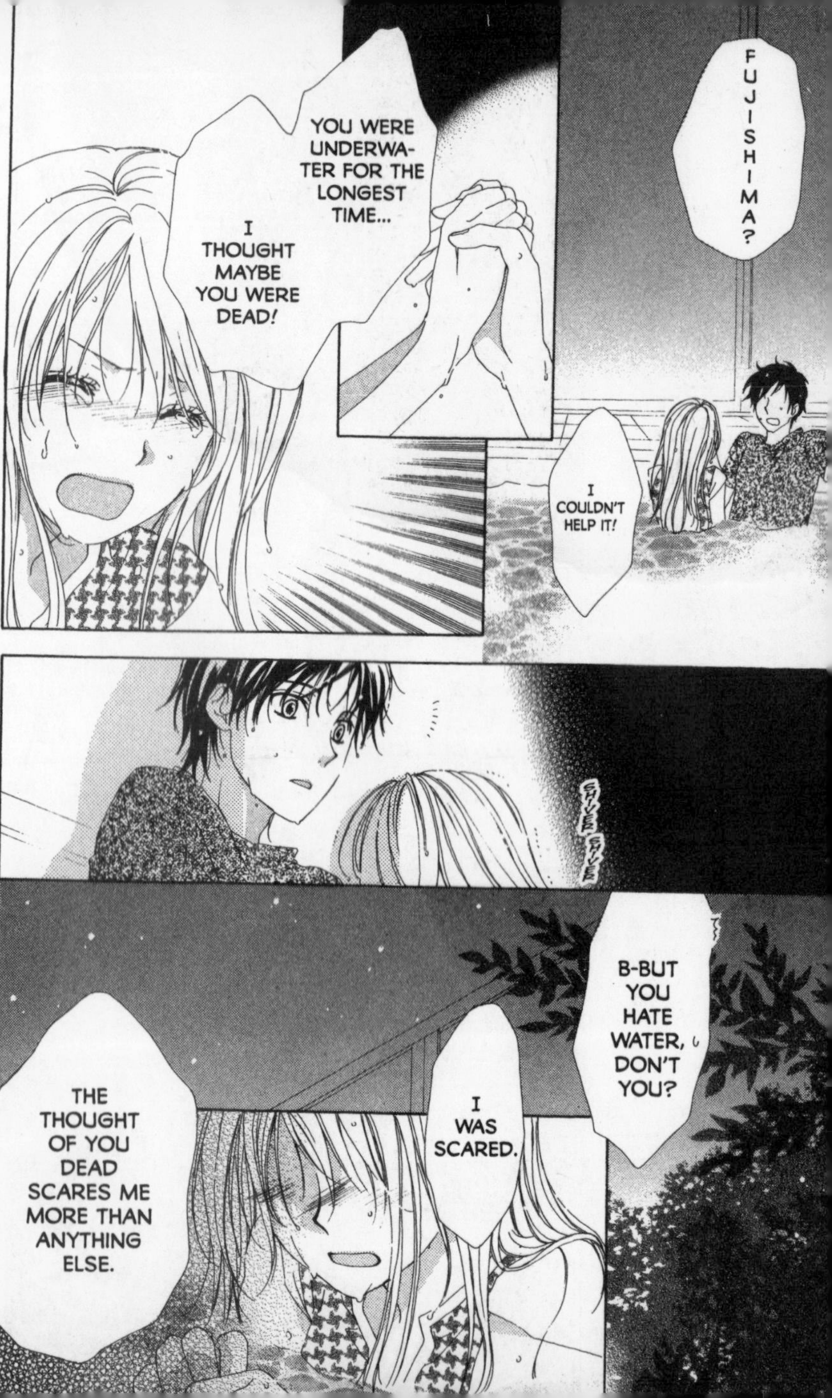
FUJISHIMA?
I COULDN'T HELP IT!
YOU WERE UNDERWATER FOR THE LONGEST TIME...
I THOUGHT MAYBE YOU WERE DEAD!
SHIVER SHIVER
B-BUT YOU HATE WATER, DON'T YOU?
I WAS SCARED.
THE THOUGHT OF YOU DEAD SCARES ME MORE THAN ANYTHING ELSE.

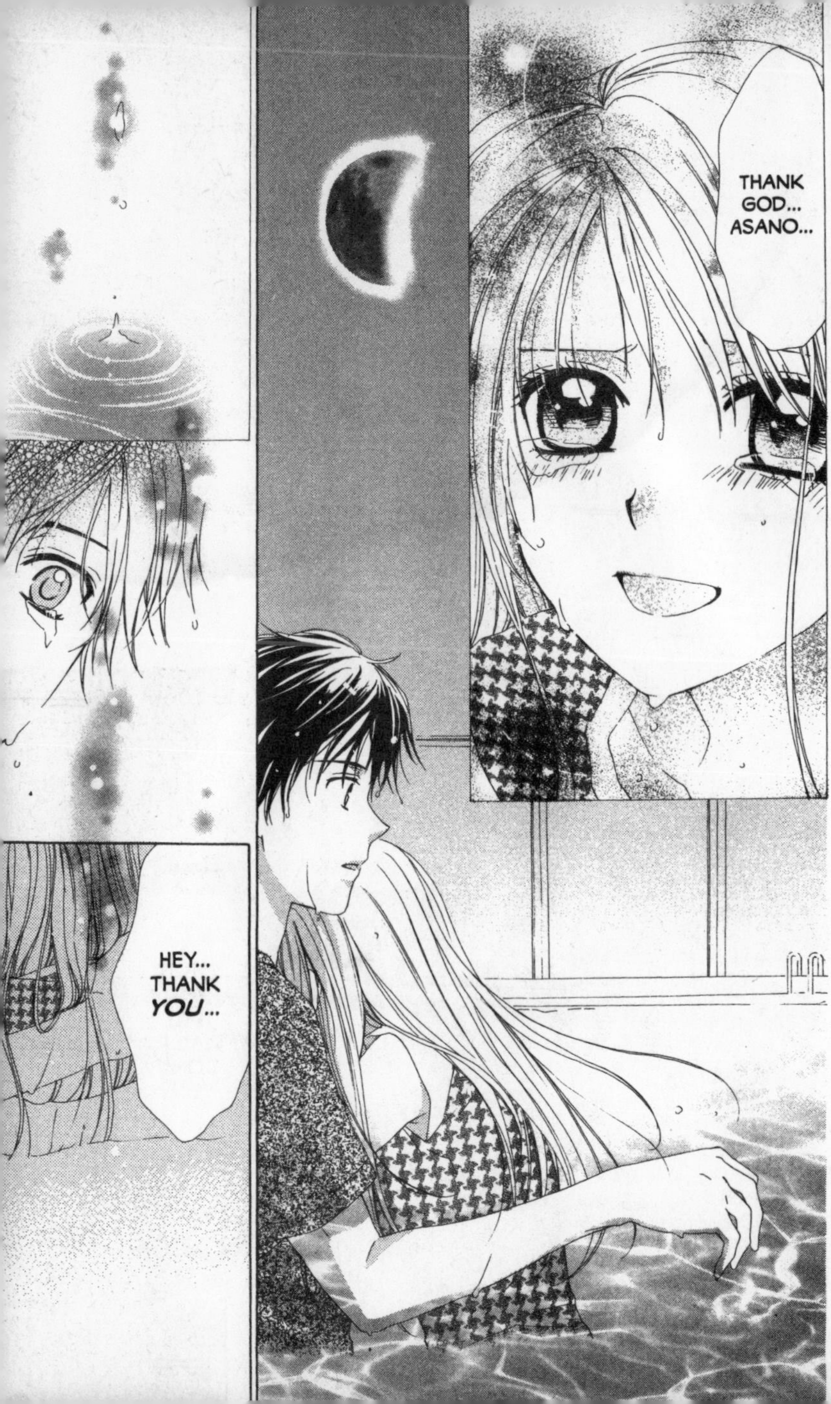
THANK GOD... ASANO...
HEY... THANK *YOU*...

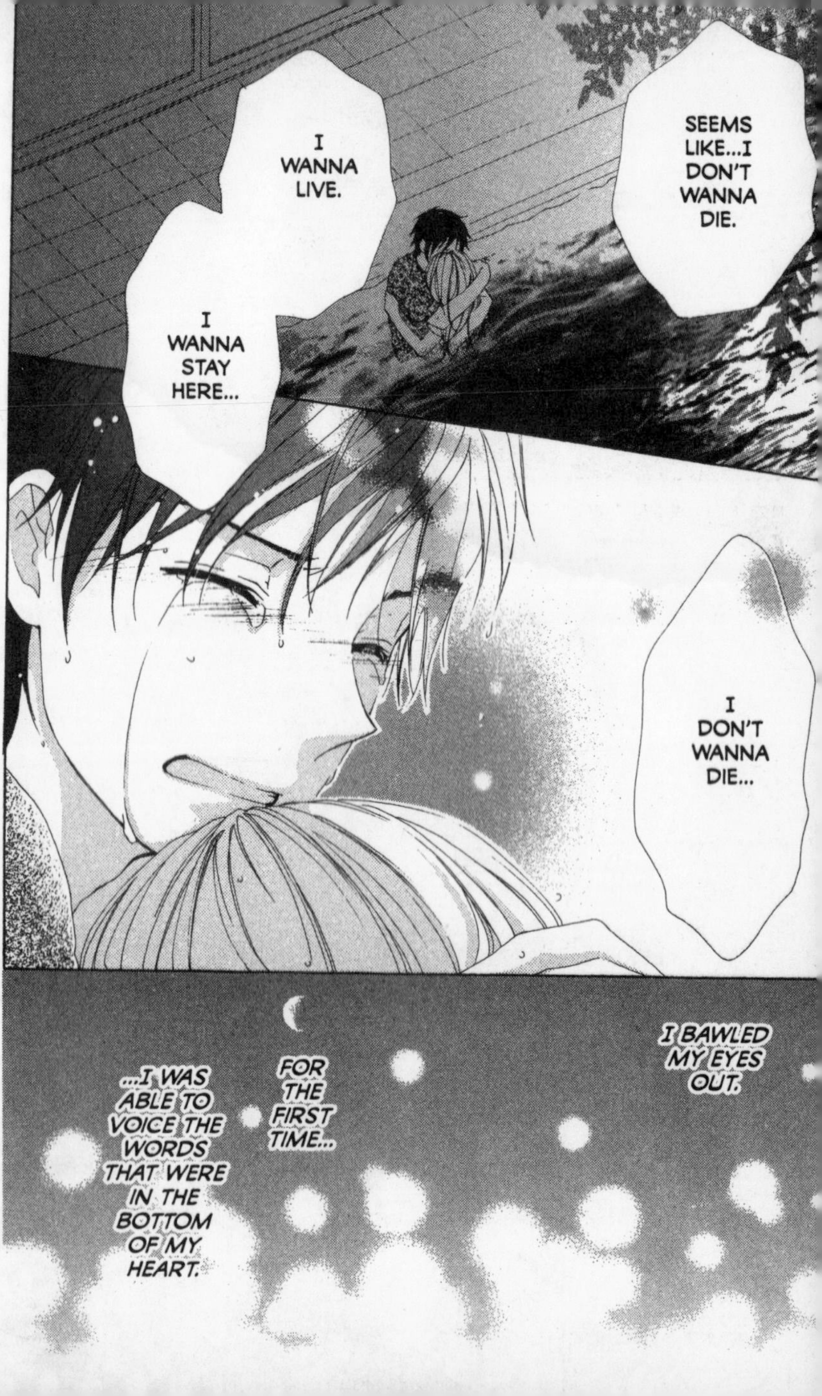
SEEMS LIKE...I DON'T WANNA DIE.
I WANNA LIVE.
I WANNA STAY HERE...
I DON'T WANNA DIE...
I BAWLED MY EYES OUT.
FOR THE FIRST TIME...
...I WAS ABLE TO VOICE THE WORDS THAT WERE IN THE BOTTOM OF MY HEART.

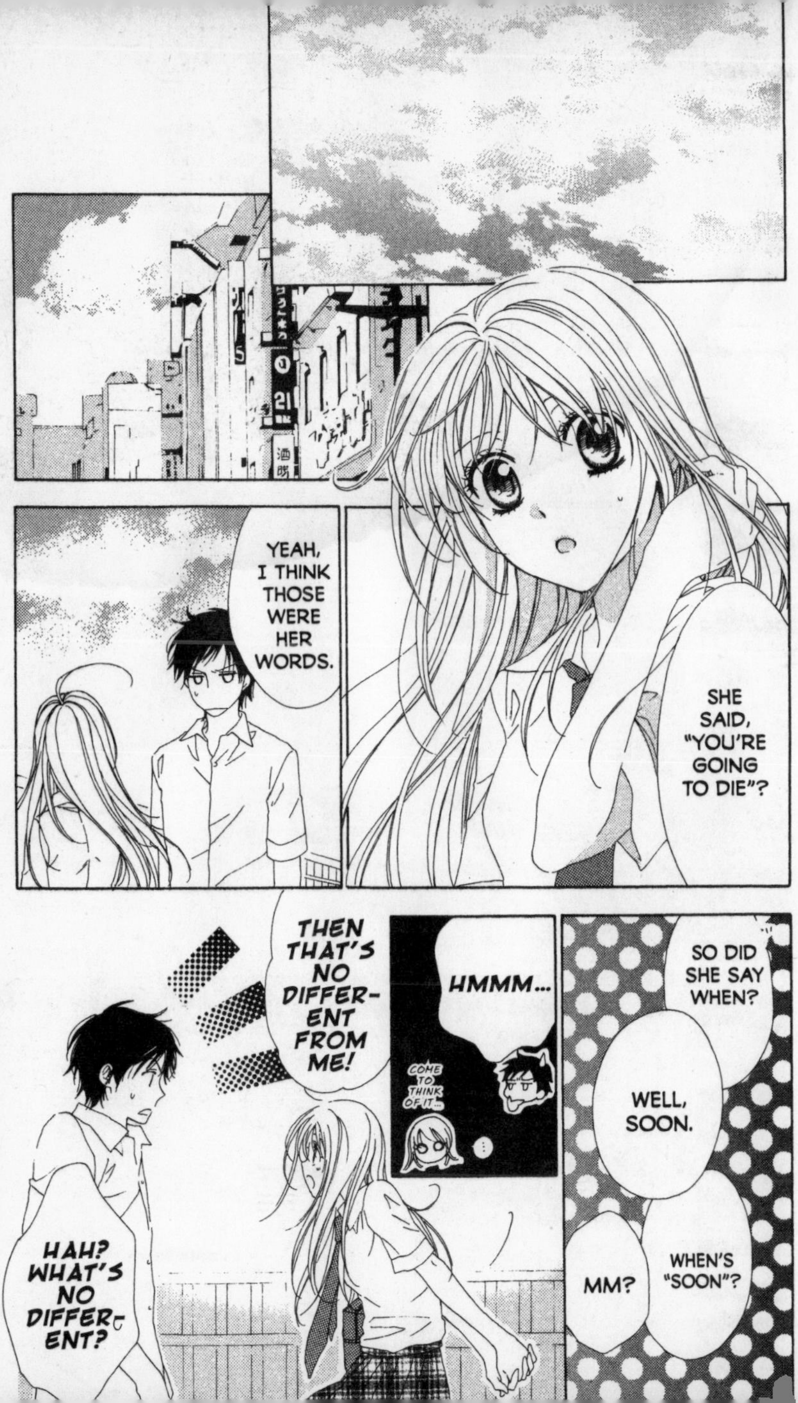
SHE SAID, "YOU'RE GOING TO DIE"?
YEAH, I THINK THOSE WERE HER WORDS.
SO DID SHE SAY WHEN?
WELL, SOON.
WHEN'S "SOON"?
MM?
HMMM...
COME TO THINK OF IT...
...
THEN THAT'S NO DIFFER-ENT FROM ME!
HAH? WHAT'S NO DIFFER-ENT?

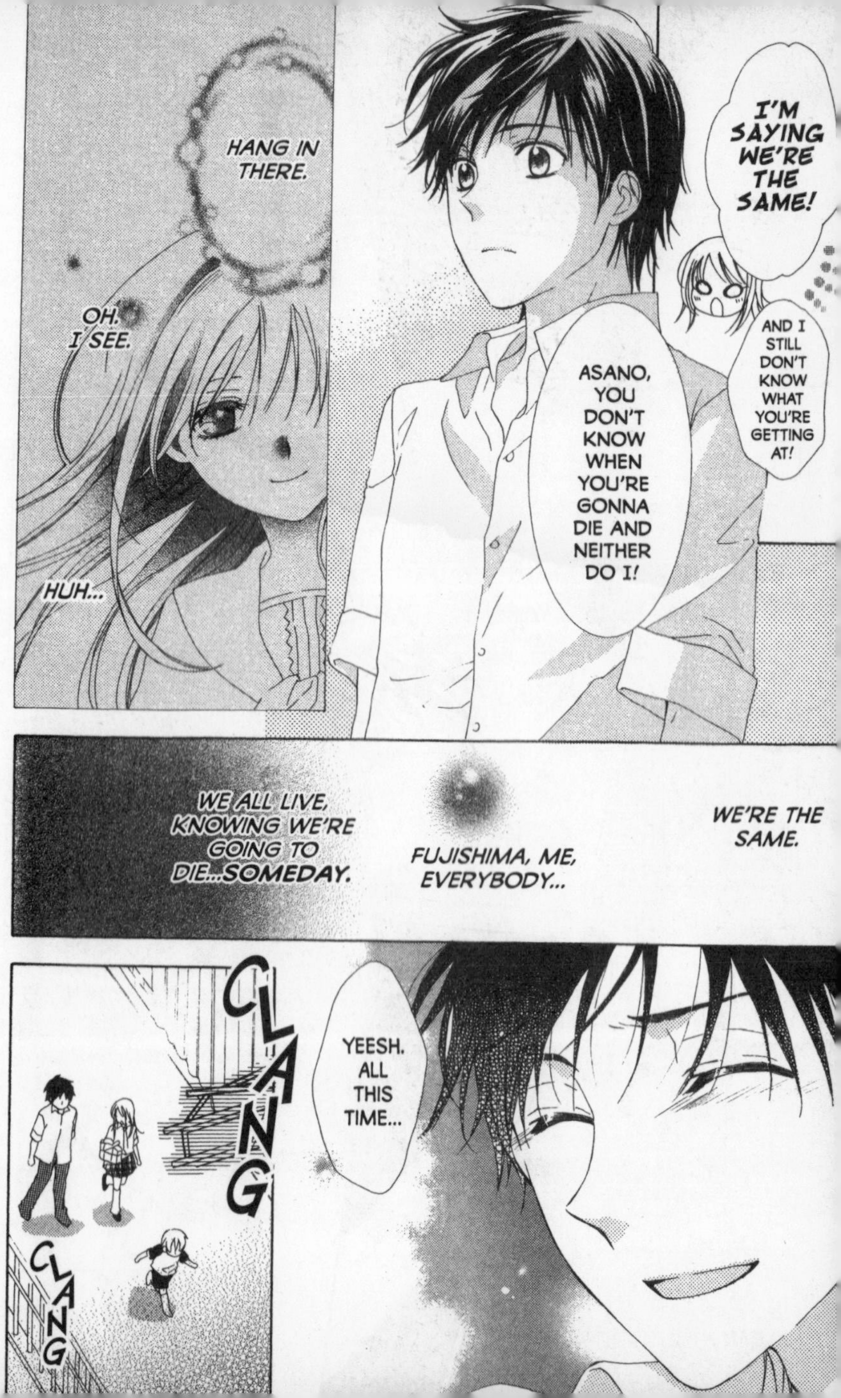
I'M SAYING WE'RE THE SAME!
AND I STILL DON'T KNOW WHAT YOU'RE GETTING AT!
ASANO, YOU DON'T KNOW WHEN YOU'RE GONNA DIE AND NEITHER DO I!
HANG IN THERE.
OH. I SEE.
HUH...
WE'RE THE SAME.
FUJISHIMA, ME, EVERYBODY...
WE ALL LIVE, KNOWING WE'RE GOING TO DIE...SOMEDAY.
YEESH. ALL THIS TIME...
CLANG
CLANG

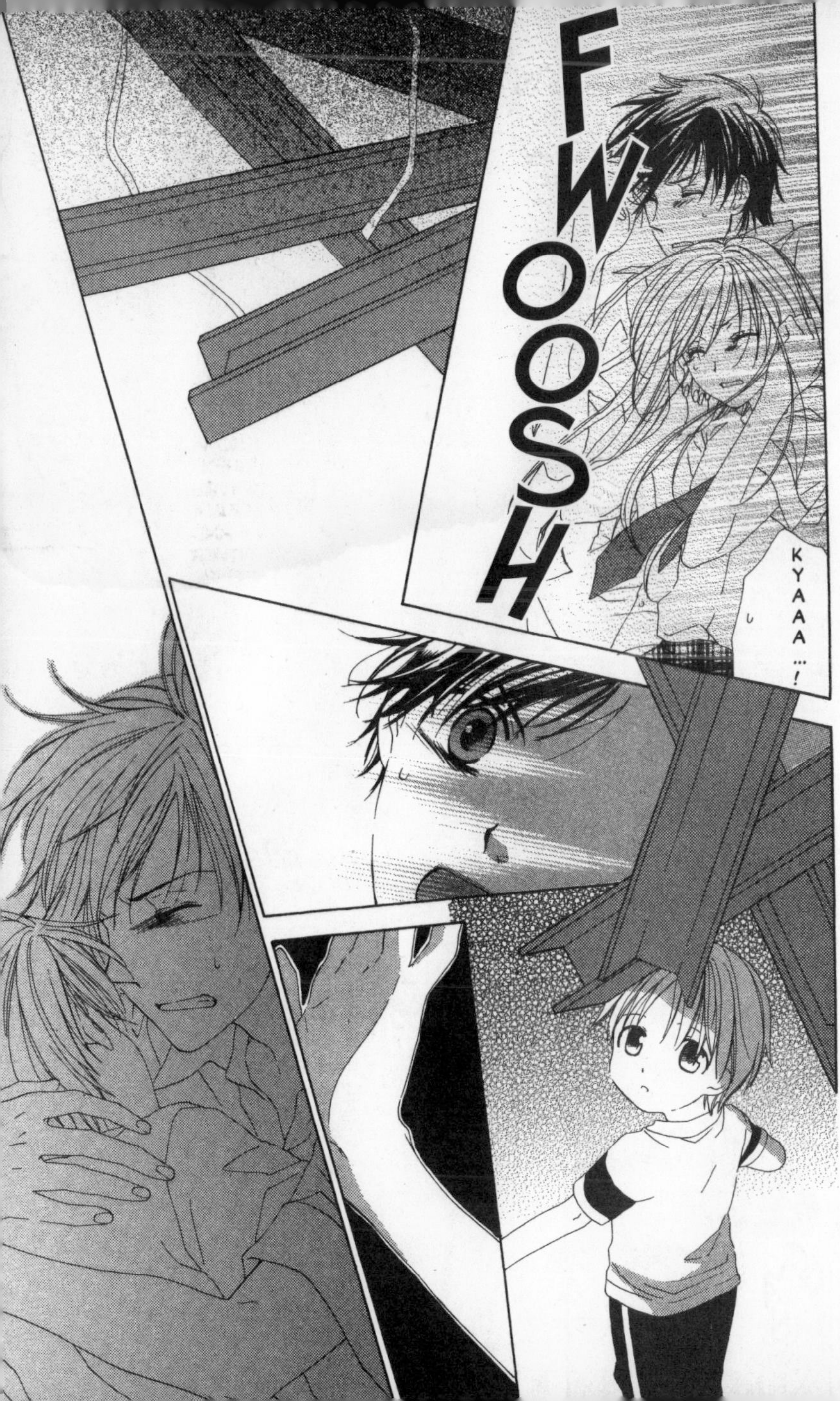
FWOOSH
KYAAA...!

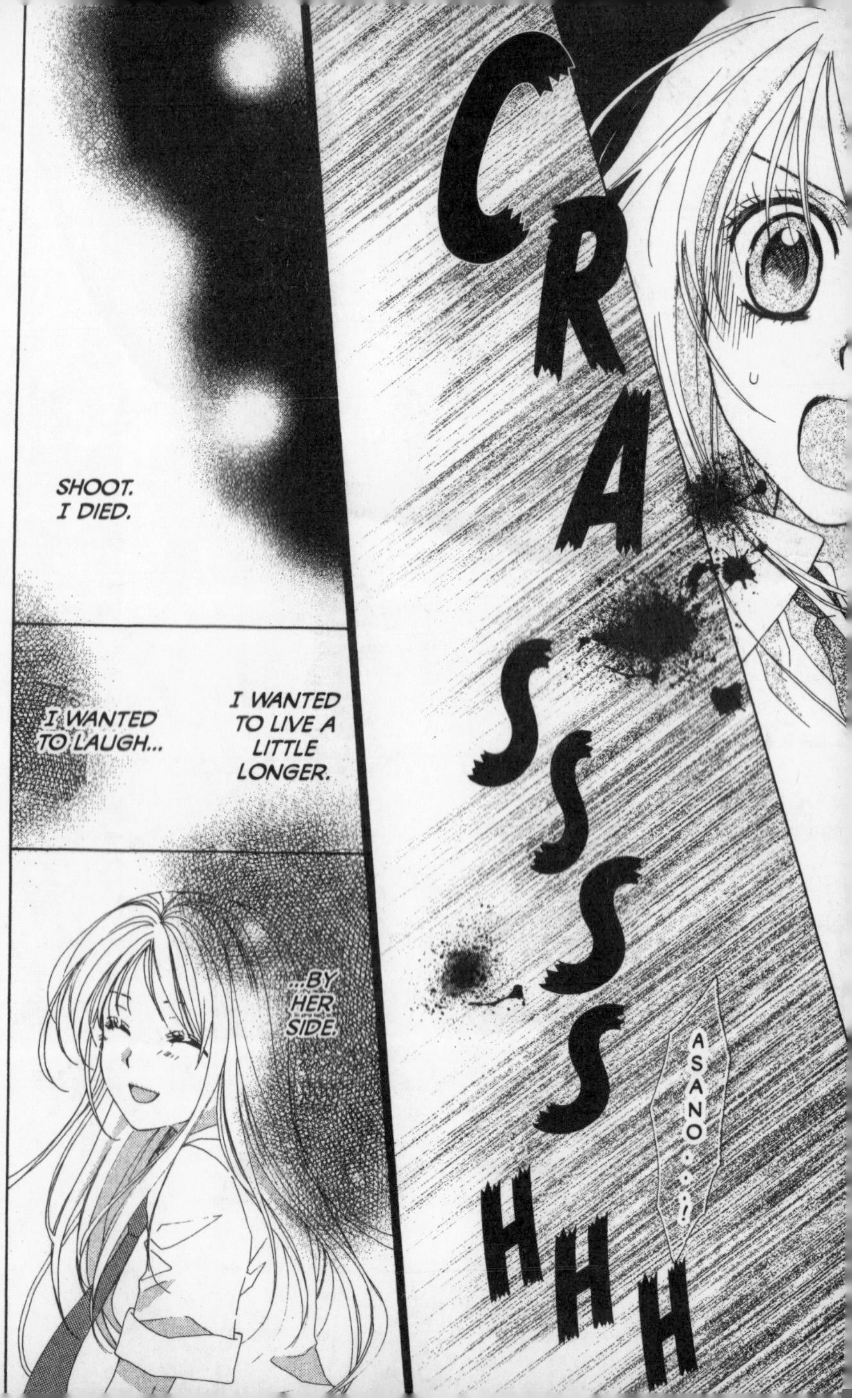
CRASSSHHH
ASANO...!
SHOOT. I DIED.
I WANTED TO LIVE A LITTLE LONGER.
I WANTED TO LAUGH...
...BY HER SIDE.

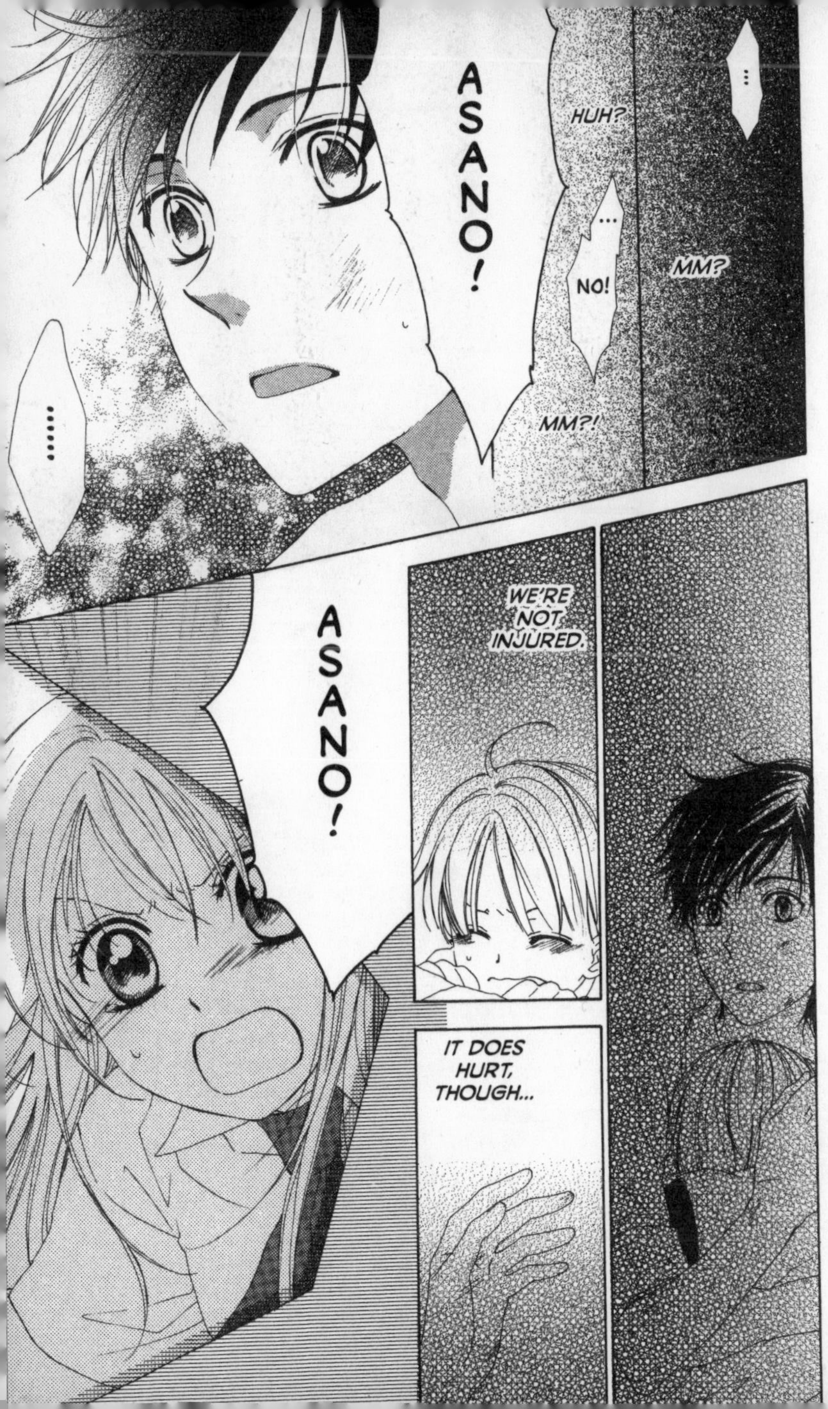
...
MM?
HUH?
... NO!
MM?!
ASANO!
......
WE'RE NOT INJURED.
IT DOES HURT, THOUGH...
ASANO!

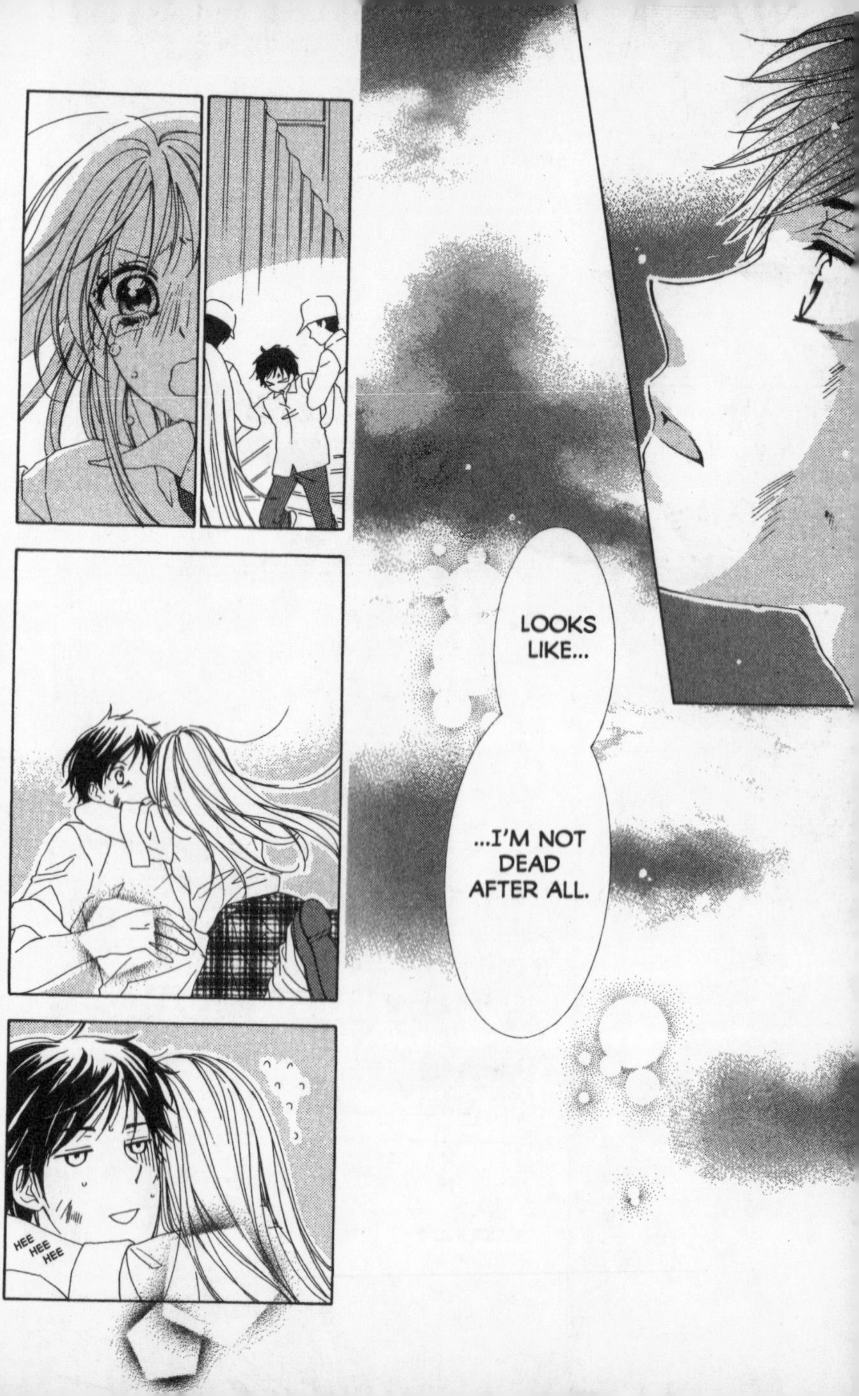
LOOKS LIKE...
...I'M NOT DEAD AFTER ALL.
HEE HEE HEE

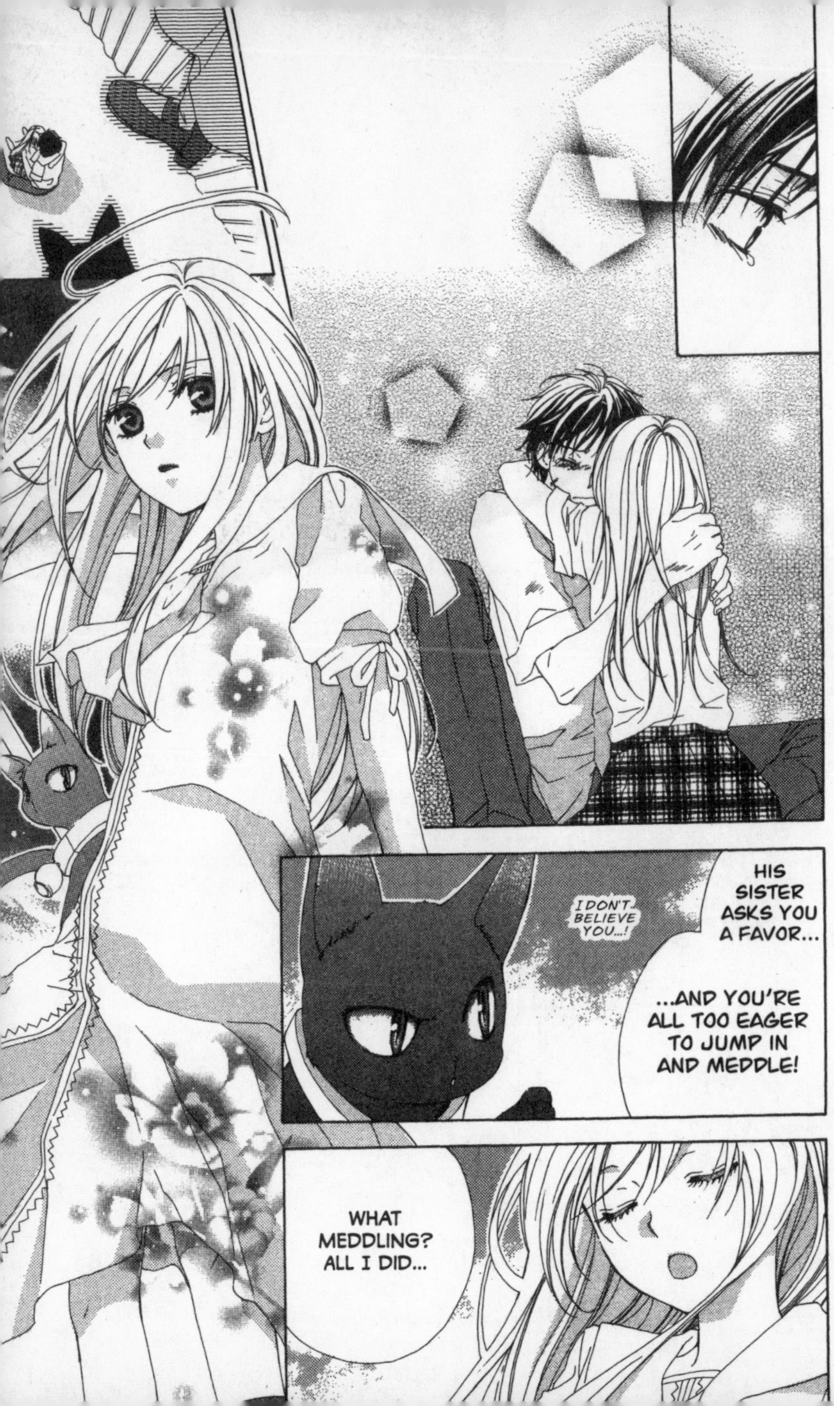
HIS SISTER ASKS YOU A FAVOR...
I DON'T BELIEVE YOU...!
...AND YOU'RE ALL TOO EAGER TO JUMP IN AND MEDDLE!
WHAT MEDDLING? ALL I DID...

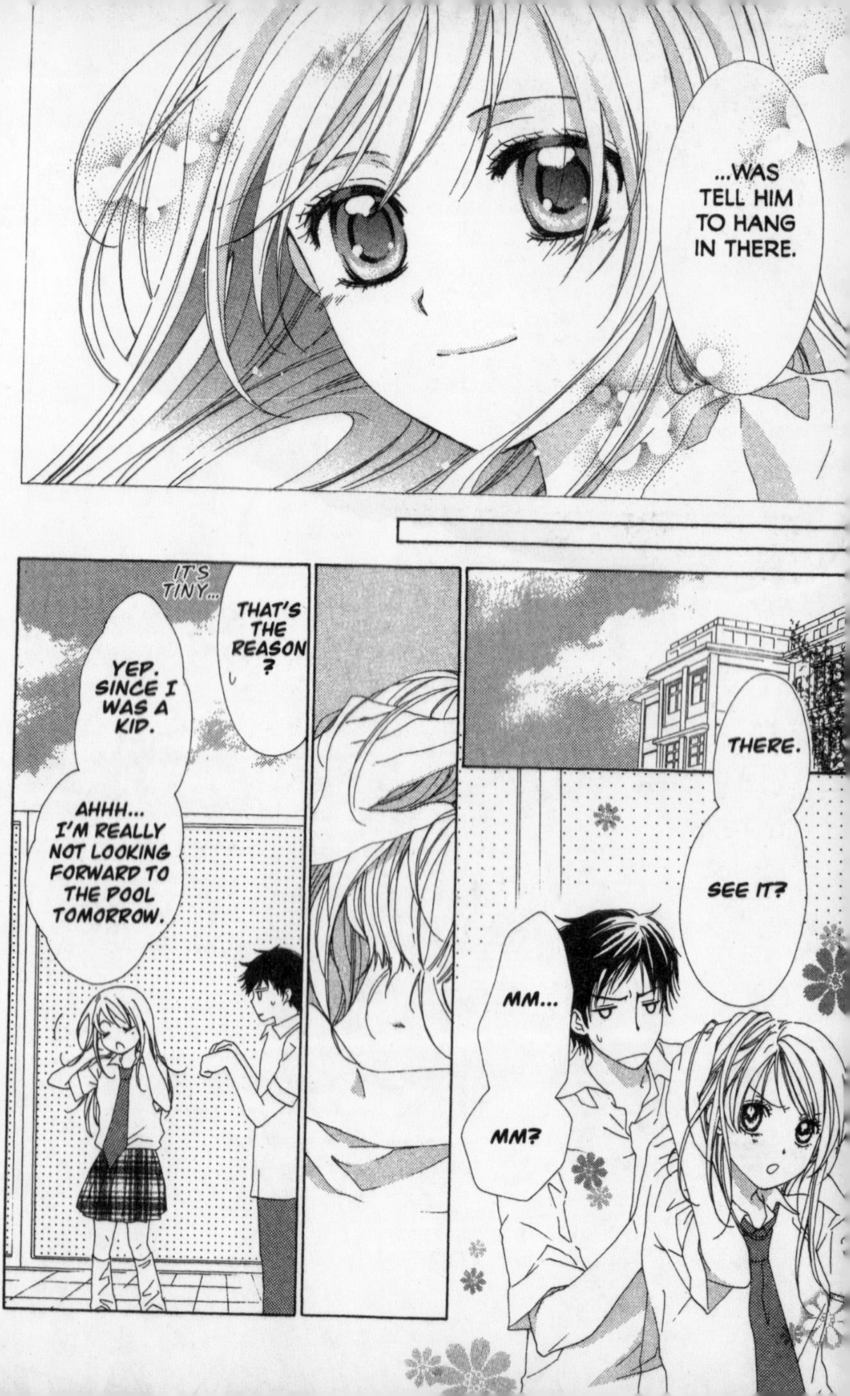
...WAS TELL HIM TO HANG IN THERE.
THERE.
SEE IT?
MM...
MM?
IT'S TINY...
THAT'S THE REASON?
YEP. SINCE I WAS A KID.
AHHH... I'M REALLY NOT LOOKING FORWARD TO THE POOL TOMORROW.

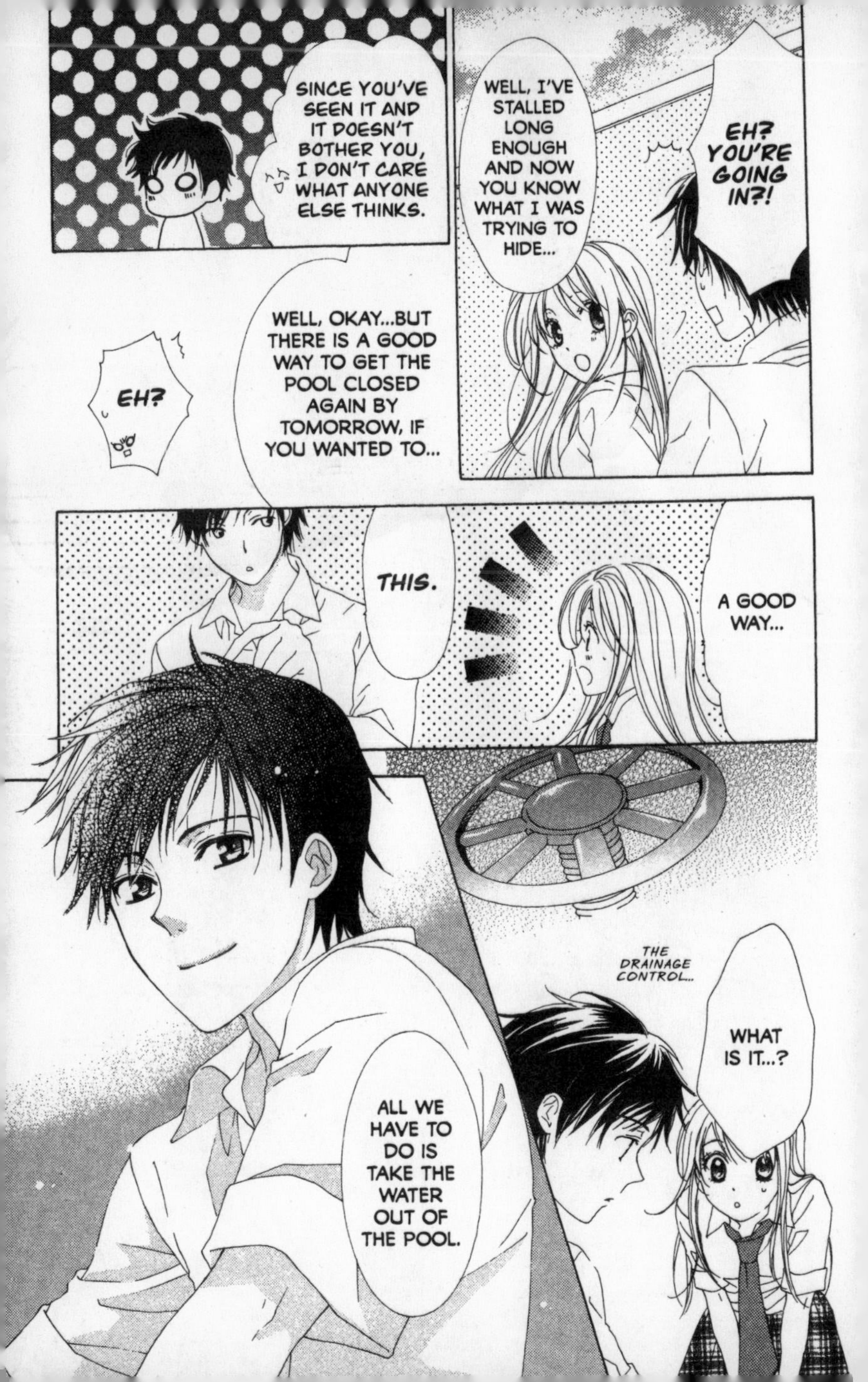
EH? YOU'RE GOING IN?!
WELL, I'VE STALLED LONG ENOUGH AND NOW YOU KNOW WHAT I WAS TRYING TO HIDE...
SINCE YOU'VE SEEN IT AND IT DOESN'T BOTHER YOU, I DON'T CARE WHAT ANYONE ELSE THINKS.
WELL, OKAY...BUT THERE IS A GOOD WAY TO GET THE POOL CLOSED AGAIN BY TOMORROW, IF YOU WANTED TO...
EH?
A GOOD WAY...
THIS.
WHAT IS IT...?
THE DRAINAGE CONTROL...
ALL WE HAVE TO DO IS TAKE THE WATER OUT OF THE POOL.

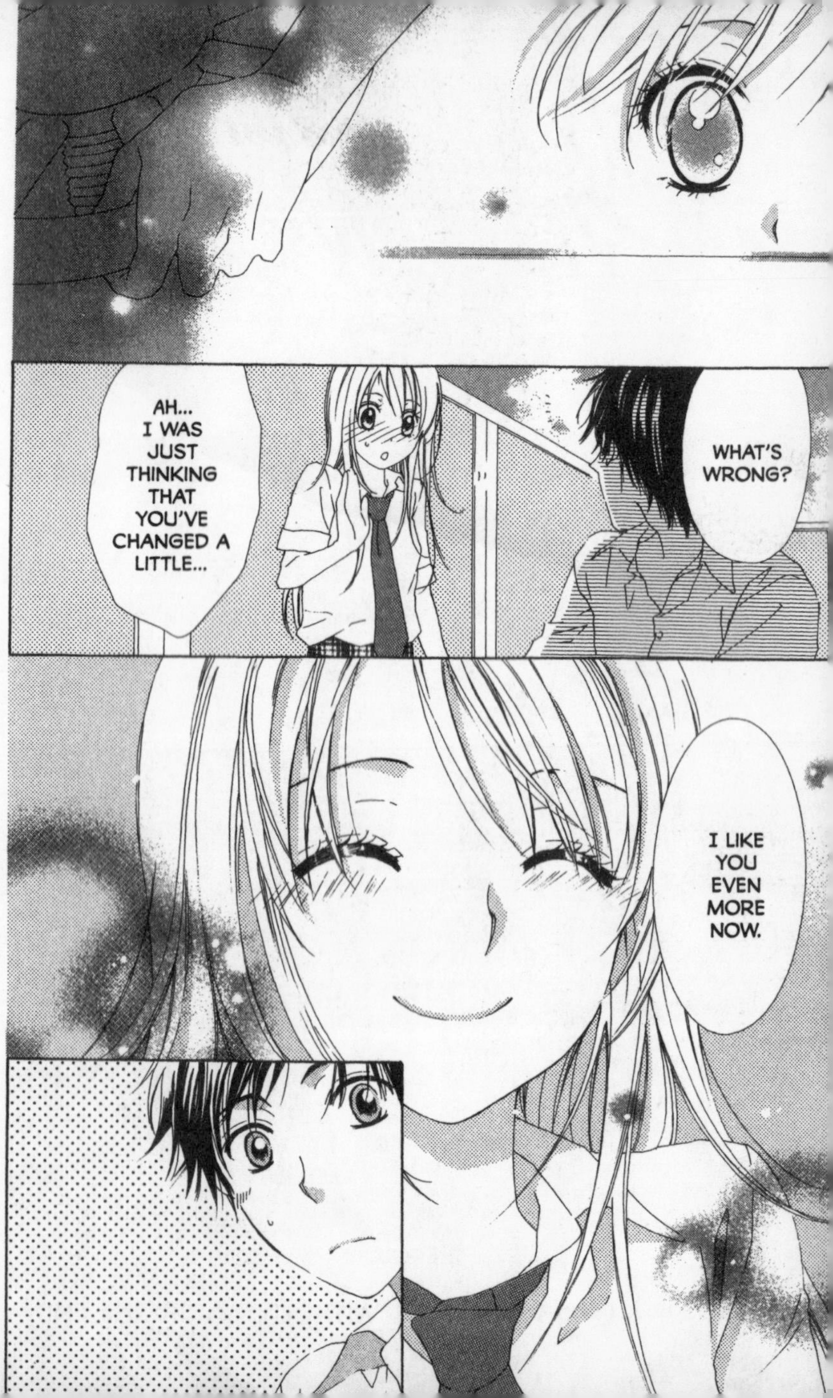
WHAT'S WRONG?
AH... I WAS JUST THINKING THAT YOU'VE CHANGED A LITTLE...
I LIKE YOU EVEN MORE NOW.

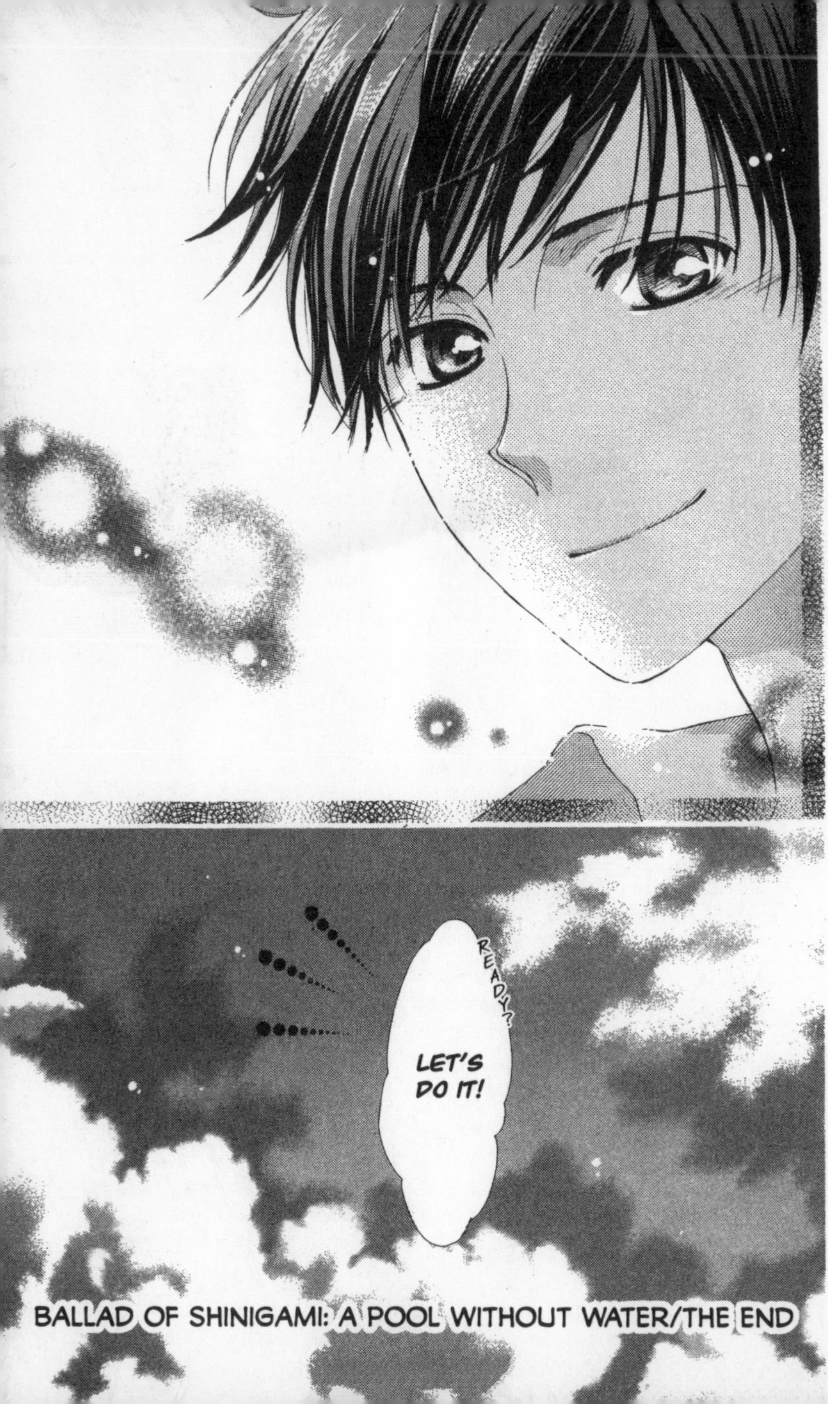
READY?
LET'S DO IT!
BALLAD OF SHINIGAMI: A POOL WITHOUT WATER/THE END

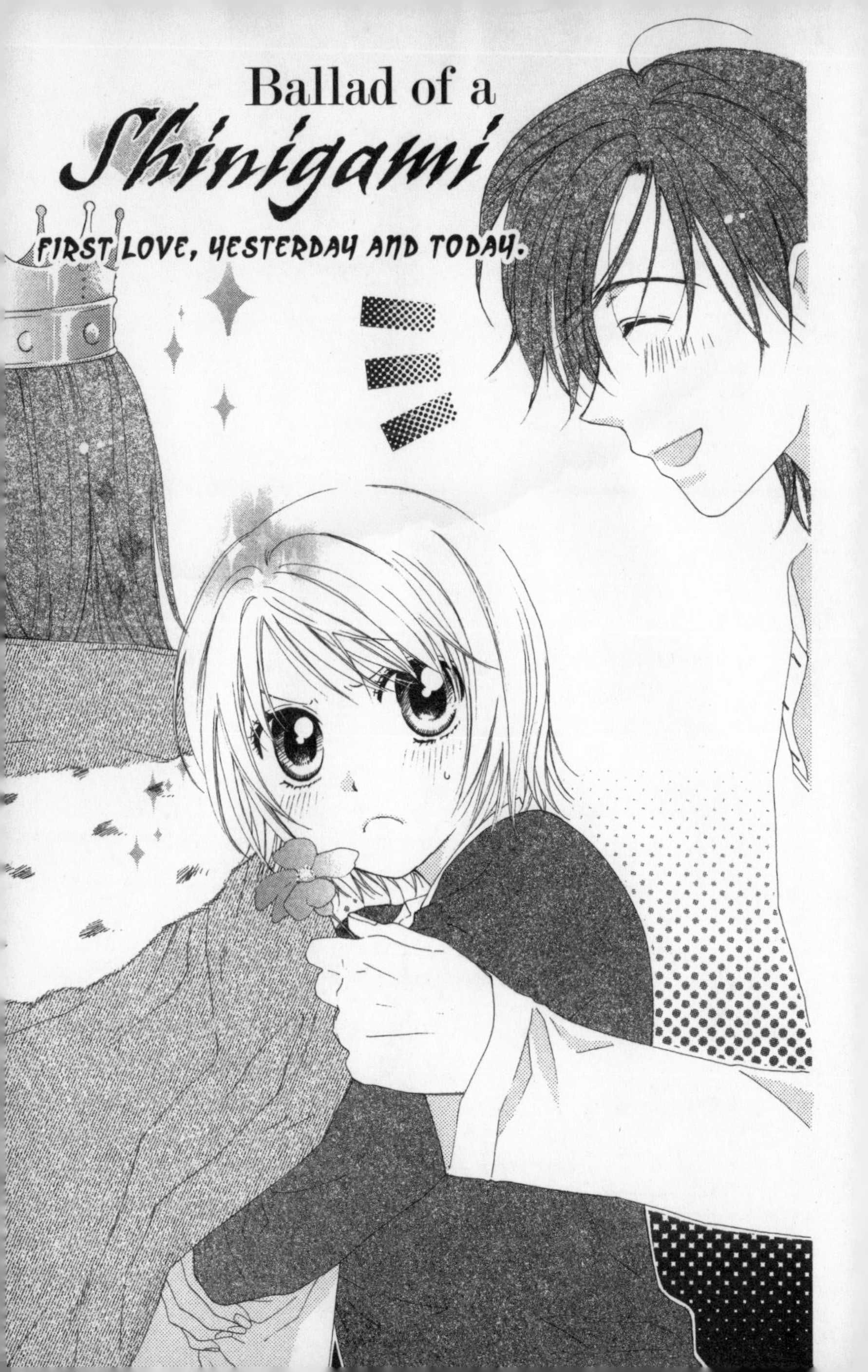
Ballad of a
Shinigami
FIRST LOVE, YESTERDAY AND TODAY.

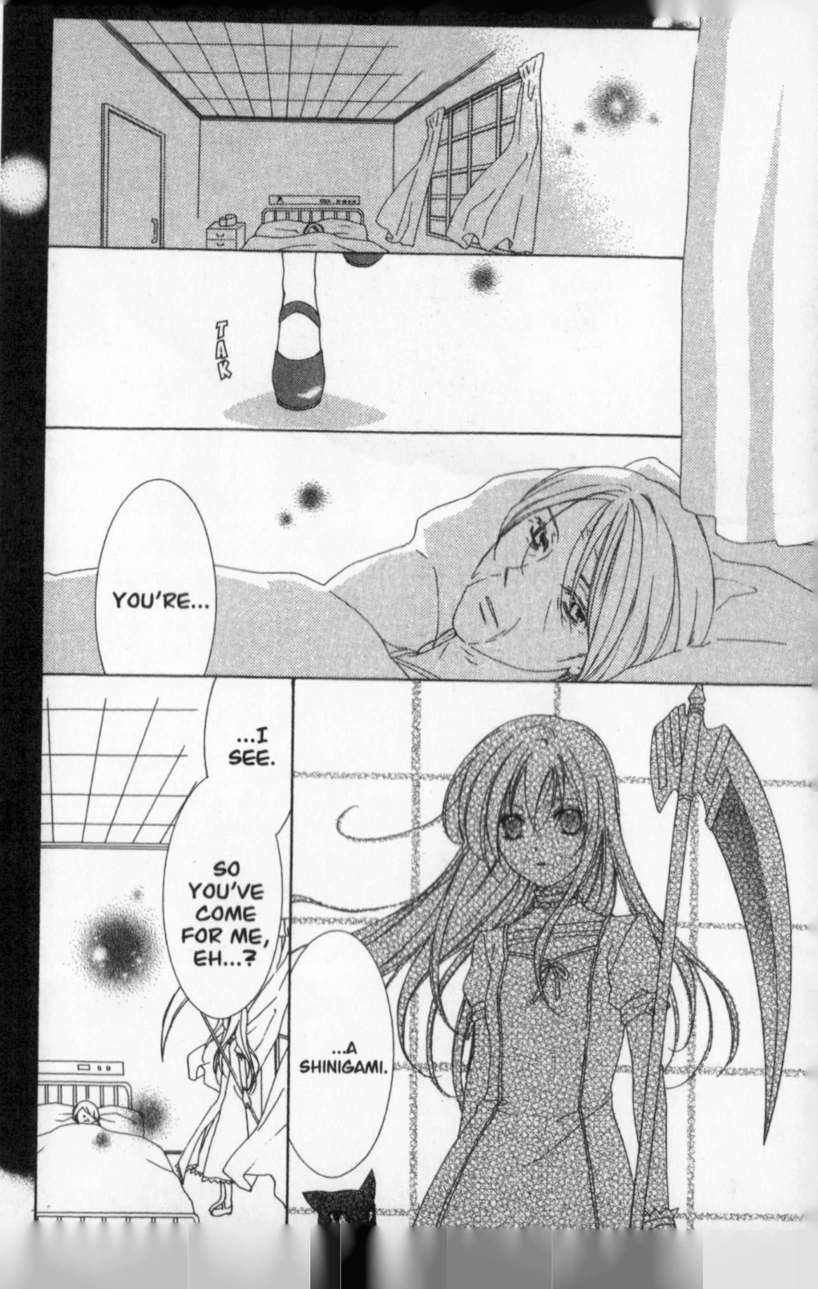
TAK
YOU'RE...
...A SHINIGAMI.
...I SEE.
SO YOU'VE COME FOR ME, EH...?

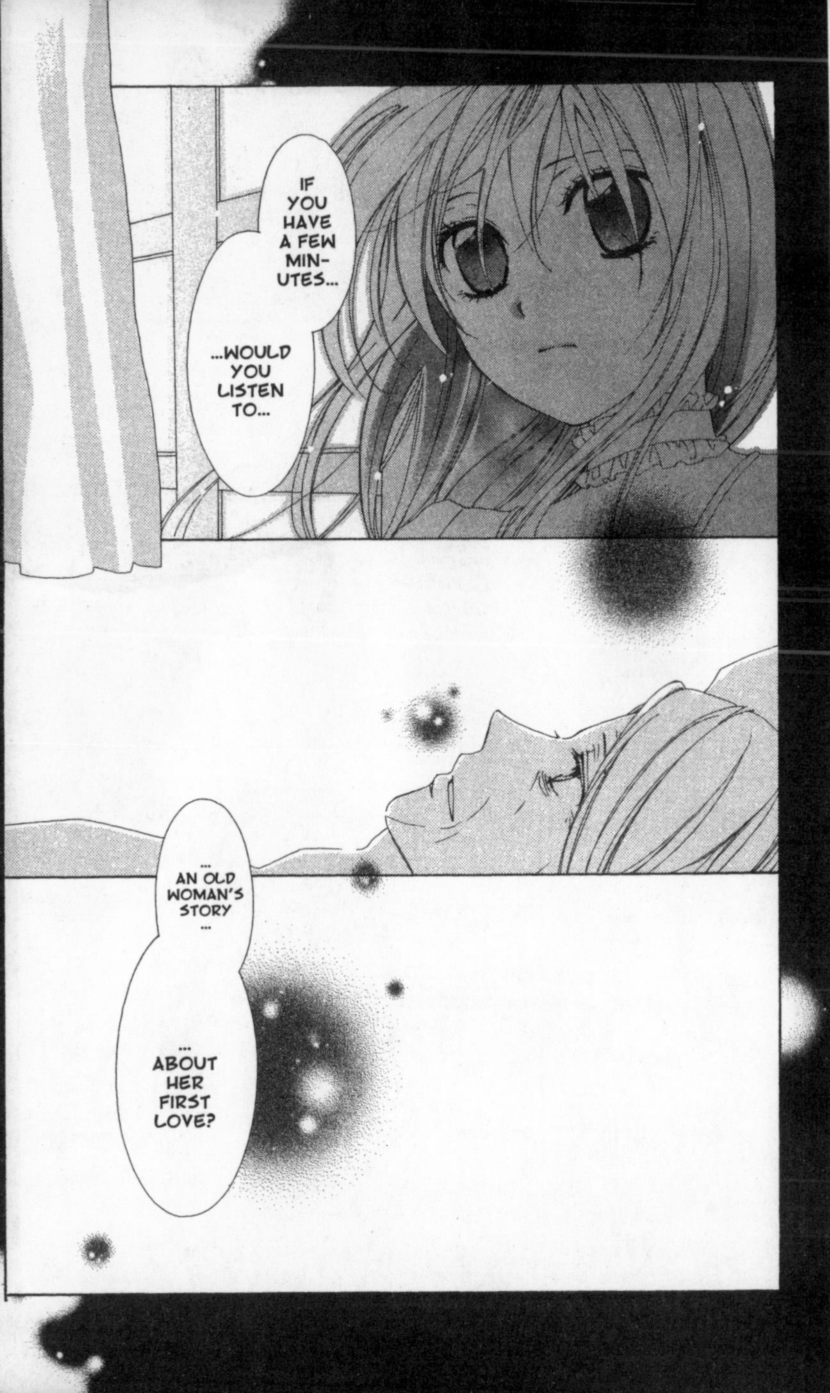
IF YOU HAVE A FEW MIN-UTES...
...WOULD YOU LISTEN TO...
... AN OLD WOMAN'S STORY ...
... ABOUT HER FIRST LOVE?

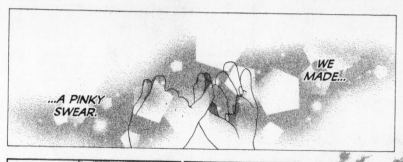

...A PINKY SWEAR.

WE MADE...

WHA--?!

RATTLE

THAT STORY AGAIN?

JEEZ, YAE, YOU'RE SUCH A DREAMER!

TINY

(4 FT. 9 IN.)

I-IT'S NOT A DREAM!

HE MADE A SOLEMN OATH!!

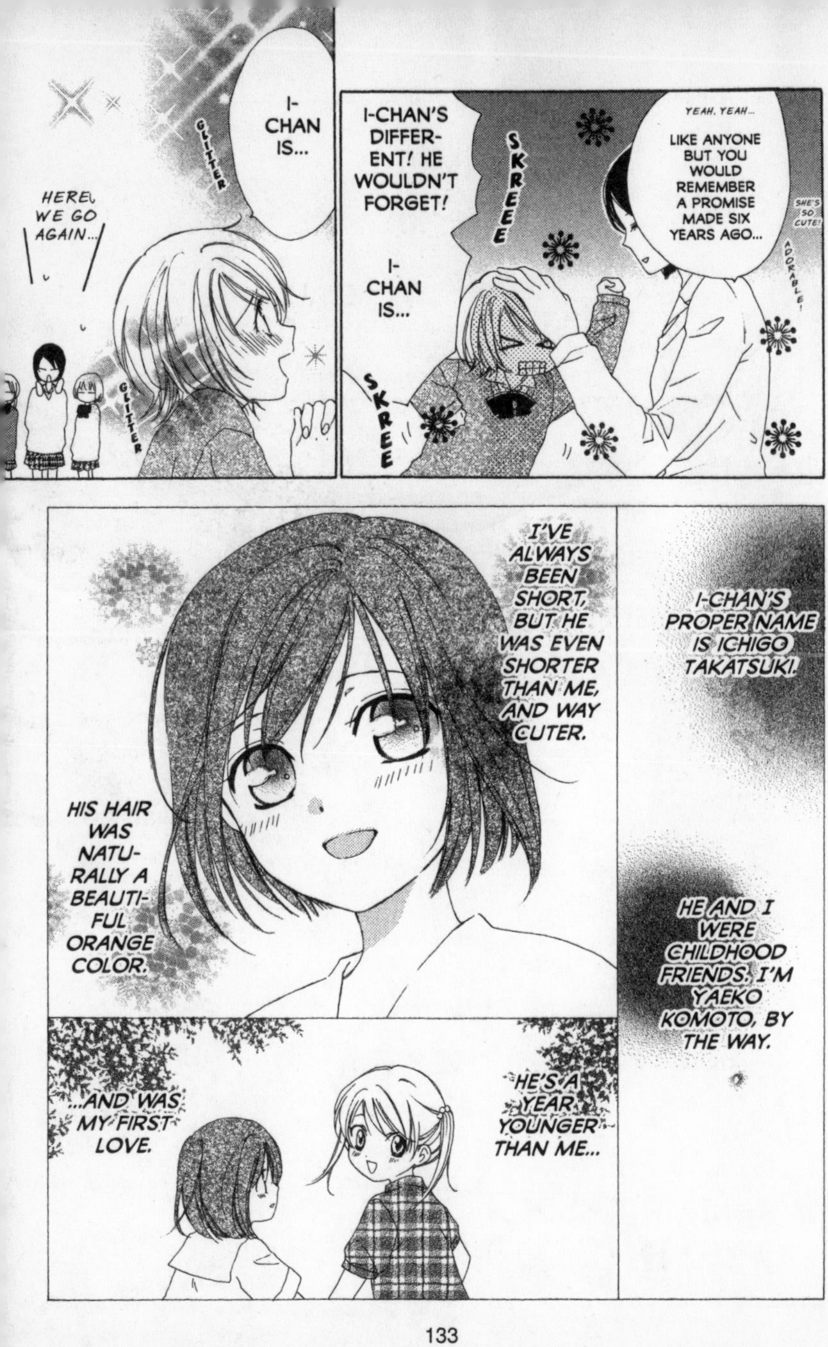
YEAH, YEAH...
LIKE ANYONE BUT YOU WOULD REMEMBER A PROMISE MADE SIX YEARS AGO...
SHE'S SO CUTE!
ADORABLE!
I-CHAN'S DIFFER-ENT! HE WOULDN'T FORGET!
SKREEE
I-CHAN IS...
SKREEE
I-CHAN IS...
GLITTER
GLITTER
HERE WE GO AGAIN...
I-CHAN'S PROPER NAME IS ICHIGO TAKATSUKI.
HE AND I WERE CHILDHOOD FRIENDS. I'M YAEKO KOMOTO, BY THE WAY.
I'VE ALWAYS BEEN SHORT, BUT HE WAS EVEN SHORTER THAN ME, AND WAY CUTER.
HIS HAIR WAS NATU-RALLY A BEAUTI-FUL ORANGE COLOR.
HE'S A YEAR YOUNGER THAN ME...
...AND WAS MY FIRST LOVE.

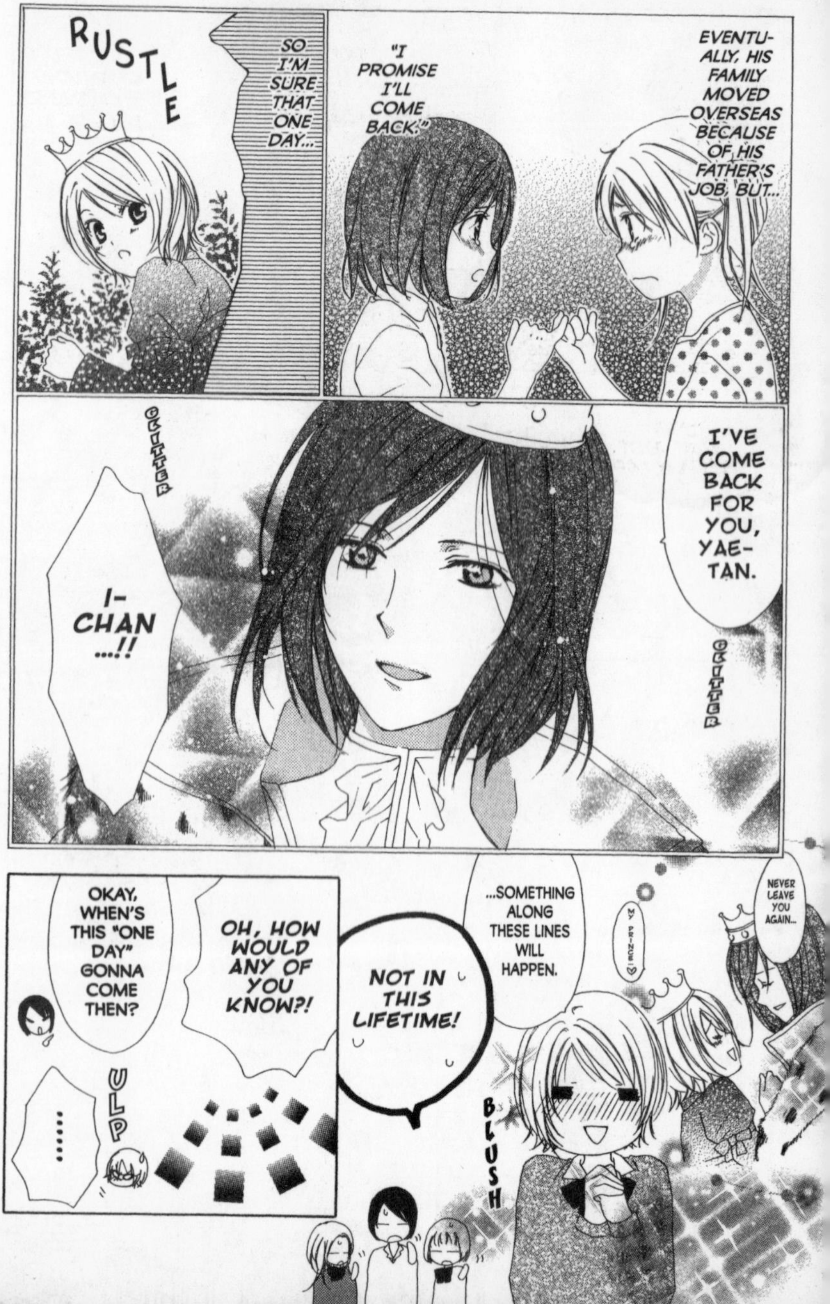
EVENTUALLY, HIS FAMILY MOVED OVERSEAS BECAUSE OF HIS FATHER'S JOB, BUT...
"I PROMISE I'LL COME BACK."
SO I'M SURE THAT ONE DAY...
RUSTLE
I'VE COME BACK FOR YOU, YAE-TAN.
GLITTER
GLITTER
I-CHAN...!!
NEVER LEAVE YOU AGAIN...
MY PRINCE♥
...SOMETHING ALONG THESE LINES WILL HAPPEN.
BLUSH
NOT IN THIS LIFETIME!
OH, HOW WOULD ANY OF YOU KNOW?!
OKAY, WHEN'S THIS "ONE DAY" GONNA COME THEN?
ULP
......

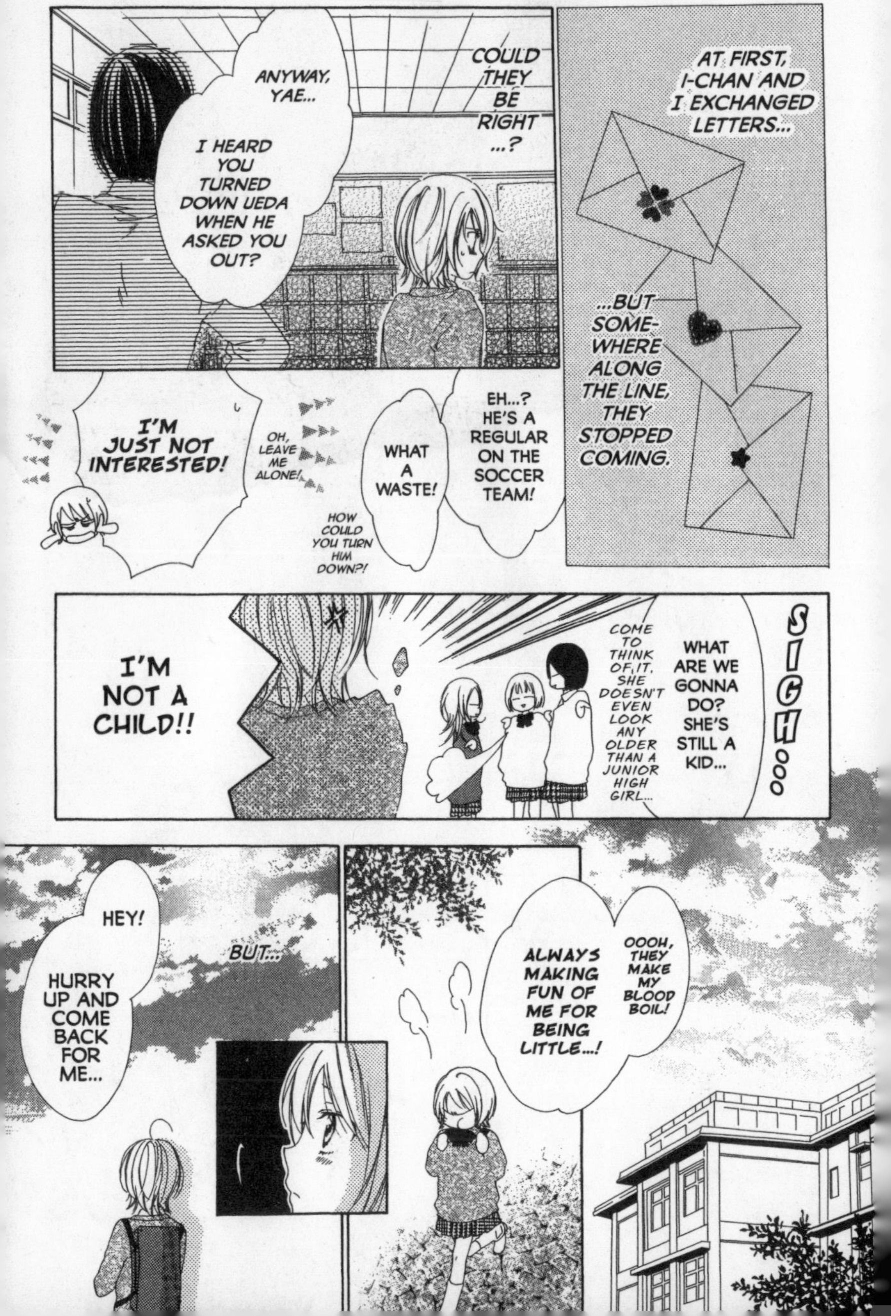
AT FIRST, I-CHAN AND I EXCHANGED LETTERS...
...BUT SOME-WHERE ALONG THE LINE, THEY STOPPED COMING.
COULD THEY BE RIGHT ...?
ANYWAY, YAE...
I HEARD YOU TURNED DOWN UEDA WHEN HE ASKED YOU OUT?
EH...? HE'S A REGULAR ON THE SOCCER TEAM!
WHAT A WASTE!
HOW COULD YOU TURN HIM DOWN?!
OH, LEAVE ME ALONE!
I'M JUST NOT INTERESTED!
SIGHooo
WHAT ARE WE GONNA DO? SHE'S STILL A KID...
COME TO THINK OF IT, SHE DOESN'T EVEN LOOK ANY OLDER THAN A JUNIOR HIGH GIRL...
I'M NOT A CHILD!!
OOOH, THEY MAKE MY BLOOD BOIL!
ALWAYS MAKING FUN OF ME FOR BEING LITTLE...!
BUT...
HEY!
HURRY UP AND COME BACK FOR ME...

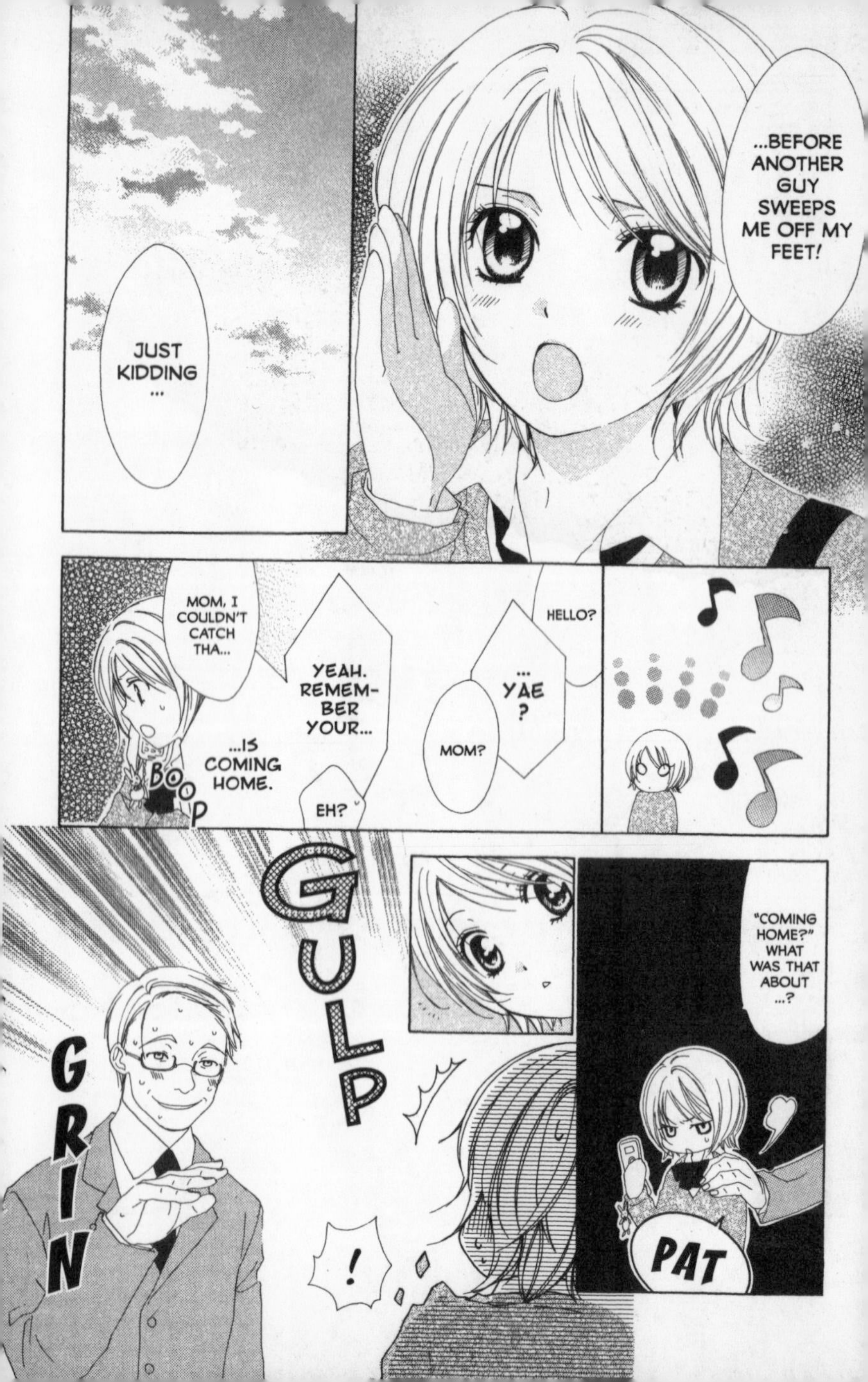
...BEFORE ANOTHER GUY SWEEPS ME OFF MY FEET!
JUST KIDDING ...
HELLO?
... YAE ?
MOM?
YEAH. REMEMBER YOUR...
EH?
...IS COMING HOME.
MOM, I COULDN'T CATCH THA...
BOOP
"COMING HOME?" WHAT WAS THAT ABOUT ...?
PAT
!
GULP
GRIN

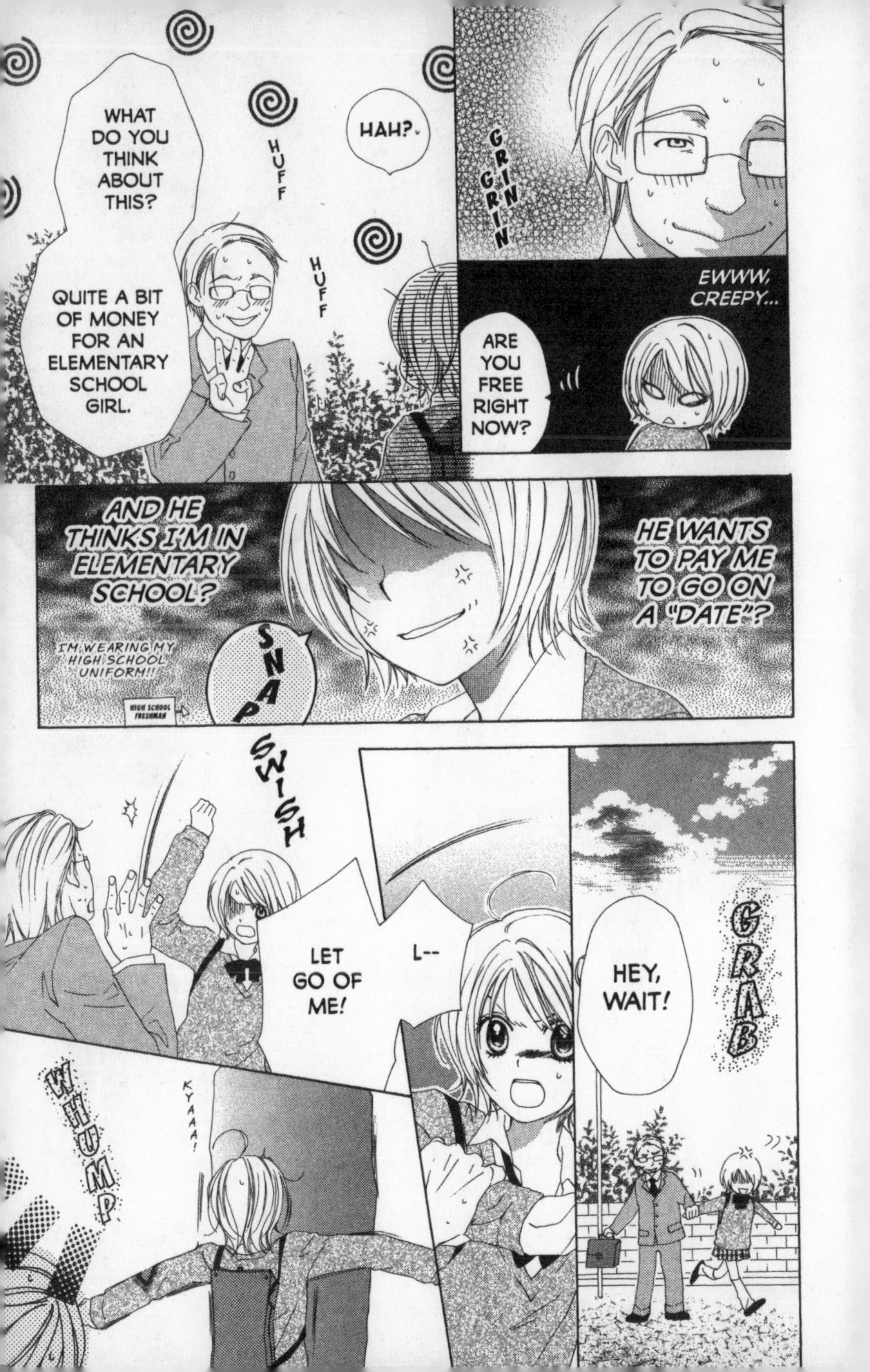
GRIN GRIN
EWWW, CREEPY...
ARE YOU FREE RIGHT NOW?
HAH?
HUFF
HUFF
WHAT DO YOU THINK ABOUT THIS?
QUITE A BIT OF MONEY FOR AN ELEMENTARY SCHOOL GIRL.
HE WANTS TO PAY ME TO GO ON A "DATE"?
AND HE THINKS I'M IN ELEMENTARY SCHOOL?
SNAP
I'M WEARING MY HIGH SCHOOL UNIFORM!!
HIGH SCHOOL FRESHMAN
GRAB
HEY, WAIT!
L--
LET GO OF ME!
SWISH
KYAAA!
WHUMP

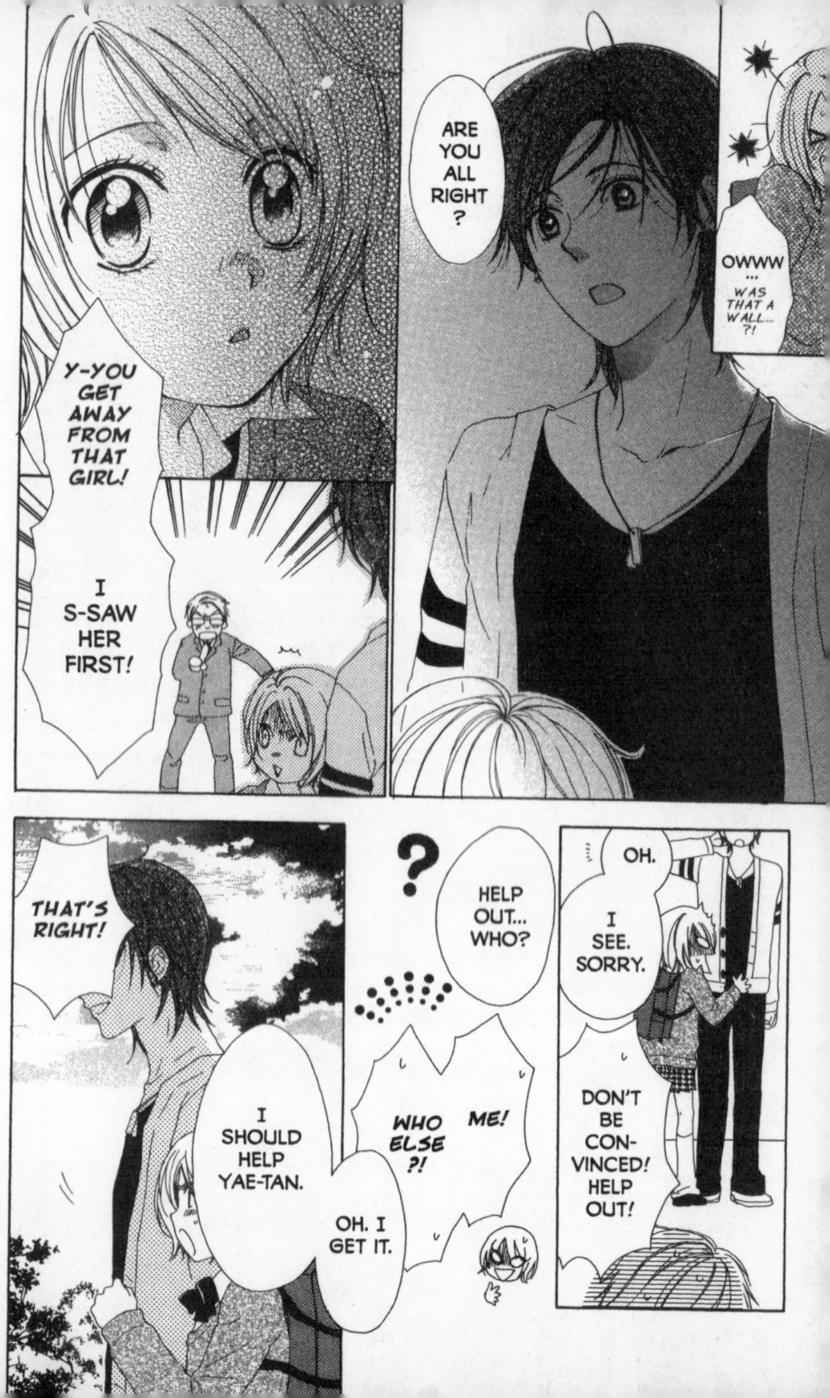
OWWW... WAS THAT A WALL...?!
ARE YOU ALL RIGHT?
Y-YOU GET AWAY FROM THAT GIRL!
I S-SAW HER FIRST!
OH.
I SEE. SORRY.
DON'T BE CON-VINCED! HELP OUT!
HELP OUT... WHO?
WHO ELSE?! ME!
OH. I GET IT.
I SHOULD HELP YAE-TAN.
THAT'S RIGHT!

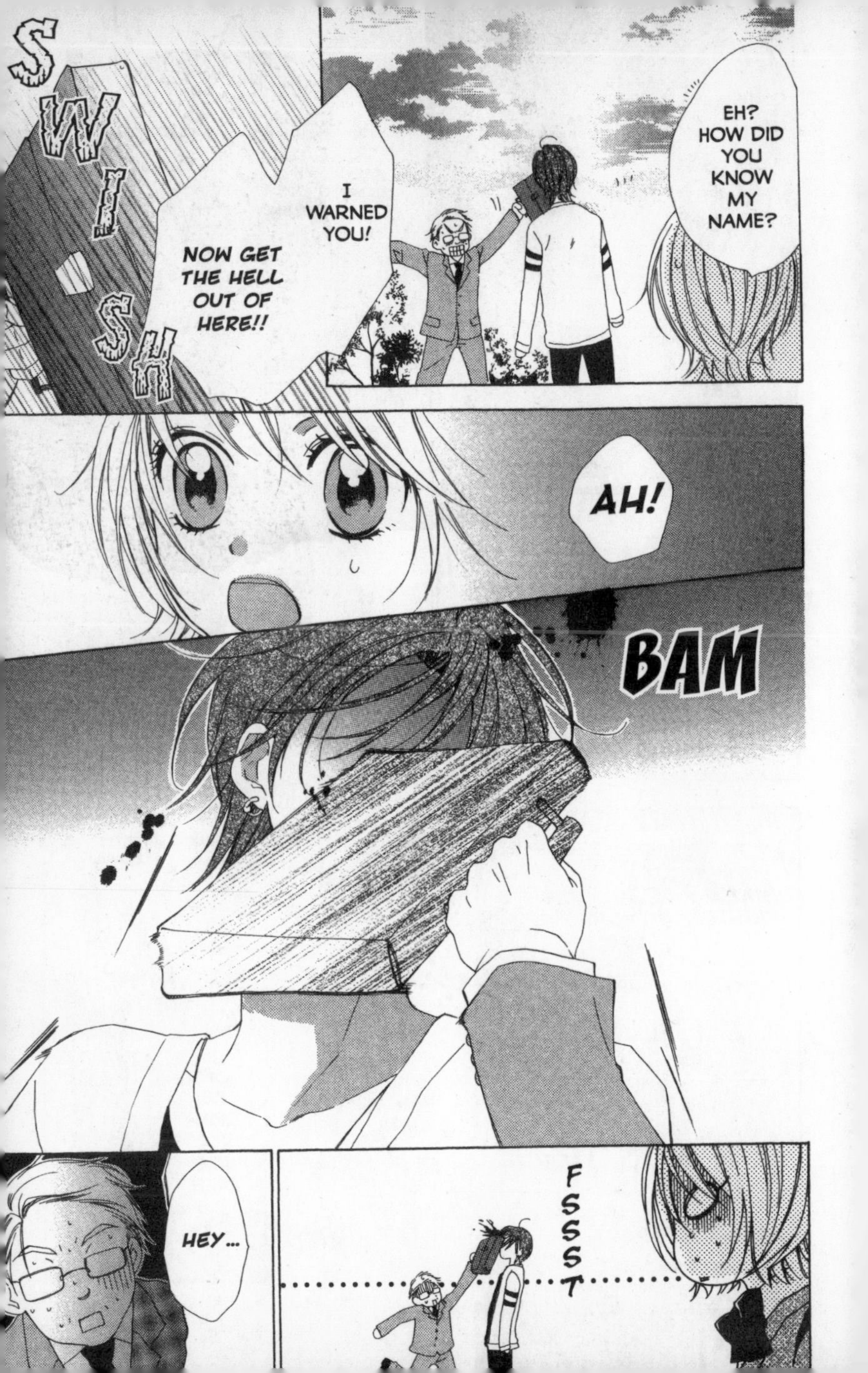
EH? HOW DID YOU KNOW MY NAME?
I WARNED YOU!
NOW GET THE HELL OUT OF HERE!!
SWISH
AH!
BAM
FSSST
HEY...

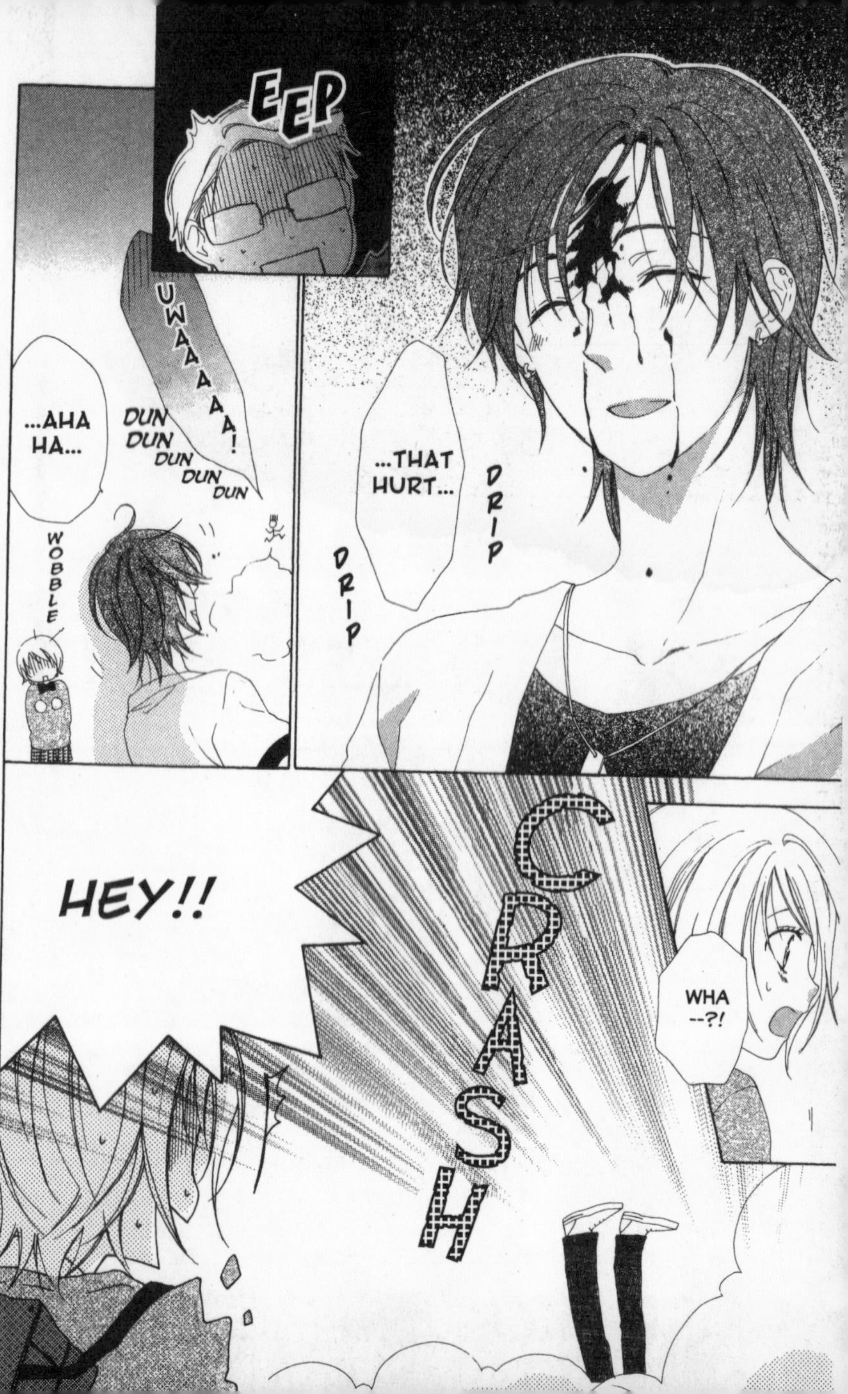
...THAT HURT...
DRIP
DRIP
EEP
UWAAAAAA!
DUN DUN DUN DUN DUN
...AHA HA...
WOBBLE
WHA--?!
CRASH
HEY!!

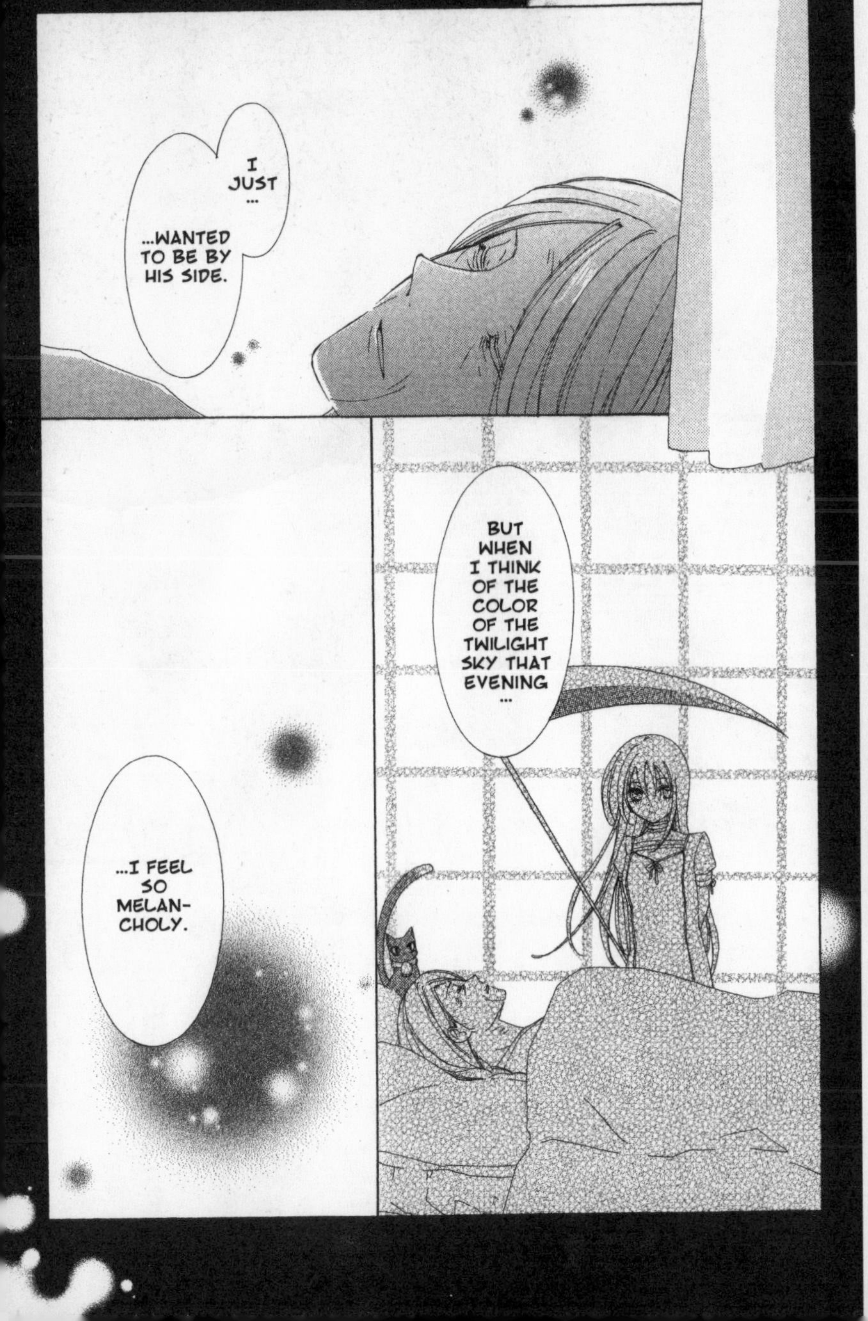
I JUST ...
...WANTED TO BE BY HIS SIDE.
BUT WHEN I THINK OF THE COLOR OF THE TWILIGHT SKY THAT EVENING ...
...I FEEL SO MELAN-CHOLY.

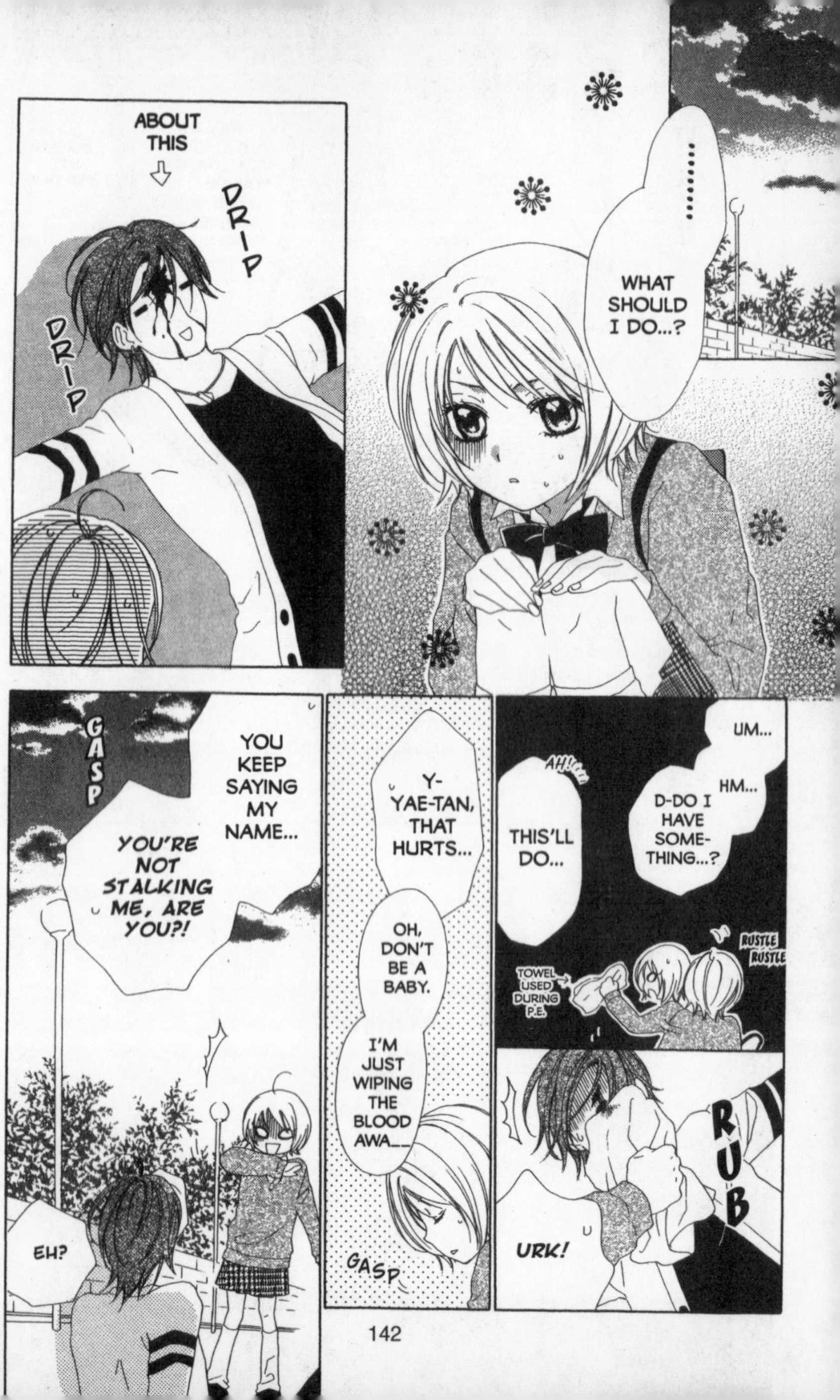
......
WHAT SHOULD I DO...?
ABOUT THIS
DRIP
DRIP
DRIP
DRIP
UM...
HM...
D-DO I HAVE SOMETHING...?
AH!
THIS'LL DO...
RUSTLE
RUSTLE
TOWEL USED DURING P.E.
RUB
URK!
Y-YAE-TAN, THAT HURTS...
OH, DON'T BE A BABY.
I'M JUST WIPING THE BLOOD AWA—
GASP
GASP
YOU KEEP SAYING MY NAME...
YOU'RE NOT STALKING ME, ARE YOU?!
EH?

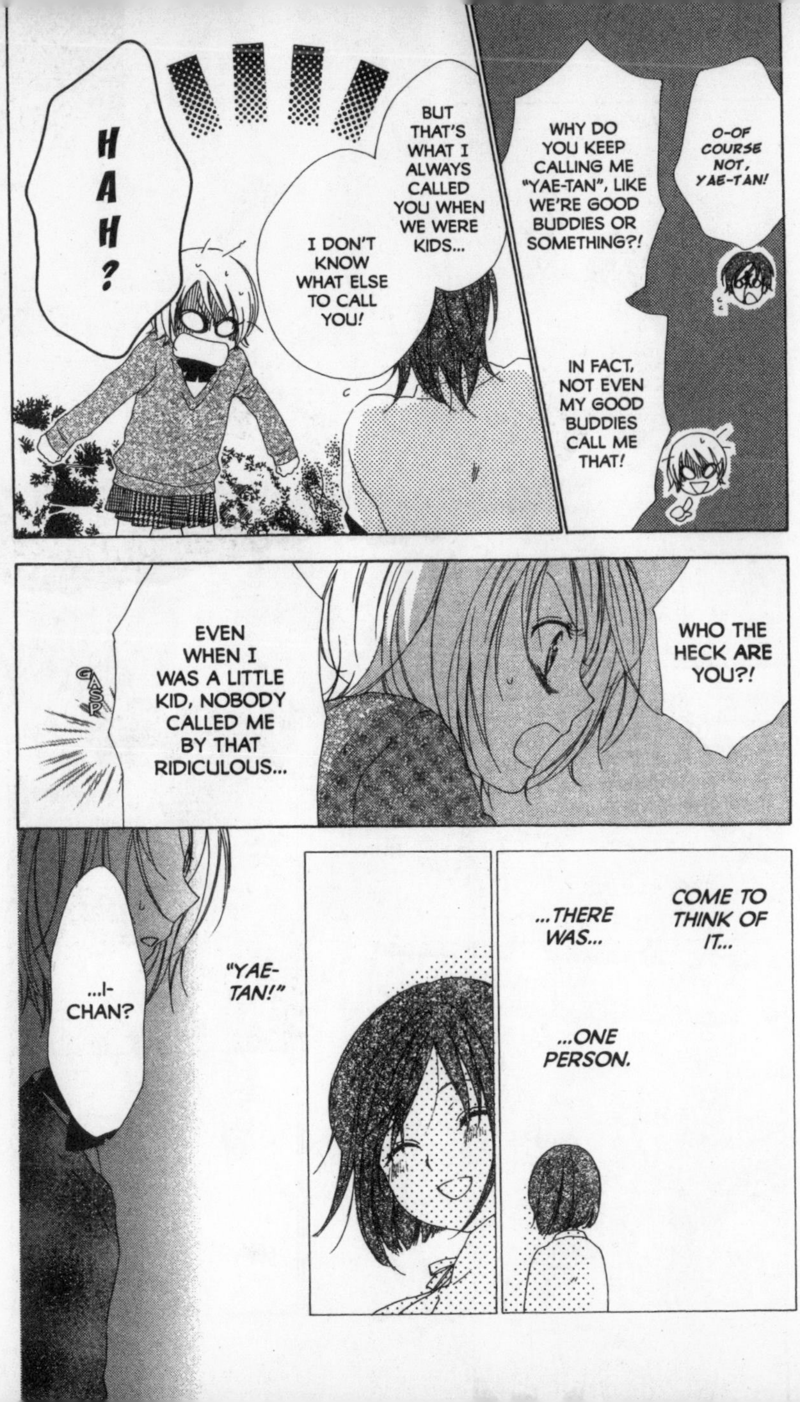
WHY DO YOU KEEP CALLING ME "YAE-TAN", LIKE WE'RE GOOD BUDDIES OR SOMETHING?!
O-OF COURSE NOT, YAE-TAN!
IN FACT, NOT EVEN MY GOOD BUDDIES CALL ME THAT!
BUT THAT'S WHAT I ALWAYS CALLED YOU WHEN WE WERE KIDS...
I DON'T KNOW WHAT ELSE TO CALL YOU!
HAH?
WHO THE HECK ARE YOU?!
EVEN WHEN I WAS A LITTLE KID, NOBODY CALLED ME BY THAT RIDICULOUS...
GASP
COME TO THINK OF IT...
...THERE WAS...
...ONE PERSON.
"YAE-TAN!"
...I-CHAN?

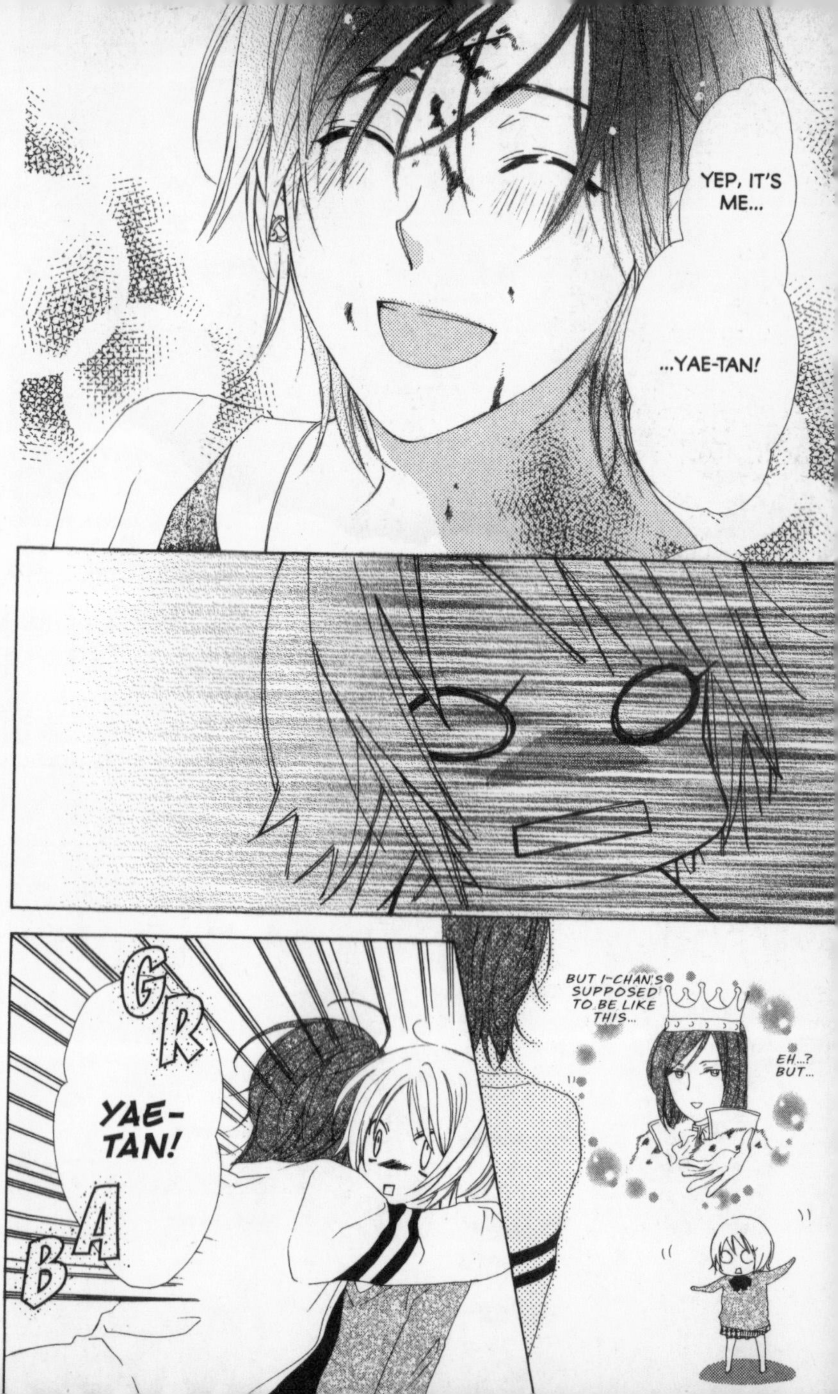
YEP, IT'S ME...
...YAE-TAN!
BUT I-CHAN'S SUPPOSED TO BE LIKE THIS...
EH...? BUT...
GRAB
YAE-TAN!

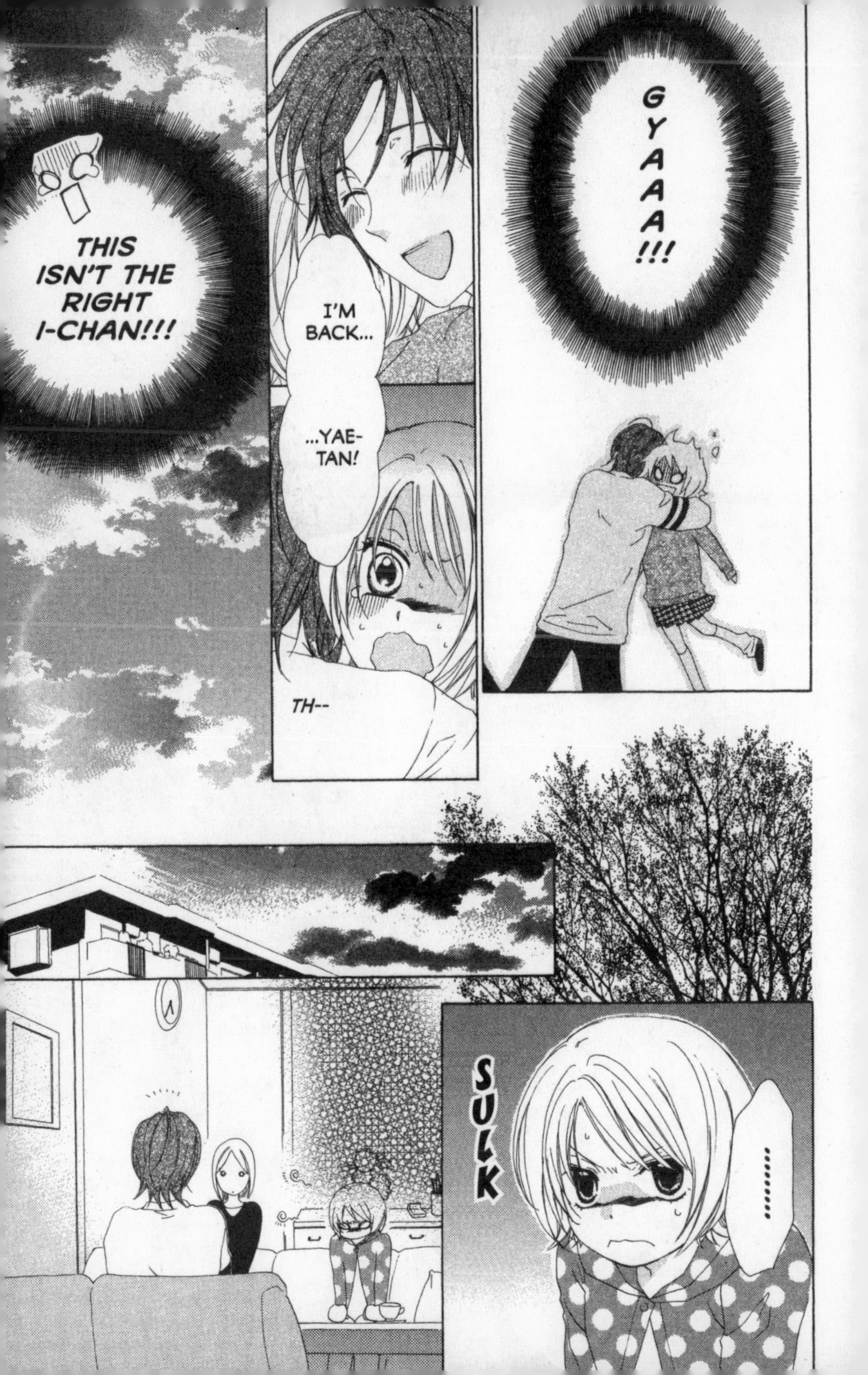
GYAAA!!!
I'M BACK...
...YAE-TAN!
TH--
THIS ISN'T THE RIGHT I-CHAN!!!
SULK
....

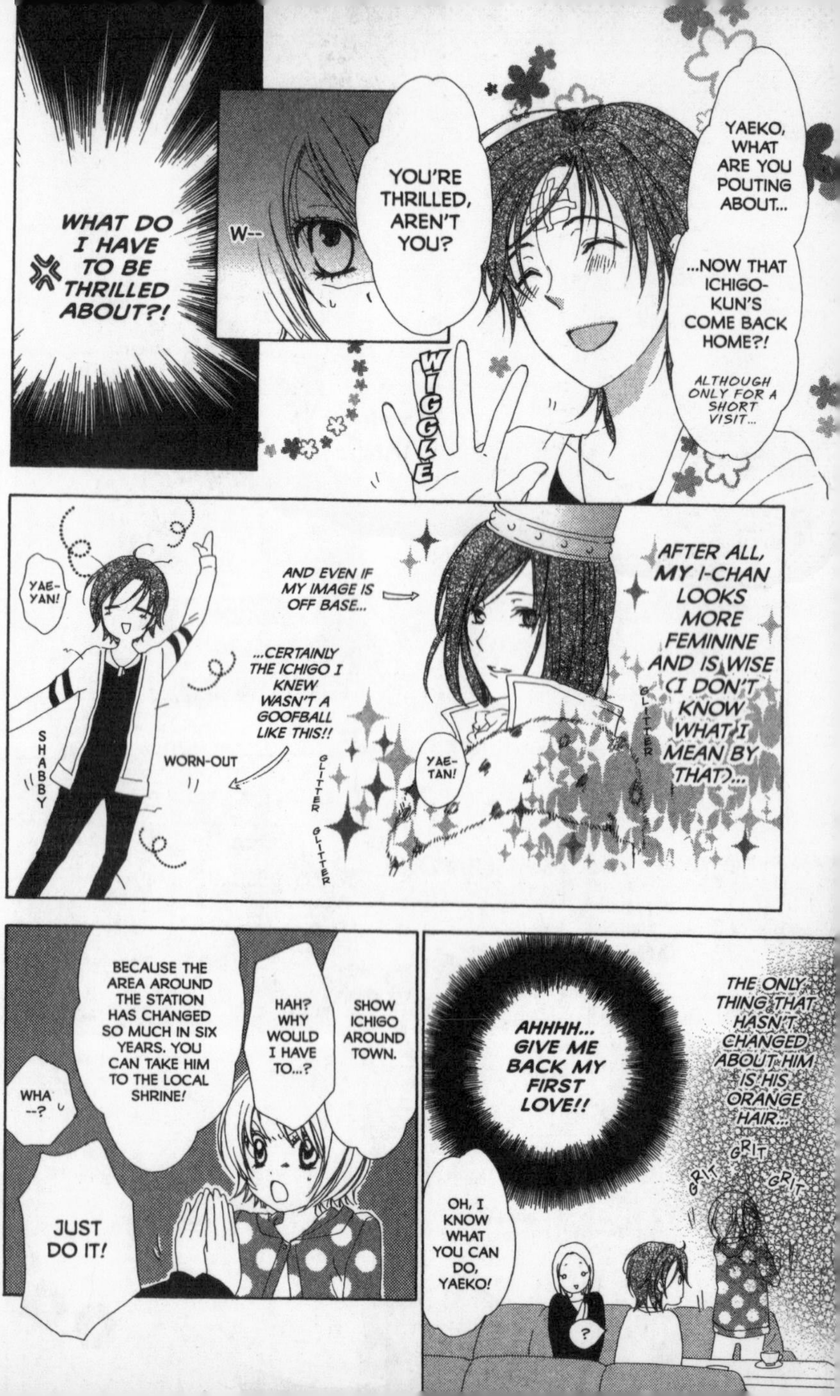

YAEKO, WHAT ARE YOU POUTING ABOUT...
...NOW THAT ICHIGO-KUN'S COME BACK HOME?!
ALTHOUGH ONLY FOR A SHORT VISIT...
YOU'RE THRILLED, AREN'T YOU?
WIGGLE
W--
WHAT DO I HAVE TO BE THRILLED ABOUT?!
AFTER ALL, MY I-CHAN LOOKS MORE FEMININE AND IS WISE (I DON'T KNOW WHAT I MEAN BY THAT)...
GLITTER
YAE-TAN!
AND EVEN IF MY IMAGE IS OFF BASE...
...CERTAINLY THE ICHIGO I KNEW WASN'T A GOOFBALL LIKE THIS!!
GLITTER GLITTER
WORN-OUT
YAE-YAN!
SHABBY
THE ONLY THING THAT HASN'T CHANGED ABOUT HIM IS HIS ORANGE HAIR...
AHHHH... GIVE ME BACK MY FIRST LOVE!!
GRIT GRIT GRIT
OH, I KNOW WHAT YOU CAN DO, YAEKO!
?
SHOW ICHIGO AROUND TOWN.
HAH? WHY WOULD I HAVE TO...?
BECAUSE THE AREA AROUND THE STATION HAS CHANGED SO MUCH IN SIX YEARS. YOU CAN TAKE HIM TO THE LOCAL SHRINE!
WHA--?
JUST DO IT!

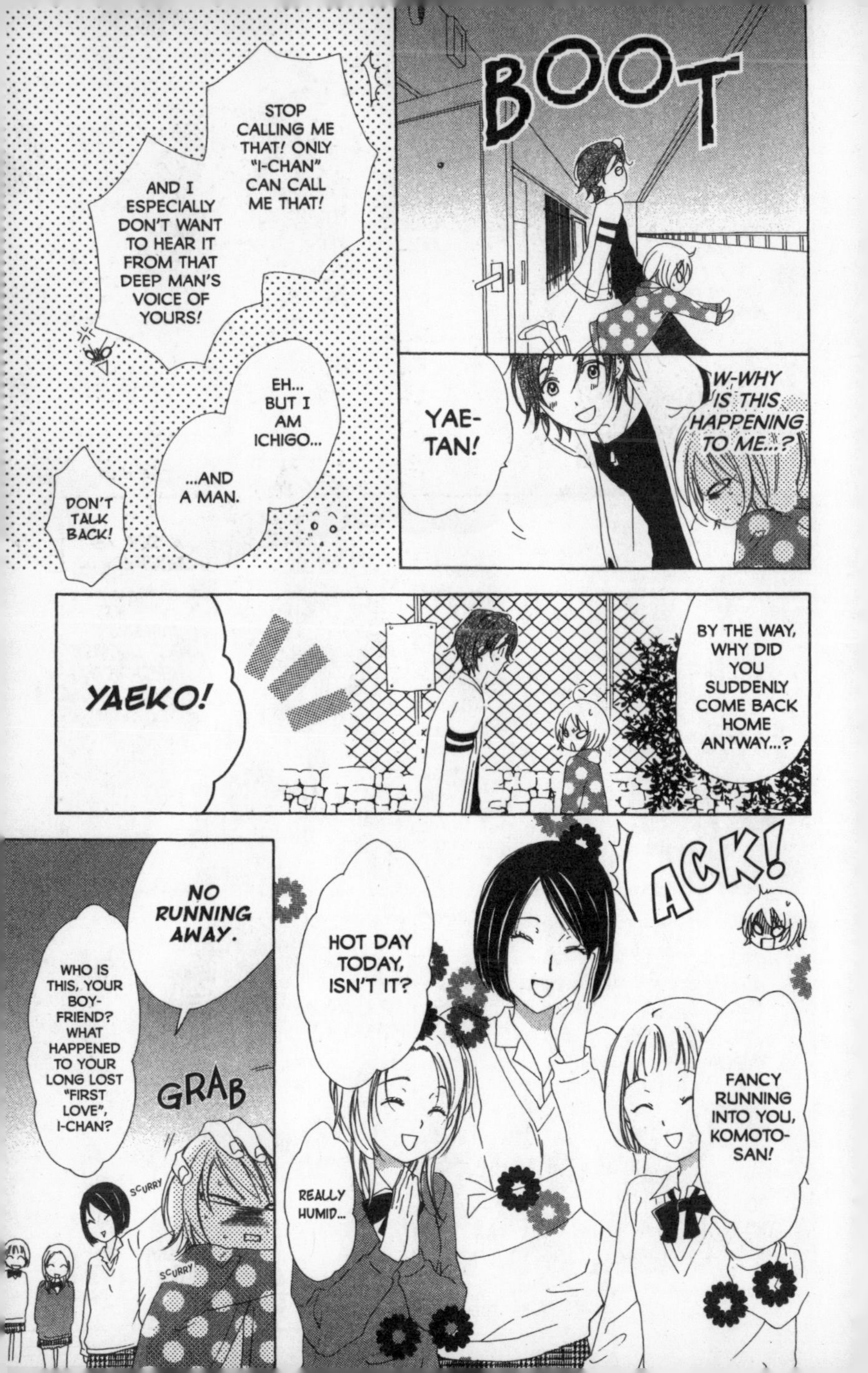
BOOT
W-WHY IS THIS HAPPENING TO ME...?
YAE-TAN!
STOP CALLING ME THAT! ONLY "I-CHAN" CAN CALL ME THAT!
AND I ESPECIALLY DON'T WANT TO HEAR IT FROM THAT DEEP MAN'S VOICE OF YOURS!
EH... BUT I AM ICHIGO...
...AND A MAN.
DON'T TALK BACK!
BY THE WAY, WHY DID YOU SUDDENLY COME BACK HOME ANYWAY...?
YAEKO!
ACK!
FANCY RUNNING INTO YOU, KOMOTO-SAN!
HOT DAY TODAY, ISN'T IT?
REALLY HUMID...
NO RUNNING AWAY.
WHO IS THIS, YOUR BOY-FRIEND? WHAT HAPPENED TO YOUR LONG LOST "FIRST LOVE", I-CHAN?
GRAB
SCURRY
SCURRY

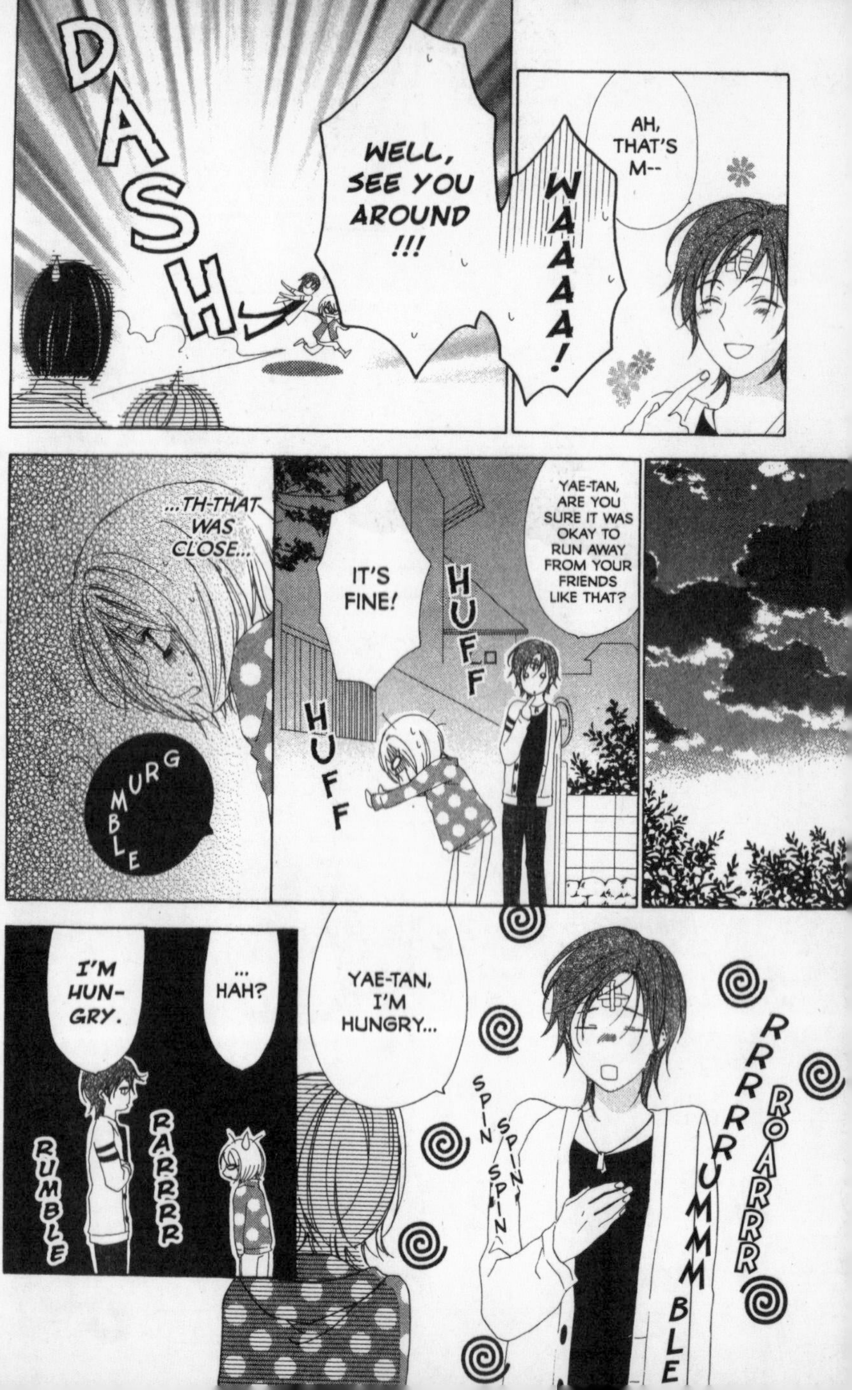
AH, THAT'S M--
WAAAA!
WELL, SEE YOU AROUND!!!
DASH
YAE-TAN, ARE YOU SURE IT WAS OKAY TO RUN AWAY FROM YOUR FRIENDS LIKE THAT?
HUFF
IT'S FINE!
HUFF
...TH-THAT WAS CLOSE...
MURGBLE
RRRRRRUMMMBLE
ROARRRR
SPIN
SPIN
SPIN
YAE-TAN, I'M HUNGRY...
...HAH?
I'M HUNGRY.
RARRRR
RUMBLE

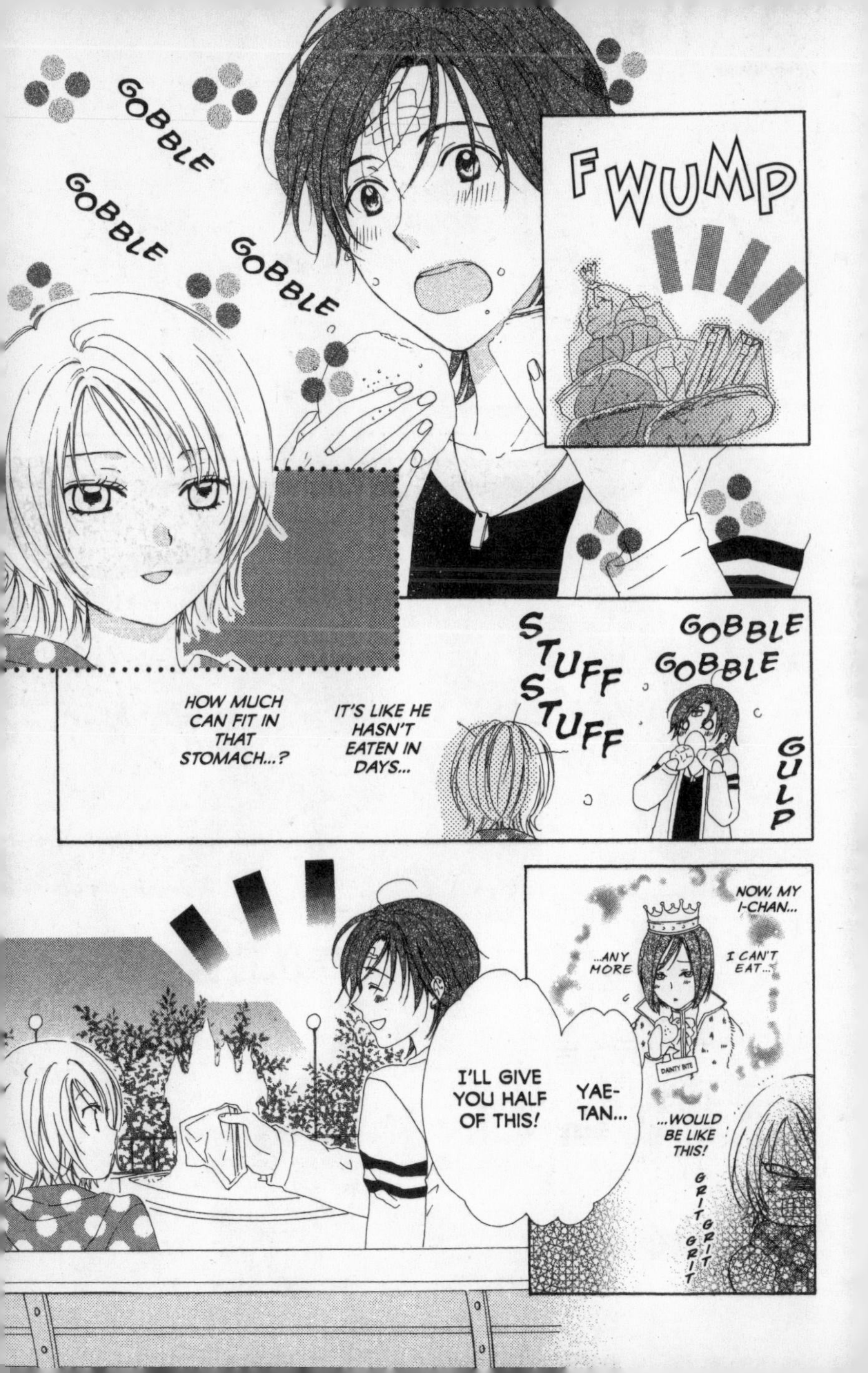
FWUMP
GOBBLE GOBBLE GOBBLE
GOBBLE GOBBLE
GOBBLE
GULP
STUFF STUFF
IT'S LIKE HE HASN'T EATEN IN DAYS...
HOW MUCH CAN FIT IN THAT STOMACH...?
NOW, MY I-CHAN...
I CAN'T EAT...
...ANY MORE
...WOULD BE LIKE THIS!
GRIT GRIT GRIT
DAINTY BITE
YAE-TAN...
I'LL GIVE YOU HALF OF THIS!

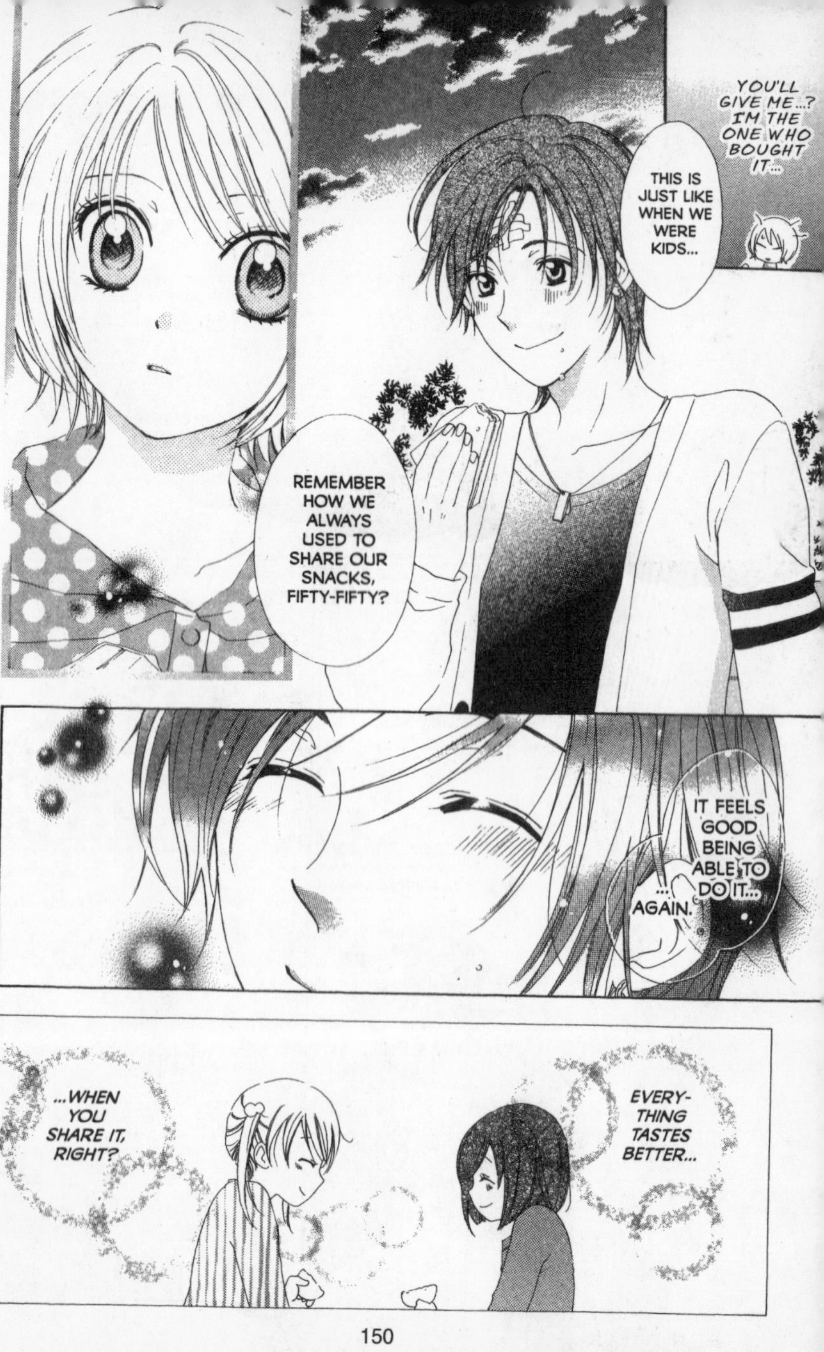
YOU'LL GIVE ME...? I'M THE ONE WHO BOUGHT IT...
THIS IS JUST LIKE WHEN WE WERE KIDS...
REMEMBER HOW WE ALWAYS USED TO SHARE OUR SNACKS, FIFTY-FIFTY?
IT FEELS GOOD BEING ABLE TO DO IT...
...AGAIN.
EVERY-THING TASTES BETTER...
...WHEN YOU SHARE IT, RIGHT?

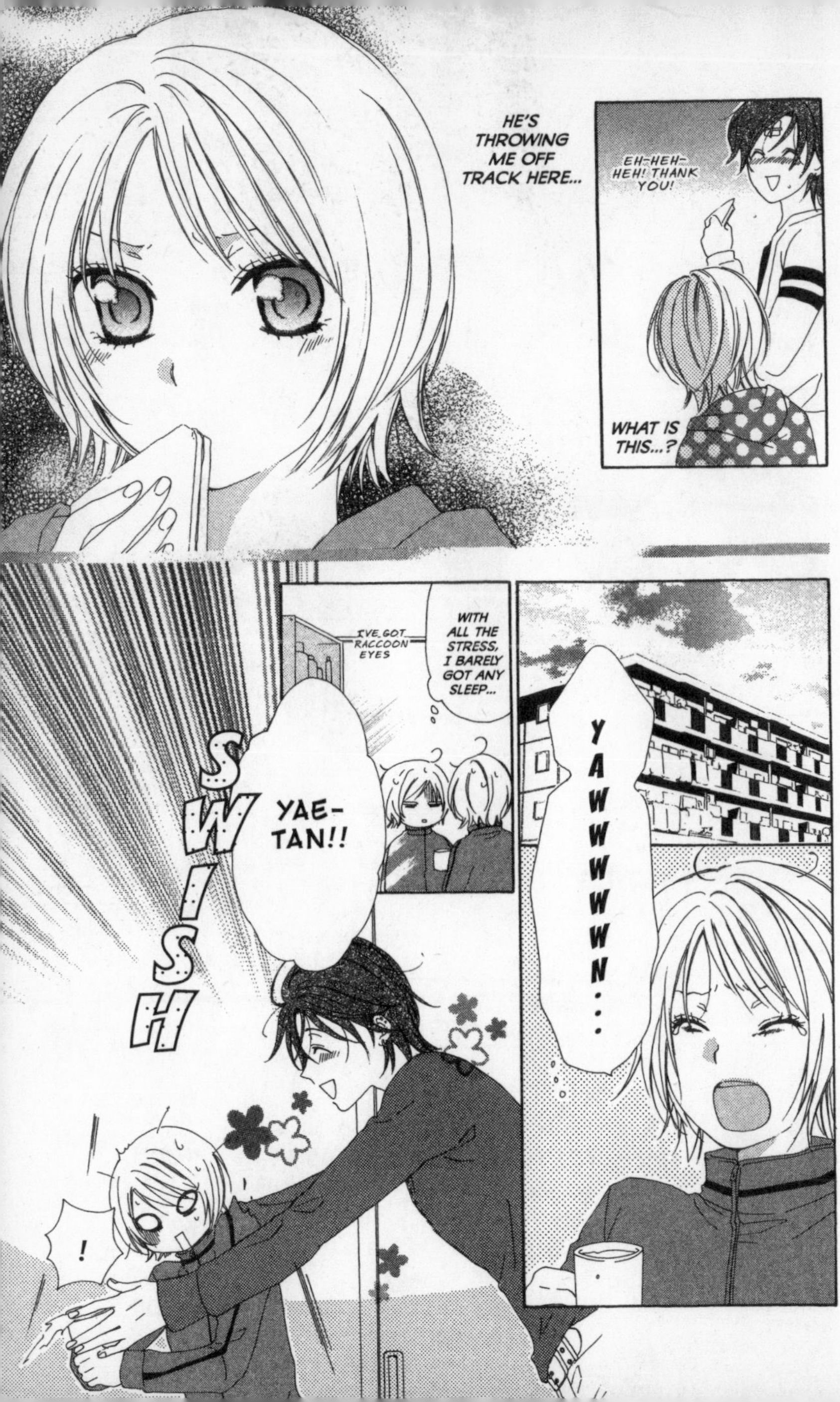
EH-HEH-HEH! THANK YOU!
WHAT IS THIS...?
HE'S THROWING ME OFF TRACK HERE...
YAWWWWWWN...
WITH ALL THE STRESS, I BARELY GOT ANY SLEEP...
I'VE GOT RACCOON EYES
YAE-TAN!!
SWISH
!

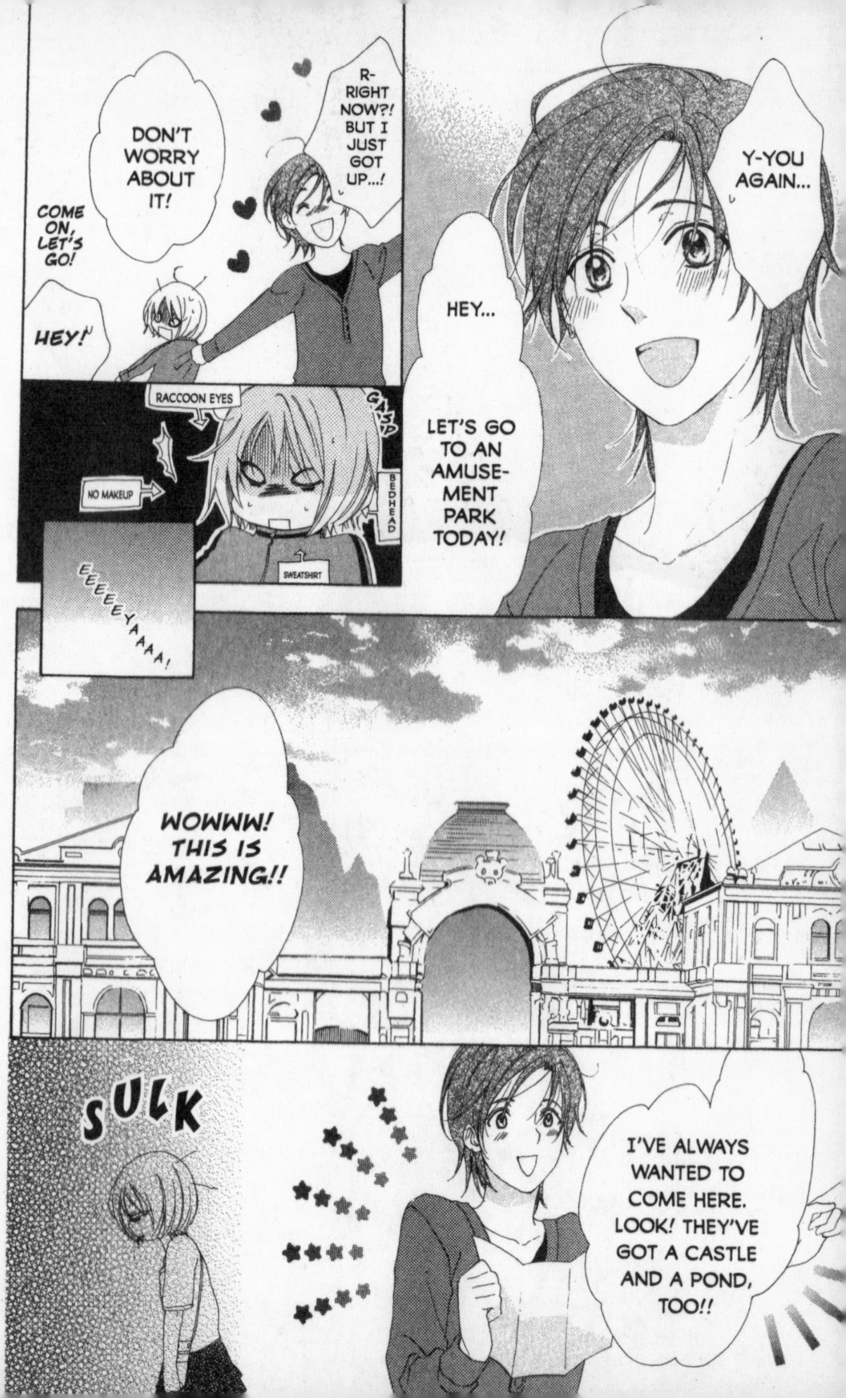
Y-YOU AGAIN...
HEY...
LET'S GO TO AN AMUSEMENT PARK TODAY!
R-RIGHT NOW?! BUT I JUST GOT UP...!
DON'T WORRY ABOUT IT!
COME ON, LET'S GO!
HEY!
GASP
RACCOON EYES
BEDHEAD
NO MAKEUP
SWEATSHIRT
EEEEEYAAAA!
WOWWW! THIS IS AMAZING!!
I'VE ALWAYS WANTED TO COME HERE. LOOK! THEY'VE GOT A CASTLE AND A POND, TOO!!
SULK

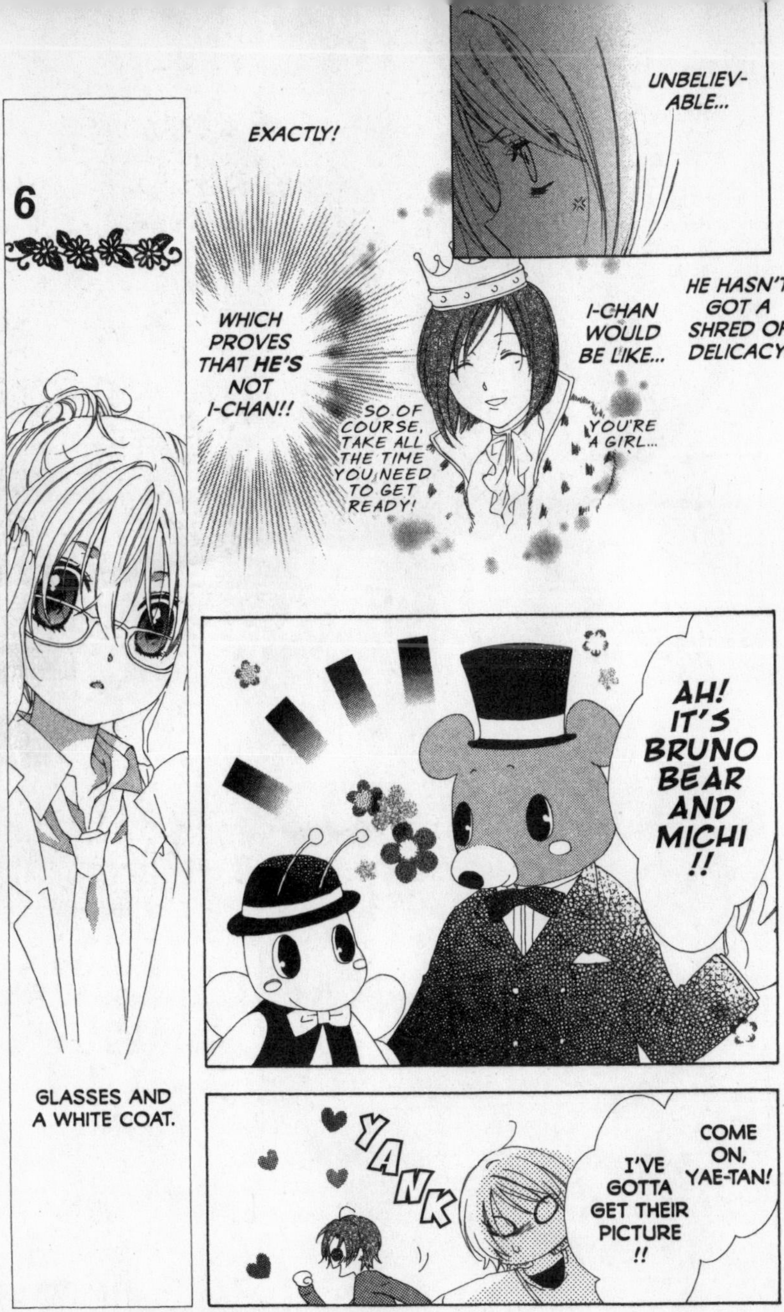
UNBELIEVABLE...
HE HASN'T GOT A SHRED OF DELICACY.
I-CHAN WOULD BE LIKE...
YOU'RE A GIRL...
SO OF COURSE, TAKE ALL THE TIME YOU NEED TO GET READY!
EXACTLY!
WHICH PROVES THAT HE'S NOT I-CHAN!!
AH! IT'S BRUNO BEAR AND MICHI!!
YANK
COME ON, YAE-TAN!
I'VE GOTTA GET THEIR PICTURE!!
6
GLASSES AND A WHITE COAT.

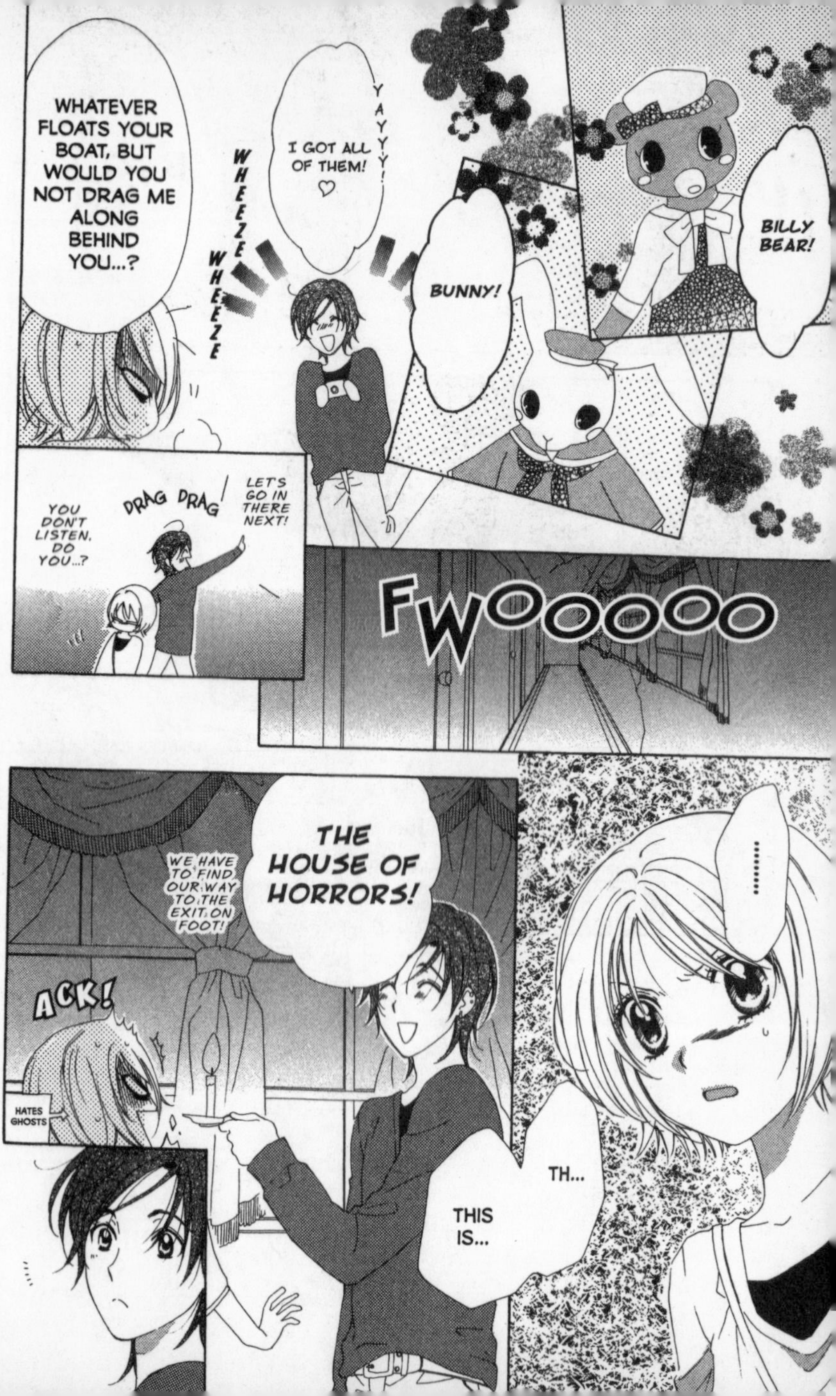
BILLY BEAR!
BUNNY!
I GOT ALL OF THEM! ♡
YAYYYY!
WHEEZE WHEEZE
WHATEVER FLOATS YOUR BOAT, BUT WOULD YOU NOT DRAG ME ALONG BEHIND YOU...?
FWOOOOOO
LET'S GO IN THERE NEXT!
DRAG DRAG
YOU DON'T LISTEN, DO YOU...?
....
TH...
THIS IS...
THE HOUSE OF HORRORS!
WE HAVE TO FIND OUR WAY TO THE EXIT ON FOOT!
ACK!
HATES GHOSTS

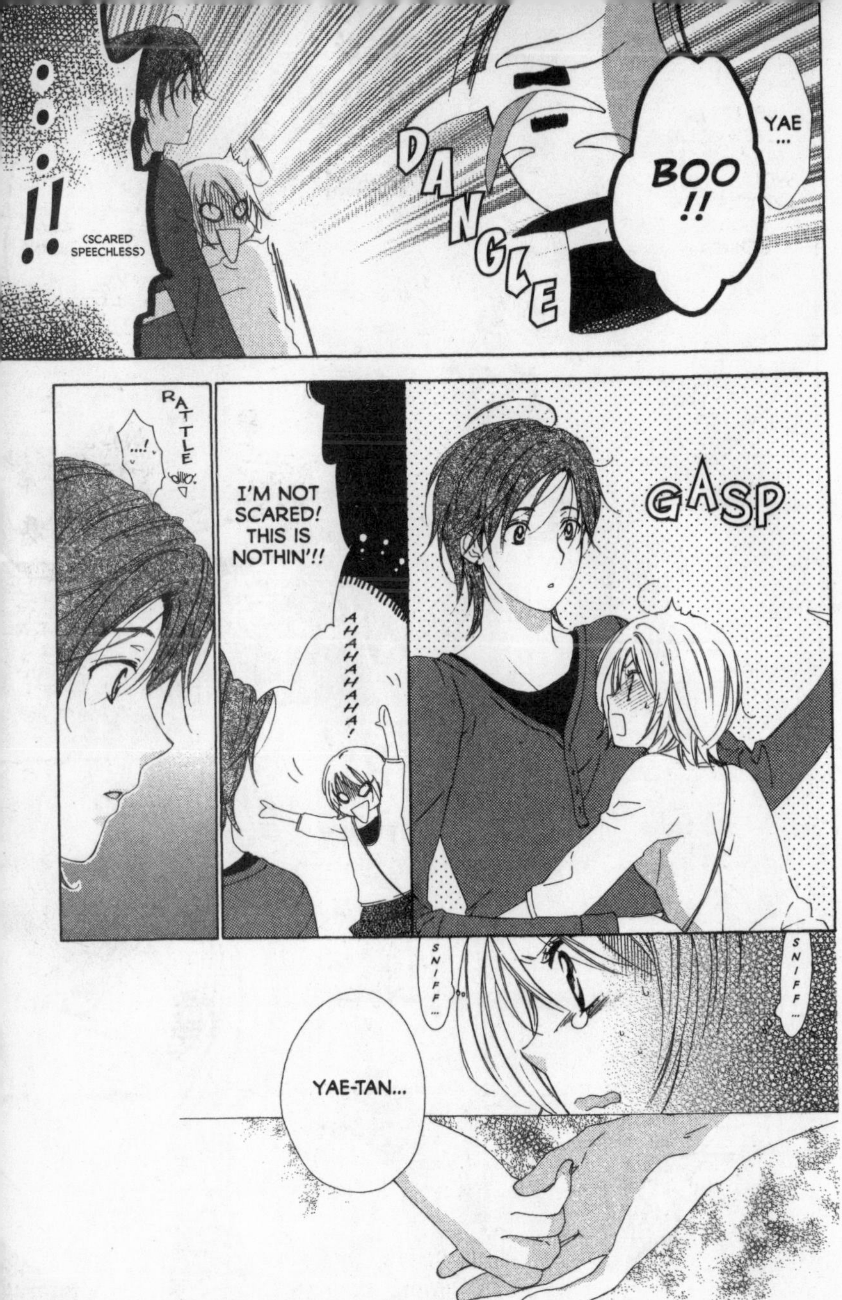
YAE...
BOO!!
DANGLE
....!!
(SCARED SPEECHLESS)
GASP
I'M NOT SCARED! THIS IS NOTHIN'!!
AHAHAHAHAHA!
RATTLE
...!
SNIFF...
SNIFF...
YAE-TAN...

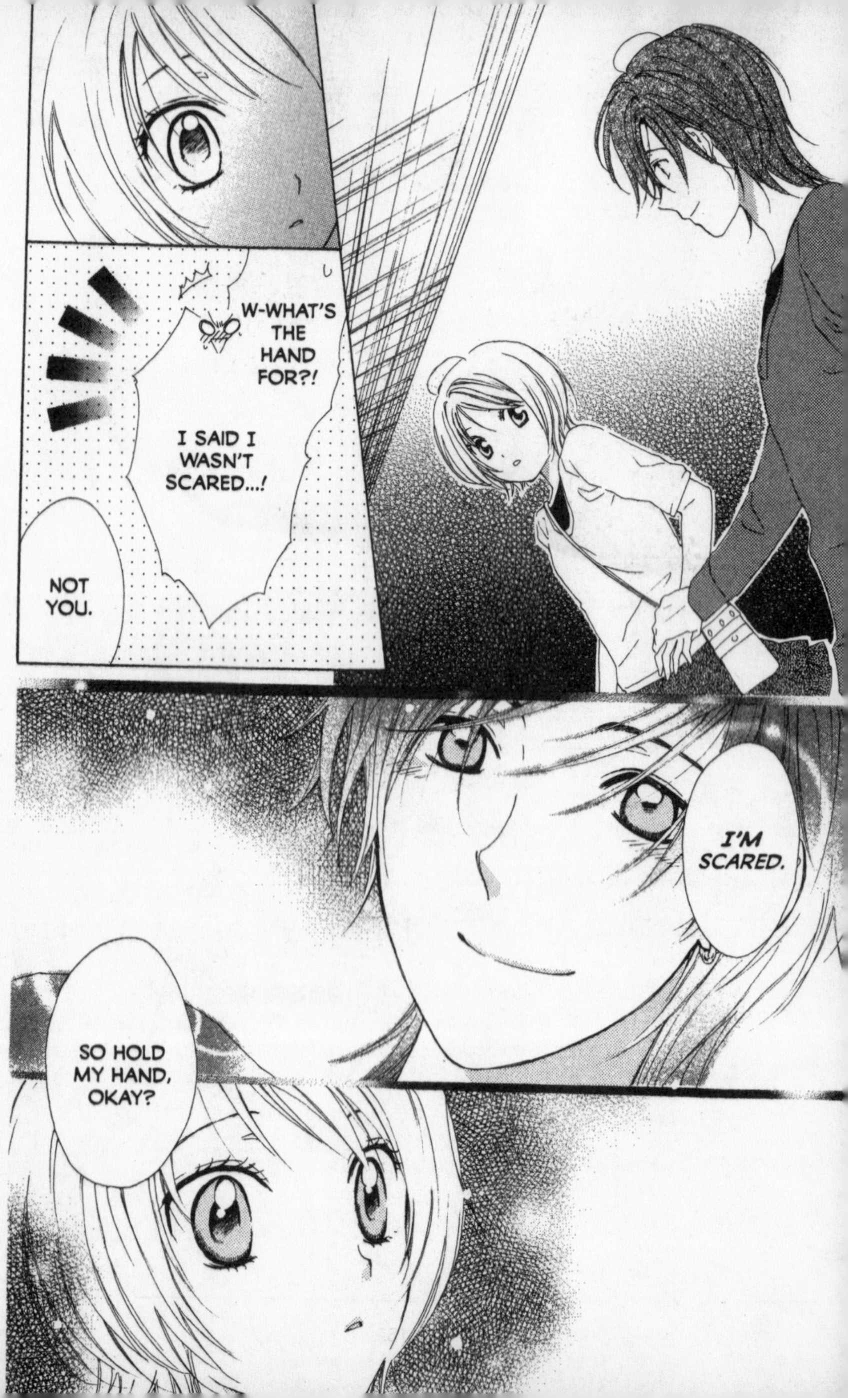
W-WHAT'S THE HAND FOR?!
I SAID I WASN'T SCARED...!
NOT YOU.
I'M SCARED.
SO HOLD MY HAND, OKAY?

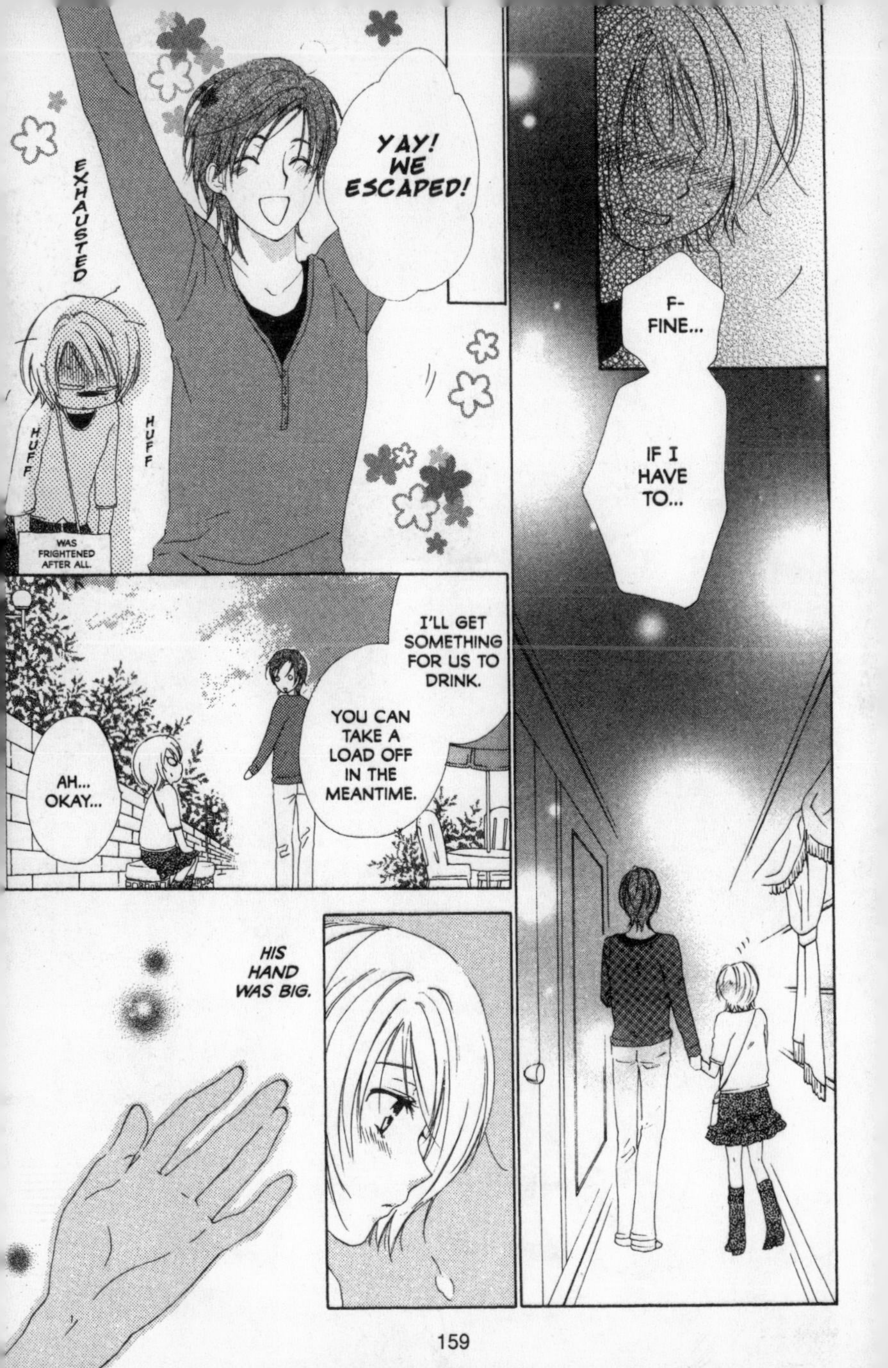
F-FINE...
IF I HAVE TO...
YAY! WE ESCAPED!
EXHAUSTED
HUFF HUFF
WAS FRIGHTENED AFTER ALL.
I'LL GET SOMETHING FOR US TO DRINK.
YOU CAN TAKE A LOAD OFF IN THE MEANTIME.
AH... OKAY...
HIS HAND WAS BIG.

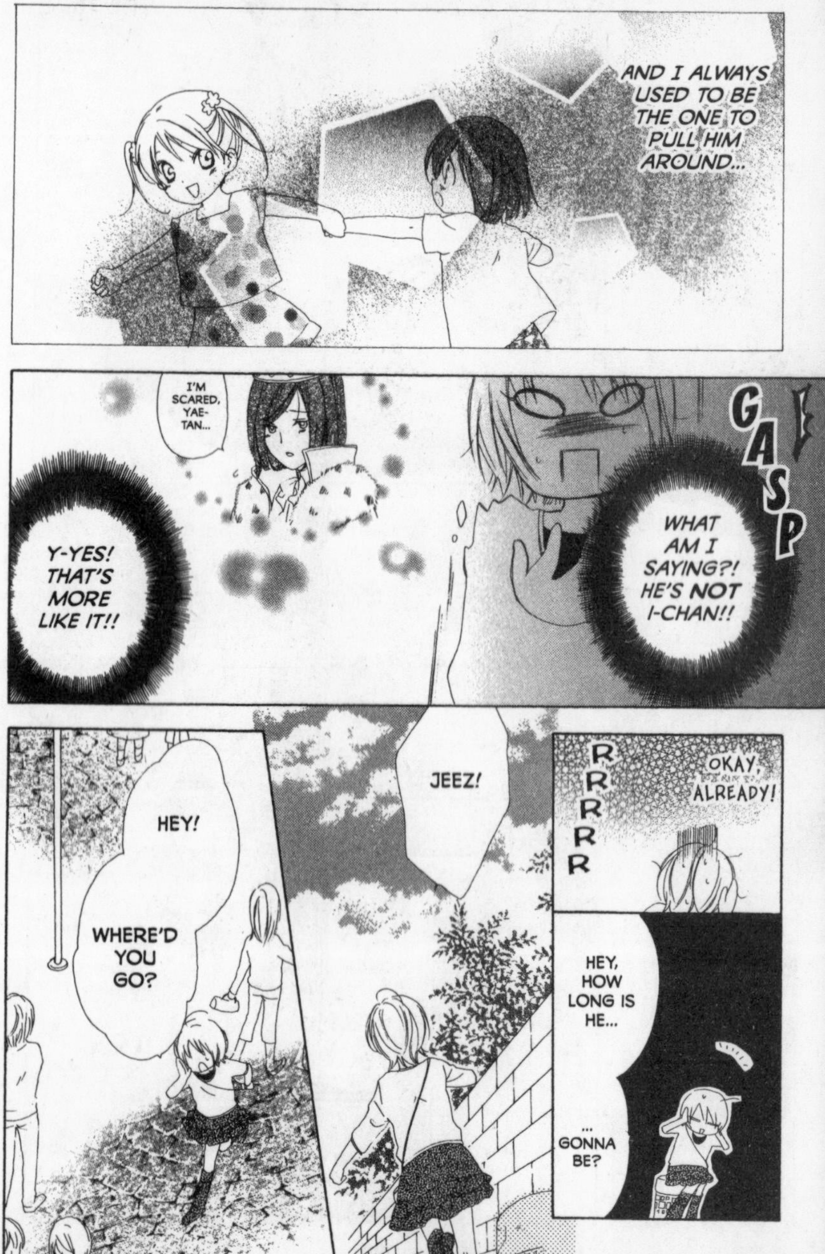
AND I ALWAYS USED TO BE THE ONE TO PULL HIM AROUND...
I'M SCARED, YAE-TAN...
Y-YES! THAT'S MORE LIKE IT!!
GASP
WHAT AM I SAYING?! HE'S NOT I-CHAN!!
OKAY, ALREADY!
RRRRR
HEY, HOW LONG IS HE...
... GONNA BE?
JEEZ!
HEY!
WHERE'D YOU GO?

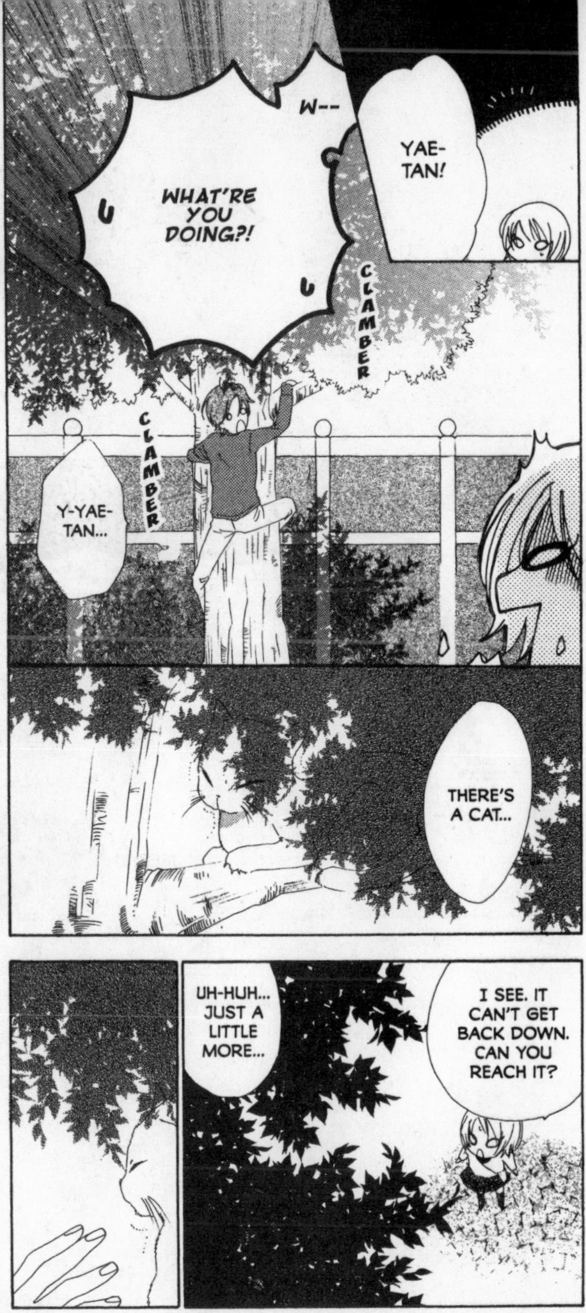
YAE-TAN!
W--
U
WHAT'RE YOU DOING?!
U
CLAMBER
CLAMBER
Y-YAE-TAN...
THERE'S A CAT...
I SEE. IT CAN'T GET BACK DOWN. CAN YOU REACH IT?
UH-HUH... JUST A LITTLE MORE...

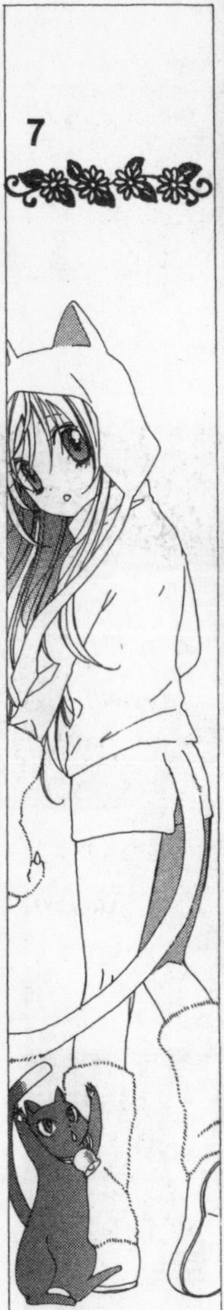
7
WHITE CAT AND BLACK CAT.

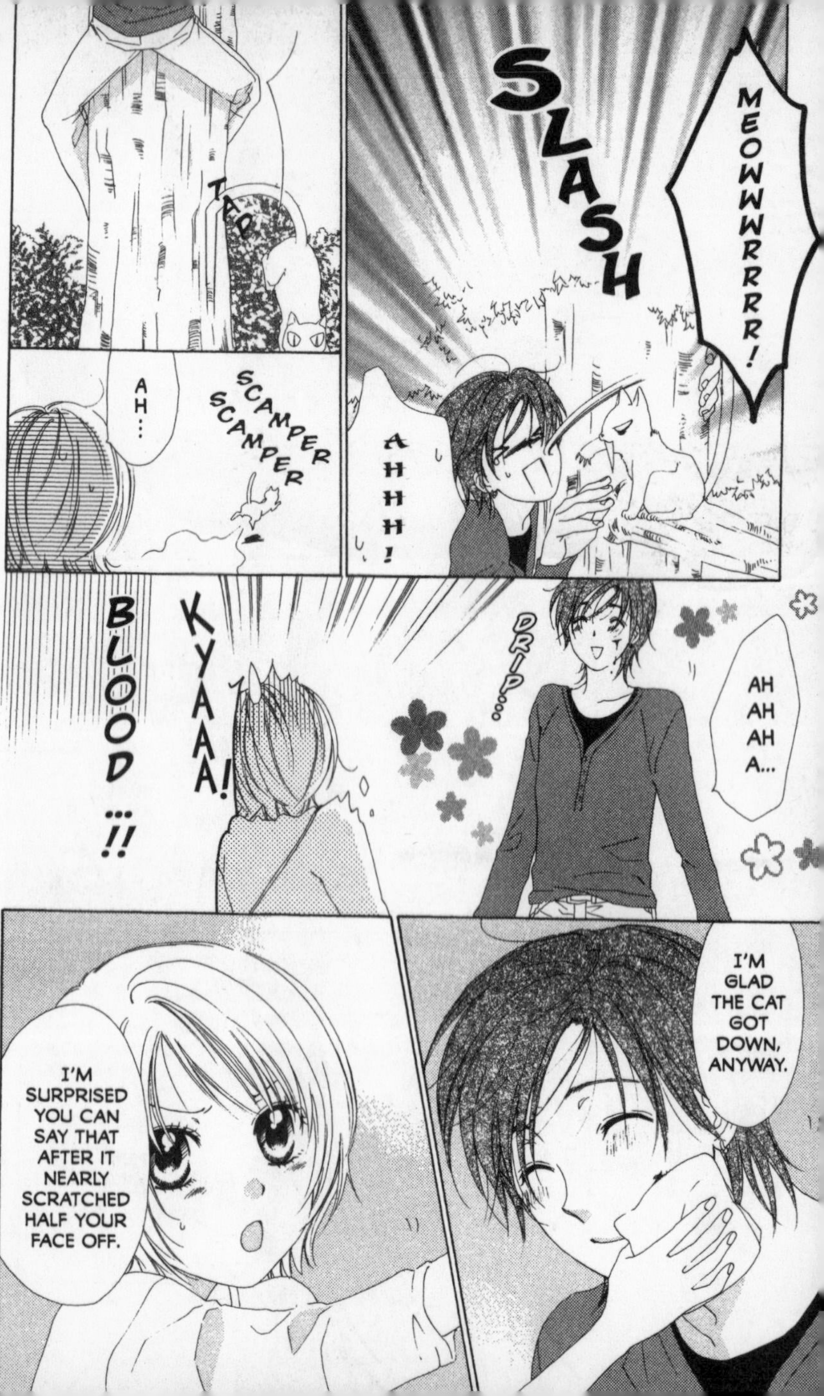
MEOWWWRRRR!
SLASH
AHHHH!
TAP
AH...
SCAMPER SCAMPER
AH AH AH A...
DRIP...
KYAAA!
BLOOD...!!
I'M GLAD THE CAT GOT DOWN, ANYWAY.
I'M SURPRISED YOU CAN SAY THAT AFTER IT NEARLY SCRATCHED HALF YOUR FACE OFF.

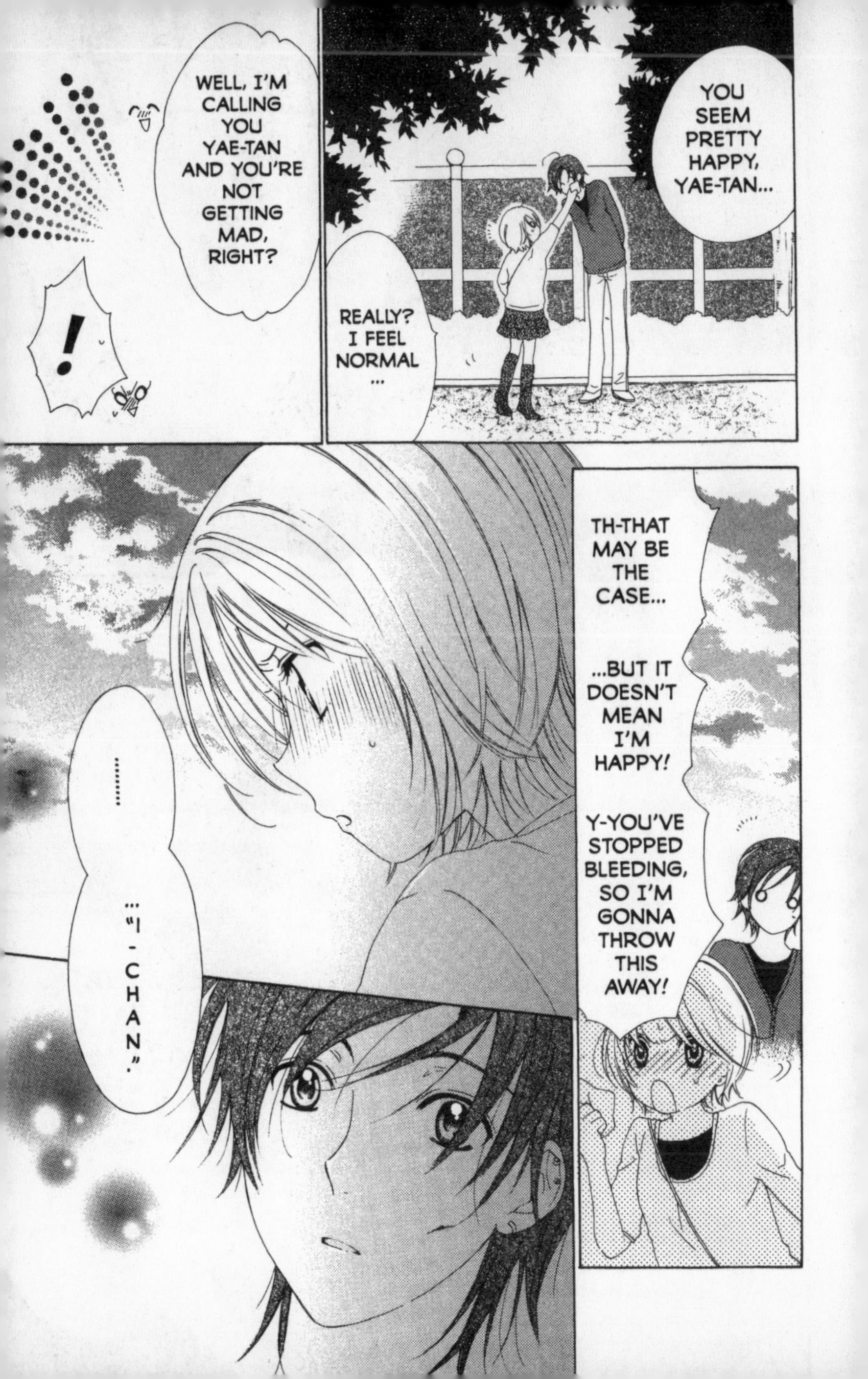
YOU SEEM PRETTY HAPPY, YAE-TAN...
REALLY? I FEEL NORMAL ...
WELL, I'M CALLING YOU YAE-TAN AND YOU'RE NOT GETTING MAD, RIGHT?
!
TH-THAT MAY BE THE CASE...
...BUT IT DOESN'T MEAN I'M HAPPY!
Y-YOU'VE STOPPED BLEEDING, SO I'M GONNA THROW THIS AWAY!
....
...“I-CHAN.”

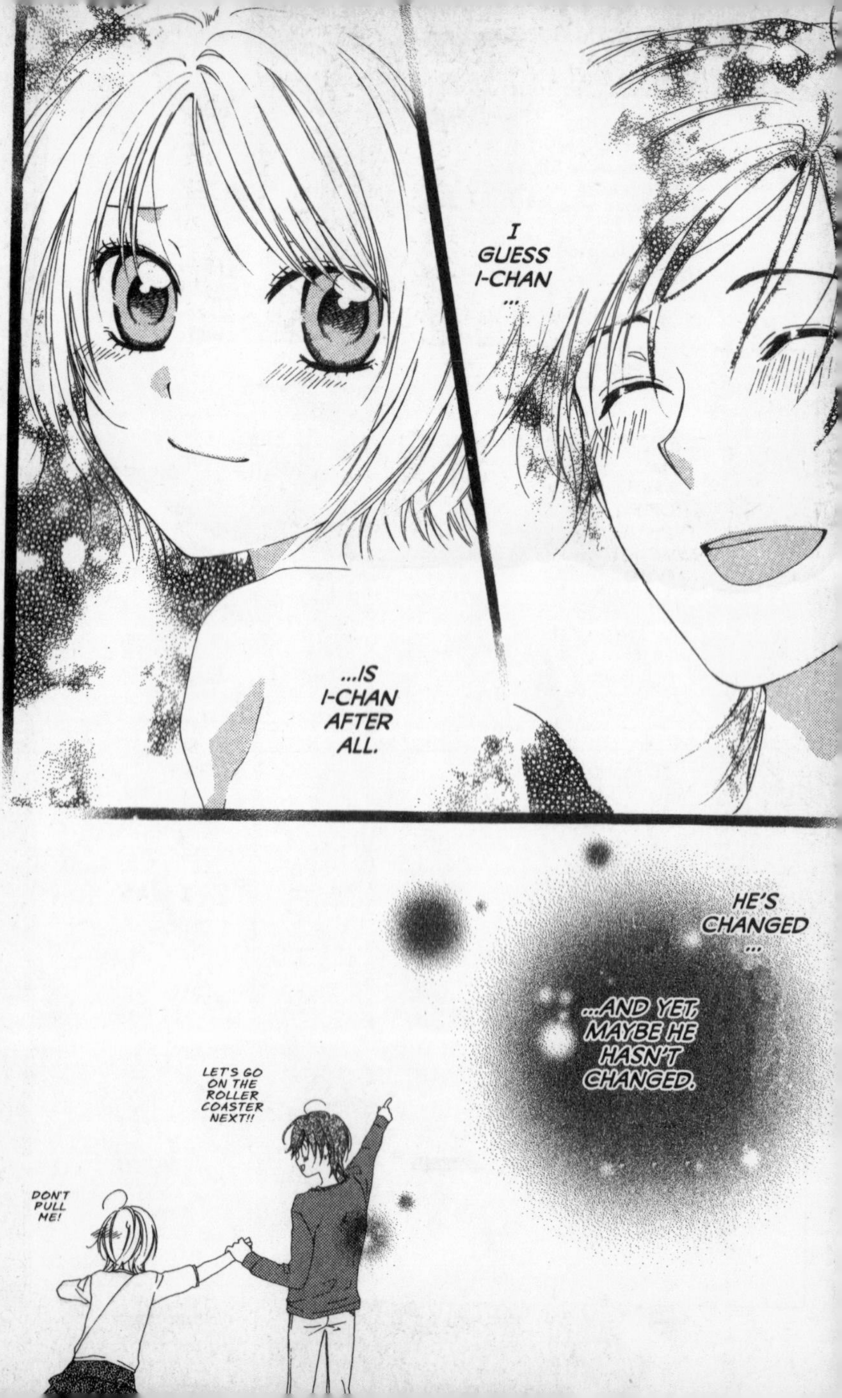
I GUESS I-CHAN ...
...IS I-CHAN AFTER ALL.
HE'S CHANGED ...
...AND YET, MAYBE HE HASN'T CHANGED.
LET'S GO ON THE ROLLER COASTER NEXT!!
DON'T PULL ME!

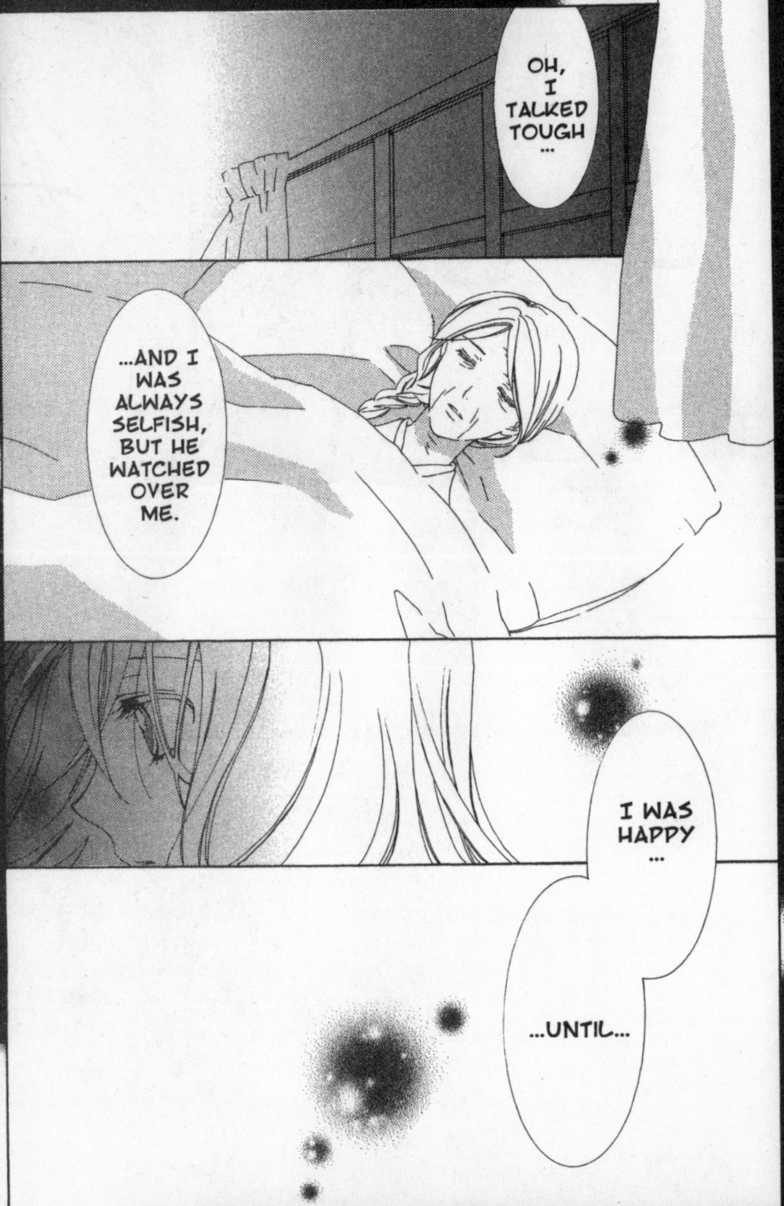
OH, I TALKED TOUGH ...
...AND I WAS ALWAYS SELFISH, BUT HE WATCHED OVER ME.
I WAS HAPPY ...
...UNTIL...

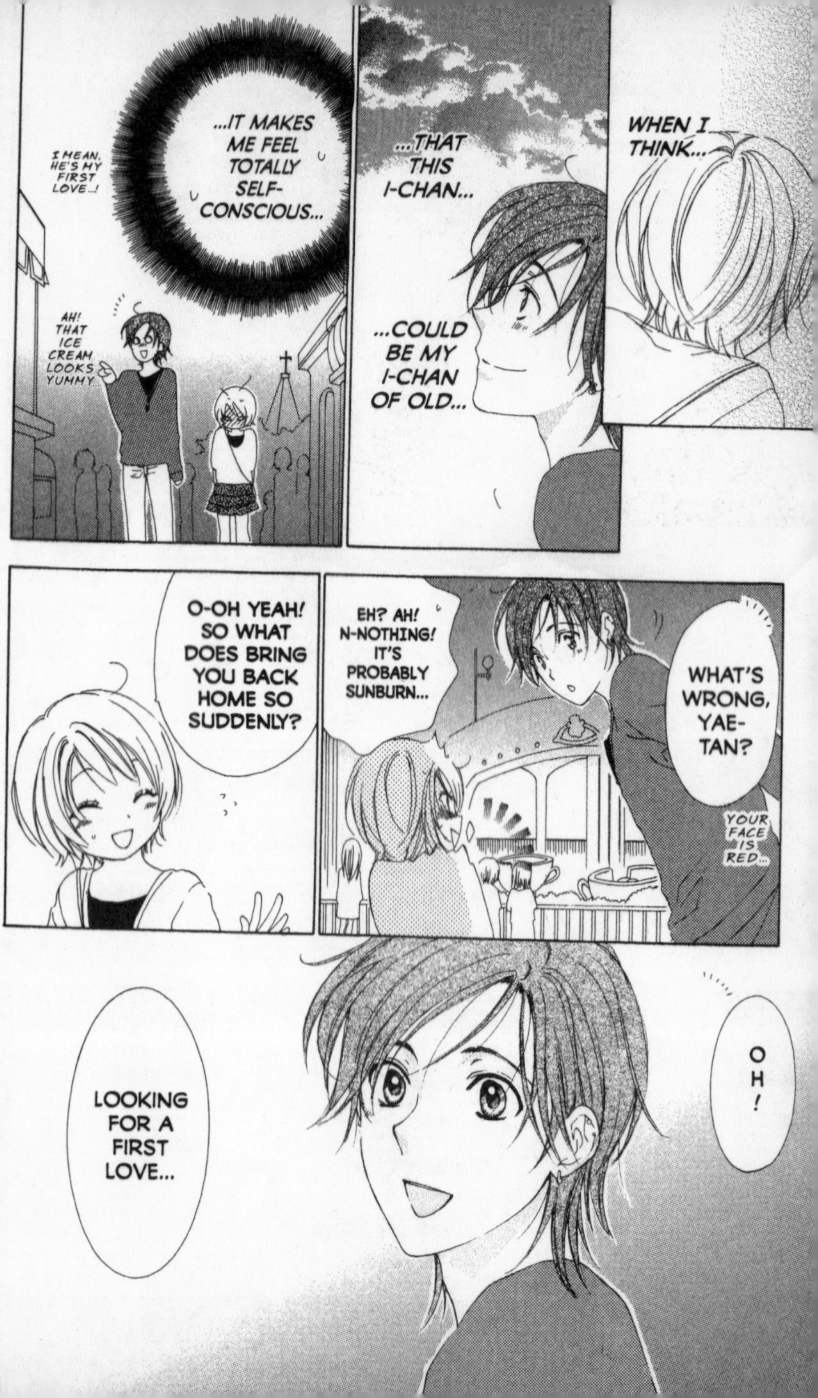
WHEN I THINK...
...THAT THIS I-CHAN...
...COULD BE MY I-CHAN OF OLD...
...IT MAKES ME FEEL TOTALLY SELF-CONSCIOUS...
I MEAN, HE'S MY FIRST LOVE...!
AH! THAT ICE CREAM LOOKS YUMMY...
WHAT'S WRONG, YAE-TAN?
YOUR FACE IS RED...
EH? AH! N-NOTHING! IT'S PROBABLY SUNBURN...
O-OH YEAH! SO WHAT DOES BRING YOU BACK HOME SO SUDDENLY?
OH!
LOOKING FOR A FIRST LOVE...

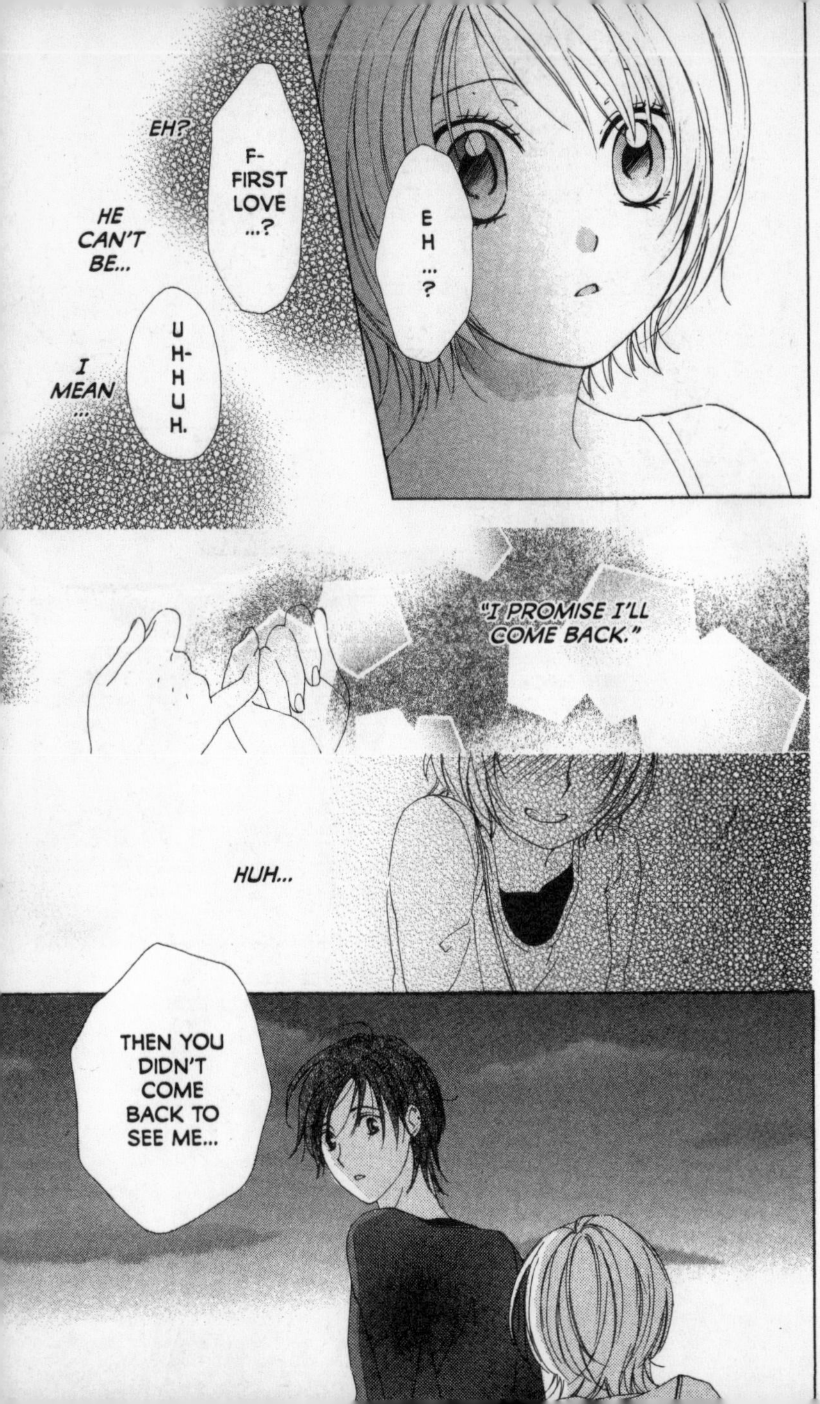
EH ...?
F-FIRST LOVE ...?
EH?
HE CAN'T BE...
UH-HUH.
I MEAN ...
"I PROMISE I'LL COME BACK."
HUH...
THEN YOU DIDN'T COME BACK TO SEE ME...

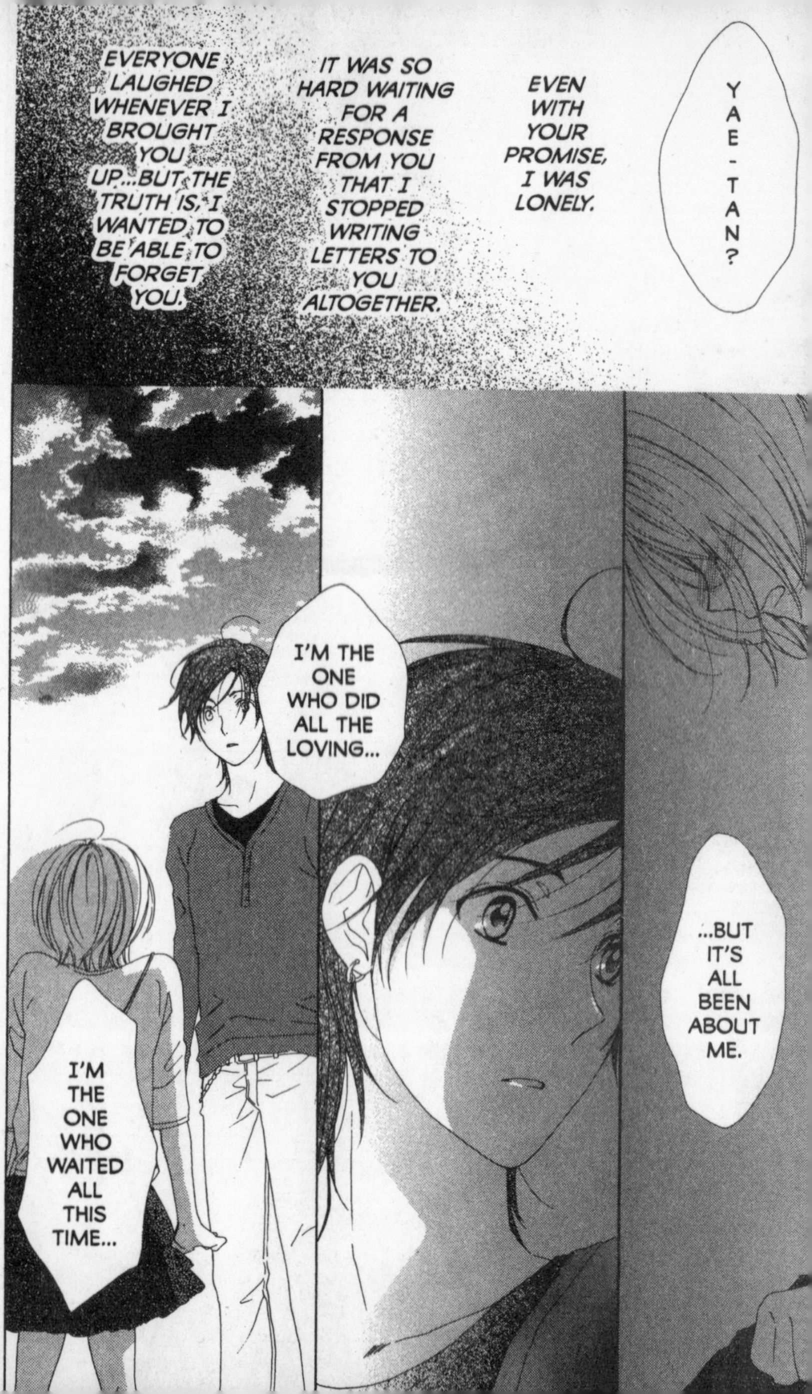
YAE-TAN?
EVEN WITH YOUR PROMISE, I WAS LONELY.
IT WAS SO HARD WAITING FOR A RESPONSE FROM YOU THAT I STOPPED WRITING LETTERS TO YOU ALTOGETHER.
EVERYONE LAUGHED WHENEVER I BROUGHT YOU UP...BUT THE TRUTH IS, I WANTED TO BE ABLE TO FORGET YOU.
...BUT IT'S ALL BEEN ABOUT ME.
I'M THE ONE WHO DID ALL THE LOVING...
I'M THE ONE WHO WAITED ALL THIS TIME...

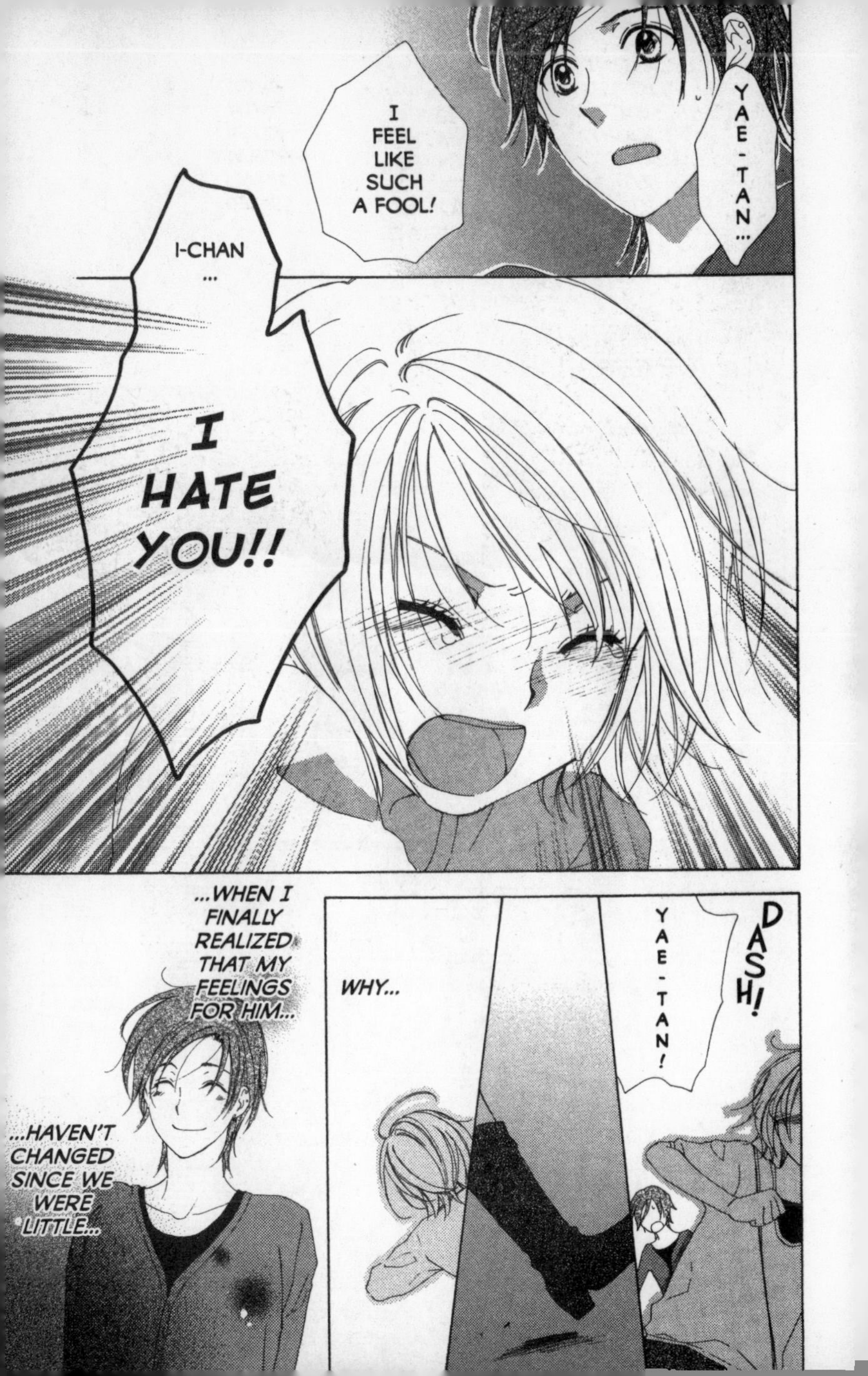
YAE-TAN...
I FEEL LIKE SUCH A FOOL!
I-CHAN ...
I HATE YOU!!
DASH!
YAE-TAN!
WHY...
...WHEN I FINALLY REALIZED THAT MY FEELINGS FOR HIM...
...HAVEN'T CHANGED SINCE WE WERE LITTLE...

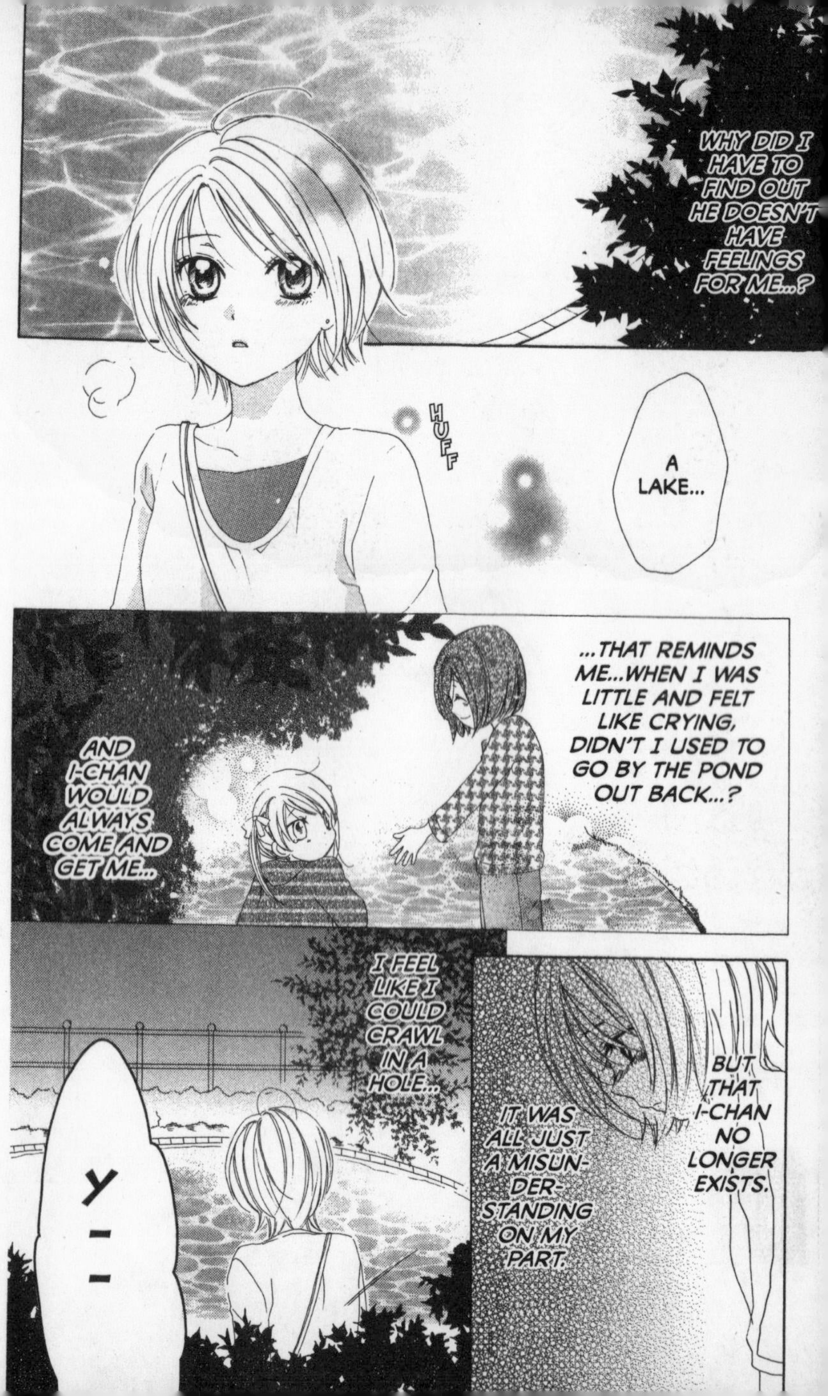
WHY DID I HAVE TO FIND OUT HE DOESN'T HAVE FEELINGS FOR ME...?
A LAKE...
HUFF
...THAT REMINDS ME...WHEN I WAS LITTLE AND FELT LIKE CRYING, DIDN'T I USED TO GO BY THE POND OUT BACK...?
AND I-CHAN WOULD ALWAYS COME AND GET ME...
BUT THAT I-CHAN NO LONGER EXISTS.
IT WAS ALL JUST A MISUNDER-STANDING ON MY PART.
I FEEL LIKE I COULD CRAWL IN A HOLE...
Y--

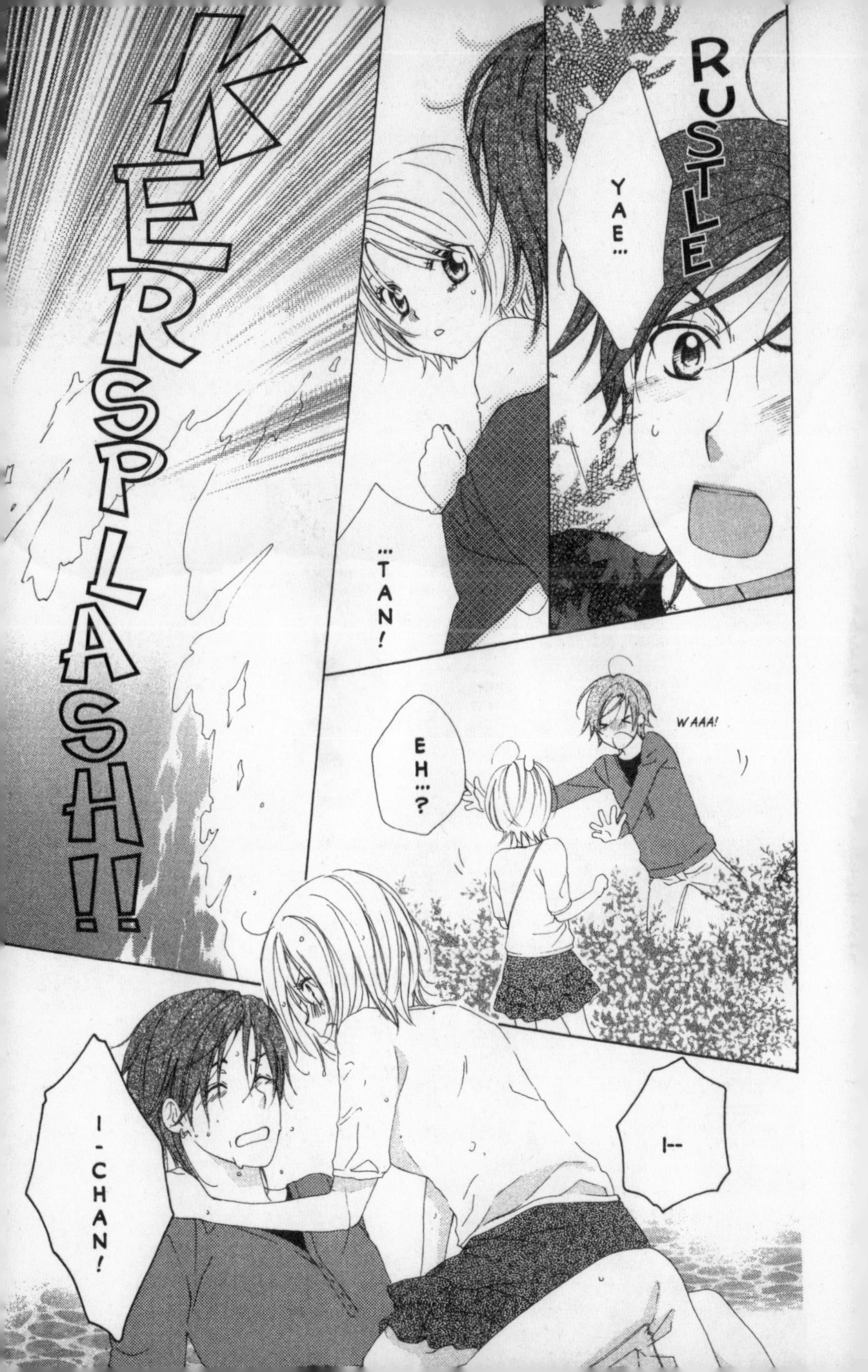
RUSTLE
YAE...
...TAN!
WAAA!
EH...?
KERSPLASH!!
I--
I-CHAN!

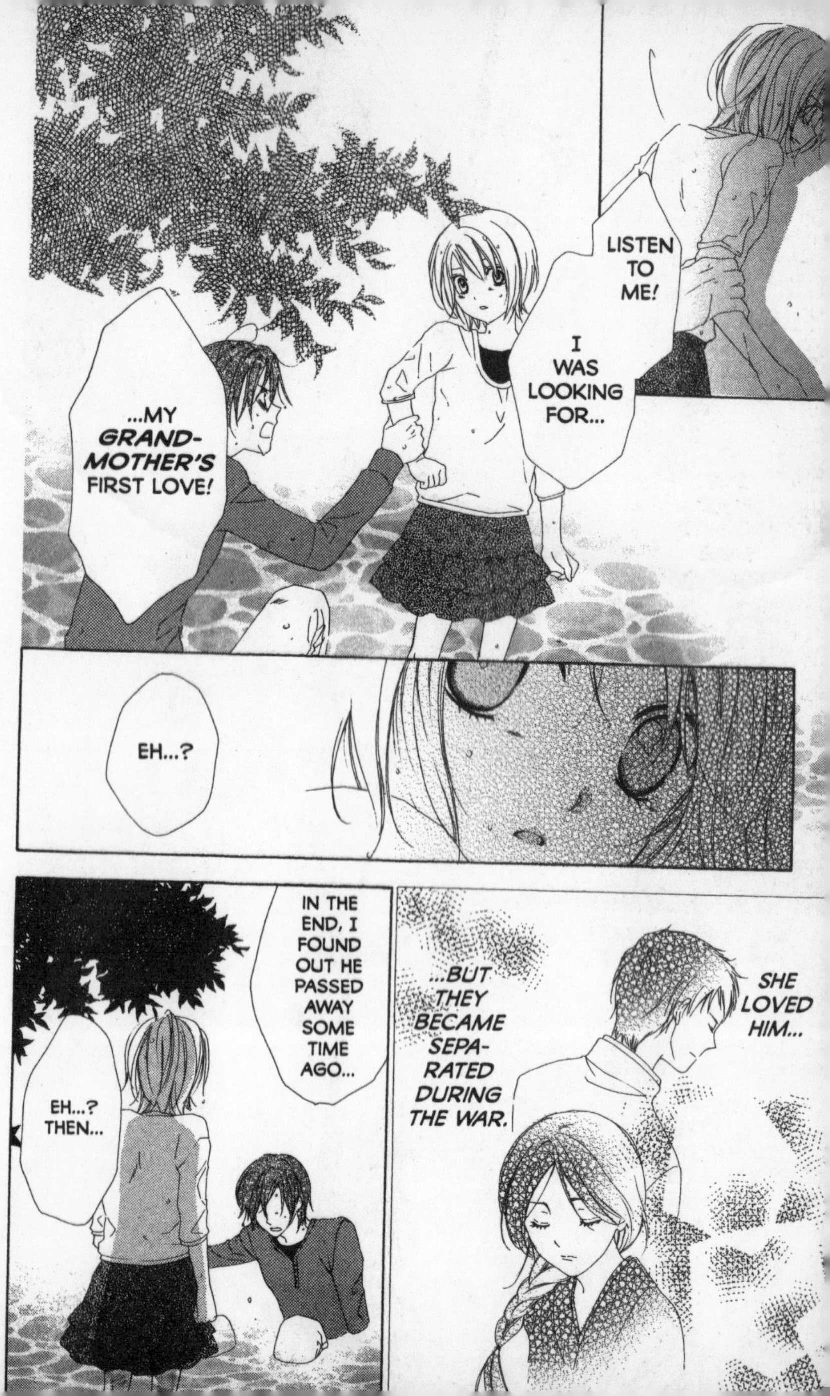
LISTEN TO ME!
I WAS LOOKING FOR...
...MY GRAND-MOTHER'S FIRST LOVE!
EH...?
SHE LOVED HIM...
...BUT THEY BECAME SEPA-RATED DURING THE WAR.
IN THE END, I FOUND OUT HE PASSED AWAY SOME TIME AGO...
EH...? THEN...

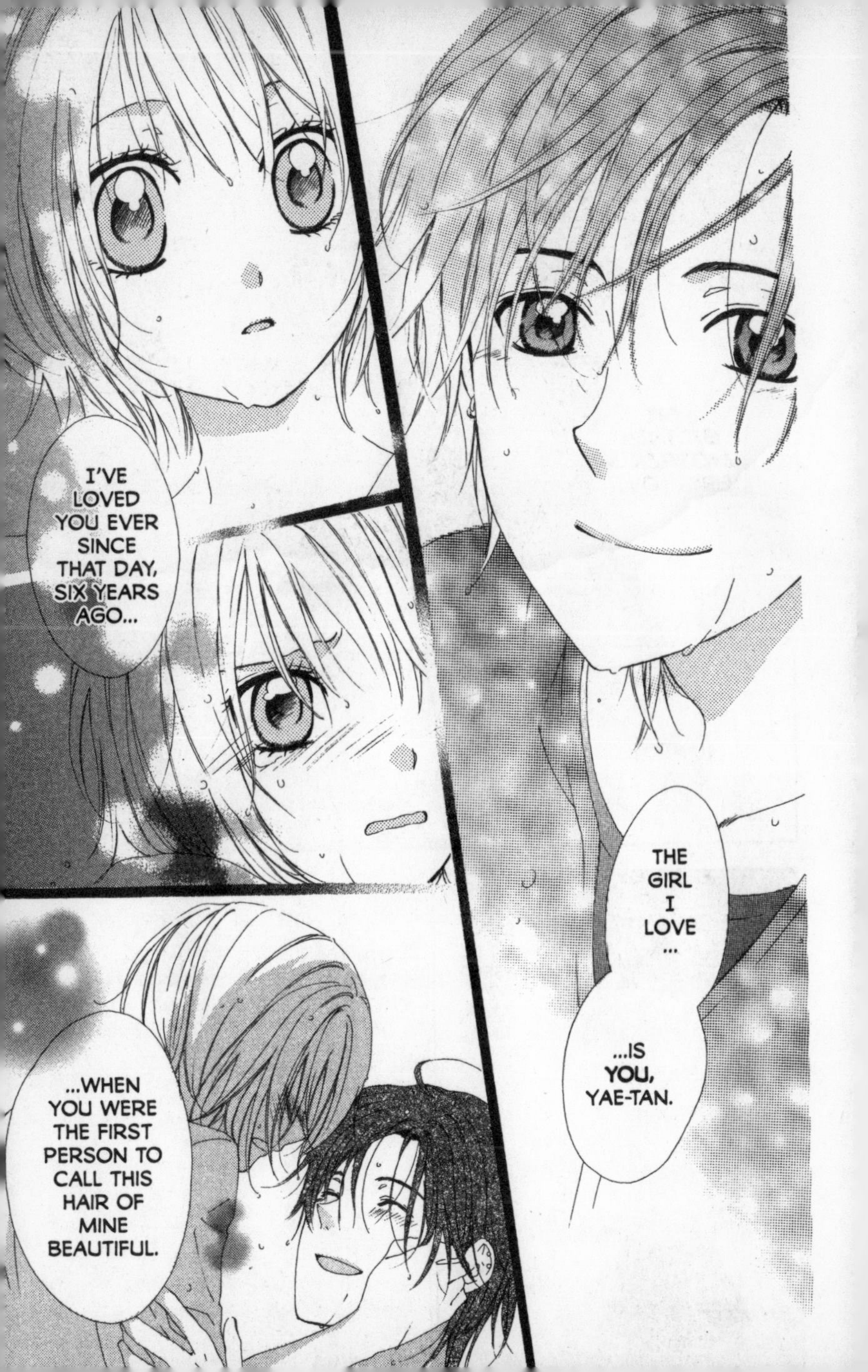
THE GIRL I LOVE ...
...IS YOU, YAE-TAN.
I'VE LOVED YOU EVER SINCE THAT DAY, SIX YEARS AGO...
...WHEN YOU WERE THE FIRST PERSON TO CALL THIS HAIR OF MINE BEAUTIFUL.

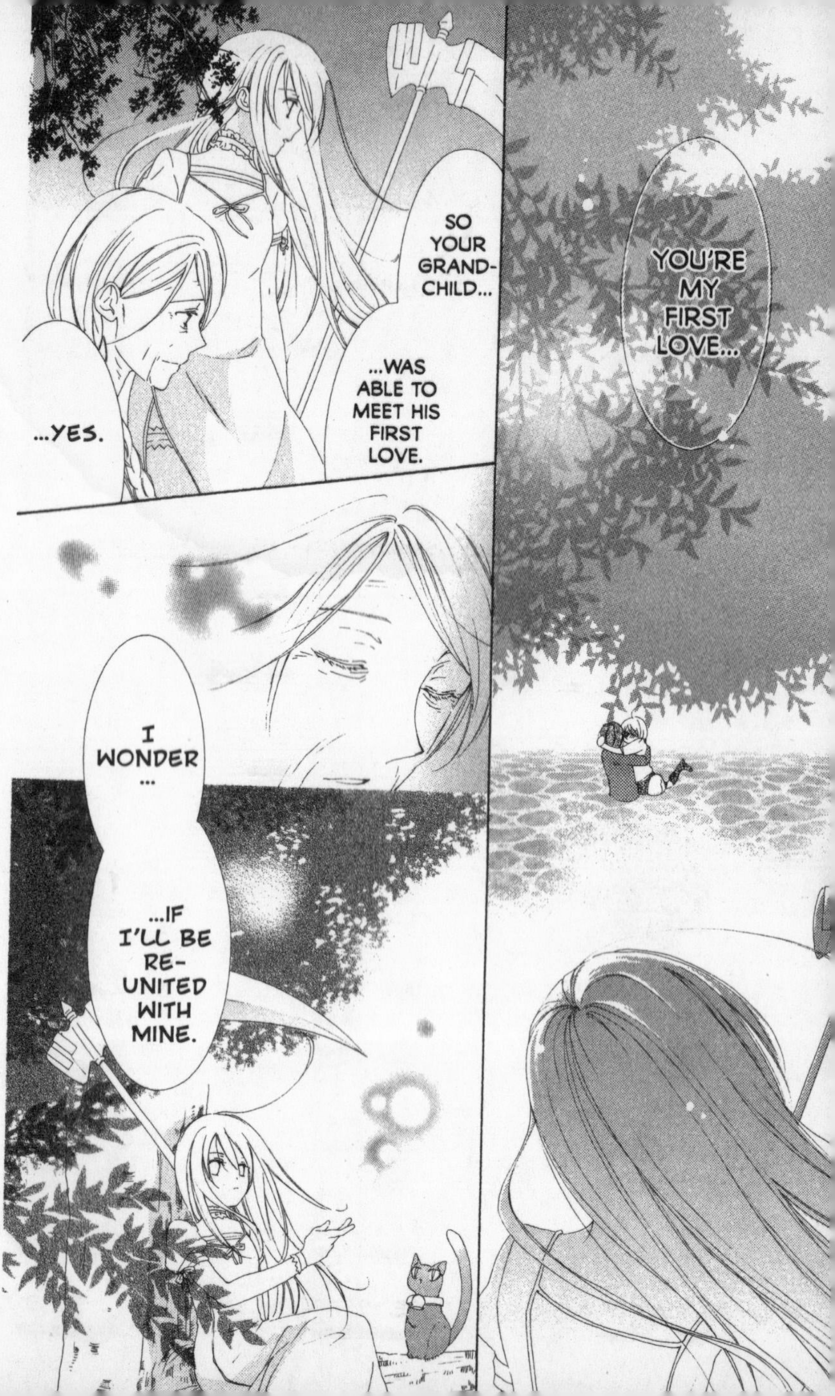
YOU'RE MY FIRST LOVE...
SO YOUR GRAND-CHILD...
...WAS ABLE TO MEET HIS FIRST LOVE.
...YES.
I WONDER...
...IF I'LL BE RE-UNITED WITH MINE.

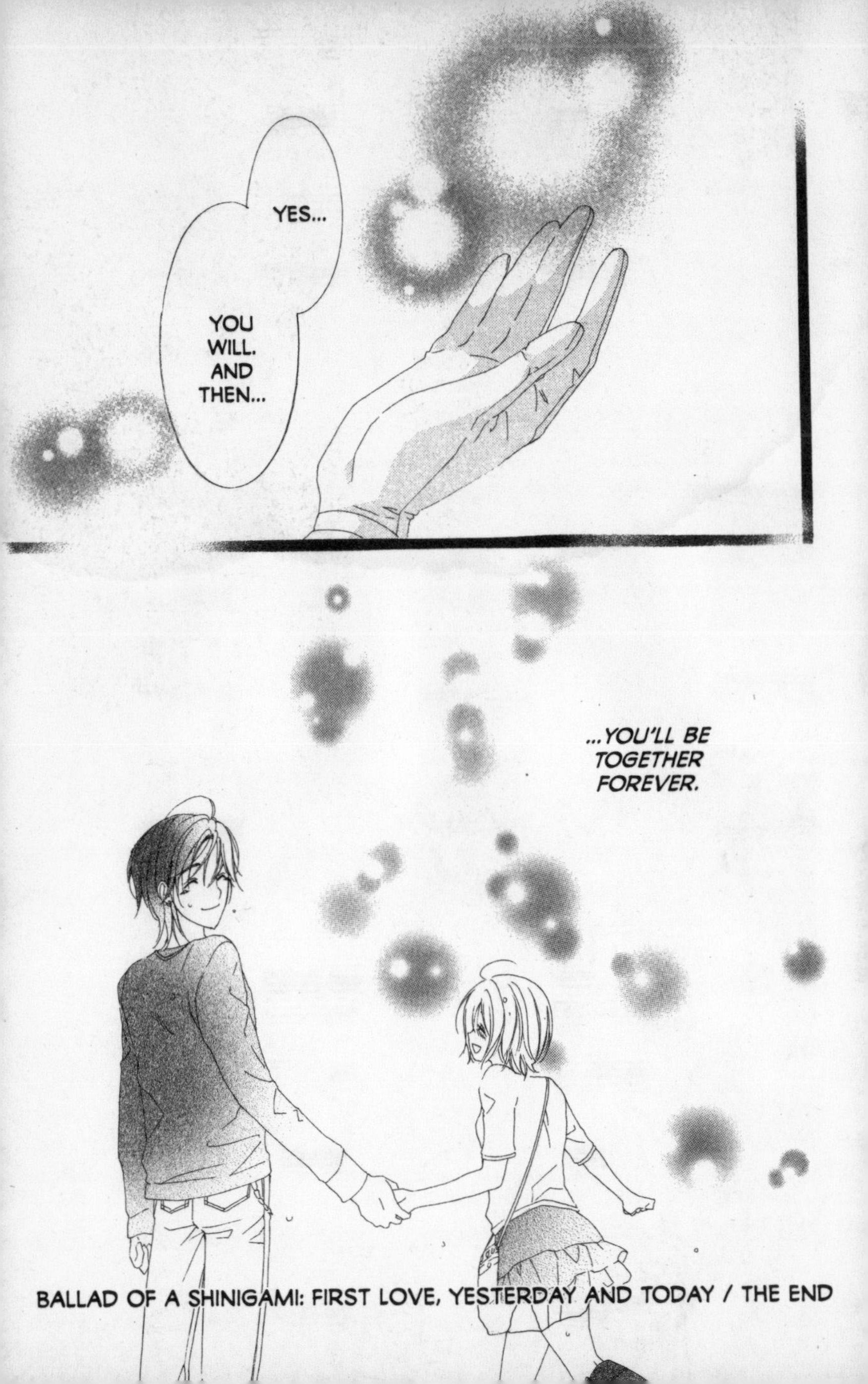
YES...
YOU WILL. AND THEN...
...YOU'LL BE TOGETHER FOREVER.
BALLAD OF A SHINIGAMI: FIRST LOVE, YESTERDAY AND TODAY / THE END

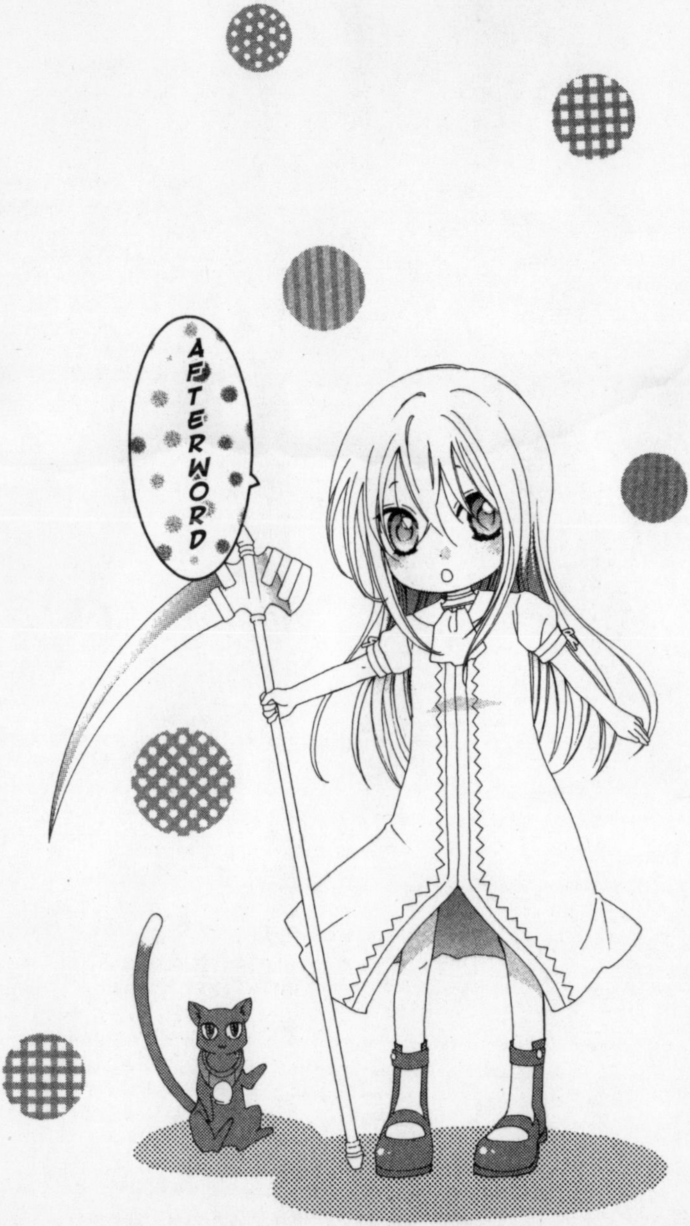
AFTERWORD

THANK YOU FOR READING THIS FAR.

I DIDN'T KNOW WHAT I WAS DOING WHEN I BEGAN ADAPTING A NOVEL INTO MANGA FORM, BUT THROUGH THE GRACIOUS HELP OF VARIOUS PEOPLE, I WAS ABLE TO PRODUCE THIS VOLUME.

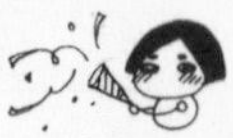

← THE GIRL ON THE LEFT APPEARS IN THE NOVEL. SHE'S THE MYSTERY SHINIGAMI, "ANN". IF YOU'RE INTRIGUED BY HER, BY ALL MEANS, READ THE NOVEL.

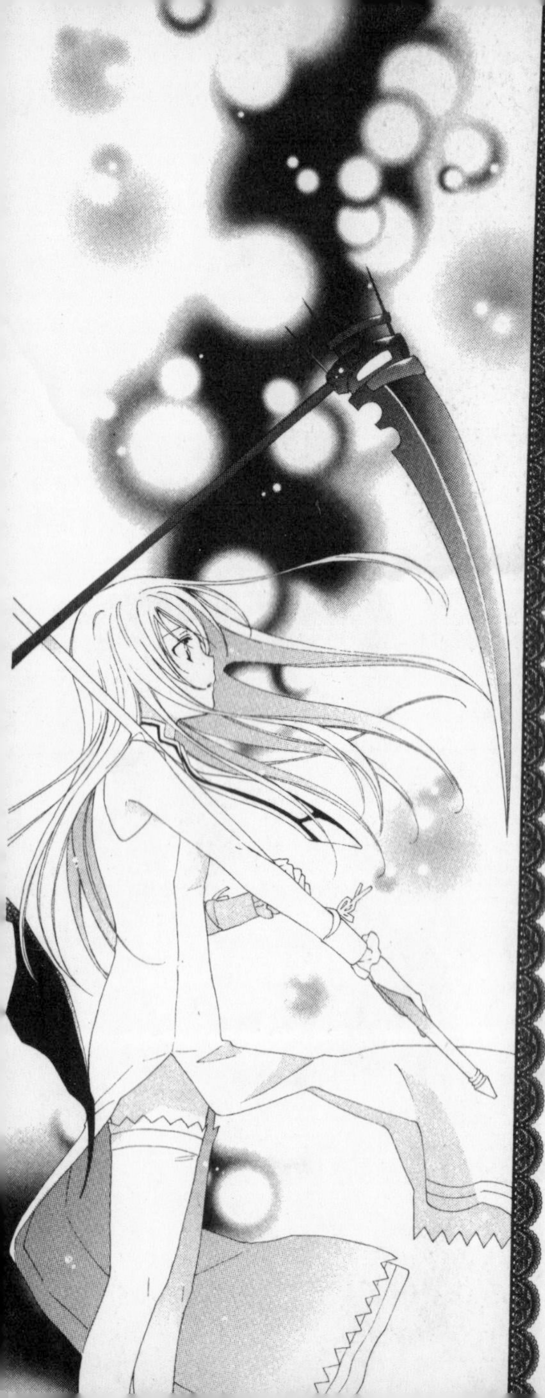

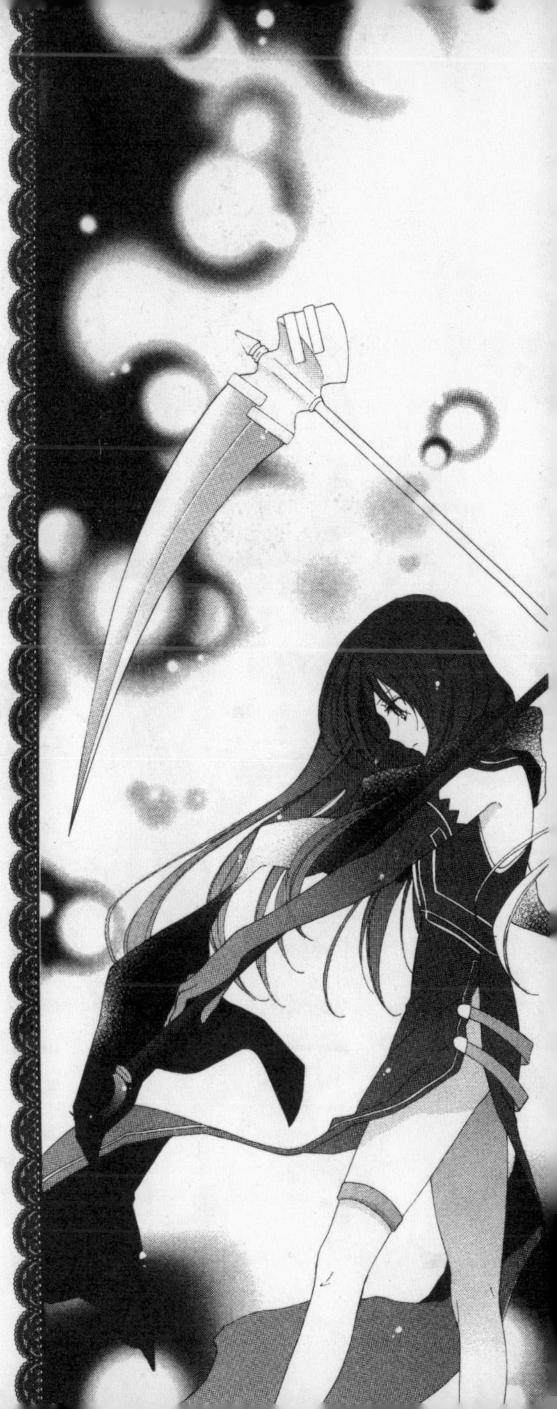

I HOPE TO BE ABLE TO TELL MORE TALES IN THE "SHINIGAMI" WORLD.

THANK YOU VERY MUCH!

ASUKA IZUMI

IF YOU'D LIKE TO SHARE YOUR THOUGHTS, SEND TO:

ASUKA IZUMI
C/O
CMX
888 PROSPECT
STREET
SUITE 240
LA JOLLA CA
92037

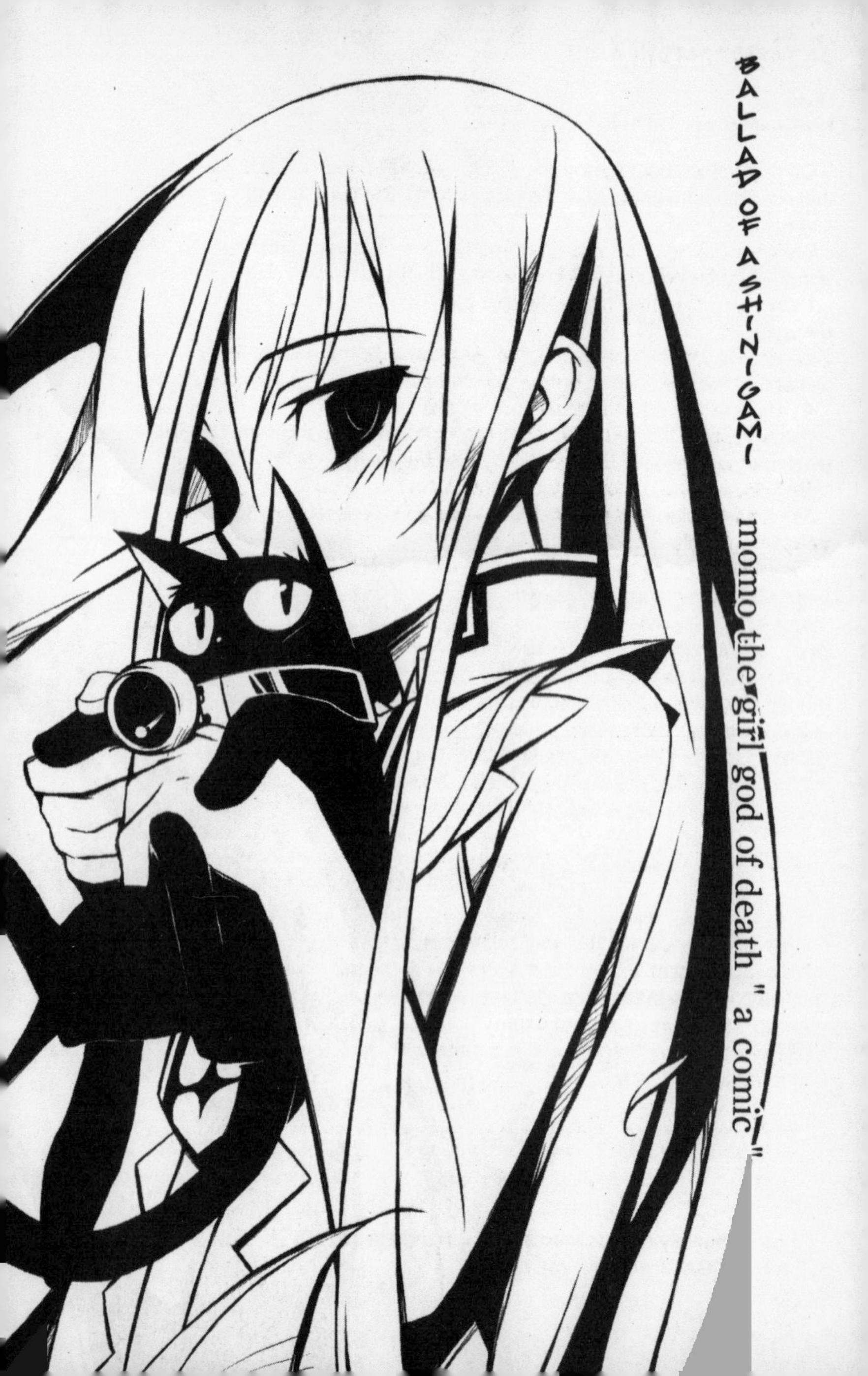
BALLAD OF A SHI-NI-GAMI
momo the girl god of death "a comic"

Afterword

Hello.
Nice to meet you. I'm Keisuke Hasegawa.

Originally, the editor for my novel, BALLAD OF A SHINIGAMI told me that it wouldn't be adapted into a manga form. But then, one day, he changed his mind.

We were talking and he said something like, "Y'know, I was thinking about a manga version of SHINIGAMI…" (LOL)

I screamed in reply, "You're the one who said there wasn't gonna be a manga!"
Now usually, I'm the dense one that gets verbal barbs sprung on him, but this time, I felt like I had to be the one that lashes out with the comeback.

At any rate, my editor explained it like this:

"What I meant then was there wouldn't be a 'boys' manga version. But a girls' manga (shojo) of SHINIGAMI. would be great."

Eh? Shojo? And published by Hakusensha? in *La La**?

Even now, I clearly remember that I was so surprised that I was trembling slightly.

I was bowled over by the prospect of having my work transposed to the pages of *La La* magazine; I mean, I'd read Hakusensha manga before.

And so, SHINIGAMI manga has been published in *La La, La La DX*, and now, collected in paperback form.

Congratulations and thank you.

I can say without a doubt in my head that Asuka izumi-san and Hakusensha collectively changed the mind of my editor, who once so firmly declared that SHINIGAMI. wouldn't be a manga.

When I think that the whole process has resulted in this book being in your hands right now, it feels like I've been blessed with a miracle.

I hope you've enjoyed it and feel like it was created just for you…

Hello, I'm Nanakusa, the illustrator of the original novel.
It's a blast getting to see the characters I drew in the novel being given "new life" in manga form. I waited for each new episode with bated breath.
I'd like to take this space to express my gratitude.
Asuka izumi-san, thank you and congratulations on the publication of this collection.

Keisuke Hasegawa & Nanakusa (Dengeki Bunsho/Mediaworks)

*La La: A monthly manga magazine published in Japan, where BALLAD OF A SHINIGAMI was first serialized.

Special thanks to
K-Ske Hasegawa
Nanakusa
Kazuma Miki(Media Works)
And You

MOMO CONTINUES HER HELPING MISSION IN OCTOBER!

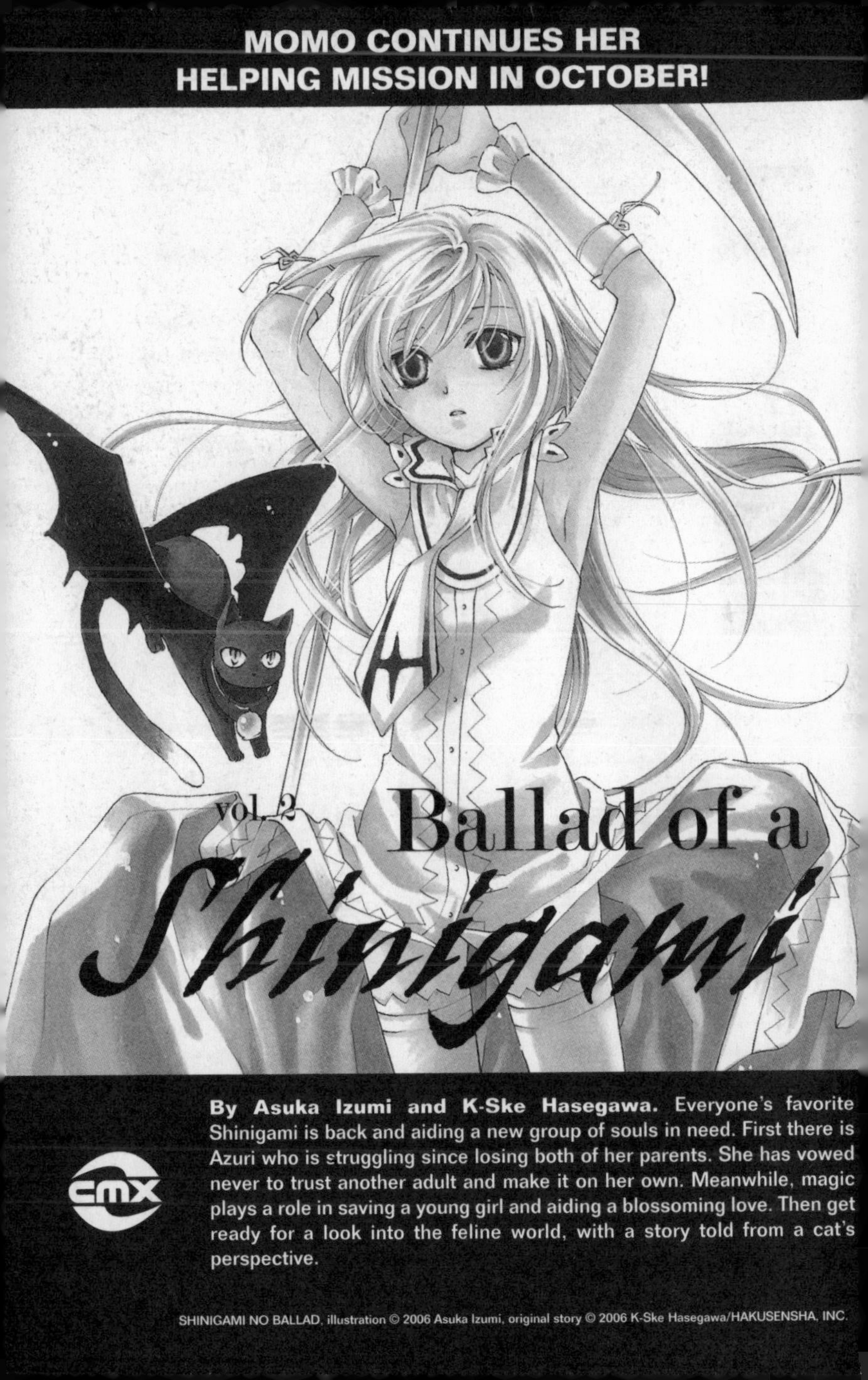
vol. 2
Ballad of a
Shinigami

By Asuka Izumi and K-Ske Hasegawa. Everyone's favorite Shinigami is back and aiding a new group of souls in need. First there is Azuri who is struggling since losing both of her parents. She has vowed never to trust another adult and make it on her own. Meanwhile, magic plays a role in saving a young girl and aiding a blossoming love. Then get ready for a look into the feline world, with a story told from a cat's perspective.

CMX

Moon Child

Volume 13

By Reiko Shimizu. Teruto's plot reaches its peak as the nuclear reactor in Chernobyl goes critical! As Seth and Shonach visit the power plant and do their best to stop the disaster the mer-people predicted, Seth discovers that their rash actions have had *unusual* consequences. Meanwhile, Art fights for his life in the hospital, and Benjamin's actions will determine if a happy ending is possible for any of them!

Jim Lee
  Editorial Director
Hank Kanalz
  VP—General Manager, WildStorm
Paul Levitz
  President & Publisher
Georg Brewer
  VP—Design & DC Direct Creative
Richard Bruning
  Senior VP—Creative Director
Patrick Caldon
  Executive VP—Finance & Operations
Chris Caramalis
  VP—Finance
John Cunningham
  VP—Marketing
Terri Cunningham
  VP—Managing Editor
Amy Genkins
  Senior VP—Business & Legal Affairs
Alison Gill
  VP—Manufacturing
David Hyde
  VP—Publicity
Gregory Noveck
  Senior VP—Creative Affairs
Sue Pohja
  VP—Book Trade Sales
Steve Rotterdam
  Senior VP—Sales & Marketing
Cheryl Rubin
  Senior VP—Brand Management
Jeff Trojan
  VP—Business Development, DC Direct
Bob Wayne
  VP—Sales

SHINIGAMI NO BALLAD, illustrated by Asuka Izumi,
original story by K-Ske Hasegawa. Illustration © 2006 by
Asuka Izumi. Original story © 2006 by K-Ske Hasegawa. All
rights reserved. First published in Japan in 2006 by
HAKUSENSHA, INC. Tokyo.

BALLAD OF A SHINIGAMI Volume 1, published by Wild-
Storm Productions, an imprint of DC Comics, 888 Prospect
St. #240, La Jolla, CA 92037. English Translation © 2009.
All Rights Reserved. English translation rights in U.S.A. And
Canada arranged with HAKUSENSHA, INC., through Tuttle-
Mori Agency, Inc., Tokyo. CMX is a
trademark of DC Comics. The stories, characters, and
incidents mentioned in this magazine are entirely fictional.
Printed on recyclable paper. WildStorm does not read or ac-
cept unsolicited submissions of ideas, stories or artwork.
Printed in Canada.

This book is manufactured at a facility holding chain-of-
custody certification. This paper is made with sustainably
managed North American fiber.

DC Comics, a Warner Bros. Entertainment Company.

Shel Drzka – Translation and Adaptation
MPS Ad Studio – Lettering
Larry Berry – Design
Sarah Farber – Assistant Editor
Jim Chadwick – Editor

ISBN: 978-1-4012-2058-7

All the pages in this book were created—and are printed here—in Japanese RIGHT-to-LEFT format. No artwork has been reversed or altered, so you can read the stories the way the creators meant for them to be read.

RIGHT TO LEFT?!

Traditional Japanese manga starts at the upper right-hand corner, and moves right-to-left as it goes down the page. Follow this guide for an easy understanding.

For more information and sneak previews, visit cmxmanga.com. Call 1-888-COMIC BOOK for the nearest comics shop or head to your local book store.

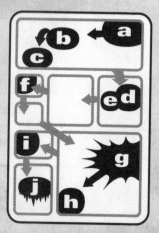